Documenting the Undocumented

UNIVERSITY PRESS OF FLORIDA

Florida A&M University, Tallahassee
Florida Atlantic University, Boca Raton
Florida Gulf Coast University, Ft. Myers
Florida International University, Miami
Florida State University, Tallahassee
New College of Florida, Sarasota
University of Central Florida, Orlando
University of Florida, Gainesville
University of North Florida, Jacksonville
University of South Florida, Tampa
University of West Florida, Pensacola

DOCUMENTING THE UNDOCUMENTED

Latino/a Narratives and Social Justice
in the Era of Operation Gatekeeper

MARTA CAMINERO-SANTANGELO

University Press of Florida
Gainesville · Tallahassee · Tampa · Boca Raton
Pensacola · Orlando · Miami · Jacksonville · Ft. Myers · Sarasota

Copyright 2016 by Marta Caminero-Santangelo
All rights reserved
Printed in the United States of America on acid-free paper

Under the Feet of Jesus by Helena María Viramontes (copyright © 1995 by Helena María Viramontes) used by permission of Dutton, an imprint of Penguin Publishing Group, a division of Penguin Random House LLC.

This book may be available in an electronic edition.

22 21 20 19 18 17   6 5 4 3 2 1

First cloth printing, 2016
First paperback printing, 2017

Library of Congress Cataloging-in-Publication Data

Names: Caminero-Santangelo, Marta, 1966– author.
Title: Documenting the undocumented : latino/a narratives and social justice in the era of Operation Gatekeeper / Marta Caminero-Santangelo.
Description: Gainesville : University Press of Florida, [2016] | 2016. | Includes bibliographical references and index.
Identifiers: LCCN 2015047964 | ISBN 9780813062594 (cloth: alk. paper)
ISBN 978-0-8130-6456-7 (pbk.)
Subjects: LCSH: American literature—Hispanic American authors—History and criticism. | Immigrants' writings, American—History and criticism. | Illegal aliens—Government policy—United States. | Social justice in literature. | Operation Gatekeeper (U.S.) | Mexican-American Border Region. | Border patrols—Mexican-American Border Region.
Classification: LCC PS153.H56 C35 2016 | DDC 810.9/868073—dc23
LC record available at http://lccn.loc.gov/2015047964

The University Press of Florida is the scholarly publishing agency for the State University System of Florida, comprising Florida A&M University, Florida Atlantic University, Florida Gulf Coast University, Florida International University, Florida State University, New College of Florida, University of Central Florida, University of Florida, University of North Florida, University of South Florida, and University of West Florida.

University Press of Florida
15 Northwest 15th Street
Gainesville, FL 32611-2079
http://upress.ufl.edu

To my children, Nicola and Gabriel

Contents

Acknowledgments ix

Introduction 1

1. Narrating the Non-Nation: Literary Journalism and "Illegal" Border Crossings 33

2. The Lost Ones: Post-Gatekeeper Border Fictions and the Construction of Cultural Trauma 56

3. The Caribbean Difference: Imagining Trans-Status Communities 107

4. Selling the Undocumented: Life Narratives of Unauthorized Immigrants 149

5. Unauthorized Plots: Life Writing, Transnationalism, and the Possibilities of Agency 194

6. Undocumented Testimony: American DREAMers 222

Conclusion 261

Notes 265

Works Cited 271

Index 285

Acknowledgments

This book was made possible by the support of the University of Kansas at various stages in its development. I benefited from a sabbatical awarded by the College of Liberal Arts and Sciences in fall 2012, and in 2008 I was the recipient of a research fellowship from the Hall Center for the Humanities, which afforded me a research-intensive semester. The book was also supported by grants from the University of Kansas General Research Fund, allocation numbers 2301619 and 2301341. A Latino Studies Research Fellowship from the Smithsonian Institution provided me with the opportunity to investigate archives in Washington, D.C., to observe a national DREAM Act protest and demonstration that converged on the capital, and to travel to Mexico in order to work with a migrant aid center for recently removed/deported immigrants. The photographs on the book cover were taken during those two trips.

Earlier versions of chapters have appeared elsewhere previously. A short version of chapter 1 originally appeared in *Arizona Quarterly* 68 (Autumn 2012) as "Narrating the Non-Nation: Literary Journalism and 'Illegal' Border Crossings." The revised and expanded version included here is printed by permission of the Regents of the University of Arizona. A short version of chapter 2 entitled "The Lost Ones: Post-Gatekeeper Border Fictions and the Construction of Cultural Trauma" appeared in *Latino Studies* 8 (Autumn 2010). And a section of chapter 4 appeared in the Biographical Research Center journal *Biography: An Interdisciplinary Quarterly* 35 (Summer 2012) as "Documenting the Undocumented: Life Narratives of Undocumented Immigrants." I thank all the editors and publishers for permission to include the revised and expanded material in this book. In addition, my thanks to Ana Castillo, Helena María Viramontes, Penguin Random House LLC, and Aunt Lute Publishing for permission to reprint the epigraphs in the introduction.

Thanks to my editor, Sian Hunter, for taking on the project and guiding it through the review process in a calm and levelheaded manner. I also wish to thank my external readers for the University Press of Florida, including Debra Castillo and the anonymous reviewer, who gave me incredibly useful feedback and made the book a much better final product. My deep appreciation goes to my amazing Latina/o Studies colleagues across the country, including especially Ylce Irizarry, Elena Machado Saez, Rafe Dalleo, Marion Rohrleitner, and Marisel Moreno—thank you for all you do! A special thank you to the young DREAM activists who were gracious enough to be interviewed for chapter 6. You have my particular admiration.

As always, I am profoundly grateful for the support of friends and family. My thanks and love to the "girls," Anna Neill, Katie Conrad, Laura Hines, Giselle Anatol, and Yo Jackson, as well as to my running / writing / drinking buddies (and so much more), Stuart Day, Darren Canady, Ben Eggleston, and Misty Schieberle, and to Becca Peterson, who dragged me through many a pre-dawn run when I didn't want to. All of them have been there for me (with wine) through many a rough patch; I consider myself exceptionally lucky to have been surrounded with such wonderful and dear friends and loved ones as my "colleagues." You have enriched my life in inexpressible ways. Thanks also to Sarah Thailing, my beloved friend and anchor for over twenty-five years. Finally, my love always and forever to my father Rafael Caminero, my brother Ralph, my sister Mary Ann Cucuzza, and my beautiful, smart, and kind children, Nicola and Gabe, who are growing up to be such wonderful human beings.

Introduction

> I walk through the hole in the fence
>   To the other side.
> . . . .
> Beneath the iron sky
> Mexican children kick their soccer ball across,
> Run after it, entering the U.S.
>
> Gloria Anzaldúa, *Borderlands/La Frontera*, 1987

> The border patrol, she thought, and she tried to remember which side she was on and which side of the wire mesh she was safe in.
>
> Helena María Viramontes, *Under the Feet of Jesus*, 1995

> The borderlands have become like the Bermuda Triangle. Sooner or later everyone knows someone who's dropped outta sight.
>
> Ana Castillo, *The Guardians*, 2007

We tend to think of the border today as "written in stone," metaphorically if not literally. But in fact that stone has become reified over time in the public mind and in public discourse, from something resembling Gloria Anzaldúa's representation of flux and permeability to the rigid ideological barrier that it is now. How did we get from there to here—from Anzaldúa's version of an artificial borderline effortlessly defied to Ana Castillo's vision of the borderlands as a menacing death zone almost mythological in its proportions? Anzaldúa's border was simultaneously a dividing line and a crossing point, a line drawn in the sand that her own images of fluid movement back and forth across borders flouted and attempted to erase.[1] A *Los Angeles Times* article in 2004 recalled in a similar vein: "For years, Calexico and Mexicali seemed like one city. The chain-link fence between the two was so flimsy that people would pull it aside and walk into the United States. Agents were often nowhere to be seen, and immigrants could easily cross the border" (Marosi, qtd. in Nevins, *Dying* 116). But by 2014, according to *USA Today*, even though $126 million had been spent on border enforcement and security in the previous decade alone, and then–Homeland Security secretary Janet Napolitano reported to Congress that the border was more secure than it had ever been, any serious talk of comprehensive immigration reform was invariably accompanied by the rhetoric of securing the border *first* (Ortega and Kelly), as though the border were an actual physical structure with leaks or holes that needed, at all costs, to be made impermeable. And increasingly, fiction and nonfiction written on *this* side of the U.S.-Mexico border detailed a litany of deaths and disappearances of those who did, in fact, try to cross: "Many travelers have disappeared and never been heard from again" (Bencastro 29). It is worth interrogating the developments that, over three decades, gave shape to this changing border landscape.

The Gatekeeper Era: Enforcement and the Immigration Debates

Anzaldúa's *Borderlands* was published on the heels of the 1986 Immigration Reform and Control Act (IRCA), passed under President Ronald Reagan, which made it illegal for employers to knowingly hire undocumented immigrants. Anzaldúa decried, "It is illegal for Mexicans to work without green cards ... big farming combines, farm bosses and smugglers who bring them in make money off the wetbacks' labor—they don't have to pay federal minimum wages or ensure adequate housing or sanitary conditions" (34). IRCA also notoriously granted "amnesty" to approximately three million immigrants already present in the United States.[2] The conflicting mandates—for legalization and for increasing enforcement—created a profound paradox with long-lasting effects (Kanstroom 95–96). In the immediate wake of the amnesty bill, however, anti-immigrant rhetoric temporarily receded into the background, though it would begin to rise anew in the early 1990s, as numbers of apprehensions of illegal crossings rose once again and as the 1992 election approached (Ellingwood 25; Nevins, *Dying* 106; Chavez, *Covering* 132–34; Andreas 39).[3]

According to Joseph Nevins, an ongoing economic recession in the early 1990s, a renewed rise in unauthorized crossings, and some high-profile incidents involving undocumented immigrants worked in tandem to fuel the flames of anti-immigrant sentiment and rhetoric. Republicans saw the anti-immigrant platform as an opportunity to distinguish themselves from Democrats in the presidential elections of 1992 and 1996 and the congressional elections of 1994. Indeed, the anti-immigrant platform was a centerpiece of California governor Pete Wilson's bid for reelection in 1994, and California simultaneously considered passage of Proposition 187, the "Save Our State" initiative, a ballot measure that sought a hard line against illegal immigration (Nevins, *Dying* 105–8; *Operation Gatekeeper* 84–92). Several observers credit the Proposition 187 campaign and Wilson's own dramatic advertisements, depicting unauthorized migrants as an infestation and menace ("They keep coming"), with the successful turnaround of Wilson's reelection campaign (Ellingwood 31; Andreas 87).

The heated rhetoric escalated. A letter in the *New York Times* warned, "By flooding the state with 2 million illegal aliens to date, and increasing that figure each of the following ten years," Mexicans in the state could become a majority, vote to secede from the United States, and become part of Mexico (qtd. in Ellingwood 30)—the infamous threat of the "Mexican takeover" corresponding to the warlike metaphor of the "invasion" of Mexican immigrants, now packaged as a phenomenon that could in fact lead to a loss of national sovereignty to a foreign power. Leo Chavez has documented that a flurry of popular news magazine covers featured immigration as a prominent topic in the years leading up to and including 1994, suggesting that immigration was once again a "hot-button political issue" (*Covering* 135). Some of these covers were decidedly "alarmist" in nature—for instance, the *Newsweek* cover in 1993 that depicted a drowning Statue of Liberty, surrounded by rickety wooden boats filled, presumably, with immigrants, and a headline that read "60% of Americans Say Immigration Is 'Bad for the Country'" (Chavez, *Covering* 162). A member of the organization STOP-IT (Stop the Out-of-Control Problems of Immigration Today) was quoted in a 1993 *Progressive* article as saying, "Just by being here they are criminals. We believe we're being invaded and we're out to stop it. . . . American citizens don't like some of the neighborhoods . . . being taken over by illegals. . . . I have to stop our members from taking up weapons. . . . White American citizens got guns to fight back against the illegal aliens and the criminals." A member of Light Up the Border raised the possibility of a "border war," adding, "We're very serious about our sovereignty here and our families" (Conniff 26, 29; qtd. in Chavez, *Covering* 166). Undocumented immigrants were portrayed as *by definition* "criminals" as well as enemy aliens threatening both a national takeover and the destruction of American "families." *Forbes* senior editor Peter Brimelow's book *Alien Nation* was hailed by *Newsweek* as "one of the most widely discussed books of 1995" (Adler). Brimelow argued that recent immigration numbers were unprecedented and constituted a distinct threat to the United States both culturally and in terms of its national sovereignty. He singled out Latinos as constituting a "strange anti-nation inside the United States" and warned of the dire consequences of "Any change in the racial balance . . . of the American nation," advocating a dramatic decrease or perhaps a temporary halt in legal immigration and a full-scale effort—amounting to a "second Operation Wetback"—to stop illegal immigration (218, 259–64).[4] Several commentators homed in on Brimelow's overtly and unapologetically racialist arguments as particularly incendiary.[5]

In 1993, in an effort to preempt Republicans from gaining too much political traction from the issue of "cracking down" on undocumented immigration, the Clinton administration announced in a news conference a "strong and clear message: We will make it tougher for illegal aliens to get into our country" (Andreas 89). In 1994, Operation Gatekeeper was launched at the San Diego border with Mexico—modeled on a much more local effort, Operation Blockade, implemented in 1993 at the El Paso border by its border patrol chief, Silvestre Reyes (Ellingwood 32; Nevins, *Dying* 107–8). The plan was part of a larger national strategy to beef up policing at the border in order to make it much more difficult for migrants to pass through heavily trafficked crossing points. The year 1995 saw the initiation of Operation Safeguard at the Nogales, Arizona, crossing point; in 1997 Operation Río Grande was launched in Texas. Operation Gatekeeper and Operation Hold-the-Line were also expanded in 1996–97 to cover more territory. As Peter Andreas writes in *Border Games*, "The unprecedented expansion of border policing . . . has ultimately been less about achieving the stated instrumental goal of deterring illegal border crossers and more about politically recrafting the image of the border and symbolically reaffirming the state's territorial authority" (85). The border was being reified into an "imaginary" line with real material gravity, whose crossing signaled criminal and life-threatening trespass.

As some scholars have pointed out, the implementation of Gatekeeper tactics occurred at the same time as the passage of the North American Free Trade Agreement (NAFTA); that is, boundary enforcement increased just as the promoted "free" flow of goods and commerce across borders made it likely that migration flows north would correspondingly increase. Indeed, some have speculated, Gatekeeper could be interpreted as a preemptive response to this very possibility.[6] U.S. officials "predicted that the 'territorial denial' strategies embodied by Operation Gatekeeper and similar operations in the Southwest would . . . push migrants into mountain and desert areas where they would make a rational cost-benefit analysis in the face of adverse conditions and decide to give up and return home" (Nevins, *Dying* 116). However, Gatekeeper and similar border enforcement strategies also had a strong rhetorical effect; they reified the nation-state boundary as an imaginary line meant to be impermeable, inviolable—to demarcate clearly who did and didn't belong in the nation. Néstor Rodríguez has argued persuasively that while national borders exist legally and politically, the symbolic meanings they acquire are constructed over time and through particular practices (223). Gatekeeper and similar efforts constituted precisely such practices and ensured that national unbelonging would be, for the foreseeable future, metonymically linked with what lay outside the "gate." Those who crossed this line could now be positioned, within U.S. discourse, not just as unauthorized crossers but as enemy aliens, as threats to the nation itself.

The Human Costs of Enforcement

With the advent of the Gatekeeper era, deaths of migrants attempting to cross the border through difficult and hazardous terrain escalated dramatically (Eschbach et al. 430–31; Nevins, *Operation Gatekeeper* 124–25, 144, 146). No More Deaths, a humanitarian aid organization with the mission of preventing migrant deaths due to environmental factors in the Arizona Sonora Desert, was founded in 2004. Longtime NMD volunteers have a standard stock of stories about victims of border crossing. In Warsaw Canyon, a "stretcher" made of belts and branches was used by a migrant group in the summer of 2005 to carry a woman who could no longer walk to reach medical assistance; she died despite their efforts. A marker by a creek bed in the desert near Arivaca signals the place where a fourteen-year-old Salvadoran girl, Josseline Jamileth Hernández Quinteros, died in February 2008. (Her body was found by No More Deaths volunteers.) In the summer of 2008, NMD volunteers came upon a migrant by the side of the road who had been lost in the desert for three days, abandoned by his group and without food or water. In his disoriented state, he asked the volunteers if they were angels, *angelitos*. Without their assistance, the man would almost certainly have died (Caminero-Santangelo, "Responding" 113–14).

Other developments in immigration policy, enforcement, and legislation set the stage for other kinds of trauma quite far from the deadly border region. In 1996, Congress passed the Illegal Immigration Reform and Immigrant Responsibility Act (IIRIRA). Under the provisions of this new law, deportations became mandatory in cases involving aggravated felony, even if the conviction had happened before the law's passage (Golash-Boza, *Due Process Denied* 27). For mixed status families, the law was, in its own way, deadly. The law's removal of judicial review of case sentencing made it impossible to argue for leniency on the grounds of subsequent rehabilitation (a judge could not take into consideration, for instance, that a particular offense may have taken place decades ago and that the offender had been a teenager at the time) or of long-standing and deep-rooted family ties or contributions to the community since the time of the offense. In practice, those caught in the net of IIRIRA enforcement were at times ripped from spouses and children to be returned to countries they barely remembered. Children were left without a parent and provider (Golash-Boza, *Due Process* 27–28, 30–34).

With the terrorist attacks of September 11, 2001, any possibility for easing of the vitriolic anti-immigrant rhetoric—or a loosening of restrictions—disappeared. "Securing our borders" acquired the status of an antiterrorist mantra, even though none of the terrorists involved in 9/11 had entered the United States illegally, nor had they entered through the land "border" with Mexico (Doland). Budget appropriations for all activities related to border control rose sharply (Migration Policy Institute 2, 4). In 2005, the U.S. Congress debated HR 4437, the Sensenbrenner Bill—a piece of anti-immigrant legislation that many immigrants and immigrant rights supporters saw as draconian because it would have made unauthorized presence in the United States a felony subject to imprisonment; it would arguably also have criminalized humanitarian or charitable assistance to the undocumented (Johnson and Hing 100; O'Rourke 201–4, 207–8). The bill sparked outrage among immigrant and Latino/a communities and prompted the largest nationwide immigrant rights protests in history in spring 2006, with hundreds of thousands of people in Chicago, Los Angeles, and other cities marching in support of immigrants (Johnson and

Hing 99). The New Sanctuary Movement (NSM), an interfaith, nationwide coalition of churches and synagogues modeled somewhat loosely on the 1980s Sanctuary Movement, was launched in May 2007.[7] It constituted another response to the escalating pitch of rhetoric marked by the Sensenbrenner Bill. The movement attempted to address what participants now perceived as a grave humanitarian crisis: the separation of families through detention and deportation (Caminero-Santangelo, "The Voice").

The Literary Response

This sketch of roughly two decades of developments in immigration legislation and enforcement, as well as of escalating and vitriolic rhetoric and the efforts of an emerging immigrant rights movement to counter it, goes some way toward explaining why Latino/a writers in the United States increasingly turned their attention to the topic of the undocumented in the years following the implementation of Operation Gatekeeper and IIRIRA. The "unauthorized" journey north along with accompanying issues of deaths and disappearances during border crossings, the threat of deportation once in the United States, familial separation, and the existential trauma of being "illegal" became the focus of a flurry of books published in the 1990s and early 2000s by U.S. Latino/as as well as by some non-Latino/as. Among these are works of narrative journalism including *Dead in Their Tracks: Crossing America's Desert Borderlands* (1999) by John Annerino; *Crossing Over: A Mexican Family on the Migrant Trail* (2001) by Rubén Martínez; *The Devil's Highway* (2004) by Luis Alberto Urrea; *Dying to Cross: The Worst Immigrant Tragedy in American History* (2005) by Jorge Ramos; and *Enrique's Journey* (2007) by Sonia Nazario. In addition to journalistic accounts, there are memoirs and oral histories recounted by the undocumented, including *Diary of an Undocumented Immigrant* (1991, published in the original Spanish as *Diario de un mojado* in 2003) by Ramón "Tianguis" Pérez and *Undocumented in L.A.* (1997) by Dianne Walta Hart. Shorter life narrative fragments published in collections include *La Migra me hizo los mandados* (2002) (translated as *The Border Patrol Ate My Dust*, 2004) edited by Alicia Alarcón; *Underground America: Narratives of Undocumented Lives* (2008) edited by Peter Orner; *Underground Undergrads: UCLA Undocumented Immigrant Students Speak Out* (2008) published by the UCLA Center for Labor Research and

Education and compiled by the students themselves (Madera et al.); *We ARE Americans: Undocumented Students Pursuing the American Dream* (2009), by William Perez; *Crossing with the Virgin: Stories from the Migrant Trail* (2010) edited by Kathryn Ferguson, Norma A. Price, and Ted Parks; and *The Death of Josseline: Immigration Stories from the Arizona-Mexico Borderlands* (2010) edited by Margaret Regan. A plethora of fiction (both short stories and novels) offers significant treatments of undocumented characters, unauthorized border crossings, and/or the very issue of "illegality," including *The Lonely Crossing of Juan Cabrera* (1993) by J. Joaquín Fraxedas; *Under the Feet of Jesus* (1995) by Helena María Viramontes; *The Tortilla Curtain* (1995) by T. C. Boyle; *Drown* (1996) by Junot Díaz; *Odisea del Norte* (1999; published first in translation as *Odyssey to the North* in 1998) by Mario Bencastro; *Esperanza's Box of Saints* (1999) by María Amparo Escandón; *Highwire Moon* (2001) by Susan Straight; *Stars Always Shine* (2001) by Rick Rivera; *Desert Blood: The Juárez Murders* (2005) by Alicia Gaspar de Alba; *Across a Hundred Mountains* (2006) by Reyna Grande; *A Handbook to Luck* (2007) by Cristina García; *The Guardians* (2007) by Ana Castillo; *Into the Beautiful North* (2009) also by Luis Alberto Urrea; and the young adult novel *Return to Sender* (2010) by Julia Alvarez. This flurry of literary representation of the issue of unauthorized crossing, "illegal" immigration, and the very category of "illegality" is the subject of this book.

Representing the Nation and the Non-Nation

My approach to this emerging body of literature takes as its starting point Homi Bhabha's postulation that "nation" is brought into being largely by *stories*, including shared histories and myths as well as a "national literature." In Bhabha's well-known formulation, "Nations, like narratives, . . . only fully realize their horizons in the mind's eye. . . . [The nation is an] idea whose cultural compulsion lies in the impossible unity of the nation as a symbolic force" (1). That is to say, nations are *imaginative* constructs rather than somehow natural, pre-given entities, characterized by a "compulsion" for coherence and cohesion which is, in fact, always impossible to achieve. Put another way, because stories of nation strive for homogeneity (something the people of the nation have "in common"), they inevitably obscure or leave out elements that do not easily fit into the imagined community (Benedict Anderson's famous coinage) of the nation. As Bill Ashcroft, Gareth Griffiths, and Helen Tiffin have explained in their gloss on Bhabha and other theorists of nation, "specific identifiers are employed to create exclusive and homogeneous conceptions of national traditions. Such signifiers of homogeneity always fail to represent the diversity of the actual 'national' community for which they purport to speak and, in practice, usually represent and consolidate the interests of the dominant power groups within any national formation" (150).

An emblematic example of this hegemonic construction of the "nation" through particular narratives is Samuel Huntington's *Who Are We? The Challenges to America's National Identity*, published in 2004, the same year that No More Deaths was founded to address the "collateral damage," in human lives, of border enforcement strategies. A political science professor at Harvard, Huntington lent academic legitimacy to the view that Latin American immigration was a profound threat to America's core cultural identity, which, he argued, was built on a foundation of Anglo-Saxon culture and Protestant Christianity. Huntington's tome thus became part of a larger tapestry of "ideas, laws, narratives, myths, and knowledge production" that together worked to construct perceptions of Latinos as a national threat (Chavez, *Latino Threat* 22).

In this book, I attend to the stories told both by and about so-called illegal aliens—the term itself designating this population as *not fitting* into the narratively constructed boundaries of the American "nation."[8] (In April 2013, the Associated Press changed its style guide so that "illegal immigrant" would no longer be standard terminology.) Indeed, as George Lakoff and Sam Ferguson have astutely observed, by framing the "problem" as "illegal immigration," dominant discourse places limits around what will be understood as the sources of the problem and allows us to consider only specific, narrowly defined solutions. The problem becomes one of legal and even criminal culpability (immigrants are doing something "illegal" by coming), rather than of a number of other factors, including high demand for cheap, exploitable labor (why does the term "illegal employers" not exist?), foreign affairs (e.g., consideration of treaties such as NAFTA and their impact on immigration, the U.S. role in supporting oppressive governments that people must flee), and human rights (e.g., the right to mobility, basic livelihood, family unity, and so on). The rhetoric of the "illegal alien" ensures that the unauthorized migrant is seen as (1) breaking the law and (2) *essentially*—rather than just incidentally or temporally—not belonging in the nation. Solutions to the "problem" must then, logically, be focused on correcting both the individual immigrant's violation and his/her "trespassing" in a meaningful space where s/he does not belong (Lakoff and Ferguson).

Further, the status of being "illegal" drastically limits the power of the undocumented to "speak for themselves" and *make themselves* heard in American popular discourse. As journalist David Bacon points out, "Those who live with globalization's consequences are not at the table, and their voices are generally excluded" (*Illegal People* viii). In a related vein, Nancy Fraser argues that the noncitizen *has no voice* recognizable in the "public sphere" as it has been historically conceived—that metaphorical space in which matters of the social and political good are debated and "public opinion" is derived—since theoretical formulations of the public sphere have generally assumed that citizenship is the delimiting principle for participation (*Scales* 4–5). Thus Fraser delineates her understanding of "subaltern counterpublics" as "parallel discursive arenas where members of subordinated social groups invent and circulate counterdiscourses, which in turn permit them to formulate oppositional interpretations of their identities, interests, and needs" ("Rethinking" 67–68). Some undocumented voices are in fact challenging their exclusion from the public sphere. These emerging stories inspire the larger question: How have Latino/a and non-Latino/a narratives about being "illegal" contested the very parameters of that definition and its consigning into unhearability of the immigrant's narrative? How have they constituted what Nancy Fraser might call a "subaltern counterpublic" that challenges the terms of its own conscription to silence ("Rethinking" 67–68)? How do the stories by Latino/a writers and by unauthorized immigrants themselves attempt to negotiate and perhaps even to redraw the boundaries of "nation"? How and when do they attempt a "reframing" of the issue of immigration so that we may begin to imagine other possibilities?

As Latino/a and popular U.S. literature representing the issue of undocumented immigration has burgeoned, literary critics too have begun to turn their attention to how literary texts respond to and challenge hegemonic narratives about immigration. Until quite recently, scholarship did not substantially address representation of "illegality" in literature at all, even when its central concerns would have seemed to lend themselves naturally to such an exploration. For example, Teresa McKenna's 1997 *Migrant Song: Politics and Process in Contemporary Chicano Literature* argued that "migration is an appropriate root metaphor for Chicano writers" (4) yet nowhere substantively addressed the issues specific to unauthorized migration across borders or to literary representations of these. In his groundbreaking *Border Matters: Remapping American Cultural Studies* (1997), José David Saldívar posits border crossing as a space of "liminality" that becomes more than a transitional space between nations or states of being, but is rather its *own* mode of existence—particularly (if not exclusively) for those who remain undocumented: "liminality is thematized not as a temporary condition of the displaced but as a permanent social reality" characterized by "intercultural and transnational experiences" (104, 107). In *Feminism on the Border: Chicana Gender Politics and Literature* (2000), Sonia Saldívar-Hull similarly treats the border as a geopolitical space where Chicana writers negotiate a feminist, "transnational solidarity" with working-class and third-world subjects: immigrants, farmworkers, refugees, and others. Saldívar-Hull briefly discusses the label *illegal immigrants* as a racialized term signifying "alterity"—"the Other"—as well as the issue of exploited undocumented labor (77, 144–45, 148), but otherwise she does not address the specific issues raised by representations of (or by) the undocumented. In *Border Fictions: Globalization, Empire, and Writing at the Boundaries of the United States* (2008), Claudia Sadowski-Smith considers literature of both the U.S.-Mexico and the U.S.-Canada borderlands, exploring how the literature represents and imagines "diverse *contemporary* border communities and their attempts to articulate experiences with U.S. empire and repressive state-sponsored nationalisms" (55). Such literature, Sadowski-Smith argues, can also posit new forms of counterhegemonic nationalism that resist being defined and constrained by the nation-state (7). Again, however, the issue of *unauthorized* border dwellers is not an extended focal point of study.

In *Border Women: Writing from La Frontera* (2002), Debra Castillo and María-Socorro Tabuenca Córdoba are concerned with how short fiction and fragmentary narratives by women on *either* side of the border imagine and represent it based on their own locatedness. Castillo and Córdoba are highly sensitive to the fact that the border "means" differently depending upon which side you "belong" to; movement across it is far more circumscribed for Mexican women than it is for Chicanas. As a result, the "border" and "borderlands" are treated more theoretically and metaphorically by Chicana writers than they are by Mexican writers, for whom the border is more material and more of a barrier. (This unevenness of meaning is replicated by Western scholars, they add, who often discuss the theoretical valences of the borderlands at the expense of their material realities.) This insight is essential to an understanding of the unequal privilege that marks the "borderlands" and its effects on literary production. Indeed, in a trenchant critique of much recent border theory, Manuel Luiz Martinez has argued that the border becomes largely a "symbolic place" designating "a purely discursive form of 'opposition' in the U.S. Mexico borderlands"—an opposition to hegemonic constructions of nation. As Martinez notes, "The borderlands have become the new poststructural geographical trope that is populated by liminal figures, hybrid border-crossers, and migratory subjects." But such conceptualizations quite problematically can render the border trope "disconnected from its material location and its history of repression." The privileging of border-crossing and the movement of migrants across borders utterly obscures the importance of geographical stability and arrival for undocumented migrants themselves ("Telling" 53–57). This is a crucial point to consider for my own project; I argue that, in the Gatekeeper era of border enforcement escalation, Chicana/o and other Latina/o writers increasingly represent the border with all its material and concrete effects, with a corresponding waning in the use of "borderlands" to refer primarily to hybrid/impure identities, to generalized group or nation "outsiders," or to other more strictly metaphorical valences of the border.

In *Rethinking the Borderlands: Between Chicano Culture and Legal Discourse,* Carl Gutiérrez-Jones explores the ways in which Chicano authors challenge structures of thought produced and promoted by legal rhetoric and the operations of the law—for example, ascriptions of "criminality" to Mexican immigrants and Mexican Americans that are "often accompanied by calls to 'close' the border or to 'repatriate' Chicanos and Mexicanos" (2). Like some of the critics referred to above, Gutiérrez-Jones sees the borderlands as primarily metaphorical, referring to the terrain on which legal and larger ideological battles regarding Mexican American rights, citizenship, and belonging are fought. Taking his cue in part from critical legal studies, which addresses the power of law to shape social thought, Gutiérrez-Jones sets out to explore the ways in which "Chicano artists project their own versions of the courtroom, and of legal culture in general, as a critical arena of resistance" (4, 13–14). If, as Castillo and Córdoba have suggested, the "theoretically conceived border" of Chicano/a studies "serves as an objective correlative for discussions of U.S. dominant culture and its resistant spaces" (3), then for Gutiérrez-Jones the courtroom *is* the "borderlands" under discussion, because it is a primary resistant space where struggles over hegemonic frames and alternative interpretations are waged. Gutiérrez-Jones's approach valuably opens the way for us to attend to current immigration law as not merely regulatory but as also a *constitutive* force which has shaped and reified convictions about immigrant nonbelonging within the U.S. nation. Immigration law and the system by which immigration cases are adjudicated encourage the production of certain types of narratives about immigrants over others; as we shall see, many of the writers I discuss here challenge these dominant, "law-and-order" based narratives in different ways, but many also attend much more concretely to the lived experience of the border's materiality.

Other scholars share with Gutiérrez-Jones and Sadowski-Smith a concern with examining Latino/a literary responses to hegemonic narratives, particularly narratives of American nation. Paul Allatson, in *Latino Dreams: Transcultural Traffic and the U.S. National Imaginary*, understands "border logics"—with reference to both the land border between Mexico and the United States, and to the more amorphous water "border" between the continental United States and the Caribbean—as a space which symbolically connotes the *conceptual* limits of the hegemonic U.S. nation (29). U.S. Latino/a writers, in Allatson's view, engage with dominant U.S. mythologies through a process of transculturation that can take various forms, not all of them necessarily contestatory (44–45). Debra Castillo's *Redreaming America: Toward a Bilingual American Culture* is an effort to consider the intertwined questions of how literature written in Spanish within the United States might have "real transformatory effects in the nation's sense of itself" (2), as well as in the construction and (self) representation of Latin America as a coherent region. Like Allatson, Castillo is interested in how claims about and representations of social reality engage "with an exclusionary system that defines an inside and an outside, a really real and an 'other' reality that lies outside the established boundaries" (10). The questions Castillo raises take on added significance if we consider the position of undocumented storytellers and narrators, many of whom understand themselves as firmly rooted "inside" the United States, even if their origins are elsewhere.

For Castillo as for Allatson, representation may engage with the bounded, imagined community of the nation in a broad spectrum of ways from acquiescence and complicity to direct challenge.[9] Furthermore, given engagement with a whole host of sometimes competing popular narratives, any given representational strategy might be resistant and challenging in certain aspects at the expense of complicity in others. This interpretational nuance is one that I wish to preserve in my own study. It is worth noting that while scholars including Castillo, Allatson, Saldívar, and others emphasize the transnational dimensions of literature of the "border" (whether geopolitical or more metaphorical), *some* undocumented narratives strategically downplay the transnational aspects of migrant experience, instead demanding a recognition of where they *are now* (existentially as well as territorially) and of where and how they have taken root (see, for example, my discussions of Orner's *Underground America* in chapter 4 and of undocumented youth narratives in chapter 6). Thus, arguably, they accede to a paradigm of singular national identification even while they challenge the way the nation's boundaries—who belongs and who does not—are imaginatively constituted. Scholars such as Allatson, Gutiérrez-Jones, and Castillo have done much to advance understanding of the ways in which Latino/a literary texts reimagine the U.S. nation; what remains to be substantially addressed is the ways in which the undocumented—as figures in literary texts and/or narrators of their own life stories—posit potential challenges to the imagined boundaries of the United States.

Despite the ascendance of borderlands scholarship, literary criticism dealing specifically with the representation of the undocumented in Latino/a writing is significantly more scarce. Alberto Ledesma, one of the few to examine the issue of undocumented immigration in Latino/a literature, takes Chicano/a literary critics to task for not attending to representations of undocumented immigration as a fundamental and essential part of what he calls the "Chicano experience" ("Narratives" 331). Yet as Ledesma himself points out elsewhere, Chicano/a *writers* have historically tended to shy away from explicit representation of undocumented immigration because of its negative social valence ("Undocumented Crossings" 88). Indeed, Ledesma argues that "undocumented immigrant subjects . . . [in Chicano narratives] are kept quiet by a pattern of silences and omissions about their experience" ("Undocumented Crossings" 88; see also "Narratives" 332).

Further, Ledesma's insistence that the undocumented experience is part and parcel of Chicano identity, even if unrecognized as such, threatens to conflate the two groups in ways that risk eliding some important differences, both in terms of the privileges of citizenship and of historical tensions between "Chicanos" and the undocumented.[10] In a later essay

Ledesma examines Richard Rodriguez's representation of undocumented immigrants, arguing that Rodriguez simultaneously identifies with the undocumented on the basis of enforced social silence and yet fails to understand the material conditions which allow him speech while the undocumented remain silent ("Narratives" 337–39, 344–46). Such a reading has the potential to shed light precisely on the sorts of material and concrete conditions, more generally, which separate Mexican Americans who are U.S. citizens from unauthorized Americans.

My own argument is that the escalation of urgency and sense of crisis in the 1990s and 2000s has seen a changed landscape in Chicano/a writing, which increasingly takes undocumented immigration quite explicitly as its subject. Stories by Chicano/a writers of 1990 and beyond portraying undocumented immigration, in particular, are replete with the trauma of border crossing, of living an unauthorized presence within the new country, and of the threat of loss of loved ones through familial separation. Further, as I will explore, Chicano/a writers are increasingly quite sensitive to concrete material conditions that impact undocumented lives in ways quite distinct from Chicano/a lives, even while they also recognize the damage inflicted on entire Mexican American communities by restrictive immigration legislation, border enforcement, and deportations.

While direct analyses of the theme of the undocumented in literature are still scant, scholars have increasingly looked at representations of unauthorized migrants in other forms of popular culture, in both Mexico and the United States. María Herrera-Sobek, for instance, writes on Mexican film; L. S. Kim has examined the figure of the undocumented maid on television; several scholars have written a volume on the 1977 film *Alambrista!* about an undocumented migrant (Groody). In general, such approaches have tended to either read representation in terms of its "progressive" potential or to comment on its reinscription of hegemonic narratives of immigration and nation. Representations themselves, of course, frequently function in more complex ways than this loose dichotomy allows, including by resisting certain narratives while affirming others; by narrating forms of collective history (including traumatic history) that are themselves instrumental in constructing group identities; by contributing to oppositional and subaltern counterpublics that attempt to make interventions into policy debates; and by calling readers to forms of ethical engagement and social action. These are the lines of inquiry I follow.

In this book, I attend to narratives, both fictional and nonfictional, that represent the personal experience of undocumented immigration. Three terms come up repeatedly as nodal points in my analysis around which the discussion tends to circulate: trauma, testimony, and ethics. I do not mean to suggest here that this framework applies equally to all chapters; rather, these terms recur throughout the project, sometimes in relative isolation and sometimes in close interrelation with one another, in what might be characterized as a literary *movement* to represent this hitherto unrepresented issue within a responsible, ethical, and sometimes even interventionist framework.

Trauma

To begin with, the effects of immigration enforcement on human lives (raids, border deaths and disappearances, family separations, generalized anxiety regarding deportation) are usefully approached through the lens of trauma. Cathy Caruth, one of the foremost trauma scholars, has defined trauma as "an overwhelming experience" characterized by an "often delayed," "intrusive," and "uncontrolled" response (11). Trauma haunts its victims long after the event itself. This definition might certainly apply to workplace raids, in which the traumatic aftereffects of sudden removal and deportation and/or of unexpected separation from children/parents might well outlast the immediate event of the raid itself.

And yet the everyday usage of the adjective *traumatic* to express something along the lines of what happens to communities in the wake of immigration raids (as a case in point) does not fit as easily as it might with much of the standard scholarship on trauma studies. Stef Craps and Gert Buelens have noted that "the founding texts of the field . . . are almost exclusively concerned with traumatic experiences of white Westerners" (2); many of the foremost trauma theorists consider primarily individual forms of trauma (especially childhood trauma) via methodologies that continue to bear the stamp of Freudian psychoanalysis. Even scholars interested in broader forms of cultural trauma tend to fall back on psychoanalytic frameworks. Take Irene Wirshing's study of national trauma in Latin American literature, which she begins by glossing trauma as follows:

> The natural response to trauma is to bury it deep in the unconscious. But trauma does not fade away into nothingness; it does not

permanently disappear. It lies dormant within the unconscious until it is triggered. It can take years, but survivors will inevitably reenact the trauma itself. Reenactments are the repeated actions of past trauma in the present lives of survivors, usually accompanied by the same psychological and emotional intensity. (1)

Wirshing's references to "unconscious" repression and to compulsive reenactment by "survivors" suggests a model of trauma in which, even when the trauma is experienced by many, the survivors' responses are still, at base, individual ones. In contrast, cultural trauma demands a broader and somewhat different conceptualization—beginning perhaps with something like Kai Erikson's postulation that "By collective trauma . . . I mean a blow to the basic tissues of social life that damages the bonds attaching people together and impairs the prevailing sense of community" (*Everything* 153–54). In this reformulation, it is the *community* (not just an aggregate of individuals within a community) that experiences trauma: "when the community is profoundly affected one can speak of a damaged social organism in almost the same way that one would speak of a damaged body" (Erikson, "Notes" 188).

Further, while Holocaust studies serve as the paradigm for exploration into collective forms of trauma, this too serves in some ways to limit our understanding of what "trauma" might by definition entail. Some trauma studies scholars have argued that we must "expand our understanding of trauma from sudden, unexpected catastrophic events" to take account of more slow and insidious forms of trauma—to take account, for instance, of "the chronic psychic suffering produced by the structural violence of racial, gender, sexual, class, and other inequities" (Craps and Buelens 3). "The collective trauma," Erikson explains, "works its way slowly and even insidiously into the awareness of those who suffer from it, so it does not have the quality of suddenness normally associated with 'trauma'" (*Everything* 153–54). Cultural trauma, in other words, need not stem from a specific historical "event" (e.g. the Holocaust). Taking the African American case, Evelyn Schreiber writes, "In a culture where whiteness is the norm, black identity is marginalized, and the nuances of this marginalization suggest a range of trauma associated with black experience" (1). Here "range of trauma" in a more generalized "experience" has replaced a singular traumatic "event." Such an understanding could similarly be applied to any marginalized or oppressed culture, traumatized not by one event but by a range of experiences—from apparently "neutral" legal systems that support the well-being of some groups over others, to difficult choices about which necessities to pay for and which to forgo, to the impracticalities of political activism and protest in the face of such obstacles (see Povinelli on indigenous activism in Australia, esp. 101–30). The move to conceptualize pervasive sociohistorical *conditions,* as well as events, as potentially traumatic constitutes a significant addition to trauma studies, with direct and obvious implications for an understanding of U.S. Latino/a and Latin American communities impacted by large-scale migration north and by U.S. policies that render that migration "illegal." (Strikingly, however, several cultural trauma scholars who acknowledge the possibility of more ongoing and pervasive forms of trauma persist in using "event" language in their formulations.)

We may do well to consider the possibility of Gatekeeper era immigration enforcement and control as increasingly in the nature of a trauma inflicted on immigrant Latino/a *communities* in the United States. Kaplan posits that trauma should be understood not only as the *direct infliction of injury* but also as the "suffering [of] terror" (1), a definition which might usefully be expanded to allow for a consideration of chronic forms of trauma historically inflicted on people of color (e.g., the perpetual threat of violence under slavery or of lynching in the Jim Crow South). Understanding "trauma" to include collective, social "terror" also allows us to consider, under the "trauma" rubric, migrant communities who live in fear of their family members being deported or of dying during a border crossing. Such trauma does not affect exclusively the individuals who are subjected to specific "events" (the victims of raids, the people actually crossing the border); its effects ripple outward to the larger communities. Indeed, because of such ripple effects, it can be difficult to make a neat and clear distinction between individual trauma and cultural trauma, as Kaplan herself readily acknowledges (1–2).

Another crucial aspect of the definition of trauma advanced by trauma scholars emphasizes the ways in which trauma poses a challenge to our meaning-making capacities. Because traumatic events and experiences "defy understanding and representation" (Craps and Buelens 1)—because in the immediate face of trauma we do not "understand" it—we cannot integrate it into a coherent causal narrative (history). In Caruth's famous explication,

> Trauma is not locatable in the simple violent or original event in an individual's past, but rather . . . the way that it was precisely *not known* in the first instance . . . returns to haunt the survivor later on. . . . [Trauma] is always the story of a wound that cries out, that addresses us in the attempt to tell us of a reality or truth that is not otherwise available. . . . [Because] traumatic experience . . . is not fully assimilated as it occurs, . . . it simultaneously defies and demands our witness. (4–5)

That is to say, the marker of trauma is not the measure of violence of the event so much as the way in which it disrupts the victim's ability to know, understand, and (self-)represent what has happened. As Susan J. Brison eloquently puts it, "Trauma undoes the self by breaking the ongoing narrative, severing the connections among remembered past, lived present, and anticipated future" (41).[11] Trauma, according to this line of thought, interrupts and dislodges the "history" or cause-and-effect narrative through which we have previously understood and given meaning to our lives. Once again, however, this understanding of trauma needs to be modified and expanded to consider not only its effects on the narrative of the individual victim but also on collective cultural narratives—and not only the effects of the traumatic catastrophic event but also those of ongoing, systemic forms of trauma such as colonialism, slavery, or contemporary racism. Cultural trauma, Ron Eyerman writes in his discussion of African American slavery, "refers to a dramatic loss of [group] identity and meaning, a tear in the social fabric, affecting a group of people that has achieved some degree of cohesion" (61); that is, the group's stories about its own collective identity are interrupted by trauma.

If trauma severs our ability to shape meaningful narratives out of a usable past, then narrative-making serves as trauma's counterbalance. Mieke Bal contends that "to enter memory, the traumatic event of the past needs to be made 'narratable'"; that is to say, it needs to be made to "make sense" in the present (x). Kathleen Brogan, writing on ethnic U.S. literatures, also deploys the distinction between "traumatic memory" and "narrative memory" to signal the effort to reconstitute severed cultural/historical memory (via slavery, migration, diaspora, assimilation): "Traumatic memory can be defined as the reexperiencing of an event too overwhelming to be integrated into understanding," while "narrative memory reshapes and gives meaning to past experience" (73, 70). Notably, in cultural trauma studies, it is *social* forms of narrative memory that rise to the fore (rather than the more psychoanalytically derived emphasis on an individual retrieving and recounting the traumatic memory). Along lines similar to Brogan, Eyerman observes that "Resolving cultural trauma can involve the articulation of collective identity and collective memory, as individual stories meld into collective history through forms and processes of collective representation" (74). According to Bal, the narrative-making of trauma is both fundamentally social and socially constitutive, in contrast to the socially severing nature of trauma itself:

> Narrative memory fundamentally serves a social function: it comes about in a cultural context . . . in which, precisely, the past makes sense in the present, to others who can understand it, sympathize with it, or respond with astonishment, surprise, even horror; narrative memory offers some form of feedback that ratifies the memory . . . as it calls for political and cultural solidarity in recognizing the traumatized party's predicament. (x)

That is to say, narrative memory at the collective level *constructs* a social context of "solidarity."

Jeffrey Alexander goes a step further to argue that cultural trauma is *produced through the process of representing something as "traumatic."* That is, an understanding of an event or historical situation as a form of "cultural trauma" only arises as a result of social narratives that *represent* it as profoundly damaging, as Erikson might say, to the "basic tissues of social life" and the fundamental bonds of a community:

> Events are one thing, representations of these events quite another. Trauma is not the result of a group experiencing pain. It is the result of this acute discomfort entering into the core of the collectivity's sense of its own identity. Collective actors "decide" to represent social pain as a fundamental threat to their sense of who they are, where they came from, and where they want to go. ("Toward a Theory" 10)

In Alexander's theory, social conditions can be experienced in the moment as distressing, painful, even agonizing—but only the cumulative collective stories told about those conditions will determine whether they are "traumatic" per se. Such stories can have the effect simultaneously of constructing trauma and of constructing (or reconstructing or reconfiguring) community in the wake of trauma. Certainly, as larger numbers of people are affected by draconian enforcement measures, Latino/a communities increasingly regard immigration as a communal and collective trauma necessitating address in the public sphere, rather than as one which affects only those deported (or dead) and their families. It is precisely for this reason that the two decades since Operation Gatekeeper's implementation have seen a groundswell of Latino/a writing representing this issue—a phenomenon that can be identified as a form of literary solidarity.

Testimony

To attend to the issue of how to make narrative out of trauma is to immediately invoke the second term in my field of nodal points: testimony. Indeed, perhaps one of the very markers of trauma may be the urgency to *narrate* after the fact—to bear witness. In *That the World May Know*, a study of storytelling and testimony in the wake of large-scale human rights crises (e.g., the Rwandan genocide, South African apartheid), James Dawes poses the question, "How do we make comprehensible stories out of incomprehensible atrocities? . . . [H]ow [do] we make stories (pleas, arguments, cases, testimonies, memoirs, novels) out of catastrophic violence, out of events that by their very nature resist coherent representation" (22)? How do individual victims or collective groups reach a point where they can provide "coherence" and meaning to the unfathomable, can "explain" it through a new narrative framework? Though trauma is marked by the *difficulty*, perhaps even impossibility, of telling, it is also marked by the compulsive *need* for telling. In the words of James Young,

> It is almost as if violent events—perceived as aberrations or ruptures in the cultural continuum—demand their retelling, their *narration*, back into traditions and structures they would otherwise defy. . . . [T]he more violently wrenched from a continuum a catastrophe is perceived to be, the more desperate—and frustrated—the writer's attempts become to represent its events *as* discontinuous [that is, as traumatic]. (404)

The effort to reincorporate the rupturing event or conditions back into a narrative of collective identity with explanatory power is one of the hallmarks of trauma.

The move from "trauma" to "testimony" implies certain concomitant shifts in emphasis, however. Testimony marks a transition from being subjected to the violence of social catastrophe to being the subject (author, narrator) of the history of that catastrophe—from witnessing to bearing witness. To refocus our attention on testimony is to begin to take into account the rhetorical purpose of narrative, outward to others not directly or vicariously involved in the experience of trauma itself. Testimony, by its nature, implies giving information to those that would otherwise not have access to it. It constructs a rhetorical relationship between victims and observers, bystanders, readers: an audience to the testimony. In the case of immigration narratives, it implies that the perhaps interested but largely uninformed audience of middle-class, non-Latino, U.S. readers has now become the imagined addressees.

At its most basic level, testimony (as in legal testimony) involves reporting what has been observed or experienced (bearing witness, as in a court of law). Such reporting may serve a variety of functions. It may involve an intentional challenge to willful historical amnesia or to imposed silences. In *That the World May Know: Bearing Witness to Atrocity*, James Dawes discusses the official silencing that was part and parcel of the Rwandan genocide: "Key public voices (journalists, activists, opposition politicians) were targeted for execution, domestic telephone lines in Kigali were cut, and curfews and roadblocks prevented public protests. . . . The government worked hard . . . to silence its opponents and victims" (41–42). In the face of such silencing, bearing witness may mean simply telling the silenced story. Linda J. Craft, in *Novels of Testimony and Resistance from Central America*, suggests along similar lines that the crucial characteristic of Latin American literature of testimony is that it attempts to give voice to the voiceless—the subaltern, whose own counternarratives and unofficial versions of history are not otherwise generally heard (188–89).

Texts under discussion in this study that resist salient recent narratives regarding unauthorized immigration or that offer perspectives of the undocumented themselves can be understood as forms of "testimony" under the rather expansive description I have given above. For instance, the life narratives discussed in the last three chapters of this book counter assumptions about encroaching and invasive "illegals" through resolutely transnational visions and the dream of return "home"—or, alternatively, through insistent challenges to the exclusion of unauthorized immigrants from the parameters of "American" inclusion. Caribbean writers discussed in chapter 3—including Cristina García, Julia Alvarez, Junot Díaz, and Achy Obejas—may be seen as offering a form of fictional testimony that corrects an overly homogenizing view of "Latinos" in which all recent Latino immigrants have fundamentally the same relationship to U.S. immigration law. These authors explore the ways in which differing access to legal status in the United States creates surprising alignments and communities, or equally surprising divisions among Latinos of differing national origin.

In almost all the cases I examine in this book, however, Latino authors respond to the escalation of anti-immigrant rhetoric and the militarization of the border with a pressing sense that the situation calls for an ethical and communal response. In doing so, they adapt the Latin American literary mode of *testimonio*. While the Spanish word *testimonio* means "testimony," invocation of the literary genre carries significant additional weight. *Testimonio* is of course giving testimony to trauma, but its central and underlying concern is less the traumatic past than the future; its self-positioning is less one of victimization than of political agency and empowerment. Scholars of the genre of *testimonio* repeatedly emphasize that it is intended to go beyond bearing witness—beyond mere testimony—to have real world impacts. John Beverley remarks that "testimonio aspires not only to interpret the world but also to change it" (xvi, 32). Narrators of deliberative *testimonio*, Kimberly Nance points out, "declare emphatically that their projects neither end with the production of the text nor even with its enthusiastic reception. Instead, they describe the texts as intermediate steps in a process directed toward producing change in the lifeworld" (*Can Literature* 14). *Testimonios* must be understood as "texts that present themselves as instruments to drastically influence the social flow of events" (Dorfman 154, qtd. and trans. in Nance, *Can Literature* 20).

In this book, then, I follow these scholars' insistence on the genre's aspirations to solicit change. When I use the broader term *testimony* I mean to suggest the act of bearing witness to social crisis, for whatever reason, whether in fiction or nonfiction; when I refer to *testimonio*, I invoke this understanding of *testimonio* as a form of testimony which seeks to *affect the world*, to change oppressive circumstances, through the power of storytelling. Linda Craft uses the term *testimonial function* to describe novels that do some of the same work as first-person *testimonio*; I have modified her phrase to *testimonio function* in my own usage because the term *testimonial* has quite different connotations (e.g., vouching for someone or something, attesting to its value) that do not at all convey *testimonio*'s concerns with addressing and changing situations of injustice and oppression. *Testimonio* that is aimed at changing the responses of the reader to a particular situation implies the third term in my triad—*ethics*—since ethics highlights the question of what *ought to be done*.

Ethics

Although my discussion thus far has focused on the telling of trauma, one development in trauma studies "calls into question the adequacy of narrative alone to enable healing and the restoration of agency" and suggests, instead, that "such recovery of language must be joined by material compensation and a fundamental refiguring of socio-spatial relationships" (Graham 129). Of course, this understanding is particularly pertinent to forms of collective and cultural trauma which demand not only stories, but also social and historical change. Can the *story* in and of itself set us free, in the absence of more profound social and/or economic changes that enact substantive correction of the *material* effects of cultural trauma? This form of critique, with its challenge to individual and psychoanalytic approaches to trauma as well as to the contention that narrative alone can heal, brings us to questions of ethical responsibility.

The imperative to give testimony to trauma is one form of ethical response that is implied or explicit in some of the narratives that I discuss in the following pages. One cannot *ethically* "witness" social crisis without also bearing witness in some form. When marginalized and oppressed populations bear witness to their own conditions—either through individual forms of *testimonio* or through collective political activism (which can, of course, include *testimonio*), and often at significant material, physical, psychological, or legal costs to themselves—they are performing ethical acts, translating trauma into a vision of action.[12] In the case of the undocumented, youth activists have been particularly notable in their activist response to this sense of responsibility in the face of what they view as the moral crisis of immigration restriction—through online *testimonio*, public protest, symbolic demonstrations (e.g., DREAM "graduations"), and audiences with political representatives.

Of course, the telling of a story—even a story that challenges dominant representations or seeks political change—is not in itself a guarantor of change. This is a point that Kimberly Nance has made forcefully, and it suggests that narrative is part of a much longer process of social transformation rather than an end in itself:

> Critical formulations that have confused writing with concrete action in the world appear to have taken at face value . . . that to write one's own history is to triumph politically. . . . [T]he very act of speaking or writing that something happened can be in itself a form of resistance. But to speak the truth while oppressors are still in power is merely to join in the contest to shape world opinion, not to win it, and much less to guarantee social action. (*Can Literature* 34)

In order to create the change that is sought, social movements generally need converts—they need to persuade a large audience of people with greater social power, who are not themselves directly affected, to act on behalf of a greater social good. Concerned with the "real world" effects of narrative, Nance contends, "As part of a social project, testimonio is . . . [a matter] of speaking of one's suffering in such a way that readers will be induced to act against the injustice of it" (*Can Literature* 90). Other scholars, too, have recently been quite concerned with the power (or failure) of narratives to move readers to action and to generate social change. According to Kay Schaffer and Sidonie Smith, "Published life narratives have contributed directly and indirectly to campaigns for human rights . . . through acts of speaking out that shift attention to systemic causes of violation" (28). James Dawes, who explores the role of fiction in human rights struggles, notes that stories may well have the power to "move" us emotionally—but "what is the line that separates those who are merely moved from those who are moved to act" (7)?

Such commentary implicitly calls forth the question of the ethical obligations *of readers*, since it is readers whose attention will be called to systemic violations, readers who will be moved (or not) to act to change the suffering depicted in the text. Ethics, by definition, invokes actions, behavior, and conduct; ethical judgments are "decisions about what to do" (Caputo 112). Dawes explicitly articulates his object of study as "the relationship between aesthetics and ethics" (6). Schaffer and Smith advance an "ethics of recognition": they suggest that stories which circulate as part of larger human rights discussions generally are those which "invite an ethical response from listeners and readers" (4). As such commentary suggests, a readerly ethics extends beyond emotion and knowledge to force a consideration of how particular values or principles shape what we *do* in the world as moral agents (LaFollette 1–2).

Of course, if we consider literary *testimonio* about immigration in the framework of ethics, then we must also contemplate the possibility that, while *testimonio* in and of itself constitutes an ethical act, the narratives in question might *fail* to have significant real-world effects on their readers. This, too, is a possibility of which some scholars are powerfully cognizant. Dawes is acutely aware of the potential "impotence of representation," the possibility that stories may fail to have concrete effects for the worlds they represent (10). Craps and Buelens have rightly noted that some *scholarly* models for conceptualizing the giving of testimony to trauma may themselves inhibit a thorough engagement with ethics. They are particularly wary of models that draw heavily on a psychoanalytic framework, in which

> The respective subject positions into which the witness and the listener/reader are interpellated are those of a passive, inarticulate victim on the one hand and a knowledgeable expert on the other. The former bears witness to a truth of which he or she is not fully conscious, and can do so only indirectly, making it impossible for his or her testimony to act as a political intervention. The [listener/reader].... responds to the witness's testimony by showing empathy, a reaction that supposedly obviates any need for critical self-reflection regarding his or her own implication in ongoing practices of oppression and denial, let alone political mobilization against those practices. (4–5)

This discussion suggests the need for alternative models for literary testimony besides a merely therapeutic one—models (like *testimonio*) which conceptualize the possibility that literary testimony might in fact constitute a "political intervention."

Many scholars are skeptical of the provocation of "empathy" in the reader of *testimonio* narratives, if this is understood as an end in itself; in various ways, they seek to supplement empathy with a more critical positioning of the reader. In a gloss on Bakhtin's notion of "exotopy," Kimberly Nance says, "When empathy is conceived as an end in itself, rather than only a preliminary to ethical action, there is no expectation of ever returning to one's own place, . . . [leaving] the reader with[out] any compelling standpoint for action" (*Can Literature* 128; Nance cites Lerner, 76–77, 128).

In order to truly respond ethically, we must on the contrary "consider the unique ways in which . . . [our own] position enables [us] to assist others" (Nance, *Can Literature* 63). Craps, similarly, suggests that trauma literature can ideally "complicate the pursuit of imaginative identification, inviting critical reflection on the potentially harmful consequences of the drive to fully imagine another's reality or voice" (197). "A listener's appropriate response" to testimony of cultural trauma might be "open and accepting but [also] respectfully acknowledging unbridgeable distances" (Craps and Buelens 9). In concerning themselves not just with the literary but also with its possible real world effects, such scholars integrate a humanistic study of fictional and nonfictional texts, and of narrative more generally, with a much larger, interdisciplinary attention to pressing issues of social justice and to how, as a society, we might address these.

Documenting the Undocumented

Since the implementation of Operation Gatekeeper in 1994, Latino/a writing has been marked by a profound shift in attention and sensibility in reaction to the multifaceted nature of the crisis of escalating immigration enforcement—a crisis including increasing deaths at the border (as well as rape, dismemberment, and other life-threatening hazards), familial separations due to deportation, labor exploitation and human trafficking, and a generalized culture of anxiety. In response, while the topic of undocumented immigration was largely absent from an earlier canon of U.S. Latina/o literature, the corpus of Latino/a letters since 1994 represents the crisis in a multitude of texts, through numerous modes of writing, and across several distinct national origin groups. Deaths and deportations are represented as issues that touch *all* Latino communities (regardless of how particular groups may choose to respond to it). Even when the narrative representation depicts characters that resist or deny their connection to the crisis (as in *Drown*, where Yunior insistently separates his father from "illegals" and groups him instead with "legal" Latinos, or the writing of Achy Obejas, in which Cuban American characters repeatedly underscore a history of Cuban access to the United States without questioning or problematizing that particular form of immigrant privilege), most of the authors I examine suggest, through their attention to the nuances of difference in legal status, that they are staking a claim to panethnic solidarity around the issue.

In *Documenting the Undocumented*, accordingly, I study some of the many counternarratives offered by (primarily) Latino/a writers and journalists as well as by the undocumented themselves. I bring to bear a literary analysis, paying close attention to metaphorical language, the entire arc of a story (plotting), and particular models of narrative structure, as a way of getting at larger issues regarding the nature of a particular narrative's intersection with current immigration rhetoric and debates. Following critics including Castillo and Allatson, I attempt to be sensitive to the varying registers of counternarrative, recognizing that texts do not necessarily work in monolithic ways and that they may offer challenges to some forms of hegemonic representation or dominant narrative while reinscribing others. I consider representation of border crossing and undocumented existence as psychologically damaging, dehumanizing, and traumatic; suggest ways in which the narratives attempt to serve a *testimonio* function regarding this (collective) trauma; and discuss the implicit calls to ethical action.

In chapters 1 and 2, I consider the ways in which Latino/a narrative representations of undocumented immigration in the new era of escalating border security and militarization shift the meanings of the border. The texts I examine in these chapters represent a post-Gatekeeper shift in sensibility from transnational identification—the cultural legacy of the Chicano Movement and of paradigmatic works such as Rodolfo "Corky" Gonzales's epic poem "I am Joaquin"—to what we might call (following Bakhtin) "exotopy." Increasingly, post-Gatekeeper texts tend to recognize and even dwell on the materiality of the border as a point of demarcation with devastating consequences, and to invest it with meanings that emphasize its impact and its dangers. In chapter 1, "Narrating the Non-Nation: Literary Journalism and 'Illegal' Border Crossings," I consider works of narrative journalism including Luis Alberto Urrea's *The Devil's Highway* (2004), Rubén Martínez's *Crossing Over: A Mexican Family on the Migrant Trail* (2001), and Sonia Nazario's *Enrique's Journey: The Story of a Boy's Dangerous Odyssey to Reunite with His Mother* (2006). Such works capitalize on a culture in which "life narratives" have become not only instrumental in discourses on human rights but also eminently marketable. The authors of the border crossing texts that I examine here clearly seek to counter the strident narrative of immigration as a threat to the existence of the nation by offering alternative narratives in which undocumented people are *not* imagined, first and foremost, as "aliens."

These texts reframe the story of immigration in terms that shift the focus from the borders of "our" imagined community, to construct alternative notions of ethical communities—although not without their own problematic reinstantiations of national identity, as we shall see.

In chapter 2, "The Lost Ones: Post-Gatekeeper Border Fictions and the Construction of Cultural Trauma," I consider several novels that represent border crossing deaths and missing or disappeared loved ones in terms of the border. I argue that the three novels which are the central focus of this chapter—by two Chicanas and an Anglo-American writer, Susan Straight—share a sensibility of cross-border solidarity and peoplehood, but they also mark a shift in U.S. border fiction by attending squarely to the traumatic effects of increased border security measures. In this chapter, I follow theorists such as Jeffrey Alexander and Neil Smelser, who argue that cultural trauma is not inherent in events themselves but is, rather, *constructed* through repeated representations of particular events as *fundamental* injuries to a "people." I argue that border fiction written in the years after Operation Gatekeeper appropriates the notion of the "disappeared"—with all its connotations of state violence—from its Latin American context, to construct migrant disappearances as a cultural trauma that violently separates families and introduces profound instability into notions of individual and group identity.

In chapter 3, "The Caribbean Difference: Imagining Trans-Status Communities," I extend my analysis of a developing, constructed sense of group identity around issues of the trauma of illegality by turning to another group not often highlighted in discussions about unauthorized immigration: Caribbeans. Given that Latino national-origin groups from the Caribbean—and in particular from Cuba and Puerto Rico—have strikingly different relationships to the possibilities of legal status and even citizenship in the United States than do Mexicans, how have Caribbean Latino/a writers recorded and negotiated these significant differences among groups in their writing? I argue that, in different ways, Dominican American and Cuban American writers including Junot Díaz, Cristina García, and Julia Alvarez seek ways of extending a group identity so that it tentatively includes both undocumented immigrants and other groups of Latinos who, by virtue of different national origin, are not subjected to the conditions and risks of "illegality." Junot Díaz's story "Negocios" (in his 1996 debut collection, *Drown*) puts the trope of family at the center of contested versions of *latinidad* that might, or might not, successfully create communities of solidarity around both U.S. citizens and undocumented Latinos. García's *A Handbook to Luck* (2007) and Alvarez's young adult novel *Return to Sender* (2010) are highly attuned to the differences of status which divide "Latino" immigrant populations. Drawing on Kwame Anthony Appiah's explication of the notion of "partial cosmopolitanism," I argue that the latter two authors construct an ethics of solidarity *across difference* that recognizes immigration status as a problem which requires an ethical response across national-origin lines.

In the final three chapters of the book, I examine the experience of so-called illegality in life narratives and personal testimonies. Turning to the voices of the undocumented themselves, this section approaches undocumented testimony as a new manifestation of *testimonio* that challenges prevailing discourses on immigration and even seeks to move readers to new forms of civic engagement with this issue. I also consider how, in certain instances, first-person narrative might fall short of the promise of the *testimonio* genre. In chapter 4, "Selling the Undocumented: Life Narratives of Unauthorized Immigrants," I discuss two collections of first-person oral testimonies of the undocumented: Alicia Alarcón's *La Migra me hizo los mandados* (2002) and Peter Orner's *Underground America: Narratives of Undocumented Lives* (2008). While both texts contain narratives that bear witness to immigration-related trauma, the packaging and editing of the testimonies is crucial in providing cues to readers for how to *read*—and thus respond ethically to—these testimonies. I argue that the marketing and covert forms of editorial manipulation in *Border Patrol* most often work to depoliticize the content of the narratives, capitalizing on readerly interest in undocumented immigration while potentially undermining the *resistant testimonio* functions of the text. In *Underground America*, comparatively, the quite prominent editorial matter mediates the first-person testimonies more overtly than *Border Patrol*, but at the same time constructs a particular readerly context for the accounts as *testimonio*—a context in which moral and ethical considerations are explicitly invoked.

In chapter 5, "Unauthorizied Plots: Life Writing, Transnationalism, and the Possibilities of Agency," I examine two extended life narratives by undocumented subjects: Ramón "Tianguis" Pérez's memoir, *Diario de un Mojado* (*Diary of an Undocumented Immigrant*, 1991, published in the original Spanish in 2003), and the oral history of Yamileth, an undocumented Nicaraguan immigrant, recorded by Dianne Walta Hart in *Undocumented in L.A.* (1997). Neither Yamileth nor Pérez plans to be a permanent immigrant (illegal or otherwise). Thus, while both texts resist certain strands of dominant discourse about "illegal" immigrants, they also express a transnational sensibility that exhibits a strong sense of agency about the plotting of their own life stories, even while it might simultaneously confirm negative rhetoric about recent immigrants' unwillingness to assimilate to "American" culture or to be fully incorporated into U.S. society.

Finally, in chapter 6, "Undocumented Testimony: American DREAMers," I consider recent life narratives by undocumented youth who are activists for the DREAM (Development, Relief, and Education for Alien Minors) Act, including the UCLA students' compilation *Underground Undergrads: UCLA Undocumented Immigrant Students Speak Out* (2008) and William Perez's *We ARE Americans: Undocumented Students Pursuing the American Dream* (2009), as well as my own interviews of undocumented (and formerly undocumented) students. These student narratives constitute a very recent challenge to Luis Alberto Urrea's statement that "undocumented immigrants have no way to tell you what they have experienced, or why, or who they are, or what they think" (in his foreword to *Underground America*). DREAM activists *do* tell what they have experienced and who they are, engaging in an ethical intervention (at considerable risk) into immigration debates through their insistence on "coming out of the shadows." I examine how these youth have shaped their stories for particular rhetorical and political ends, creating out of the raw material of their lives plots and themes that are remarkably consistent across stories (despite differences of situation or country of origin) and that are clearly crafted to achieve a *testimonio* function, to move people to (a very specific) action: support of the DREAM act. The DREAMers, as they call themselves, thus constitute a visible counterpublic that challenges norms and assumptions about who can be a *subject* and *agent* of political activism and change.

Recent narratives about and by undocumented immigrants contribute in significant and varied ways to a larger conversation. The nature of the conversation, and thus of the contributions, is complex and at times contradictory. Because I, like *testimonio* scholars Beverley and Nance, am concerned with "real" effects and what these might be, I do not wish to suggest that literature, all by itself, *is* the effect. It is my hope that the narratives, taken as a whole, may have some "real world" effects and shift attitudes, at least for some; but this hopeful vision cannot be assumed a priori, in part because to do so would be to negate the very real work to be done.

Narrating the Non-Nation

Literary Journalism and "Illegal" Border Crossings

The twenty-first century has been hailed as ushering in a new era of globalization and "post-nationalism," in which the nation-state is becoming an increasingly "obsolete" category (Appadurai 169). Such grand claims are belied, however, by the strong wave of resurgent nativism in the United States that has accompanied immigration reform debates of the last decade—vividly manifested in Arizona's notorious SB 1070 and similar legislative efforts in other states[1]—as well as by the accompanying escalation in militarization of the border. In the words of Joseph Nevins, "While many would have us believe that globalization is making the modern territorial state and its boundaries redundant, the U.S.-Mexico boundary enforcement apparatus is stronger than it has ever been, a manifestation . . . of growing state power" (*Operation Gatekeeper* 158–59).

Operation Hold-the-Line (1993) and Operation Gatekeeper (1994), which escalated border security at the highly trafficked crossing points of El Paso and San Diego, implemented a new regime of border militarization. The number of border patrol agents rose from 4,200 in fiscal year 1994 to almost 8,000 four years later and—just in the San Diego sector—from 998 in October 1994 to 2,264 in June 1998; fencing and border walls in the sector went from 19 miles to over 45; the number of underground sensors went from 448 to 1,214 and that of infrared scopes from 12 to 59. The Immigration and Naturalization Service (INS) budget for border enforcement in the Southwest rose from $400 million in FY 1993 to $800 million in FY 1997 (Nevins, *Dying* 114, 187–89; Nevins, *Operation Gatekeeper* 3–4; Ellingwood 34; Andreas 90).

With the intensified security measures, the risks of illegal border crossing also skyrocketed. Migrant border crossing deaths doubled between 1995 and 2005, though there was no corresponding rise in illegal entries. More than three-fourths of the increase is attributable to deaths in Arizona, where the Sonora Desert makes environmental conditions particularly dangerous; crossing attempts could lead to dehydration, suffocation (in overheated vehicles), hypothermia, and hyperthermia (U.S. Government Accountability Office, 2006). As Nevins argues, "By knowingly 'forcing' people to cross risky terrain, [border security policies are] contributing to the numerous deaths that have resulted." Yet, to judge from some media coverage of these deaths, "No one . . . [says] anything that would suggest that the INS and its practice of boundary control had anything to do with the death[s]" (*Operation Gatekeeper* 145-46; see also Hing 202–4).

In response to the growing crisis, the last decade has seen a flurry of books on the subject of undocumented immigrant crossings and deaths (many by Latino/a writers) including *Dead in Their Tracks: Crossing America's Desert Borderlands* (1999), by John Annerino; *Crossing Over: A Mexican Family on the Migrant Trail* (2001), by Rubén Martínez; *The Devil's Highway* (2004), by Luis Alberto Urrea; *Dying to Cross: The Worst Immigrant Tragedy in American History* (2005), by Jorge Ramos; *Enrique's Journey: The Story of a Boy's Dangerous Odyssey to Reunite with His Mother* (2006), by Sonia Nazario; and *The Death of Josseline: Immigration Stories from the Arizona-Mexico Borderlands* (2010), by Margaret Regan. These texts reframe the immigration debate through graphic narrative accounts of the human costs of our border policy, and they emphasize the pressing urgency of the crisis through the haunting leitmotif of border deaths.

The title of this chapter clearly takes its cue from Homi Bhabha's postulation that "nation" is constituted through "narration." Stories (history, myth, fiction) can construct a sense of what a national people have in common; they also operate on a principle of exclusion, by which *some* people are represented as not belonging to the national body. The now standard labeling of undocumented immigrants as "illegals" suggests the degree to which this population has been narratively constructed as *not fitting* into the boundaries of the American "nation"—indeed, as fundamentally threatening that nation. Perceptions of Latinos as a national threat, Leo R. Chavez argues, have been shaped by "a history of ideas, laws, narratives, myths, and knowledge production in social sciences, sciences, the media, and the arts" that constitute a powerful set of "discursive formations" (*Latino Threat* 22; Hall 6, qtd. in Chavez). In the wake of 9/11, for instance, titles linking immigration to threats to America's national security and even survival have proliferated.[2]

The authors of the works of narrative journalism that I examine in this chapter clearly seek to intervene in this strident narrative of immigration as a threat to the existence of the nation by offering alternative narratives in which undocumented people are *not* imagined as "aliens." These texts offer counterdiscourses, reframing the story of immigration in terms that shift the focus from the borders of "our" imagined community, to construct alternative notions of ethical communities. As works of literary journalism, these accounts capitalize on a culture in which "life narratives" have become not only instrumental in discourses on human rights but also eminently marketable (Schaffer and Smith 7, 25, 27). The current popularity of life writing suggests the degree to which these books might be instrumental in advocacy by reaching privileged readers (in this case, U.S. citizens) with the power to affect the course of policy through voting, campaign contributions, protests, e-mails to congressional representatives, and other forms of pressure. Yet, despite obvious pro-immigrant sympathies and appeals to readerly empathy and identification, such texts often reinstate a problematic politics of place that diffuses a sense of urgency and crisis needing address.

In *Can Literature Promote Justice?* Kimberly Nance has considered the ways in which literary representations of crisis might spur ethical responses on the part of Western readers. Central to Nance's analysis is an interrogation of both the possibilities and the pitfalls of readerly identification with the "I" of *testimonio*. In a similar vein, John Beverley has suggested that such identification is the lynchpin to the social justice functions of *testimonio*—that is, to moving readers to (new kinds of) action to further a just society: "The complicity a testimonio establishes with its readers involves their identification—by engaging their sense of ethics and justice—with a popular cause normally distant, not to say alien, from their immediate experience" (37). Nance, drawing on Lerner's *Belief in a Just World*, as well as upon Mikhail Bakhtin's writings, has also noted that identification, or empathy, is a crucial starting point in reorienting readers from an alienating distancing to involvement. Indeed, Jeffrey Alexander, in a discussion of the construction of cultural trauma, contends that it was narratives which solicited *identification* with the Jewish victims of the

Holocaust that "stimulated an unprecedented universalization of political and moral responsibility" and paved the way for an understanding that "morality must be universalized beyond any particular time and place" ("On the Social Construction" 229), that is, beyond the strictures of national identity that might place limits on those to whom we feel ethically responsible.

Yet there also exists profound scholarly wariness, if not skepticism, about the political project of soliciting identification. As Nance notes in a discussion of Lerner's studies, unqualified empathetic responses actually "made witnesses more likely to reject" those whom they saw as victims (*Can Literature* 71; Nance cites Lerner on 76–77, 128). Bakhtin, likewise, theorizes that ethical responses to the witnessing of injustice must follow identification with exotopy: "My projection of myself into [the victim] must be followed by a *return* into myself, a *return* to my own place outside the suffering person" (Bakhtin 25–26). Nance, glossing Bakhtin's concept of exotopy, posits that empathy is at best only a starting point for ethical action, which ultimately requires a purposeful inhabiting of our own social positionings. Only through a return to the particularity of the reader's own subject position can he or she begin to conceive of how acting *from that position* (as a U.S. citizen, as a voter, as a consumer, as economically, racially, or socially privileged, etc.) might in fact make a difference, however small, to the situation under consideration.

Doris Sommer, in her discussions of *testimonio*, has been even more stridently suspicious of identification and empathy. As Sommer warns, empathy "involves a dissolution of difference between reader and writer" and thus "cancels any need to appreciate a different interiority" ("Taking a Life" 921, 925). If we truly want to engage ethically with the subaltern subject of *testimonio*, Sommer insists, we need "to safeguard distance [from the speaker] as a condition of possibility" (926). Texts intended to take on a *testimonio* function, then, apparently need to navigate between the Scylla of alienation and the Charybdis of identification.

Although the texts I examine in this chapter would not be recognized as *testimonios* by the common scholarly understanding of that term (i.e., first-person accounts of "witnesses" of crisis and repression [Yúdice 54]), the discussions above have obvious implications for the stories of unauthorized immigrants, almost invariably imagined by U.S. audiences as outsiders to the nation, not properly belonging to it, even when they are located within its geographical borders. In what follows, I closely analyze three texts by U.S. Latino/as—Martínez's *Crossing Over*, Nazario's *Enrique's Journey*, and Urrea's *The Devil's Highway*—as particularly salient accounts that present counterhegemonic narratives of unauthorized immigration. What might it mean to apply *testimonio* theory to this new category of literary narrative? For while none of these are first-person narratives told by the witness-participants themselves, they do have certain similarities. Consider the definition of *testimonio* outlined by Cuba's Casa de las Américas when it instituted a new literary prize for the genre: to be eligible for consideration, *testimonios* must

> document, from a direct source, an aspect of reality.... By "direct source" we mean [firsthand] knowledge of the facts by the author, or the collection by the latter of stories or records obtained from the persons in question, or from suitable witnesses. In both cases, reliable documentation is indispensable.... The form is at the discretion of the author, but the literary quality is also indispensable. (Qtd. in Sklodowska, *Testimonio* 56; my translation)

According to such a definition (which scholars have admittedly criticized as overly broad and general), the texts of literary journalism I examine here could indeed conceivably qualify as *testimonio*.[3] To wrest the term from its firm identification with Latin American contexts of human rights abuses, disappearance, torture, and even genocide at the hands of repressive governments in the 1970s and 1980s, and from its corresponding interrelation with larger corrective structures of justice including tribunals, truth commissions, and international human rights law, to the new context of immigration to the United States *from* Latin America most assuredly constitutes a rather stark decontextualization. Nonetheless, such a strategic shift also *insists* that we continue to apply notions of urgency, immediate crisis, human rights issues needing address, and even oppressive state power to the new U.S. context. In other words, my application of the term *testimonio* to many of the texts in this book is a deliberate and self-conscious mechanism for underscoring my contention that, although the historical period, situation, and geographical contexts are different, the rhetorical imperative of the urgency to communicate human rights crises through narrative testimony can be understood to be shared.

Further, like *testimonio*, these early twenty-first-century texts about

U.S. immigration ask us to hear the voices of the subaltern that are usually unhearable—even if the giving voice is highly mediated (something often true as well of *testimonio* proper). As Sommer insists, "Learning to listen to subalterns is an ethical and political imperative" ("No Secrets" 134). Again, my suggestion that we apply a *testimonio* framework to this new corpus of texts is at bottom a mechanism for insisting that listening to the undocumented is also an "ethical and political imperative," even if a less immediately apparent one, because the forms of violence are less overtly physical.

Given the emphasis in many definitions of *testimonio* on the relationship between speaker and mediator or interlocutor, however, one crucial distinction between *testimonio* "proper" and literary journalism of the kind I examine here lies in that relationship. Instead of one informant who serves a representative, collective function, there are in these texts many informants (thus enhancing, if anything, the narrative's collective function). Instead of erasing the interlocutor's tracks to create an "illusion of immediacy" with the subaltern speaker (Sommer, "No Secrets" 131), the journalistic narratives I examine foreground the voice, the perspective, and the interpretive lens of the *interlocutor*, with the result that readers are much less likely to mistake his or her own textual strategies for those of the subaltern themselves. Instead, the interlocutor's textual politics—the underlying assumptions that undergird his or her narrative choices—are far more prominent than in Latin American *testimonio*. All three journalistic texts clearly seek to make a contribution to current, vociferous immigration debates and have received notable critical attention and praise.[4] All three have been positioned by the media in terms of their sympathetic reframing of the issue, as well as by immigrant advocacy groups such as No Más Muertes [No More Deaths], on whose volunteer training list of recommended reading all three books have appeared.[5]

In what follows, I consider some of the ways in which these accounts address and solicit their imagined U.S. readers. While anti-immigrant activism frequently adopts the rhetoric of national defense and patriotism, the narratives I examine here are notable for their engagements with a more generalized rhetoric of humanism and human rights that resists dominant constructs of the "nation," encouraging readers to "identify" with migrants who are normally treated as ethnic and cultural "others" in dominant discourse. Nonetheless, the invitation to readers to identify with the subaltern brings its own grave pitfalls for projects of immigrant advocacy, as I will show. Further, all three texts are still firmly located in a politics of nation; in different ways they paradoxically also function to interpolate U.S. readers within their national "place."

Globalization and Transnationalism: *Crossing Over*

Rubén Martínez's lengthy chronicle *Crossing Over: A Mexican Family on the Migrant Trail* (2001) takes migrant border crossing deaths as his point of departure—specifically the deaths of three brothers of the Chávez family from Michoacán, Mexico, along with five other migrants in a truck camper as a result of a high-speed border patrol chase. Martínez's story turns its attention away from these deaths fairly quickly, however, to focus on the surviving family members who come to the United States themselves. Through their intertwined stories, as well as a whole host of other individual "cameos," *Crossing Over* delineates the circuits of capital and labor under late twentieth-century globalization that have profoundly impacted even small, indigenous towns like Cherán in Michoacán, creating deeply entrenched migration patterns but also "assimilating" remote indigenous peoples to "American" ways of life before they have even arrived in the United States. Martínez's narrative suggests the degree to which immigrants are "familiar" to us—are, indeed, only another version of "Americans." But it also places readers in a position of estrangement with respect to the immigrants. This rhetorical movement between the poles of estrangement and familiarity, I wish to argue, ultimately reinstitutes a potentially problematic politics of nation.

Like their U.S. counterparts, Martínez suggests, undocumented immigrants are participating in the "American Dream": "One of the defining characteristics of the American middle class is the ideal and practice of mobility in pursuit of the bigger house, the nicer neighborhood, the family vacation, and a golden retirement. In this sense, the Enríquezes are profoundly American" (115). Like "us," Cherán migrants want amenities that signal an upwardly mobile, middle-class standard of living: "The Cortéz kitchen [in St. Louis, Missouri] is equipped with a microwave oven, an Osterizer food processor, and an electric can opener.... The nineteen-inch RCA TV receives, via cable hooked up for a small fee . . . HBO, Showtime, and Cinemax" (279). On some level migrants are "just like us"; they share the same middle-class aspirations and therefore are "profoundly American." Readers, that is, are invited to identify with the undocumented via their consumerism and middle-class aspirations.

Such a possibility of identification clearly blunts discourses suggesting that recent waves of migrants are antiassimilationist or unassimilable (Chavez, *Latino Threat* 37–40). Indeed, these communities, Martínez implies, started "assimilating" to American lifestyles while they were still in Mexico. Nonetheless, identification on the basis of middle-class amenities provides highly problematic grounds on which to construct a counterhegemonic vision of imagined community. Martínez's extended representation of middle-class aspirations to some degree already achieved by revolving-door migrants in Cherán diffuses any sense of urgency that needs to be addressed. For one thing, *Crossing Over* underscores that these movements of people and culture have already happened and are here to stay; but as Nance notes, such a sense of inevitability "appear[s] virtually guaranteed to let the general reader off the hook" (*Can Literature* 92). For another, the narrative of the "American Dream," in itself, makes no particular demands on readers. Although effective *testimonio* aims to persuade its audience that the subjects represented "are actually suffering in this situation" (74), consumerism suggests ambition, not suffering. In the absence of crisis, *why* ought U.S. Americans to rethink their deeply held notions of nation? One can well imagine the resistant response: "What? We're supposed to let in millions of 'illegals' so that they can have big-screen TVs and nice cars?" The narrative of middle-class aspiration and the American Dream invites identification without positing any particular sense of ethical responsibility.

The identificatory impulse in *Crossing Over*, furthermore, is accompanied by an opposing but more subtle thrust in the text: the exoticizing of immigrant "informants." In many ways, even while working very hard to redraw the imagined boundaries of the nation, the text distances readers from the plight of migrants that it portrays. Perhaps the most profound illustration of this distancing is the strong visibility of the journalistic eye, combined with a recurring emphasis on observation of the indigenous "other" culture in Cherán, which potentially underscores the separation of Anglo-American readers from migrants. Recall that according to Nance, a key step in leading readers through an "ethical" response to the plight of the subjects is imaginative empathy or identification with those subjects; they must respond "as readers imagine that they themselves might behave in the same circumstance" (*Can Literature* 75). In Martínez's depiction of Cherán, readers are repeatedly solicited to identify not so much with the migrants themselves—who are inhabiting and adapting an "ancient" indigenous culture that is sure to be perceived as quite "other" to most Anglo-Americans—but with the observing perspective of Martínez, the interlocutor-journalist, who both documents and exoticizes this culture. Martínez describes, for example, how the local *bruja* or witch (the term used in the text for indigenous healers) will treat a baby's cough by "work[ing] her white magic against the black that's gotten hold of the child.... She'll seek out a friendly eagle or owl to take hold of and fly ... directly to the child's bedroom, where she will reappear in her grandmotherly form, placing the palm of her hand on the child's forehead to cast out the blackness" (80). Such ethnographic details, arguably, encourage not empathy or exotopy but *absenting* on the reader's part:

> Absenting assumes an incommensurable difference between speaker [or subject] and reader, an uncrossable distance across which it is prohibitively difficult or even impossible to communicate. Absenting may be facilitated by critiques that emphasize the localization of [subjects] in their own cultural and geographic contexts, to the point of isolation. (Nance, *Can Literature* 55)

Martínez's magical, shape-shifting witch turns the indigenous other into an exotic spectacle for U.S. readers. As Arnaldo Cruz-Malavé has observed, "The point of acknowledging difference" is to "engage with that difference" (119; see also Sommer, "Taking a Life" 925–26); exoticization of the kind that "fetishize[s] otherness" (Yúdice 57), rendering it in the eminently consumable terms of magical realism, works against such engagement.

Martínez's explicit and frequently intrusive presence in the text, as interviewer, observer, commentator, and not-quite-participant, also adds a layer of distancing between subject and reader. Martínez's own perspective and position often injects itself into the text; but unlike narrators of *testimonios*, who are both witness to and participant in the injustices being recounted and who serve as a synecdoche for a larger collective, Martínez's observing presence is always rhetorically set apart from those he is writing about. This is, ironically, never more the case than when Martínez is actually attempting to engage in "participatory journalism," in which he will supposedly experience what his subjects experience—such as in his attempts to accompany a group of migrants and a coyote across the border in an "illegal" crossing. When he is told that the group "probably won't leave until after Christmas," he "mull[s] it over. Wait another ten days in Cherán or head to L.A. to spend Christmas with my family? . . . Family wins out. 'I'll be back a couple of days after Christmas,' I tell him" (174). This choice is one marked by privilege; unlike the migrants who must wait until the coyote is ready to cross illegally, Martínez can cross the border at any time. He can go "home" to L.A. for Christmas (surely something many U.S. readers will easily identify with), and then cross back for his stint as an "illegal." The incident both highlights the distance between Martínez's position and that of his subjects and takes the focus off of the undocumented migrant experience, inviting readerly identification instead with Martínez, the Mexican American journalist-observer, in his casual deliberations to go or to stay. Not surprisingly, he misses the migrants' departure and does not accompany them.

No Child Left Behind: *Enrique's Journey*

Enrique's Journey, about a Honduran teenager who works his way through Mexico and into the United States to be reunited with his mother, makes its social agenda explicit from the start. Nazario wants to "humanize" immigrants coming to the United States in order to make them more than just "cost-benefit ratios" in the reader's mind (xiv). That is, she wants to reframe the immigration issue in such a way that strict financial calculations, such as use of social services which cost U.S. taxpayers money, need not be the sole or even the primary determinate of policies. This articulated goal implies that the desired response on the reader's part is a change in attitude toward nativist, anti-immigrant legislation. The "troubles and triumphs" of immigrants, Nazario insists, are "a part of this country's future" (xxv); in this way she reinscribes the undocumented within the boundaries of our nation's imagined community.

Nazario's narrative recounts the odyssey of a boy searching for his mother and encountering in the process one life-threatening obstacle after another. As in *testimonio* proper, Enrique's experiences are synecdochic, meant to stand for a larger and generalized migrant experience. Boys like Enrique who try to hop trains heading north through Mexico may face mutilation of limbs, if not death:

> They pick up three migrants mutilated by the train in as many days. One loses a leg, another his hand; the third has been cut in half. Sometimes the ambulance workers must pry a flattened hand or leg off the rails.... In April, a Honduran broke his foot falling from the train. In May, a Honduran had a fractured right clavicle. In June, a Nicaraguan had a broken right rib. In July, a seventeen-year-old Honduran lost both legs. In August, a Salvadoran arrived with his leg hanging by a bit of skin and muscle. (58)

Nazario uses a catalogue style to generalize the risks that Enrique faces, detailing what happened to "one ... another ... a third" and punctuating a chronological string of months with the accidents that marked each. The incantatory quality of the lists of broken bones and mutilations emphasizes a state of humanitarian crisis and underscores the representative nature of particular instances, pointing readers to the significant and generalized human costs of migration north.

Nazario clearly means to elicit a compassionate response to such suffering. To this end she includes an ethical exemplar in which she recounts unexpected aid coming from the most unlikely of places—poor rural Mexican communities surrounding the railroad tracks in Oaxaca and Veracruz: "Not long after seeing the statue of Jesus, Enrique is alone on a hopper.... He looks over the side. More than a dozen people, mostly women and children, are rushing out of their houses along the tracks, clutching small bundles" (103). The bundles, containing food, water, and clothing, are thrown to the top of the train to aid the largely Central American migrants. The figurative connection to the statue of Jesus is unmistakable, but Nazario underscores it by including the religious rhetoric used by the locals to explain their acts of giving: "God says, when I saw you naked, I clothed you. When I saw you hungry, I gave you food. That is what God teaches" (106). In such justifications, state boundaries, national identities, and economic cost-benefit analyses are deemphasized as the Mexican speakers make an imaginative leap to *identify* with Central American migrants, based on a much more amorphous "imagined community," rendered metaphorically as "your neighbor." The deployment of religious discourse by the Mexicans providing "aid" to *their* "illegals" resonates strongly with the language used on the U.S. side of the border by groups such as Humane Borders, the New Sanctuary movement, and No Más Muertes / No More Deaths, which have, in the past decade, described their activities at the border in just such terms. A Franciscan nun and Humane Borders cofounder has put it this way: "If I'm driving through the desert and it's 107 degrees outside and I see someone in need, there's no way I can't stop. I'll give them water. I'll give them food. . . . I think, if Jesus were in this car and it was me sitting out there by the side of the road, would he drive away from me? I don't think so" (Van Denburg; Interfaith Worker Justice). The scene of aid in Nazario's text dramatizes a faith-based and humanitarian response, rather than a nationalistic one, to unauthorized immigrants and implicitly solicits readers to live up to this particular measure of the "good."

To the end of humanizing her subjects and inviting readerly identification, Nazario opens her story with Enrique's separation from his mother, who goes to the United States in search of the economic means to support the children she leaves behind. The separation, which Enrique experiences as an abandonment, is related in an emotionally charged sequence:

> The boy does not understand.
>
> His mother is not talking to him. She will not even look at him. Enrique has no hint of what she is going to do.
>
> Lourdes knows. She understands, as only a mother can, the terror she is about to inflict, the ache Enrique will feel, and finally the emptiness.
>
> What will become of him? Already he will not let anyone else feed or bathe him. He loves her deeply, as only a son can. . . . "*Dame pico, mami.* Give me a kiss, Mom," he pleads, over and over, pursing his lips. . . .
>
> Slowly, she walks out onto the porch. Enrique clings to her pant leg. Beside her, he is tiny. Lourdes loves him so much she cannot bring herself to say a word. She cannot carry his picture. It would melt her resolve. She cannot hug him. He is five years old. . . .
>
> It is January 29, 1989. His mother steps off the porch.
>
> She walks away.
>
> "¿Dónde está mi mami?" Enrique cries, over and over. "Where is my mom?" (3–5)

The language of the passage is notable for its attempt to "make drama out of the observable world of real people," as Robert Vare puts it. As an aspect of this narrative mode, the roles of mother and son in the story seem to acquire a universalized quality. The passage begins not with the names but with the roles—the "boy" and his "mother"—and then goes on to detail the presumably easily identifiable emotions felt by each person within their "role": Lourdes understands "as only a mother can" the trauma her departure will inflict; Enrique loves her "as only a son can." Spanish phrases that might work to highlight difference between Central American subjects and privileged U.S. readers are immediately translated into familiar English phrases common to Anglo-American children: "give me a kiss" or "where is my mom?" Like Enrique's pleas to his mother, the passage's physical images (the "tiny" Enrique "clings to her pant leg") serve to highlight the young boy's extreme vulnerability, in a transparent appeal to western readers that the child, as a figure of helpless innocence, is in need of protection. The text thus solicits identification with its "characters" through a recognition of, and empathy with, those emotions that attach to their generalized familial roles. The affective quality of this opening scene is emphasized throughout. Readers are invited to place themselves in the scene's rather decontextualized *present* and to empathetically conjure the emotions of the experience.

Yet, while on some level the text invites us to respond humanely to those risking their lives to cross the border, Nazario's solicitation of readerly identification with her subjects also falls prey to what Sommer calls the "dissolution of difference between reader and [subaltern subject]" and thus "cancels any need to appreciate a different interiority" ("Taking a Life" 921, 925). The ways in which Nazario structures her narrative suggest precisely the problems of which Sommer warns, I suggest, because Nazario ultimately betrays a remarkably "American" inability to understand and accept the decision of the Central American mother to leave her children.

On the face of it, Nazario clearly hopes to lead readers to understand how Mexican and Central American mothers—mothers who love their children—could "abandon" them to come to the United States, precisely *out* of love for them. Nazario herself starts out in this position of incomprehension, as she signals through the opening of her text. She traces the origin of her project to a recollected conversation with her housekeeper, Carmen, in which Carmen revealed she had left four children behind in Guatemala, twelve years earlier. The youngest was only one year old at the time. "Twelve years? I react with disbelief. How can a mother leave her children and travel more than two thousand miles away, not knowing when or if she will ever see them again? What drove her to do this?" (x). Here Nazario posits *herself* as a former naïve addressee to the story of children left behind. The task of her narrative will ostensibly be to explain how a loving mother could do such a thing to her children. Carmen provides an answer in brief:

> She worked hard but didn't earn enough to feed four children. "They would ask me for food, and I didn't have it." Many nights, they went to bed without dinner. She lulled them to sleep with advice on how to quell their hunger pangs. "Sleep facedown so your stomach won't growl so much," Carmen said, gently coaxing them to turn over.
>
> She left for the United States out of love. She hoped she could provide her children an escape from their grinding poverty, a chance to attend school beyond the sixth grade. (x)

While Martínez's text invites identification via the immigrants' middle-class aspirations and desires for U.S.-style consumerism, Nazario's opens by suggesting incommensurable difference between her subjects and her privileged readership; while "we" can afford to buy the book in our hands (and to read it in our leisure time), Nazario's subjects face "grinding poverty" and real "hunger pangs." Indeed, Carmen herself, anticipating American women's alienation from her understanding of her role as a mother, challenges, "What's really incomprehensible . . . are middle-class or wealthy working mothers in the United States. These women, she says, could tighten their belts, stay at home, spend all their time with their children. Instead, they devote most of their waking hours and energy to careers. . . . Why, she asks, with disbelief on her face, would anyone do that?" (xi). This early, framing scene highlights readerly estrangement; we (privileged readers) are not in Carmen's place; our circumstances are not hers; we do not understand her choices, nor does she apparently understand ours.

I suggest that Nazario's text ultimately does not invite recognition of a *different* ethical system applicable under different conditions of existence. Instead, it seems to confirm Nazario's early verdict that the mother's abandonment of her children is wrong. The coda to Carmen's story is that her own son Minor undertook the dangerous journey north in the following year to find his mother. In Nazario's recounting, "Minor's friends in Guatemala envied the money and presents Carmen sent. 'You have it all. Good clothes. Good tennis shoes,' they said. . . . Minor answered, 'I'd trade it all for my mother.... You can never get the love of a mother from someone else'" (xii). Mother love, then, trumps economic advancement or social opportunities; the fact that Minor was given the latter apparently does not justify the absence of his mother, which has, so to speak, the last word. By universalizing "mother love" into something that would presumably look the same across places and situations, Nazario falls into the trap outlined by Sommer, who warns us away from assuming readerly intimacy, "lest our enlightened and universalizing drives presume to offer a better understanding than [that of the subaltern woman] ... and lest we therefore proceed to make moral and strategic decisions in her stead" ("Taking a Life" 931).

Nazario herself notes in her preface that she hopes Latin American immigrant women who are leaving their children behind will "make better-informed decisions" (xxv) as a result of reading her text. Though Nazario does not explicitly say so, her narrative framing obviously implies that "better-informed decisions" means *not* coming to the United States, *not* leaving one's children behind. As Nazario puts it, "These separations almost always end badly" (xxv). The question of what the children's fate might have been in the absence of their mother's relocation to the United States for work is never seriously taken up by Nazario.

The "plotting" of the narrative ultimately works to reinstall Nazario, the first-world journalist and interlocutor of her subaltern subjects, as moral and ethical arbiter. A narrative emphasizing the horrors of familial separation wrecked by impossible-to-navigate immigration laws might have been expected to conclude with the happy reunification of mother and son. But instead of ending *Enrique's Journey* there, Nazario extends her chronicle of Enrique and his family for another seventy-seven pages—close to a third of the total narrative. After the reunion scene, Nazario writes:

> *The Odyssey*, an epic poem about a hero's journey home from war, ends with reunion and peace....
> Enrique's journey is not fiction, and its conclusion is more complex and less dramatic. But it ends with a twist worthy of O. Henry.
> Children like Enrique dream of finding their mothers and living happily ever after. For weeks, perhaps months, these children and their mothers cling to romanticized notions of how they should feel toward each other.

> Then reality intrudes. The children show resentment because they were left behind. They remember broken promises of return and accuse their mothers of lying. (190–91)

It can fairly be noted that ending with a happy reunion between Enrique and his mother would be a fiction, an artificial and calculated "end," for strategic rhetorical purposes, to a story that in fact continues. But in this sense, the story of Enrique and his mother *has* no "conclusion"; like all stories of living people, it continues. The choice of how to conclude the narrative of *Enrique's Journey* to find his mother is *inevitably* a *choice*, rather than natural or inherent in the story—and the choice is revealing of Nazario's own privileged position. In Nazario's remaining narrative, what is emphasized is the discord between Enrique and his mother once the reunion period is past; the resurfacing of Enrique's serious problems attributed to his early "abandonment" by his mother, including drug use; and Enrique's encouraging of his girlfriend to leave their infant daughter behind in Honduras and join him in the United States, which she eventually does.

The narrative thus concludes not with reunion but with a different resolution altogether: after visiting her mother in the United States, Lourdes's daughter, Belky, "boards an airplane back to Honduras. Back to her son" (267). Through this narrative closure, Nazario privileges not reunification but *return*. That this is the "happy ending" with which the narrative concludes its odyssey strongly implies that the mother's return is the correct moral and ethical resolution. Belky's son will not be abandoned as Enrique was; the cycle will not repeat. Nazario never contemplates, however, the possibility of what would have happened to Enrique if she had not gone to the United States.

The closing pages of the narrative, which generalize from Enrique's story to larger implications, present the results of a Harvard University study which "found that immigrant children in U.S. schools who spent time separated from parents are often depressed, act up, have trouble trusting anyone, and don't respond to the authority of parents they weren't raised with" (248). How are such negative social results to be addressed? Nazario presents the following commentary on the situation:

> [Gabriel Murillo, a Los Angeles school counselor, concludes]: "The parents say: I had to do it. But that's not enough for these children. All of them feel the resentment." Special education teacher Marga

Rodriguez adds, "This isn't worth it. In the end, you lose your kids." . . . Oscar Escalada Hernández, director of the Casa YMCA shelter for immigrant children in Tijuana, Mexico, agrees. "People are leaving behind the most important value: family unity." (248–49)

Regardless of circumstances, the collective and accumulated commentary puts the weight of responsibility on the *act* of immigration, on the parents' physical *leaving* behind of their children, suggesting that this decision is a flawed one. The naïve North American addressee's reaction, "How can a mother leave her children?" (x) is thus ultimately supported, rather than challenged, by the overall thrust of the text. It is not just the "costs" of immigration for U.S. citizens that are too high—it is also the "costs" for the immigrants themselves.

How is it that Nazario's text fails to deliver on its implied promise to bring readers to a position where they can understand Lourdes's apparently incomprehensible decision to leave her children? I would suggest it is *precisely* through an overemphasis on reader empathy. As Nance has eloquently argued, an ethical response to suffering *cannot* stop with empathy or identification (*Can Literature* 128). Readers who are asked only to *identify* with mother love, as a seemingly universal category without historically and situationally specific manifestations, need not consider specific differences of class or privilege that might produce different forms of loving parenting. "Universal" mother love, as a basis for identification, also becomes the yardstick by which readers will judge the narrative's protagonists, since economic differences (and the real, ethical difference they make) have now been effaced. Indeed, empathy with a victim can work to obscure any responsibility that the reader might have for the *structural* conditions under which the victim suffers. Paradoxically, Nazario's effacing of the determinant effects of place serves to reinscribe these effects, via a preservation of the U.S. reader's (or journalist's) privileged position and the power it affords to determine "universal" ethical models. Aside from the question of situational specificity, such a rendering elides any sense that the reader "is in any way responsible, whether through commission or omission, for that suffering" (Nance, "Let Us Say" 66); that is to say, it elides U.S. complicity in the position of these mothers.

Nazario's commitment to family unification might just as easily have led her to engage in an explicit critique of immigration policies—policies that have been allowed to remain in place by a largely indifferent or even actively supportive U.S. electorate. She might have targeted our current rigid system of border enforcement that, likewise, makes mothers unwilling to permit their children to make the treacherous journey to rejoin them. After all, it is such policy initiatives as Operation Gatekeeper and Operation Hold-the-Line that resulted in a "resident" undocumented population much less willing to make return trips across the border (Durand and Massey 247), therefore making it *more* likely that mothers would not return to their children. She might have discussed current deportation laws, which have come under widespread fire from immigration rights activist groups such as the New Sanctuary movement *precisely* because they separate parents from citizen children. Instead, Nazario renders the factors that separate mother from son as primarily a matter of personal shortcomings and flawed decisions, rather than of the reverberations of U.S. immigration policy. Thus even while we are asked to empathize with the separated families of migrants, we are also left secure in our comfortable (and ethically superior) positions as U.S. readers.

Who Is the "You"? *The Devil's Highway*

Of the three texts under discussion here, Luis Alberto Urrea's *The Devil's Highway* is in my view the most successful both in encouraging empathetic identification and then in relocating readers in their "own place," in ways that promote exotopy as a grounds for reevaluation and civic action rather than a mere reinscription of national privilege. *The Devil's Highway* recounts the story of one of the best publicized of mass border deaths in the new millennium, in which fourteen men died trying to enter the United States by crossing through the Arizona desert in 2001. Urrea is well known as a novelist as well as a writer of nonfiction, and *The Devil's Highway* bears this literary stamp; his "True Story" (the subtitle of his book) transforms the materials of nonfiction into a text as gripping as any suspense novel, in part by imagining deeply into the experiences of the desert victims. The invitation to identification is followed by a move back to the particularities of citizenship and its implications via a reconsideration of immigration policy and border enforcement issues. That is, Urrea draws attention to our (national) place and to the forms of civic engagement that it can entail.

Like *Enrique's Journey*, *The Devil's Highway* opens with a story that universalizes (or, at least, momentarily abstracts) the experience of its "protagonists," identified only as "five men." Urrea is seemingly determined to postpone for as long as possible identifying information that might designate these men as Mexican or as illegal; for the moment, all identifying tags are left off. The five men, when their voices are represented, seem to be talking and thinking in English: "They were walking now for water, not salvation. Just a drink. They whispered it to each other as they staggered into parched pools of their own shadows, forever spilling downhill before them: Just one drink, brothers. Water. Cold water!" (4). Slowly, as though it were a camera lens, the narrative voice backs away, increasing, ever so slightly, the distance between reader and subject, by making more visible the process of imagining what the men imagined: "In the distance, deceptive stands of mesquite trees must have looked like oases. . . . [It] must have seemed like another bad dream" (4–5). Instead of hearing immediately the men's whispers, readers have now been removed to the level of conjecture: this is what it *must have felt like*. But in that removal process, readers are also being invited specifically to *engage* in conjecture, to imagine what the men felt. Not until near the end of this introductory scene setting, in which the men have already been trekking through deadly desert heat for days, does one of the men even speak in Spanish: *Pinches piedras* [Too many damned rocks] (5).

Urrea's invitation to readers to inhabit the perspective of desert crossers unfolds through a strategic shifting and fluidity of pronouns—of the "you" that his text addresses, and an occasional merging of that "you" with the "he" or "they" of his subjects. The first time Urrea makes this narrative move is in his depiction of the U.S. Border Patrol, often a vilified entity for pro-immigrant politics: "Like the other old boys of Wellton Station, you love your country, you love your job, and though you would never admit it, you love your fellow officers. . . . You can always come in to the clubhouse and find someone to talk to. Somebody who votes like you, talks like you" (23). Someone to talk to, in this hypothetical scene, is configured here as a priori *not* the "illegals." Readers are shown, as in a mirror, their possible predisposition toward identifying with a comforting "Americanness." In Urrea's appeal to our sympathies, he begins by allowing readers to occupy a "you" with which Anglo-American readers, at least, might feel an easier initial identification—with someone who speaks in English.

From here, Urrea guides his sympathetic readers to other, potentially more difficult identifications. Just as the narrative of slow death of the border crossers has barely gained traction—Urrea notes that on the morning of the second day of the trek, "they had already begun to die" (here the undocumented are, however sympathetically, still "they")—he interrupts his narrative, slowing it down: "not only Mexicans die in this desert" (117). He then reverts, for several pages, to stories of "mainstream" U.S. citizens of nondescript ethnicity also dying in the desert. Lisa Scala and Martin Myer went off-roading in sand dunes during a camping trip; the steering arm of their jeep broke, and they died because they could not reach water. Joseph and Laura Popielas "went for a walk in the park" to climb Picacho Peak and never made it; Joseph was found within sight of their car, which he was probably trying to reach to get help for his wife (119). Urrea concludes this section with the terse statement, "In the desert, we are all illegal aliens" (120), resituating the pronoun "we" so that the former "they" is also included—a "we" with boundaries flexible and fluid enough that "illegal aliens" and U.S. citizens can inhabit it simultaneously. What happened to them could, given the wrong set of circumstances, happen to "us."

Urrea now launches into another narrative interruption, in which he asks readers literally to imagine their own deaths in the desert: "Experts can't give a definitive schedule of doom. Your own death is largely dictated by factors outside of your control. . . . All sources say you will die in a period of time that can vary from hours to days" (120). Each stage of hyperthermia is described in excruciating and relentless detail, all while using the pronoun "you," directed presumably *at the reader*: "Sooner or later, you understand that you have to drink your own urine" (126). National and racial identifiers are deliberately stripped away: "It doesn't matter what language you speak, or what color your skin" (120). Scenes of increasing disorientation are rendered in second person, as though the reader were experiencing them: "You don't know much anymore. You are confused; your memories are conflated with your dreams. . . . The only clear thought in your mind now is: I'm thirsty, I'm thirsty" (125). So is the scene of death itself, when consciousness is extinguished: "Proteins are peeling off your dying muscles. Chunks of cooked meat are falling out of your organs. . . . Your brain sparks. Out. You're gone" (129).

Elaine Scarry, in her landmark work *The Body in Pain* (1985), has noted that the inherent difficulty in representing *the pain of another person* in words (because pain is not visible and is intensely private, contained within the individual body) must be overcome in order for humanitarian and political efforts to ameliorate the sources of pain to be successful. Discussing organizations such as Amnesty International, Scarry insists that "the act of verbally expressing pain is a necessary prelude to the collective task of diminishing pain" and that, furthermore, "the relative ease or difficulty with which any given phenomenon can be verbally represented also influences the ease or difficulty with which that phenomenon comes to be politically represented" (9, 12). Though surely most of Urrea's readers have not thought for prolonged periods about what it might *feel like* to die in the desert of dehydration and hyperthermia, Urrea's text insistently renders visible this invisible and interior physical pain, caused by no wound and undetectable by external bodily signs (at least by an unexpert eye). From the introduction of the migrants' deaths, to the description of U.S. tourist deaths, to the description of "your" deaths, the central section of *The Devil's Highway*, entitled "Killed by the Light," unremittingly asks readers to close the distance between migrants and themselves, to imagine desert deaths—with their attendant and necessarily bodily pain and anguish—as something that *could happen to them*.

But, of course, the circumstances would be markedly different for readers than for undocumented migrants; dying in the desert as a tourist is not the same exact experience as dying while trying to cross to the United States in search of economic subsistence for one's family. This is a point that John Annerino makes forcefully in *Dead in Their Tracks*:

> [Unauthorized migrants] will be wearing cheap rubber shower sandals and ill-fitting baseball cleats to protect their feet from rocks, thorns, hot sand, and lava, not form-fitting one hundred dollar hiking boots; they will carry their meager rations of tortillas, beans, sardines, and chilis in flimsy white plastic bags, not freeze-dried gourmet meals cooked over shiny white gas stoves carried in expensive gortex backpacks. And they will sleep on the scorched bare earth in thin cotton T-shirts, not in cozy two hundred dollar down sleeping bags. . . . They will cross a merciless desert for jobs, not for scenic vistas. (40–41)

Differences of privilege and circumstance make it more likely that unauthorized migrants will die than that tourists will. What for a tourist might be a horrible accident is, for migrants, a recognized hazard and increasingly a form of cultural trauma.

Thus Urrea does not just leave us with facile desert humanism. Rather, from the point of most intimate readerly identification and empathy with desert crossers, Urrea solicits his readers to move back to exotopy—to their own position as U.S. citizens and the attendant capacity to act in particular ways to change the ending of the story. Just as Nazario does, Urrea includes a segment that apparently "models" ethical behavior; but while Nazario's description of rural Mexican humanitarians is ultimately subsumed by the thrust of her concluding pages, Urrea's ethical "modeling" comes near the very end of his text—and in the surprising form of the border patrol. As the concluding pages of *The Devil's Highway* point out: "One thing Yuma and Wellton [border patrol agents] understood immediately from the disaster in May was that the way things worked didn't work. If they were to hope for a change in the fate of the Devil's Highway and all the lost souls walking it, they would have to become proactive, not reactive" (212). He describes a series of towers, built to be visible "day and night" in the desert, with warning signs and panic buttons to summon help (213). Further, although "conservative pundits try to get their constituents to believe [that] the American Taxpayer . . . is funding lifesaving towers foisted on them by the lily-livered INS," Urrea notes, "In fact, the towers are built, raised, maintained, and paid for out-of-pocket by those bleeding-heart liberals, the Border Patrol agents themselves" (214). As a result of border patrol interventions in Yuma, while the migrant death tally in the neighboring Tucson sector for the following season continued to escalate, the Yuma sector brought its total down to *nine* (214). Urrea's inclusion of this unexpected bit of information might be understood as its own form of rhetorical call to action: if border patrol agents, so often portrayed as the villains of this story, are willing to pay for towers with their own personal salaries to save the lives of illegals, what are *you* willing to do?

* * *

My intent in this chapter has been to offer a consideration of the ethical implications of these journalistic representations of "Others" positioned as outside of the nation-state. My underlying assumption is that literary texts, as sustained narratives consumed over time and thus significantly engaging the imagination, can have a particular role to play in the shaping of public discourse. It is beyond the scope of this chapter to make a case for the *actual* effects of each of these texts based upon a sufficiently representative sample of readers (though that might certainly be an interesting study). That said, one piece of anecdotal evidence about possible "real world" effects might be of interest, by way of conclusion. In the spring of 2008, I assigned *The Devil's Highway* to a class of honors students. As part of our discussion, I invited a former No Más Muertes volunteer to come to the class to speak about his experiences in the field; students also participated in a viewing of the documentary film *Crossing Arizona* and a discussion afterward with its director, Dan DeVivo. Afterward, two of my nine students informed me that they planned to volunteer for No More Deaths during the coming summer. I have no way of knowing, of course, what tipped the scales for these particular students, but clearly *The Devil's Highway* was part of a larger cluster of "listening practices" that turned out to have a *testimonio* function for them.

Literature does not exist in isolation. There are books, then there are conversations about books (a cultural phenomenon spawned on a large scale by Oprah's book selections), and there are also movies, television, news magazines, websites, and so on—all offering their little piece to the public conversation. There is, alas, no scientific way to predict which books will make waves and which will only create ripples. But perhaps we should not underestimate the power of the ripples.

The Lost Ones

Post-Gatekeeper Border Fictions and the Construction of Cultural Trauma

In February 2008, a volunteer for the humanitarian organization No Más Muertes [No More Deaths] found the body of a fourteen-year-old girl from El Salvador in the Arizona desert.[1] A shrine now marks the isolated spot where she was discovered, and a book on undocumented immigration at the U.S.-Mexico border bears her name (Regan). In Agua Prieta, Sonora, Mexico, at a resource center operated by Frontera de Cristo in partnership with No Más Muertes that provides food, water, clothing, and first aid for just-repatriated migrants, one migrant who had been caught by the border patrol after walking through the desert reported that a member of his group had died there from a rattlesnake bite. Another reported having come across a corpse in the desert while trying to cross. Just across the border from Agua Prieta, in Douglas, Arizona, weekly vigils were held to make visible these lost and disappeared. In a new example of what Diana Taylor terms "trauma driven performances" which "address the society-wide repercussions" of politics that result in death and disappearance (1674), participants at these vigils would hold up crosses with the names of identified bodies (or sometimes with the words *no identificado* for a body never identified), read the names aloud, calling out a collective "¡presente!" after each name as a way of making visible these invisible deaths, and then lay the crosses down, one by one, on the side of the highway leading to the border. By the end of the vigil, a mile of the Pan American Avenue highway had become a temporary shrine, lined with crosses. Needless to say, for each body recovered (or not recovered) along the migrant trails of the U.S. Southwest, there is a family somewhere wondering what happened to their loved one.

"With disappearance, closure is impossible," columnist Roger Cohen wrote in the *International Herald Tribune* in 2007. Cohen (like Taylor) is referring to the "disappeared" of Latin American countries such as Argentina, Chile, El Salvador, and Guatemala in the 1970s, '80s, and early '90s at the hands of repressive military regimes. These regimes and right-wing death squads were responsible for kidnapping, torturing, and murdering thousands of their citizens, for reasons ranging from random terror to the repression of political opposition to what amounted to ethnic genocide.[2] But some contemporary writers in the United States, both Latino and non-Latino, are making the case for a possible analogy to these earlier waves of the disappeared: those who are lost through unauthorized migration. Loved ones might disappear in the process of crossing itself or through the sudden deportation of family members. Detention or deportation of undocumented adults, for instance, can and frequently does leave behind U.S. citizen children.

A report of the Urban Institute on the effects of worksite raids on children noted that they contributed to "a general sense of chaos and fear," often leading to "outright panic," in communities associated with the raids (Capps et al. 34). The report found that some arrested parents did not tell ICE agents that they had children at home, because they feared their children would then also be detained; some families of arrested workers went into hiding in the days or weeks following the raids, concealing themselves in basements or closets. In one of the work sites raided, 17 percent of the children of arrested parents had had *both* parents arrested. In communities where workplace raids had taken place, schools, churches, and social service and community agencies needed to mobilize to ensure that children of detained parents were properly cared for rather than abandoned (Capps et al. 4, 34–36, 42, 56). As the report's authors repeatedly underscored—perhaps in an attempt to rhetorically forestall indifference about psychological impacts on undocumented children—many of the children (probably close to two-thirds) were themselves U.S. citizens (9, 17–18). The authors of the report, drawing on the affective sense of affiliation, loyalty, and obligation that hegemonically attaches to the imagined community of the nation, urged readers to recognize and accept ethical responsibility for the care of these citizen children (9).

In this chapter, I argue that writers are constructing disappearance related to unauthorized crossings and deportations as a new form of cultural trauma that devastates Latino/a families and communities and necessitates a radical reconstitution of individual and collective identities. I want to attend to how crossing of the southern U.S. border has been represented in recent U.S. Latino/a fiction, as well as one non-Latina novel, Susan Straight's *Highwire Moon,* which I argue is important for the ethical call it presents for non-Latino/a readers. This body of fiction, produced in the wake of border security measures undertaken in the mid-1990s, is notable both for the ways in which it attends to the current lethal conditions of the U.S.-Mexican border *and* for its conversion of border crossing (*al otro lado*) into a new kind of metaphor that refers back to itself. It draws on a Chicano/a literary and cultural legacy of transborder solidarity. At the same time, this fiction puts increasing emphasis on what could be termed the tragedy of the U.S.-Mexican border, most powerfully emblematized in the lives lost there. For example, Ana Castillo dedicates her 2007 novel, *The Guardians,* "To all working for a world without borders and to all who dare to cross them." Castillo points simultaneously to a utopic space of borderlessness and to the undeniable fact of borders—to an ideal and to a grim reality.

When "disappearance" was the result of violence and state repression in El Salvador and Guatemala in the 1980s, Latina writers in the United States, including Demetria Martínez, Helena María Viramontes, Sandra Benítez, Carole Fernández, and Graciela Limón, responded by writing fiction that told the story of these political crises for U.S. audiences (N. Rodríguez; Lyon-Johnson). Their novels and short stories depicted characters who had lost loved ones, often without full knowledge of their fates, to death squads and terror tactics. The characters sometimes traveled north across the U.S. border, and back again, in search of these "disappeared" ones; the migrant flow northward invoked the complicity of the United States in the political situation of the "home" country.

With the advent of what I have called the "Gatekeeper era" of border enforcement, migrants were driven to take more dangerous routes, often through hostile desert conditions, with the result that deaths skyrocketed (Eschbach et al.; Nevins, *Operation Gatekeeper*). Through most of the 1990s, known migrant deaths in Arizona were in single digits (Regan xxii). But as Operation Gatekeeper and Hold-the-Line took effect, the death toll began to rise sharply. According to tallies taken from medical examiners' offices in the four Arizona border counties, Cochise, Pima,

Santa Cruz, and Yuma, death tolls of *recovered bodies* went from 163 in fiscal year 2002 to 205 in 2003, 234 in 2004, and 279 in 2005 (Regan xxiii). In total, an estimated 5,000 bodies were found in southwestern borderlands between 1994 and 2000 (Regan xxv). As a result, critics refer to the border zone as a "landscape of death" (Nevins, *Operation Gatekeeper* 144) and a "killing field" (Regan xxiii). Both fictional and nonfictional accounts detail long lists of the various perils that migrants must contend with when they cross. Major Chicana novelist Ana Castillo's latest novel, *The Guardians*, explains the hazards this way:

> You are at the mercy of everything known to mankind and nature. There is the harsh weather and land, the river and desert. The night is and is not your friend. It provides coolness and darkness to allow you to move. But you can get lost, you can freeze, you can get robbed or kidnapped, you can drown in el río. You can fall into a ravine, get bitten by a snake, a tarantula, a bat, or something else. The brutal sun comes with day and anything can happen to you that happens at night but you can also dehydrate, burn, be more easily detected by patrols and thieves. Bandits could kill you as easily as rob you of not just your life's savings but that of your whole familia. Even of your village, in cases where communities have decided that getting one person out will help them all. If you are a pollo smuggled with others in an enclosed truck you could die of suffocation. Whatever happens to men . . . is worse for women. (117)

The casual use of the second person "you" in Castillo's text follows the rhetorical strategy of Urrea's *The Devil's Highway* (discussed in the previous chapter), inviting readers to imagine the perspectives of the border crossers normally vilified and dehumanized as "illegals" in dominant American political discourse.

The many obstacles that face undocumented migrants as they attempt to cross the border are also recounted, as a litany of sorts, near the beginning of Bencastro's *Odyssey to the North*:

> "They say that the trip is full of difficulties. . . . They say many people have been abandoned, lost in strange lands."
>
> "A friend who made the trip . . . told me about the horrible things that happen on those trips. Everyone's afraid. The rumors are true! The *coyotes* abuse the women and rape them, they'll kill anyone for a

few dollars, and they abandon women and children in the desert for no good reason. Many travelers have disappeared and never been heard from again. This friend says that, the farther you get on the trip, everything you've heard pales in comparison to what's really happening.... The *coyotes* treat the people like animals." (29)

A repeated theme is abandonment—abandonment to death by the coyotes (human smugglers) and the larger, looming sense of possible abandonment by loved ones, as relatives go north, where they are often "never ... heard from again."

The border as a landscape of death and disappearance is a looming presence in several works of the last decade that explore the effects of Gatekeeper-like enforcement policies on the lives—and deaths—of migrants. Nonfictional narratives of the life-threatening dangers of crossing the border have proliferated. Simultaneously, the post-Gatekeeper era has seen the production of several novels which, in various ways, link border crossing with the disappearance of loved ones: *Return to Sender* (2009) by Julia Alvarez; *The Guardians* (2007) by Ana Castillo; *Across a Hundred Mountains* (2006) by Reyna Grande; *Esperanza's Box of Saints* (1999) by María Amparo Escandón; *Desert Blood: The Juárez Murders* (2005) by Alicia Gaspar de Alba; *Into the Beautiful North* (2009) by Luis Alberto Urrea; *The River Flows North* (2009) by Graciela Limón; and *Highwire Moon* (2001) by (non-Latina) Susan Straight.

Several post-Gatekeeper books of border crossing allude explicitly to *The Odyssey* as ur-narrative of a perilous journey beset by obstacles. These include Mario Bencastro's *Odisea del Norte* (*Odyssey to the North*); Sonia Nazario's *Enrique's Journey,* the cover of which reads, "The Story of a Boy's Dangerous Odyssey to Reunite with His Mother"; or the repeated use of the odyssey metaphor in *Crossing with the Virgin: Stories from the Migrant Trail* by Kathryn Ferguson, Norma A. Price, and Ted Parks. In these accounts, the odyssey trope is imbued with new politically and historically specific meanings even while it suggests the layering of dangers along the border-crossing journey as forms of profound trauma.

While the nonfictional and journalistic accounts tend to concentrate their attention on the most direct victims of border policies—the undocumented migrants themselves—and on the immediate trauma of crossing the border as perhaps the most "newsworthy" subject,[3] the nature of the novel as genre has always been, arguably, more conducive to explorations of broader social landscapes that include both major and minor "characters" or subjects and of situations of greater psychological complexity. The fictional texts I examine here are able to imaginatively conjure a different trauma—that of *disappearance* at the border. Disappearance implies, of course, that the perspective is no longer or not primarily that of the border crosser himself or herself; the disappeared one disappears from the perspective of those who don't know what has happened to him or her. These texts of border crossing, death, and "disappearance" suggest through their cumulative and collective weight that border disappearances are becoming a form of cultural trauma for migrants and their families and communities. In this chapter, I argue that these texts increasingly serve as forms of fiction that narrate (and in the process construct) the collective trauma resulting from the disappearances occurring during unauthorized immigration.[4] I focus in particular on the novels by Castillo, Grande, and Straight, which deal with the theme of cultural trauma—although I also briefly consider Alvarez's young adult novel *Return to Sender* (given more extended treatment in the next chapter); Alicia Gaspar de Alba's fictional narrative about the Juárez femicide, *Desert Blood*; Luis Alberto Urrea's *Into the Beautiful North*, which recounts the journey of a group of friends (three teenaged girls and one gay man) to the United States to find seven Mexican men to "return" to Mexico to repopulate a town decimated by migration northward; and Bencastro's *Odyssey to the North*, which bridges earlier Chicano/a and Latino/a works depicting Central American immigration in the early 1980s ("The Cariboo Café" by Helena María Viramontes, *Mother Tongue* by Demetria Martínez) and post-Gatekeeper fiction more focused on the dangers of the border crossing journey. The novels I examine appropriate the notion of the "disappeared"—with all its connotations of state violence—from its Latin American context, to construct migrant disappearances as a new form of cultural trauma that violently separates families and introduces profound instability into notions of individual and group identity. Taken as a whole, the novels also implicate U.S. labor dynamics, inhumane immigration and border enforcement, and racial hegemonies in a larger landscape of border disappearances.[5]

Dead Bodies and Absent Bodies

"The dead body is a political body," as Kelli Lyon-Johnson has argued (208); dead bodies can function as powerful political symbols.[6] Nonfictional, journalistic accounts of the deaths of border crossers, such as Luis Alberto Urrea's *The Devil's Highway,* Jorge Ramos's *Dying to Cross*, and John Annerino's *Dead in Their Tracks*, emphasize the dead migrant body as a focal point for the tragedy of the border. Further, by focusing on the body's agonizing torment prior to death, these writers shift the issue to human suffering rather than the legality or illegality of immigration, thus reconstructing the meaning of specific dead bodies. As Elaine Scarry has powerfully insisted, physical suffering is an intensely private phenomenon that is inordinately difficult to convey adequately in words. To become aware of the pain of others, Scarry insists, is at base a means by which "other persons become visible to us" (22). If the body itself is removed from sight, its pain becomes increasingly unimaginable. There could have been no pain—or infinite pain.

The missing body of the lost migrant, perhaps ironically, thus comes to serve as a fitting symbolic locus for the profound psychological pain of the family members left without knowledge of their loved one. The post-Gatekeeper novels of migrant disappearances turn increasingly to the trope of the absent body of the lost one. Unlike the nameless cadavers shown in the photographs of Annerino's *Dead in Their Tracks*, literature of migrant disappearance has, as its strongest visual analogy, the shrines dedicated to lost loved ones that can now be found in the Arizona desert; the person is remembered, but the body itself is removed from view. In *Highwire Moon*, the protagonist Elvia looks at "crosses, white wood, with notes and flowers attached," and she comments that "the people in the desert, somebody's taking their bodies away. And nobody will ever know how long they walked, where they came from, when they gave up" (144). The shrines—like the material bodies Verdery discusses—still serve the function of a localized claim, but they emphasize the radical unknowability of loss and absence, rather than material presence. In this way they also resist the narrative closure that might, argues Allen Feldman, be intimated by a more permanent and institutionalized memorial (166).[7] These novels render the border region as a highly politicized geographical zone where many bodies are simply never found, their very lack pointing to the deeply inhumane nature of policies that cause human beings to vanish.

The "Disappearing" Border and Cultural Trauma

Diana Taylor, among many others, has posed the question of how "society as a whole internalizes traumatic violence" (1675). The term *disappeared* calls attention not only to the missing themselves, but also to those left behind who "internalize" the ongoing effects of the violence to their loved ones. The disappeared ones are disappeared not to themselves but to their families and communities; the families of the disappeared are themselves "victims of trauma—having suffered the uncertain and thus all the more devastating loss of their loved ones" (Taylor 1676). The term *disappeared* in its Latin American context requires an onlooker, a witness for whom the beloved subject has vanished, leaving "an inconsolable absence in the place of a human being" (Cohen); it makes no sense as a term focused exclusively on the individual victim. For this reason, as Cohen astutely notes, "closure is impossible."

In representing the reverberations of border disappearances for families and communities, writers have begun to construct this ongoing "event" as a new manifestation of "disappearance" sharing a cultural and collective history with the Latin American disappearances of past decades (Castillo even employs the term *disappeared* as a transitive verb—it is coyotes, rather than military regimes and death squads, that "disappear people" now—preserving its resonance from the Latin American context), and as a form of cultural trauma affecting communities at the border and in the interior of both Mexico and the United States. At a cultural and collective level, Jeffrey C. Alexander writes, trauma is not "inherent" in events but is, rather, a "socially mediated attribution" ("Toward a Theory" 8). Certain events, but not others, will become widely represented (and thus regarded) as inflicting cultural trauma. Alexander explains that the process by which cultural trauma is *constructed* entails repeated and mutually reinforcing symbolic representation of a particular event as constituting a "fundamental injury"; widespread dissemination of such representation among group members, such that the characterization gains currency within the group; and demands for reparation ("Toward a Theory" 11). Neil Smelser elaborates that, to become established as a cultural trauma, a historical event (or sequence of events) must "be remembered, or made to be remembered" (36); that is to say, it is *narrativized* to the point where it becomes an indelible collective memory associated with profound collective pain.

If, as Sandra K. Soto contends, the cultural meanings of the border are both created and reified through the repetition of what we say about it (430), then it is arguable that recent literary representations are contributing to a new "cementing" of the border as a space inextricably associated with death and loss. El Abuelo Milton, the grandfather in Castillo's novel *The Guardians*, notes, "The borderlands have become like the Bermuda Triangle. Sooner or later everyone knows someone who's dropped outta sight" (132). In Straight's *Highwire Moon,* one character in a band of would-be crossers reports, "Down there, . . . in the desert, people die all the time because they have no water" (132). The desert itself has become a killing field of sorts; in Grande's novel *Across a Hundred Mountains*, one character muses of the missing loved one, "It is as if the earth has swallowed him" (61). In fact, the border has.[8] The protagonist Juana's trek northward in this novel is dotted by the random appearance of dead or dying bodies. Near Tijuana, a five-year-old boy dies on the bus next to his mother, who keeps urging, "We're almost there" (145). Is "there" the final destination, the border, or the afterlife? Later, as Juana and the group led by her coyote try to hide from *la migra* in the desert, she notes that "a dead man lay on the ground a few meters away from them" (209). No context for this body is ever provided; he is simply a synecdoche for the anonymous dead bodies in the desert. The dead bodies of migrants also inhabit Susan Straight's border. One character comments, "Shit. La Migra didn't get [them]. The desert did" (121).

In post-Gatekeeper era novels of the migrant disappeared, *el otro lado* becomes an almost obsessive metonym for death itself, so closely associated have the two ideas become in the minds of migrants and their families and communities. Reyna Grande's dedication to her novel *Across a Hundred Mountains* refers to "El Otro Lado" (all words capitalized) in terms of death—"to those who have perished trying to get to El Otro Lado." This novel's main character, Juana, is "afraid of dying while attempting to cross the border. . . . One never knew if they'd live to see El Otro Lado" (Grande 205). Juana's father's grave, as the novel's opening establishes, is not an actual gravesite but the U.S. border (1), which has itself become a mass gravesite. The dual meanings of crossing to the other side evolve from here. Juana's father, Miguel García, has heard from a friend who "has written to me from the other side" about a world with "riches unheard of, streets that never end, and buildings that nearly reach the sky" (27). To the humble Garcías who live in a frequently flooded shack in Guerrero, Mexico, the images might as well be of paradise as of the United States.

The title of Grande's novel is itself another metonym for *el otro lado* in both senses. When Juana's father, referred to as "Apá" in the story, is about to leave her, she asks, "Is El Otro Lado far away, Apá?" and he responds, "I won't be that far from you. When you feel that you need to talk to your Apá, just look toward the mountains, and the wind will carry your words to me" (29). The advice to his daughter, which would seem to suggest prayer to a departed loved one rather than communication between two living beings, proves prophetic, since Apá, as it turns out, never makes it past the U.S. border but dies trying to cross—though no one in the family knows this for decades. Much later, Juana sets off across the mountains in search of her father, but is told by Doña Martina, a family friend, "But your father is not on the other side of the mountains. . . . [He] is very, very far away." Doña Martina then goes on to show Juana, on a map, how far the Mexican state of Guerrero is from the U.S. border. Juana thinks to herself that "what Doña Martina said was true. Apá was not on the other side of these mountains. And in order to find him, she would have to cross not just these mountains, but perhaps a hundred more" (106). While the sense of geographical distance separating Juana from her father works on a literal level with the characters' understanding that he is in the United States, it clearly acquires a figurative resonance with the as yet unrevealed truth that he is farther away than any distance that can be traveled spatially. Although one character cavalierly responds that it is not too hard to get to "El Otro Lado"—"it's a lot of walking, but walking never killed anyone" (113)—the novel's figurative scaffolding is meant to suggest precisely how walking to *el otro lado* kills plenty of people; the journey is a metaphorical death, because it is increasingly an actual one.

Ana Castillo's novel *The Guardians* goes even further, making explicit the new, dual meaning that *el otro lado* has acquired. This novel tells the intertwined stories of an undocumented teenaged boy, Gabo, whose father, Rafa, has "disappeared" in the border region; his aunt and primary caregiver, Regina, who has legalized status; a Chicano schoolteacher, Miguel, who helps them search for their missing family member; and Miguel's Mexican American grandfather, el Abuelo Milton, who represents the novel's keeper of memory and border history. Regina clarifies that when she uses the phrase "the other side," "By that I mean here and across the border in México and I mean this life and whatever's on the Other Side" (A. Castillo 27). Regina's self-conscious elaboration suggests the ways that the two meanings have become increasingly one in narratives of border crossing; to cross the border northward inevitably carries with it the risk of death. Indeed, later in the novel crossing to "the other side" *from* the United States also becomes metonymically associated with death. Miguel's ex-wife, who does volunteer work in Mexico (but lives in the United States), disappears herself, apparently in the act of crossing over (185). The fear of losing loved ones in the desert has become so powerful that it permeates those relationships even before it has become a reality: Gabo remembers, "We used [a whistle] when we crossed the desert. In case you lost your mamá or me, hijito" (85). Castillo's novel *shapes* the collective trauma of lost ones at the border so that it has a communal and anticipatory impact (as a community, the characters come to the point where they *anticipate* disappearance and loss).

This metonymic relation of crossing the border with passing into death extends to non-Chicano/a literary texts as well. In Dominican American writer Julia Alvarez's young adult novel *Return to Sender*, the undocumented, adolescent protagonist Mari, who was born in Mexico, recalls her journey across the border in terms that refer to the United States as "the other side" (27), while elsewhere, the phrase "the other side" appears with reference to her mother's disappearance while attempting to return to the United States from Mexico: "she went to the other side of life" (118). The meaning of the phrase in this context ambiguously connotes both migration across a nation-state border *and* death, the "undiscover'd country from whose bourn/No traveller returns" (*Hamlet* III.i.79–80). As Tyler (the other young protagonist, an American farm boy in Vermont) thinks in confusion, "*The other side of life* is the way people talk about Gramps's death. But how can the girls' mother be dead and be on her way back from a trip to Mexico?" (118–19). When Tyler's mother refers to the farm's new (undocumented) workers as "our angels," because their cheap labor has helped to save the farm from foreclosure, Tyler responds, "Angels are just one step away from ghosts and the spooky thought that maybe their farm is haunted" (14), linking these undocumented angels metonymically to the afterlife. As with other fictions of border crossing, the conflation between land journey and the passage from life to death is meant to call attention to the severity of the trauma of crossing the border, both for those who risk their lives trying to cross and for those waiting for them uncertainly on "the other side," without knowing whether they "made it."

Return to Sender uses the swallow as a figure not only for Mexican migrants but also for the more general cultural paradigm of having been lost in migration. The novel's epigraph is a stanza from the song "La Golondrina" by Narciso Serradel Sevilla. Alvarez translates for her assumed largely monolingual young audience: "Swallow, why are you leaving here? / Oh, what if you lose your way in the wind / Looking for a home you will never find?" In her epilogue, Alvarez tells her young readers:

> When a Mexican dies far away from home, a song known as "La Golondrina" is sung at the funeral. The song tells of a swallow that makes the yearly migration from Mexico to *El Norte*[.] ... [S]ometimes that swallow gets lost in the cold winds and never finds its way back. This is the fear of those who leave home as well as those who stay behind awaiting their return. (322)

For Alvarez, the novel's key figure, the swallow, embodies the fears that attend migration northward—that those who stay behind will never see the return of their loved ones.

Sudden deportation can become another form of disappearance, equally devastating for family members who may have no sense of what has become of those who have vanished. In *Return to Sender*, Tío Felipe's detention results in the escalation of a "culture of anxiety" (Orner 10) among the family of unauthorized laborers working on the farm. At this point, detention and deportation, along with the concomitant trauma of disappearing family members, becomes an omnipresent threat added to the memory of Mari's mother's disappearance while crossing the border to return north to her family. Mari's Papá now insists, "We all have to be ready" (123), because he is "worried that *la migra* would raid the farm and we would come home to an empty trailer" (131). That is, he is worried about *his own* disappearance and the resulting trauma for his children.

In Straight's *Highwire Moon*, the association of the other world with the other side is repeated, once again rendered metonymically in order to contribute to the construction of *both* crossing and deportation as forms of cultural and collective trauma which—Straight suggests—pose ethical demands upon non-Latino U.S. readers. (Straight herself is obviously an outsider to the trauma she represents.) *Highwire Moon* traces the stories of Serafina, a Mexican indigenous woman who is forcibly and suddenly deported from the United States, leaving behind an infant daughter and her older daughter, Elvia, who grows up not knowing what has happened to her mother. The novel's central motif is the separation of mothers and their children; thus the smuggling across the border of "a daughter or wife searching for a loved one on the other side" is immediately juxtaposed to another kind of reunion of mothers and daughters, through death (90). When Serafina's mother in Mexico dies of cancer, she "carried with her the things she needed for her journey to the other world" (59). Near death, Serafina's mother calls out for her own dead mother—which Serafina immediately and by association connects to her own separation from her daughter Elvia, left behind in the United States:

> Her mother spoke to her own mother. "*Náá*," she said. When her mother called out the word again and again, "*Náá, Náá,*" Serafina lay on the dirt floor near the cookstove and screamed into her rebozo so no one would hear. Her daughter would have called for her over and over, screamed at the car window.... She remembered the Cap'n Crunch, the sweet corn dust on Elvia's fingers. (59)

Mothers and daughters can be separated by deportation as by death, and the separation is as complete and irrevocable, the Cap'n Crunch a memory of "the other world."

It is worth pausing here, however, to note that some critics have in fact cautioned against the attribution of deaths to *the border* itself. Soto, for instance, takes issue with certain representations of the border as deadly, such as Charles Bowden's essay "While You Were Sleeping," originally published in *Harper's* in 1996. Soto wryly observes that "fatality does not happen in Bowden's Juárez; it *is* Juárez" (Soto 424). Bowden's photographs of border casualties, Soto argues, are decontextualized and detached from a larger "systemic critique" of the operations of global capitalism which lay the conditions for violence in Juárez (427). Out of context, the border as a death zone may become fodder for alarmist anti-immigration rhetoric insisting that "we" cannot allow such disorder and violence to enter "our" boundaries. Like Soto, Joseph Nevins has cautioned against attribution of instrumentality to the territory of the border itself: "Territoriality helps to obfuscate social relations between controlled and controller by ascribing these relations to territory, and thus away from human agency" (Nevins, *Operation Gatekeeper* 147–48). Metaphors of the border as a Bermuda

Triangle, as a sinister and "swallowing" earth, or as itself some kind of afterlife, risk precisely this sort of decontextualization. If death attaches "naturally" to the border, then human-made policies and practices are off the hook. As we will see, some of the recent novels of border disappearances resist attribution of responsibility to the border.

Castillo's novel *The Guardians*, in particular, struggles against this form of metaphorical decontextualization through a strong documentary impulse. Various characters take turns serving as "expository" and teacherly narrators not only of the novel's plot but also of its historical context, as though that context is too important for readers not to "get." Castillo clearly seeks to acquaint uninformed readers with a long, enmeshed history of immigration policies, foreign policies, domestic racism, and border security which come together as contributing factors in border deaths. In *The Guardians*, it is el Abuelo Milton, the novel's "elder" figure (when he speaks within the other characters' narratives, his words are always in all capital letters), who provides much of the novel's historical memory. In the process he also voices some of the strongest expressions of a borderless *ethnic* solidarity of the sort reflected in the literature of the Chicano movement, constructing Mexicans and Mexican Americans as a single group. In one of his history lessons he notes, "The Border Patrol got started up in 1924.... That was when Mexicans got to be fugitives on our own land. Whether you lived on this side or that side, all Mexicans got harassed" (72). In another, he recalls the desperate conditions along the border during the Great Depression:

> Children were always sick of all kinds of diseases around here—smallpox... scarlet fever, diphtheria. El Río Grande was a breeding ground for mosquitoes, flies, and who knows what all. There was waste seepage... it was terrible.... The whole country was in despair but we here, los mejicanos, were really desperate.... And if los americanos were going through hard times, you best believe so were all the people escaping the ravages of La Revolución. (70)

"Los mejicanos" clearly refers both to immigrants fleeing the Mexican Revolution *and* to Mexican American border residents such as Milton himself, a single group juxtaposed with "los americanos." (Milton's son Miguel, likewise, reconnects "all Mexicans" through the trope of familial relatedness: "We felt our hermanos and hermanas on the other side had every right to be here" [124].)

Yet it is Milton who also notes the pragmatic realities of the existence of the border: "Crossing has never been easy. Let me clarify—crossing over from México has never been easy" (127). Borders are regions of unequal state power. Whether Milton feels kinship with those "on the other side" or not, the reality of the border is that he can cross over to Mexico much more easily than his "hermanos and hermanas" can come the other way. It is this unequal balance, indeed, to which the enormity of border deaths must be attributed.

Border Corpses

El Abuelo Milton's history of the border makes clear that the physical existence of human bodies, in particular physical conditions, is a crucial part of that history. Bodies are affected by diseases—smallpox, diphtheria, scarlet fever—and by the conditions of their physical environment, such as waste seepage. When bodies turn into corpses, they are reinvested with political meaning by border histories such as Milton's and by border fictions that call attention to the search for lost loved ones. Of the post-Gatekeeper texts I examine here, Alicia Gaspar de Alba's border mystery *Desert Blood: The Juárez Murders* is the most haunted by the cadaver's persistent physical materiality. *Desert Blood*, of course, tells a somewhat different kind of narrative of the border's "lost ones" (40), a phrase that, in this novel, refers most directly not to missing border crossers but rather to the hundreds of women who have been killed on the Mexican side of the border in Ciudad Juárez. Yet the targets of Gaspar de Alba's critique are remarkably similar, since at a broader level she is concerned with the various ways in which national and financial imperatives strip bodies of their humanity and render disappeared people insignificant and unworthy of redress.

In *Desert Blood*, the *rastreo*—or search for bodies to find those of the missing in the desert—conveys the urgency felt by family and community members to convert the missing and absent body to an identified body through the materiality of the corpse. When the protagonist Ivon's sister Irene, who crossed from El Paso to Juárez for an evening at a fair, goes missing, Ivon's desperate search for her pulls her to participate in a *rastreo* (23–24). As an activist informs viewers of a talk show, thanks to *rastreos* by various organizations, "many more victims have been found, and we have been able to answer the question, 'Where is my daughter?' Although the answer in many cases has been a tragic one in the form of a dead body turning up in a deserted lot somewhere" (319–20). The trauma of the missing body is mitigated by the discovery, however terrible, of the dead body; thus it is particularly horrible when—as another news segment reports—a "body was never identified" and has thus become "one more unidentified skeleton in the amphitheater" of the medical examiner's office (279). Anxiety over unidentified bodies permeates these texts of the disappeared.

On the *rastreo*, Ivon's companions do, in fact, discover a dead body, which is presented in graphic detail to the reader: "The eyes were gone. The face was completely bloated and purple, facial features erased, blistered skin crusted with sand and blood and maggots. . . . A thick black rope burn ran across the neck and teeth marks covered the chest. The bra was pushed up over the breasts. Worms oozed over the torn nipple of the left breast" (246). The corpse is so utterly unidentifiable that Ivon must ask them to examine its tongue to see if it bears a post, since her sister has a pierced tongue. The coroner's assistant notes that "the tongue was either bitten off or eaten away" (246). The emphasis throughout this description on the corpse's physicality underscores the violence done to its humanity—a violence conveyed, above all, by the stripping away of all identity markers, including facial features and even the tongue, instrument of speech. Though this corpse is eventually identified by an employee identification card found near the site (249), it is, in a more general sense, emblematic of the lack of human recognition given to the victims at the border, who are stripped of their *personhood* by much discussion of border enforcement.

The gruesome and determined physicality of corpses in *Desert Blood* serves as a useful paradigm by which to read the representation of corpses in other border fictions. *The Guardians*, too, attends to the materiality of unidentified corpses, even while shifting attention to missing and absent bodies. *The Guardians* uses an image of unidentified bodies to convey the magnitude of the "disappeared." At one point, el Abuelo Milton calls Miguel regarding news about "muertos they found out on el desierto" who are being held in a morgue in Juárez, and wonders whether the missing father, Rafa, might be among them: "The bodies are more or less decomposed from bein' out there for a while. But anyone interested can go and identify 'em" (126). The physicality of the bodies and the materiality of their suffering is emphasized, disrupting more abstract notions of (nonphysical) disappearance.

Further, the task at hand begs the question of whether, even if Rafa is among the bodies, they would be able to "identify" him if he is decomposed. As Milton comments later,

> That day at the morgue . . . los muertos were out in the open like gruesome wares at a mercado—all waiting for someone to come and give them names. In some cases even faces. You can't put that scene in your head without asking for nightmares. . . . There were not only the skeletons we went to check out but all kinds of muertos, shot-up men, lil children, and the bodies of unidentified females. Gabo was describing everything to me. "They're not really blue or wax-looking, Abuelo Milton, but like something that was never even human." . . . I reached out. Tiesos, all right, so stiff if you raised an arm it would probably have broken off at the joint. The coroner or whoever was in charge there kept saying, "Don't touch. Por favor."
> "How else am I supposed to identify anyone?" I asked. (143)

Once again the bodies' physicality—their touch, their feel beneath the fingers of the almost blind Milton—is the focus of the passage, but it serves to underscore that these are bodies detached from "names." Milton repeats this lament later, with reference to identified bodies of murdered women found near the Mexican border, "naked, tied up, stabbed . . . never get to even find out their names. It's like it don't matter" (189–90). Whether the lost bodies are murdered women in Juárez or lost and decomposing would-be migrants, the lament ends up looking remarkably similar. To be a body without a name is to be not even human—to have lost the claim to a social identity that matters. The text's repetition of nameless and unidentified bodies signals a larger, collective anxiety. What effect, the narrative asks, will this inability to identify the lost ones have on the larger community of solidarity that Milton imagines?

Collective Trauma and the Absent Body

In *Migrant Imaginaries*, Alicia Schmidt Camacho discusses the "national trauma of emigration, in which kinship ties must extend beyond the nation-space in order for the family to remain intact" (34). The "trauma" of emigration is compounded and magnified, however, when the family does *not* remain intact because migration produces death or disappearance. Writing about the relatively new phenomenon of the posting on Mexican consulate websites of pictures and descriptions of the border "disappeared," Schmidt Camacho postulates:

> Family photographs, passport pictures, and identification cards posted to sites . . . adopt both the form of official immigration documents and more personal narratives to describe the disappeared. . . . The interrupted biographies of the disappeared represent a rupture . . . for sending families and towns. For the bereft, not knowing whether the missing person is alive or dead disrupts the narrative of transnational community . . . both in its symbolic unity and in the material sense of economic survival and the futurity of family lines. (310)

When the intimate connection between physical body and larger "narratives" of identity—including familial as well as communal or regional identity—is severed, the result, constructed through "narratives" of loss that foreground interruptions, breaks, and ruptures, is a *larger collective trauma*, wherein the community's identity is also destabilized.

Gabriele Schwab and E. Ann Kaplan, among others, have posited that individual trauma can become collective precisely through the transmission of stories "from person to person and from generation to generation" (Schwab 105); the stories, in other words, give form to a traumatic history that becomes understood as collective, and not just personal, in nature. As Kaplan has written, there are various levels of intimacy in the transmission of individual trauma to a larger group, from the direct witness of another individual's trauma, to the passing down of stories of trauma generationally, to the vicarious experience of trauma through listening to a victim's personal account or, even more remotely, through watching a representation of trauma in film or other media. Further, Kaplan notes, not everyone's potential to experience vicarious trauma is the same, even given the same stimulus. A person who can connect the experience narrated in someone else's first-person account of trauma to similar stories of trauma passed down to him or her generationally by parents, for example, may be more likely to empathize with the traumatic experience than someone who has no analogous history of trauma, whether personally or communally (Kaplan 90–93). These points are provocative for a consideration of Chicana authors, in particular, because while the writers themselves may not have experienced the trauma of unauthorized border crossing or of having immediate family members lost to crossing or deportation, they have lived within and identified themselves with communities where such stories are not unfamiliar, and in some cases even have an eyewitness or a generational component. (Consider, for example, Gloria Anzaldúa's account in *Borderlands/La Frontera* of witnessing as a child the forced "repatriation" of a relative to Mexico, even though he was an American citizen [26].) Extrapolating from Kaplan's observations, we might surmise that Chicana writers such as Castillo, Grande, and Gaspar de Alba may indeed be more likely to understand and represent the trauma of border crossing as a *collective* trauma that affects entire communities, rather than only individuals. Within their novels, the effect of the trauma of disappearance ripples outwards, touching both immediate and extended family members as well as the larger community.

Kaplan's theorizing about levels of traumatic experience or empathy, however, also opens a space for understanding a text such as Susan Straight's *Highwire Moon*, since sharing a particular *group* identity with victims of trauma is not, in Kaplan's accounting, the only way in which trauma may be empathetically experienced or passed from individual to group. The complex exploration of this topic in *non*-Latino/a cultural production, via Straight's novel, attests to the degree to which this cultural trauma may well be slowly imbricating itself in the larger sociopolitical landscape and making itself felt as an urgent crisis to Anglo-Americans interested in human rights and humanitarian issues as well as to U.S. Latino/as. As my opening anecdote illustrates, humanitarian border groups such as No More Deaths, Humane Borders, Samaritans, and Frontera de Cristo—composed predominantly of non-Latino members—see themselves as in solidarity with the victims of border security policies. Pertinent here is Alexander's contention that, in the construction of cultural trauma, eventually a case must be made for the existence of trauma to those who are *not* in the "in-group" most directly affected by the trauma ("Toward a Theory" 12).

Neil J. Smelser writes that representations of cultural trauma inevitably involve a threat to individuals' *personal* identities, because collective trauma is affectively experienced at the individual level (40). The question of what the border disappearances of loved ones do to a sense of collective and individual "identity" is brought up repeatedly in the post-Gatekeeper novels of disappearance I examine here. Generally, however, the instability of identity is underscored not by the materiality of found bodies but by the *absence* of bodies to even attempt to "identify." The absence of (the crucial) physical bodies—even more than the presence of unidentified bodies—introduces an unknowability of the fate of loved ones that repeatedly shakes the very grounds of identity. Further, the new literary and cultural manifestations of disappearance as a cultural trauma bear a marked distinction from earlier Latin American political "disappearances," despite their similarities in other ways. Although the loved ones of the political disappeared knew, generally, to whom to attribute the disappearance of their family member (hence the attribution of responsibility by such groups as Comadres in El Salvador or Mothers of the Plaza de Mayo in Argentina), the nature of border disappearance is such as to render causes and explanatory narratives more uncertain and diffuse and more profoundly disruptive to the family structure.

This issue is the crux of Grande's *Across a Hundred Mountains*, in which the father's disappearance literally fragments the identities of all his family members, who cannot comprehend his silence and fear that he has abandoned them. Because he neither sends money nor communicates with his family from beyond "El Otro Lado," Amá (colloquial for "mamá," referring to the protagonist's mother and the father's wife) is forced into prostitution with the sinister Don Elías. Instead of referring to her as "Señora García," the town now calls her "Don Elías's puta," and when her personal tragedy drives her to alcoholism, her former identity is increasingly effaced: "Everyone in town had started calling Amá La Borracha, the drunk. She was no longer Doña Lupe or la señora García" (121). Textually the erasure of Amá's sense of self is formally completed through a scene in which Juana, her daughter, comes across "a woman" lying drunkenly on the ground. The "woman" is referred to only by this noun throughout a long descriptive passage, as well as by a passerby who warns Juana away from "That crazy woman"—until, at chapter's close, it is Juana herself who grants the woman recognition (since the narrator does not), picking her up and saying, "Let's go home, Amá" (124). At a formal level, Amá's identity has been so affected—we might even say traumatized—by her husband's unexplained absence that the text itself can no longer recognize her. Only Juana is willing to suggest that this (new) person shares some continuity with the mother that was.

The driving conflict in *Across a Hundred Mountains* is that Juana's own identity has been fractured by her father's disappearance. After he leaves, both Juana and Amá repeat insistently to themselves that "*Apá* [the father] *would never forget her. He would never abandon us*" as a way of countering an opposing narrative in which they are increasingly constructed by their community as "the forgotten women, the abandoned women" (37). Notably, Joanne Dreby has suggested that in the (Mexican) popular imaginary, at the very least, migration is strongly associated with family disintegration and the *fear* of abandonment—even though her own findings suggest that in many cases this is not the outcome. Dreby quotes an official from Mexican Child Protective Services as saying, "The moment that there is a migrant father or migrant mother, the family is disintegrated. . . . There are cases in which the father leaves and maybe he sends economic resources, but in many cases he leaves and the family doesn't hear from him again. . . . Families divided by borders, popular sentiment suggests, essentially fall apart" (202). This is, in fact, the strong sentiment against which the chanted repetitions position themselves as counternarratives. Nonetheless, the force of the abandonment narrative does threaten to palpably disintegrate this family.

Elzbieta Sklodowska, interestingly here, has drawn upon Steven Marcus's gloss of Freud in a discussion of Latin American *testimonio* that also has clear implications for fiction of the border: "When Freud specifies what it is that is wrong with his patient's stories, 'the difficulties are in the first instance formal shortcomings of *narrative*: the connections . . . [are] obscured and unclear,'" the timelines confused. Marcus reminds us that "Among various types of narrative insufficiency, . . . Freud lists 'amnesias and paramnesias of several kinds and various other means of severing connections and altering chronologies'" (Sklodowska 91; Marcus 162–63, qtd. in Sklodowska). It is precisely such narrative insufficiencies and apparent amnesias that structure *Across a Hundred Mountains*. Narratively, Grande's novel juxtaposes two alternating points of view (recounted in limited third person): Juana, a young child, and Adelina, a much older woman coming from the United States to Mexico in search of her own father. It is only near the novel's conclusion that it is revealed that "Adelina" is actually the adult Juana, who has literally changed her identity by stealing the identity of another woman (the "real" Adelina, who is murdered by her boyfriend/pimp on the Mexican side of the border) so that she might come to Los Angeles to continue her search for Apá. The "real" Adelina, when she finally appears in the text, tells Juana, "I'm from El Otro Lado, as you call it" (175), once again underscoring the metonymical association of El Otro Lado with death, since this Adelina's voice is heard—as it turns out—from beyond the grave. As with Amá's textual reinscription as "the woman," the narrative refers to the adult Juana as "Adelina" throughout, even when characters from Juana's childhood life recognize her as "Juana," suggesting through this formal technique the irretrievable fragmentation of Juana's identity in the wake of her father's disappearance. (In a symbolic underscoring of the novel's theme of mistaken identity, at one point police officers wrongly believe that Juana has stolen a wallet and they grab for her, saying, "We've got you now, girl," while Juana screams in response, "You've made a mistake!" [168–69]). Even Amá, when Adelina/Juana returns near the novel's conclusion, cannot recognize her daughter—"You aren't my Juana"—although the woman referred to by the narrator as Adelina insists repeatedly, "'I'm Juana. Your daughter.' . . . She wanted so desperately for her mother to see her, to see Juana" (232). To not be able to recognize Juana *as her daughter* is to not be able to recognize the *relatedness* that stitches them together as a family.

Even (perhaps especially) the identity of Apá's unborn son is cast into doubt and confusion by his absence. The boy, named "Miguelito" after his father, is assumed by all except Amá herself to be the child of Don Elías, who eventually kidnaps him to live as his son with his wife. They rename him José Alberto. At the news of her brother's baptism, with his "new" parents and under his new name, Juana thinks to herself, "*His name is Miguel García. . . . Miguel García. Miguelito García. My brother*" (137), trying rhetorically to restabilize both his identity and his relatedness through compulsive repetition. When Adelina (Juana) reappears after many years' absence and by chance meets her brother (who now bears a striking resemblance to his biological father), he has no idea who he "really" is, or that Adelina is actually his sister. The havoc rendered by disappearance is conveyed in Adelina's lament about "not knowing who you are, where you came from, or the people you loved and who loved you" (171). The "not knowing" of familial disappearance attacks the core of a sense of identity; to not know "who loved you" is intimately linked with "not knowing who you are," rendering the familial story uncertain and unreliable. (Notably, Apá's leave-taking years earlier is described in terms of the absence of *stories*—Juana asks him for a story because "she knew this would be the last story he told her before he left" [33].) In other words, the father's disappearance indeed interrupts the narrative of family history, replacing it with a narrative that constitutes both family and community in dramatically different ways.

The multiple ways in which familial and collective identity has been disrupted by the father's disappearance are the novel's most pressing theme, and the restoration of a narrative that will recognize both familial and communal bonds provides the frame of the novel. *Across a Hundred Mountains* opens with the adult Adelina insisting that she be shown what could be her father's bones, demanding, "I have to know.... For nineteen years I have not known what happened to my father. You have no idea what it's like to live like that—not to know" (3). Confirmation of her father's body beneath the "grave" of the border will resolve "not knowing" into identity. Finding his bones at the border, Adelina insists that she "will take him with me, even if I have to carry his bones on my back" (2), a Virgilian passage which suggests the degree to which finding her father's physical body (and thus learning the history of his absence) might potentially heal the wounds to collective identity by restoring a larger narrative of self and family. When Adelina subsequently returns to her mother with the bones, the family is symbolically reunited—and both Adelina and José Alberto are addressed by their "real" names (although the narrative voice continues to call them Adelina and José Alberto).

The way in which family serves as a synecdoche for a larger communal and collective disruption is also conveyed symbolically through the image of the set of dishes which were given to Amá and Apá upon their marriage, and which are promised to Juana as her "inheritance" in the familial story. In Amá's story about the plate set, "*It gave me and your father good luck, Juana. We've had a good marriage*" (254). But when Apá's absence destroys the family, Amá goes on a rampage, breaking each of the plates into "a hundred pieces" until only one plate, "the only plate left of her inheritance," remains (73–74). The familial story has been fractured, but the "hundred pieces" stand for a much larger fractured story. In one scene in the novel, Adelina meets Miguel García, a man tracked down by a private detective she has hired to search for her father. *This* Miguel García lost his memory in an accident soon after arrival in Watsonville, so he does not know whom he might have left behind—who might have been affected by his own disappearance. Meeting this Miguel García, Adelina "knew what [he] wanted of her. He wanted his identity back. He wanted all those forgotten years back. He wanted to remember, to be able to look in the mirror and know where his roots were" (172). Like her own family, Miguel García wants the narrative of his history restored into coherence. When Adelina must tell him that he is not, in fact, her father, "She saw his body tremble, saw his hopes shatter, saw Gloria [his new wife] wrap her arms around him, as if trying to hold the pieces together" (172). The obvious metaphorical resonance of the image of shattering and of holding pieces together suggests that border disappearances are a collective ill that fragments communal identity, which must be held tenuously together through the reciprocal efforts of its members. Simultaneously, of course, Grande's narrative *constructs* Mexican and Mexican American identity as a communal one through the "shared history" of disappearances at the border—much like African American collective identity has been constructed in the United States largely through a shared history of diaspora, slavery, and Jim Crow segregation laws. In Cornell and Hartmann's explanation of ethnic group identity construction, they argue that "the common history a group claims" is often deployed as one of the "symbolic elements that may be viewed as emblematic of peoplehood" (19). While the trauma of border disappearances is portrayed as fracturing community, in fact the *narration* of ongoing trauma constitutes the community that is its subject.

A remarkably similar trauma narrative is played out in Castillo's *The Guardians*. The characters in this novel represent a range of legal statuses and immigrant arrivals: from el Abuelo Milton, the Mexican American with a long memory of racism, discrimination, and the building up of the border, to Miguel, the radicalized Chicano professor, to Regina, the military widow with legalized status, to her nephew Gabo, who remains undocumented. Because *all* the characters participate in the search for Gabo's lost father, Rafa, Castillo suggests that the search is a collective one; border disappearances impact the many different members of the community. Regina, contemplating her brother Rafa's disappearance, tells readers:

> I'd rather be pricked by a thousand thorns than have to think about what my little brother may have endured. The fact is, however, that I don't know what exactly he had to endure. Sometimes I like to think

he is back in Chihuahua with a pregnant wife and that we just never heard from him because he became too selfish and didn't care about Gabo no more or his past life with Ximena. (12)

Though Regina claims that she "likes to think" this (because it opens up the possibility that her brother is still alive, that he has not crossed over to *el otro lado* in either of its senses), it is clear from the narrative she projects that this prospect is not at all desirable. The alternative story that Regina resorts to telling of her brother's disappearance interrupts any narrative of family or communal connectedness or responsibility. As she acknowledges at the novel's conclusion, whatever she may have *thought* she would like to think, "the worst part was over, the not knowing" (207).

The interrupted, severed familial narrative has particularly grave consequences for Gabo, her nephew, who is loosed from any comprehensible collective identity. As Schmidt Camacho discusses with regard to missing migrants, "Familial dislocation, occurring across national boundaries, puts children's identities . . . in crisis." Schmidt Camacho suggests that the phenomenon of migrant disappearances reveals the "profoundly unsettling ways" in which "kinship cannot mitigate against loss" (312). Gabo socially disintegrates under the pressure of losing his father: he sleepwalks, his grades dip, and he begins to associate with known drug traffickers on the (at face value) highly improbable chance that they might lead him somehow to his father. The diagnosis from the doctor that Regina consults is that Gabo is under stress from "possibly losing a second parent." Regina comments, "That's not just stress, that's trauma" (122). Finally, Gabo dons a monk's garb and begins to preach publicly in a prophetic tone that makes no social sense and is incomprehensible to those around him. Weirdly, in the final chapters Miguel is referring to him as "Gabe" at some points and as "Gabo" at others (e.g., 168–69), even though he is addressed as "Gabe" nowhere else in the novel—suggesting an irretrievably fragmented identity.

Luis Alberto Urrea's novel *Into the Beautiful North* (2009), like those of Castillo and Grande, also begins from the premise of the cultural trauma of migration and absence, and also narrates paternal disappearance through migration. This novel tells the story of a ragtag group from Mexico who become aware of the pressing absence of men from their village—almost all have migrated to the United States—and decide to go north themselves in search of seven men to bring home. Though this text is ultimately less urgent than those by Grande or Castillo in its portrayal of the scarring and fragmentation caused by migratory disappearance—thanks to its appropriation of the "road trip" genre, which lends a tongue-in-cheek humor—that trauma still looms in the background as grim specter. The central character of the group, Nayeli, is driven north as much by the need to find her disappeared father (whose last known whereabouts are in Illinois) as by the more generalized desire to restock her Mexican hometown's masculinity. Nayeli constructs a narrative about her reunion with her father, imagining it in terms of the *presence* of a formerly absent body: "Was he there? Did he share a house with other men? Was he well? Surely he would laugh when he saw her. He would hurry to her and lift her in the air and spin around like he did when she was small. He would smell of Old Spice and his whiskers would prickle her face and she would cry, ¡Papá!" (322). But minutes later her fantasy is interrupted by the reality: her father has formed a new family in the United States and is oblivious not only to her physical presence ("his eyes passed right over Nayeli" [323]) but *to the trauma of absence.* Though Nayeli tries to reassert their familial relationship by wailing, "FATHER! ... Over and Over" (323), her cries are literally unheard. Thus Nayeli's father emblematizes the threat of abandonment that is posed by so many narratives of migration north (starting, perhaps, with the now classic film *El Norte*).

Susan Straight's novel *Highwire Moon* also attests to the issues of disappearance, familial separation, and resulting trauma that are found in the Latina/o post-Gatekeeper texts. Indeed, Straight's "outsider" (that is, non-Latina) narrative is as profound and moving in its depiction of the reverberations of trauma as any of the Chicano/a novels I have examined here, while also suggesting that this trauma poses ethical demands upon *non-Latino* U.S. readers—those who would be seen as "outsiders" even to the tentatively constituted community of "Latinos." The novel is also unique in its depiction of a particular aspect of that trauma—that is, the trauma inflicted on children by the deportation of their parents. The report *Paying the Price: The Impact of Immigration Raids on America's Children* documents such raids: "For children, especially very young children, the sudden loss of a parent played out like a 'disappearance.' . . . Especially among very young children, who could not understand the concept of parents not having 'papers,' sudden separation was considered personal abandonment" (Capps et al. 50–51).

It is the effects of such trauma that *Highwire Moon* imaginatively reconstructs, through the stories of Serafina, a Mexican indigenous woman who is forcibly deported from the United States leaving behind an infant daughter, and the daughter, Elvia, who grows up not knowing what has happened to her mother. Elvia's white, U.S. citizen father Larry does not talk about her disappeared mother Serafina, with the result that Elvia, lacking any kind of narrative of her familial or ethnic origins, has a disjointed and fragmented sense of her own identity:

> She didn't look like the rich or poor blond kids or the black kids or the kids who'd just gotten here from Mexico. And everyone asked, "What are you, anyway?" . . . Someone would say, "You look Hawaiian." Elvia would shrug. Someone would sneer, "I hate when girls get green contacts that don't even go with their skin." "Try pull these out then." Elvia would fold her arms and glare. (16)

In the absence of a narrative of self, Elvia cannot answer the question "What are you," nor can she explain coherently the mixed strands of her heritage; her sense of fragmentation is conveyed metaphorically in the alluded image of bodily fragmentation, as Elvia suggests that the kids who tease her try, literally, to pull out her eyes. When she attempts to fill out a medical form she declares in frustration: "'I can't do this. . . . I don't know anything.' Mother's medical history. . . . The questions about diabetes and cancer, heart trouble" (266). (As her boyfriend Michael observes, "Who knows what you got from your moms [sic], right?" [114].) Uncertain about her past, Elvia is unable to identify *herself,* even on a physical, bodily level.

Strikingly, Serafina's grief at Elvia's absence is most often described in terms of her daughter's absent *body*, emphasizing the physical senses and their deprivation as a locus of trauma. She misses "the sweet corn dust on Elvia's fingers" (59), and she still "remembered how Elvia's breath had smelled . . . soft and milky through the baby teeth, and . . . one sharp pebble of backbone" (48). Elvia, likewise, retains a powerful memory of her mother's body, specifically of "hands always moving like trapped birds, the crescent grin of white at her brown heels" (12), and the long braid in which she used to entwine her fingers to hold on to her as a baby (15). She memorializes her longing for her own mother in a tattoo of moths that recalls her boyfriend's memory of his own dead mother, who used to rub the sparkly dust of moth wings on her eyelids; a memorial to the missing maternal body is thus literally inscribed on Elvia's body (139).

But though memories of the body speak louder than words in this novel, the sparsity of a familial narrative is a painful source of Elvia's trauma. Elvia is furious when she discovers her father has withheld from her what little he did know about her mother that might serve as evidence of her whereabouts: her full name, a picture, a plastic laminated card with what might be her address. "Why didn't you tell me?" Elvia demands. But Larry retorts: "Tell you what? . . . That when your mom bailed, she left that and some clothes and some burned-up candles? Big deal. She forgot to pack you, too" (64). Larry's narrative of Serafina remains skeletal, incomplete, ridden with gaps. He refuses to stitch the evidence into a story that will anchor Elvia. Thus Elvia is confused, for example, about whether her mother is "Indian" or "Mexican," because Larry refuses to explain that one could be both; of her own dark complexion, Larry insists, "You're just tanned" (12). (Elvia's friend Hector has a similarly failed narrative of origins. Because his college aspirations have separated him from his migrant farmworker parents, he "can't figure out what he got from his parents. He's like alien boy" [114].)

Behind this failed narrative of identity and origins is another, deeper one: Elvia cannot explain *why* her mother left her. Her own narrative of what happened to her mother, when she tries to tell it, is as skeletal as her father's: "She left me in a church parking lot, in a car with no plates, no ID, nothing. She was from Mexico" (25). The narrative gaps in her story are suggested by her compulsive and repeated questions about her mother's disappearance, never verbalized, asked only to herself: "*Had she been crying before she left me? Because she was leaving me? . . . What did I do? What did I do when I was little like this, to make her leave me? . . . Was I like this? Is that why she left? Because I drove her crazy?*" (22). She attempts to construct alternate stories of the supposed abandonment in her head: "*Someone found me, in the church parking lot. Was my mom taking me inside, to leave me on one of those benches?*" (68). Seeing a poor woman begging at the border while nursing an infant, Elvia thinks, "*That could be my mother. Is that why she didn't want me to come? Back to nowhere?*" (143). Or, looking at the corpse of a woman who has died trying to cross the border, she imagines, "*What if that's her? What if she crosses every year from Tijuana to work grapes, and now she's just bones?*" (137). To Hector, she hypothesizes, "She's probably dead. . . . That's why she never came to find me" (140). Hector offers another possibility (the real one): "What if la migra got your mom? Way back then? What if she had to go back home?" (120). But among the many narratives of Serafina's absence, this is only one possible version; Elvia has no way of determining its truth. While she is certainly lost to her mother, then, she is also—perhaps more importantly—lost to herself.

As in *testimonio*, Elvia's situation is a synecdoche for the larger situation of family separations at the border. Michael, the teenaged father of Elvia's unborn baby, offers a metaphor that suggests how Elvia's trauma is collective rather than individual: "The smoke tree drops the seeds, but they have to get beat up by rushing water, like knocked into rocks and all, before they can take root. So the babies are always like way downstream from the mom" (120). When Serafina, now in Mexico, writes to her brother Rigoberto, who has gone north for work, to inform him of their mother's terminal cancer, his response comes in a letter: "*Take her to the doctor in Oaxaca City. I cannot come home. Crossing is too hard. Do you want my face or my money?*" (51). In the wake of Gatekeeper-like enforcement strategies, the children are separated by forces "like rushing water" from their mothers. In some sense, Michael, Hector, and Rigoberto—as well as Elvia herself—are all lost children of the border.

Dis(re)membered Bodies

The wounded, fragmented, and dismembered body in several post-Gatekeeper narratives—as with the ghostly figure of Beloved in Toni Morrison's novel by that name—represents much more than one individual's traumatic response to disappearance. Amy Novak has argued that the body itself can serve as a "marred testament" to cultural trauma (Danticat 227, qtd. in Novak 103)—and perhaps all the more because the story that the body tells is "disfigured" and "flawed," like the disfigured and ruptured narrative that is the effect of trauma itself (Novak 103). Indeed, Novak points out (citing trauma theorist Cathy Caruth) that the commonly understood significance of "trauma" has evolved from the sense of a "bodily wound" to that of a "psychic wounding" (101); so bodily wounds may well serve as a powerful textual figuration of the larger "wound" to the collective psyche. The image of bodily dismemberment figures, in a variety of contexts, as insistently linked to social and collective anxieties about the ability to *remember* traumatic histories (see, for instance, Martin; Young; Koven). Indeed, if, as Christopher Forth and Ivan Crozier posit, a coherent sense of identity is largely a function of a sense of "bodily unity" as "a gestalt of corporeal wholeness constantly projected in the face of [aberrant, malfunctioning, or even missing] parts" (4), then the missing body part serves equally well to represent a sense of fractured or wounded *communal* identity which needs re-membering.

In Castillo's *The Guardians*, the loss of the missing family member is, accordingly, sometimes analogized through the figure of *someone else's* wounded or amputated body, which alludes to the loved one's missing/absent body. Miguel, contemplating the failed search for Gabo's father, must acknowledge that "Rafa is only one among hundreds every year disappearing or finally turning up dead because of heat and dehydration in the desert or foul play at the hands of coyotes. These days all I can see in my mind's eye lately is that skeleton mother with three fingers that Gabe and my grandpa saw at the city morgue in J-Town" (148). As in *testimonio*, Rafa's disappearance is a synecdoche; it is not the story of one lost individual but the story of "hundreds every year." In this passage, that synecdoche is then visually and viscerally figured in the anonymous body with missing fingers. Likewise, Regina, recollecting a doctor's warning that her mother's leg would have to be amputated, clearly comes to view that existential moment for its metaphorical value: "I've been thinking about that lately. About losing a part of yourself. But even after they cut off your leg you can still talk to people. You can tell them how you feel about them. You can live without half a leg" (137). The phrasing is clearly evocative of the loss that *cannot* be mitigated against—the missing *individuals*. As in *Beloved*, the body has become the figure for the larger communal body; the dis(re)membered body then suggests the fear of the community's fragmentation (Caminero-Santangelo, *Madwoman* 156), a fear only mitigated by the relationships and connections that remain ("you can still talk to people").

Ironically, all of the post-Gatekeeper border narratives I examine here inevitably compensate for the radical instability introduced by *not knowing* by ultimately revealing the fates of the "disappeared" ones; it is as though, narratively, the sense of trauma produced by radical and unresolved disappearance must be delimited and contained, even as the collective trauma itself is narratively constructed. Thus in *The Guardians*, the lost father Rafa's dead body is finally found in a coyote's El Paso home; in *Across a Hundred Mountains* Juana/Adelina eventually finds, and properly buries, the dead bones of her father; in *Highwire Moon* we know, even if

Elvia does not, the reasons why her mother left and her efforts to return to her daughter, with the novel strongly suggesting that they will be reunited. Likewise, in Straight's novel *Highwire Moon*, readers have all along known what happened to the disappeared mother, even if Elvia herself did not. Eventually, Elvia too learns that her mother did not intend to leave her, a healing narrative that counters Elvia's long-standing and identity-fracturing belief that she was abandoned.

Border *Testimonio*

As Alexander writes, one of the contested issues at stake in the representation of cultural trauma is the "attribution of responsibility": "Who actually injured the victim? Who caused the trauma?" ("Toward a Theory" 15). This is a point emphasized by Neil Smelser: "A historical memory is established as a national trauma for which the society has to be held in some way responsible. . . . [In cultural trauma,] the assignment of responsibility is salient. Who is at fault? Some hated group in our midst? Conspirators? Political leaders? The military? Capitalists? A foreign power? We ourselves as a group or nation?" (38, 52). In a related vein, Kimberly Nance notes that the function of "epideictic" *testimonio* is the assignation of praise and blame (*Can Literature* 23); and Susan Sontag, in a discussion of photographic museum exhibits which remember horrific occurrences of social violence and genocide, suggests that such exhibits solicit similar questions: "Whom do we wish to blame? . . . Whom do we believe we have the right to blame?" (93). To apply this interrogation to the situation of undocumented disappearances is to ask, analogously: Who is to blame for the cultural trauma of border disappearances and familial separations? How do the novels ask us to shift our gaze not outward (at those, implicitly *not ourselves*, whom we have a "right" to blame) but inward?

Earlier I suggested that the border itself becomes figured as the grounds of death, but as we saw, this representation bears the danger of attributing responsibility to mere territoriality. This is a suggestion that at least some of these border narratives actively resist. The novels by Castillo and Straight do suggest that it is "we ourselves as a group or nation" (Smelser 52), in a generalized sense, that is responsible for the current crisis. This is perhaps nowhere more powerfully conveyed than in Straight's novel, in which it is Elvia's father who is the spokesperson for U.S. racial hegemonies and intolerance, much as he loves his daughter. Scorning her long, braided hair, he repetitively scolds her, "You're not Mexican.... You're not Indian. You're American. Wear your hair like everybody else at school" (15). His words bear a frightening resemblance to those of actual anti-immigrant activists such as one man interviewed in the documentary film *Crossing Arizona*, who angrily spouts that "the schools are all going into Spanish," which irks him because "I don't want to live in a non-American neighborhood. I want to live in America." To speak Spanish, to be "Mexican" or "Indian," are posed as mutually exclusive with being "American." One cannot be both. This strain of discourse, repeatedly heard in popular media especially around immigration debates, suggests the degree to which the construct of the American "nation" has no room to accommodate either Elvia or her mother.

The scene of Serafina's arrest in the novel, further, grimly anticipates the current escalation in the cooperation of law enforcement with INS/ICE and Border Patrol, suggesting the degree to which this cooperation is complicit with the intertwined structures of racism and nationalism. Outside of the church where Serafina has been praying, police detain her and demand: "ID? ID? You got ID?" Serafina responds with a different kind of "identification," attempting to communicate that her infant daughter is still in the car parked in the church lot:

> "Mydotter! Mydotter!" She screamed the words, felt their strange shape pull the cords in her throat. "My! My dotter!"
> "Okay, okay, you need a doctor. In Mexico. Get a doctor in Mexico." He held her wrist with one hand and pulled her up slowly....
> Serafina screamed. She couldn't see the car. They were taking her away. "Elvia! *Náá*, Elvia, mommy, my dotter . . ."
> "No habla español [*sic*]," He said softly. (6–7)

The scene is remarkable for a whole host of ways in which responsibility is attributed—from the fact that Serafina is forcibly separated from her family without any opportunity to contact them or to secure substitute care for her daughter, to the officers' lack of interest in obtaining medical attention for her (although they erroneously understand her to be requesting it), to the policeman's final remark that he does not speak Spanish, when not a word of Spanish has been spoken in the entire exchange. Serafina is attempting to speak not in English but in her native Mixtec tongue. (In an analogous instance from recent events, the report "Paying the Price" notes that in several of the major raids of the 1990s, "many Guatemalans . . . spoke a Mayan dialect, not Spanish, as their first language; ICE certainly had difficulty communicating with this group" [Capps et al. 22].) In short, though the policemen who detain Serafina ask for identification, their practices work to *efface* Serafina's identity (as somebody's mother and somebody's partner; as an indigenous woman from Mexico) and thus withhold recognition from her as a human being for whom such a wrenching removal will inflict trauma. And although Callie, the sometime-girlfriend of Elvia's father, Larry, tells Elvia that her mother "lives right over the border. . . . If she wanted you, she could a came to get you" (64), the actual difficulty of Serafina's return to her daughter is underscored by repeated and explicit mentions of "Operation Gatekeeper [which] catches everybody" (143; see also 91, 140, 152).

Castillo's *The Guardians* is equally explicit in its attributions of responsibility, suggesting perhaps that the crisis is too urgent for any chances to be taken with the reader's understanding on this point. El Abuelo Milton points out the hypocrisy in an immigration enforcement policy that has varied with changing labor needs; during the Great Depression, migrants "weren't allowed to cross over precisely 'cause there was no work. Now, during the chile harvest season, La Migra turns a blind eye at all the men that come to be picked up" (132). Yet despite pressing demands for labor, our immigration policies "force people to crawl on their bellies for a chance to make it" (4). Expanding the resonance and meanings of the term *disappearance* from its context within Latin American state repression (as I have already suggested), Castillo writes that at the border it is "crooked coyotes who disappear people" (58).

At the same time, the emphasis on human smugglers as the "culprit" in border deaths and disappearances potentially serves to obscure the complicity of what Nevins calls "boundary policing" *itself* in the escalating fatality count (*Operation Gatekeeper* 67, 145–46), an argument also forcefully made by Bill Ong Hing, who points out that border security measures have in fact contributed to the growing trade in human smuggling (196). (Nevins makes a useful distinction between the "border region" and the "boundary" or nation-state line that is policed by operations such as Gatekeeper [*Operation Gatekeeper* 67]. This makes it possible for us to discuss a border ethics that is not invested in boundary lines, as I will discuss shortly.) The limitation of blame to the coyotes is one that *The Guardians* persistently pushes against; while the coyotes do indeed turn out to be the most immediate villains, Castillo's larger, contextualized narrative is about the historical factors that have given the coyotes their power. The "coyotes and narcos own the desert now" (4), Regina tells readers at the novel's opening. But the drug traffic across the border is fueled by U.S. demand (151), and the drug smugglers have gone into the business of human trafficking thanks to the more militarized border enforcement strategy which has made the human smuggling market increasingly lucrative: "What has happened is that migrants are having to try more often to get across without being apprehended, and are using different routes to do so, which are more dangerous.... [T]he only reason [Rafa] needed a coyote was that was the law of the land now. If you wanted to cross, you had to pay *somebody*" (116).

In *Highwire Moon*, likewise, the increased border security measures which have made human smuggling a powerful and profitable business also have a share in responsibility for the dangers of the border, including the increased danger of rape—Serafina is raped when she first tries to recross to return to Elvia, and she is almost raped again by the coyote who leads her second attempt. Imagining a solution to the problem of border deaths, then, would require a comprehensive understanding of many interlocked causes, rather than a simplistic pinpointing of any individual culprit, as Regina suggests in *The Guardians*: "You just have to keep taking those what-ifs to infinity. What if ... no money could be made on killing undocumented people for their organs? What if this country accepted outright that it needed the cheap labor from the south and opened up the border? And people didn't like drugs so that trying to sell them would be pointless?" (29). Regina, who, in the novel's backstory, was eventually able to legalize her status through her dead husband's military service, pinpoints immigration policies that have rendered legalization virtually impossible for most immigrants today, noting wryly that "Getting legal status was easier said than done.... That's all every immigrant in the world wants, to get her papers in order. To officially become a person" (116). To not have papers is like not being identified; the "official" denial of status is thus likened to a form of disappearance in itself, a body without a "name" to render one socially recognizable as "human."

Gaspar de Alba also casts a wide net in attributing responsibility for the various forms of death at the border. U.S. economic domination of Mexico is certainly a primary target; thus the pennies inserted into the corpses of murdered women are equated to "the *maquilas* themselves [which] have been shoved down Mexico's throat ... because of NAFTA" (251–52). Free trade benefits U.S. corporations by providing cheap labor; but these pennies earned are symbolically held accountable for the lives of the vulnerable *maquila* workers—whether or not the maquilas are directly responsible for the murders. Economic interests, further, work *in conjunction with* the cultural and racial imperatives of a hegemonic Anglo-American culture threatened by the encroaching "brown tide" (Santa Ana) of Mexican and Central American immigration. As Ivon slowly pieces together the puzzle, she thinks to herself:

> NAFTA's brought thousands of poor, brown, fertile female bodies to the border to work at a *maquiladora*. . . . Not all of them will get jobs. . . . What happens if they cross over? More illegal Mexican women in El Paso means more legal brown babies. Who wants more brown babies as legal citizens of the Promised Land? . . . Although we love having all that surplus labor to exploit, once it becomes reproductive rather than just productive, it stops being profitable. (332)

The business interests of U.S. corporations require cheap labor but *not* the demands of pregnancy-related medical care or maternity leave. The cultural imperatives of the hegemonic nation require, at the same time, that surplus labor (especially with a reproductive capacity) not flow northward. As Leo Chavez writes, anti-immigration sentiment is constructed through images which suggest the threat of an "insidious invasion" that includes, among other things, "the capacity of the invaders to reproduce themselves" (*Covering Immigration* 233). In Gaspar de Alba's fictional theory of the Juárez murders, the rape and dismembering of women's bodies serves, in part, a terrorist function to keep women from crossing the border.

Meanwhile, NAFTA's implementation is accompanied by an astronomical increase in the budget for border patrol (Gaspar de Alba 330), which is justified by new border enforcement strategies such as Gatekeeper and Hold-the-Line. *Desert Blood's* resolution of the crime of border deaths, then, is a "bilateral assembly line of perpetrators" that extends far beyond the specific violence done to the women of Juárez: "from the actual agents of the crime to the law enforcement agents on both sides of the border to the agents that made binational immigration policy and trade agreements" (335). To truly resolve these border crimes, we would have to address "the profit reaped by the handiwork of [all] the perpetrators" (335).

Like Gaspar de Alba, Castillo is interested in providing *testimonio* for a whole host of interconnected border ills that stem from the lack of recognition of humanity for those who reside there. In both novels, for instance, environmental justice for border communities is a pressing problem. In *Desert Blood*, Ivon is horrified to hear that her sister Irene was bathing in the Rio Grande at one point, because "The river stunk of sewer. Beer cans and human feces floated in the black water" (141). Ivon also registers how the "refinery smokestacks [in El Paso] stood like sentinels of death," and recalls that this place "gave [her uncle] stomach cancer and killed Granny Rosemary with tuberculosis" (295). In *The Guardians*, Miguel is agitating against the exact same "smelter company," ASARCO (American Smelting and Refining Company), which has poisoned the air in the border region and is now trying to renew its air quality permit. Regina remembers: "When I was a girl and came up to work in the fields, I'd see the humongous swirls of smoke coming up from the smelter" (51). She equated the vision in her child's mind to "the Statue of Liberty" holding a beacon for "the huddled masses" (51). The imagery underscores the ways in which the American Dream has failed to live up to its promise for immigrants coming from south of the border, not only in terms of status or opportunity but even more fundamentally in terms of basic, safe living conditions for all those within its borders.

In this sense, the "disappeared" are not just those who have lost their lives trying to cross; they also include the overlooked, the unattended to, and the unrecognized. The string of human-made and environmental ills that plague those on either side of the border are linked together by Miguel: "For days and nights we had to go outside to the bathroom. Electricity was out. La migra stopped and flashed infrared lights on people all the time" (108). As Regina notes, "We didn't forget that what brought us together in the first place was searching for my Gabo's papá. But I will be the first to say . . . that me and my sobrino are not the only ones with problems" (52). There are, apparently, many lost ones at the border, and they are lost in different ways, but all are related to economic interests and racial politics that intersect at the border zone.

The preoccupation with those who are "disappeared" by virtue of simply not registering as significant in the public sphere is also taken up in Bencastro's *Odyssey to the North*. This novel opens with a dead body—the accidental death of an unnamed and unknown undocumented immigrant working as a window washer in Washington, D.C.—but then expands its reach to other bodies and even other forms of "disappearance" related to border and immigration enforcement. Anonymous characters lament, in chorus-like fashion, that "the Wizard," a Latin American immigrant who dies in a fire in an abandoned building, had "come so far just to end up burned to a crisp in the basement of an abandoned house" (24). The culmination of the Wizard's journey in a death quite far from the border highlights the sense that crossing the border is not the successful culmination of the odyssey, which continues in different forms *within* the United States. Other characters will be "lost" because they cannot navigate the *post*-crossing process.

Leo R. Chavez, in *Shadowed Lives: Undocumented Immigrants in American Society*, provides a useful lens for understanding such representations of undocumented-immigration-as-odyssey. Chavez suggests three phases to the migration experience of immigrants in general: separation, transition, and incorporation (5, 12). Chavez is particularly interested in the "transition" phase—the phase during which immigrants move from being "temporary migrants to settlers in the United States" (12). He argues that "crossing the border marks the beginning of the transition phase, when migrants move from one way of life to another" (13). But as Chavez further remarks, "The case of undocumented immigrants . . . suggests that for some the transition phase *begins with crossing the border, but never comes to a close*; these people never accumulate enough links of incorporation—secure employment, family formation, the establishment of credit, capital accumulation, competency in English, and so forth—to allow them to become settlers and feel part of the new society" (*Shadowed Lives* 5).

Bencastro's *Odyssey to the North* suggests, precisely, that the "transition" that begins with border crossing is never complete; that the experience of "incorporation" is never reached, and that therefore the border itself stretches on into infinity, never actually crossed. The novel's depiction of a deportation hearing in which "Teresa," a Salvadoran character, appears before a judge after entering the country illegally, certainly gestures toward the threats to Teresa's physical well-being posed *during* her journey north (37); but eventually the legal system itself, which Teresa has to navigate, becomes a continuation of her odyssey from El Salvador, positing yet more Scyllas and Charybdises for her to overcome. The larger critique that Bencastro inscribes into his novel suggests that legalization is just a continuation of the crossing odyssey, and it is one as dangerous to navigate as the journey itself.

As with *Enrique's Journey,* the style of *Odyssey to the North* suggests the synecdochic nature of the characters' experiences as well as the flattening and confusion of time into an amorphous and continuing present. Time shifts from "past" to "present" take place throughout the nonchronological narrative, with sections from the past alternating with those of the present, without chapter headings or other formal markers to signal these shifts. The effect is that the narrative's "past" in the home countries of the characters is easily confused on a formal level with their "present" in Washington, D.C. Furthermore, some chapters are written as dramatic scripts: dialogue is represented, with alternating characters speaking, without any intervening narration. Yet most of these dramatic sections do not designate *which* character is speaking at any particular point (as a script would do); the speaking parts are, as it were, unlabeled. Here, for example, is a discussion among workers in a hotel restaurant about an immigration raid:

> When the *migra* arrived at the hotel, everyone panicked.
> Most of the employees escaped in the blink of an eye! I took off running.
> Me too. The only one they caught was Caremacho.
> They say he was distracted, flirting with Pateyuca.
> ....
> What could Caremacho see in Pateyuca?
> Rumor has it that he wanted to marry her just to get his green card.
> What a user!
> But it backfired on him because, while he was flirting with her, they trapped him in the kitchen and caught him.
> Because of his own stupidity he was left with nothing.
> And now the *migra* is going around checking all the restaurants and hotels in the area.
> You have to be alert at all times.
> But all the same, you have to work anyway you can, so you have to run the risk of being caught. (30)

The unattributed dialogue creates the effect that, although the undocumented speakers come from El Salvador, Chile, and Colombia, their discourse blends together into a cumulative "chorus" of the undocumented in the U.S. restaurant, each character serving as a synecdoche of the experience of being "illegal." And with *la migra* checking the restaurants in Washington, D.C., the border's characteristic threat of apprehension has now been extended outward (or inward) to the nation's capital.

Unhearable Testimony

Another significant aspect of the border's extension through time and space is the silence that continues to be imposed upon undocumented migrants. The undocumented, arguably until quite recently, have had no voice that could be heard in public discourse. In the same way that silence is a necessity while crossing the border undetected, its effects linger on into current U.S. contexts, much like the incursions of *la migra* into Washington, D.C. restaurants. In *Human Rights and Narrated Lives*, Kay Schaffer and Sidonie Smith point out that

> human rights discourses, norms, and instruments depend upon the international commitment to narratability, a commitment to provide, according to Joseph Slaughter, "a public, international space that empowers all human beings to speak." [Victims'] testimony brings into play, implicitly or explicitly, a rights claim. The teller bears witness to his or her own experience through acts of remembering elicited by rights activists. . . . As individual stories accumulate, the collective story gains cultural salience and resonance. (Slaughter 415, qtd. in Schaffer and Smith 3)

But what if the collective story *does not* gain cultural salience and resonance? What if, in fact, it fails to gain a true public hearing at all? What if the teller, for all practical purposes, cannot effectively bear witness?

Susan Bibler Coutin considers one salient example of the unhearableness of the narratives of unauthorized immigrants. Writing on Central American asylum applications in the 1980s and '90s from refugees fleeing repression and genocide in El Salvador and Guatemala, Coutin discusses how refugees had problems proving "political" persecution because, under the legal terms established in the United States, they had to establish that they were *personally* being singled out and persecuted for political beliefs or activities (65). Such a criterion obscured the way that these regimes worked through the installation of terror (they were, indeed, terrorist states). The state operated through a system of violence that was quite often indiscriminate; it was therefore difficult for asylum claimants to construct a narrative that responded to the specific criteria for asylum under U.S. law. As Coutin writes,

> Analyzing [the narratives of Central Americans] suggests that during the Salvadoran and Guatemalan civil wars, continual violence, surveillance, and interrogation made the causes of persecution unclear and defined average people as potentially subversive. In the words of one exiled Guatemalan who struggled to convey the deadly ambiguity of repression in his country, "No one is a victim, and all are victims." (75)

The difficulty facing Central American claimants underscores how the stories we tell—about ourselves, our lives, our relations to others and to the state—matter in profound ways that may well mean life or death. In this way, *testimonio* failed at the most basic level, as a form of storytelling and testimony told to enact certain ends (the ability of the Central American immigrant to remain safely on U.S. soil).

This is the point made dramatically in Bencastro's novel *Odyssey to the North* during a character's asylum hearing. Teresa, a Salvadoran immigrant facing deportation, repeatedly tells the judge that she and her husband left El Salvador because her husband, who had been in the military, was threatened with death by the guerrillas if he continued to serve in government forces. Although he left the military, he feared for his life—from the armed forces themselves, if they discovered him, and also from the guerrillas, who could not be sure he had deserted. Teresa's testimony about the Salvadoran oppression of the 1990s within a post-Gatekeeper novel about undocumented Latin American immigration in the United States deliberately brings together the earlier contexts of *testimonio* with this new genre of text advocating for immigrant human rights. Needless to say (and that is perhaps the point), a threat to Teresa's husband in a terrorist state is a threat to Teresa herself. Yet that point is not comprehended in an asylum system that demands a claim of *individual* persecution. Thus the trial attorney interjects, "Your Honor, I don't understand how these questions are relevant . . . the questions about the husband's encounters with the guerrillas" (101). Shortly thereafter, the judge concurs:

> I don't know if we're hearing her case today, or her husband's, but we're far from the central point. I would like to know why she is afraid of being persecuted in El Salvador, and I have not yet found the reason. After fifteen minutes of questioning there is nothing more than the fact that the guerrillas once threatened that if he didn't leave the army, he would be killed. . . . [T]his hearing is not about his case but about hers. (102)

The scene dramatizes the fact that Teresa's testimony is *unhearable* within U.S. asylum law. According to the judge, listening to testimony regarding her husband is not "hearing" her case but his. Thus the silencing of voice that comes through the generalized trauma of being undocumented in the United States is compounded by juridical silencing; the judge insists "I simply don't want to hear any more about this husband" (161).

Notably, it is precisely the collective, communal nature of the story that renders it unhearable, incomprehensible within the U.S. asylum framework. The trial attorney, for instance, seeks to discredit Teresa's asylum claim precisely by focusing on the fact that her story is not individual or unique but applies to others in her position as well:

> TRIAL ATTORNEY: From your testimony, it would appear that conditions in your country are dangerous. Is that a fair summary?
> TERESA: Yes.
> TRIAL ATTORNEY: And it appears that many people are in very difficult situations, isn't that right?
> TERESA: Yes. (161)

For Teresa, responding "yes" to the attorney's questions is an acknowledgment of the synecdochic nature of her experiences—she is not being singled out for persecution, because there are "many people" in her situation. But to the attorney and later for the judge, Teresa's "yes" is evidence that her story does not fit the criteria for asylum. As the judge summarizes in his finding,

> To be eligible for asylum under section 208(a) of the Act, an applicant must fit the definition of a refugee, which requires her to show persecution or a well-founded fear of persecution in her homeland. . . . In describing the amount and type of proof required to establish that a fear of persecution is well founded, the Ninth Circuit held:

> Applicants must point to specific objective facts that support an inference of past persecution or risk of future persecution. . . .
> It is only after concrete evidence sufficient to suggest a risk of persecution has been presented that the applicant's subjective fears and desire to avoid the risk-laden situation in his homeland become relevant.
> The evidence appears, frankly, to establish a case for the husband more than for the respondent. There is no testimony that the respondent was ever threatened. (175–76)

The judge, looking for "concrete evidence" that *Teresa herself* should "objectively" fear persecution, finds that Teresa's fears are "subjective" and amount to a "desire to avoid [a] risk-laden situation." A narrative of generalized, collective persecution does not fit within the legal framework of asylum law. The result is that Teresa is deported back across several borders and "mysteriously murdered" in El Salvador (124). The inability to tell her story becomes another Scylla in her odyssey—and ultimately it is the one that she (and many others) cannot survive.

The Failure of Faith

Another way in which these novels underscore the traumatic impact of undocumented disappearance is by representing the ways in which faith practices intrinsic to Latino communities fail to bear the weight of trauma or to provide avenues of redress or relief. In *God's Heart Has No Borders: How Religious Activists Are Working for Immigrant Rights*, Pierrette Hondagneu-Sotelo delineates the many ways in which traditional religious forms have been adapted in galvanizing responses to such imperatives. Indeed, Hondagneu-Sotelo contends that, more than any other form of mobilization, the immigrant rights movement has been spurred by faith-based coalitions and forms of activism. It is all the more striking, then, that in post-Gatekeeper novels of the disappeared, skepticism about traditional religious forms and rituals to successfully mediate collective trauma has become very deep indeed. These writers seem to suggest the utter failure of religious rhetoric or religious forms to adapt to these new circumstances of loss and disappearance at the border.

Susan Straight's *Highwire Moon*, notably, opens with a scene of the apparent failure of religious faith. Serafina goes to a church to pray to the

Virgen de Guadalupe about whether she should return to Mexico; her infant daughter Elvia sleeps quietly in the car while her mother prays. It is from the otherwise empty church that the policemen find and forcibly remove Serafina—she is subsequently deported back to Mexico—ignoring her attempts to explain that her daughter is still in the car. As Serafina thinks to the Virgen later, in anguish, "*I was praying to you, and they took me away. My baby was sleeping in the car. How could you be so cruel?*" (43). In the aftermath of her traumatic separation from her daughter, Serafina "kept her head turned away from la Virgen de Guadalupe, hanging over the altar" (93). Serafina's prayers were "answered" in a way she could never have imagined—by traumatic force; consequently she cannot view faith as restorative. Similarly, *Across a Hundred Mountains* strongly suggests a sense of the failure of religious symbolism to address trauma. In the absence of the father Miguel's return and the subsequent catastrophe that descends on the García household, religious symbols and rituals are depicted as without power: "Juana remembered the times of long ago when the saints and La Virgen de Guadalupe had been there for them. But now, all the statues were covered with dust" (128). The image of religious figures covered or turned away suggests a loss of faith in the power of such images to offer healing, recovery, or redress from trauma.

And yet, in her study of the use of religion in immigrant activism, Hondagneu-Sotelo has suggested that traditional religious forms *can* in fact prove adaptable and effective in religious activism for immigrant rights—which of course advocates for forms of redress. She describes, for example, a Holy Week Procession held in Santa Monica in 2001 in which an interfaith gathering took up one clergyman's call to "take your Good Friday to the streets!" (73):

> [The activists] processed through the posh streets of Santa Monica, singing songs and stopping at hotels that represented the stations of the cross. . . . At the first station, we all dropped matzo crackers in a basket, offering thanks . . . "for the sustenance of labor and the journey from oppression to liberation." When we stopped at . . . [a hotel] where a particularly nasty labor struggle was under way, we left bitter herbs as a reminder to the hotel "to not make the lives of their workers bitter anymore." (74–75)

The Santa Monica procession, which has its precedent in the march of farmworkers led by César Chávez during Holy Week of 1966

(Hondagneu-Sotelo 83), is just one recent post-Gatekeeper example of how religious symbolism, ritual, and rhetoric has been increasingly called into service in the cause of activism on behalf of Latin American immigrants.

A Holy Week procession makes a remarkably similar activist appearance in an earlier novel by Ana Castillo, *So Far from God*, which is concerned (among other things) with environmental justice at the border. In *So Far from God*, Castillo draws on the power of liberation theology to construct an argument about the suffering of human beings modeled on the suffering of Christ, interjecting stages of the cross with environmental and human ills in a Good Friday procession that is also a political protest (see Caminero-Santangelo, *On Latinidad* 153–54). I quote the scene for purposes of comparison:

> When Jesus was condemned to death, the spokesperson for the committee working to protest dumping radioactive waste in the sewer addressed the crowd. [. . .]
>
> Jesus fell,
> and people all over the land were dying from toxic exposure in factories.
>
> Jesus met his mother, and three Navajo women talked about uranium contamination on the reservation, and the babies they gave birth to with brain damage and cancer. [. . .]
>
> Veronica wiped the blood and sweat from Jesus' face. Livestock drank and swam in contaminated canals.
>
> Jesus fell for the second time.
>
> The women of Jerusalem consoled Jesus. Children also played in those open disease-ridden canals where the livestock swam and drank and died from it.
>
> Jesus fell a third time. The air was contaminated by the pollutants coming from the factories. (242–43)

Castillo's earlier novel intertwines traditional Christian, religious rituals with the activist call to take protest "to the streets," much as does Hondagneu-Sotelo's real-world example, thus seeming to reinforce Hondagneu-Sotelo's claim about religious ritual in activist imaginaries.

The difference in tenor between *So Far from God* and Castillo's post-Gatekeeper novel *The Guardians*, however, suggests a growing discomfort with *any* form of religious rhetoric to successfully advocate for progressive change or to redress collective trauma. The status of religious discourse has become much more troubling. The teenaged Gabo is the narrator of the parallel scene from the later novel:

> "The first angel poured his vial on the earth," I said, at first speaking softly, "the second on the sea, the third upon the rivers, and the fourth was poured upon the sun."
>
> (Contamination is everywhere in the environment, Padre Pío. El Chongo Man is always saying toxins are steadily killing everyone. The science teacher has told us that global warming will be the demise of the planet.)
>
> "The fifth angel poured out his vial and the kingdom was left full of darkness . . . *And I saw three unclean spirits like frogs come out of the mouth of the beast.*" (It was the day after the president gave a speech on TV . . . nothing but lies to placate the public. Yes, everywhere people were sleeping.) (164–65)

As with the earlier Good Friday scene, religious "scenes" are interspersed with the "real world" problems of those at the border. Notably, however, the difference in the way these two scenes are written is concentrated in the ridicule to which Gabo is subjected as he "preaches" to his fellow students atop a cafeteria chair, while wearing a monk's robes: "The students were mostly ignoring me. . . . Some made fun and even threw food at me. I did not care. Why should I?" (165). Unlike the Good Friday procession in *So Far from God*, which is a public protest that harnesses all the power of a community to give testimony to forms of collective trauma, Gabo is here a lone religious fanatic whose words are *incomprehensible* to those he speaks to. It is striking that (in contrast to the Good Friday procession in *So Far from God*) while the prophetic discourse in this scene is in quotation marks, the "translation" into common terms is unspoken and uncommunicated. Gabriel is aware of it; his audience is not. Religious discourse *fails* because it cannot process trauma in a comprehensible way that is meaningful to the larger community. It is instead represented as so intensely private that the building of a shared, collective narrative out of such materials seems impossible.

Other novels, too, suggest the paucity of religious ritual for bearing public witness or healing collective trauma. In *Desert Blood*, readers are told much more simply that "eight years ago, Ivon's dad had gone on a Holy Week pilgrimage . . . and lost his life" (236). So much for Holy Week pilgrimages. When one character near the end of this novel praises Jesus that Ivon's sister Irene has been found alive, Ivon's unspoken retort is, "No thanks to Jesus, she's . . . gang-banged and dog-bitten" (315). Such passages surely suggest these authors' discomfort with the use of religiosity as a tool in the battle of the border. In *Across a Hundred Mountains*, Juana's mother still thinks ahead to the potentially redeeming rituals of the "Semana Santa" [Holy Week] procession (128). But in Amá's tortured reenactment of this scene, she positions herself as the cause of her misfortunes: "*I must try to offer something more powerful than prayers. . . . But what can I offer them, Juana, for them to forgive me?*" The result is not protest but penance—Amá whips her bare back with a strap studded with nails in the hope that "her sin will be absolved" (132–33). Rather than a collective demonstration of the ways in which Amá and others have been made the victims of particularly repressive social and economic structures, Amá engages in a ritual that suggests that she is individually blameworthy. Violence and protest are directed inward, rather than outward.

Amá's self-flagellation might be understood as one effort to make comprehensible an incomprehensible series of events, but the text also suggests that the narrative woven by such self-punishment is highly counterproductive. We are told that the "image of [the *penitentes*'] bloody backs lingered in Juana's memory. She wished she'd never seen the procession. For many months afterward, she had recurring nightmares about the flagellants. She could see the whips swinging up and down in the air, digging into human flesh" (129). Juana understands, on some level, the story of sin, punishment, and redemption that the *penitentes*' practices make of their suffering, but "redemption" is missing from Juana's grasp of this narrative at a visceral level—it ends with suffering. A story which explains suffering through suffering, trauma through trauma, and which focuses inward on the individual's guilt and penance instead of outward to the healing of a community, offers no potential for redemption. In Grande's novel, as in Castillo's, the Good Friday procession has been reduced to a ritual that locks suffering in incomprehensibility.

Trauma and Narrative Breakdown

Of course, incomprehensibility is part of the nature of trauma, as Cathy Caruth has explained—trauma by its nature resists accurate narration in the moment (4, 11). We see the failure of the ability to tell the story of the lost ones repeatedly in Castillo's novel, not just in its religious discourse. Toward the conclusion of *The Guardians*, for instance—when Miguel's ex-wife has also disappeared—Regina describes the breakdown in communication between them:

> I followed him out to his car as he was leaving the building. "Wait, please!" I called. "Wait." Miguel could hear me, I was sure of it, but he kept walking. . . . "Espérate," I then called in Spanish, like it was a language problem between us and not the preponderance of tragedies in our lives building sound barriers. (182)

In a later passage, Regina describes her own faulty powers of recollection and narration: "no matter how many times I try to reconstruct it all, for the cops, for my own sake, for the sake of ever-elusive justice, there are still blanks. There will always be blanks in my recollection of Wonderland" (204). Perhaps we can understand the failure of religious discourse in terms of just such traumatic "gaps"—the gaps in Gabriel's narrative where he fails to communicate the "content" of his prophetic witness: the suffering in real people's lives. More disturbing, it may be, than Gabo's *inability* to communicate to others through his religious discourse is his *unconcern* about his failure: "I did not care. Why should I?" (165). In some sense, the larger collective trauma is a function of people's inability to realize, as Gabo suggests, why *they should care*. One alternative to a rhetoric that isolates wounded individuals is one that stitches together a community, however tentatively, out of the materials of trauma.

Narrating Collective Identity

While the trauma of border disappearances is portrayed in the texts I have examined as fracturing community, it is arguable that the *narration* of ongoing trauma simultaneously constitutes the community that is its subject. Stephen Cornell and Douglas Hartmann have postulated that "the common history a group claims" is often deployed as one of the "symbolic elements that may be viewed as emblematic of peoplehood" (19). In Castillo's *The Guardians*, Mexican and Mexican American characters are assuredly traumatized by loss and disappearance; however, they are bound together by those disappearances and the search for the missing ones. Precisely because trauma is shown to impact each character in a range of ethnonational subject positions, "the group" is constituted *through* the reverberations of trauma, even as it is ostensibly fractured by them. That is to say, Castillo's narrative *constructs* Mexican and Mexican American identity as a communal one through a complex "shared history" that includes dispossession, discrimination, exploited labor, *and* current disappearances at the border, just as African Americans share a collective history, including forced migration, slavery, segregation, discrimination, and lynching. Grande's *Across a Hundred Mountains*, similarly, suggests the ways in which recent Mexican immigrants (like Juana) and U.S. Latinos (like Juana's romantic interest, Sebastian, and his family) are stitched tenuously together in a fragile solidarity that might come to imagine and represent itself as an ethnic "family," collectively healing cultural rifts caused by impoverishment, dislocation, and migration. In these Gatekeeper-era narratives of disappearance, then, trauma is paradoxically both destructive and constitutive, a threat to communal identity and a symbolic element of communal identity that makes powerful social justice claims, underscoring yet again the ways in which the stories we tell about ourselves continue to define—and in the process to construct—who we are.

Located Humanism and an Ethics of Witnessing

Susan Straight's *Highwire Moon* and Gaspar de Alba's *Desert Blood*, in particular, take this constructed solidarity one step further, proposing an "ethics of witnessing" (Kaplan 122) that invokes a surprising, generalized *humanistic* rhetoric which is surely an ethical appeal to the hegemonic "mainstream." *The Guardians* gestures toward this humanist position as well in certain moments, such as when Regina mulls: "First one person's loved one has gone missing and before you find him, someone else's goes missing. Things that terrible don't just keep happening to people, I thought. To what people? Just people" (180). The question-and-answer structure of this meditation suggests that Regina resists the psychological defense by which we are inclined to distance ourselves from "other people's" problems by asking "what people" are injured by violence or deprivation, as though the answer (delimiting people by some sort of group identity) actually matters. Such witnessing goes beyond merely empathetic trauma; rather, predicated on a certain *distance* from the victims of trauma, witnessing as Kaplan defines it "has to do with an art work producing a deliberate ethical consciousness"; while empathy may be limited to a single individual feeling (vicariously) the pain of another, "witnessing implies a larger ethical framework that has to do with public recognition" of large-scale wounds *and with the acknowledgment of shared responsibility* for them (122).

Straight encodes such responsibility into her text both negatively (through the figure of the Anglo-American father whose lesson to his daughter is shame at her indigenous and Mexican heritage) and more positively, through the figure of Elvia's white foster mother, Sandy, who teaches her that "family" need not be based on blood ties or identity politics but may truly be writ large as a sense of mutual caretaking. Though Elvia's father derides Sandy's home as a "group home" rather than "blood family" and asks, "How could you love anybody that wasn't your own blood?" he also remembers, "When he'd first walked into that yard, seen [Elvia] with the other kids under that mulberry tree, he knew it wasn't a group home. It was a family" (220). As a figure, Sandy suggests an ethics of responsibility not based on sharing the blood of family or ethnicity.

Desert Blood gives perhaps the most extended treatment of this humanistic ethics, so I will close by discussing the vision that it presents. Ivon invokes the trope of family to imagine a connectedness that extends beyond nation-state or even ethnic backgrounds. Ivon's cousin William, who reluctantly helps her to search for her missing sister, lashes out, "She's your sister, not mine." Ivon retorts, "Hey, if it's not your sister, it's not your problem, right?" (214). Later, relieved that one of the dead bodies discovered in a *rastreo* is not her sister, she nevertheless comments, "She's someone else's sister, . . . someone else's daughter" (249), a repeated refrain in the novel with regard to the dead (see 214). The underlying assumption is that familial relatedness, even imagined relatedness, serves as a grounds for empathy. To imagine the dead corpse in a web of familial and communal relations is to reinvest it with its social meaning—indeed, with its *humanity*. To see it as only an anonymous and unidentified corpse, by contrast, would allow Ivon (and readers) to regard the body as without social meaning, to bracket the crimes done to this body and every other for which we lack context.

But while the trope of "family" has been used exhaustively as a metaphor for various sorts of "imagined communities"—including ethnic, national, or even religious ones—that extend beyond the biological reach of actual families, the condition of all such communities is that they are bounded, in some way, by some criteria. There are always, inevitably, others who are "outside" of the boundaries of any community, even an imagined one. Yet Ivon's conjuring of "family" to invoke ethical responsibility for disappeared bodies does not seem to map onto *any* imagined group categories (as el Abuelo Milton's use of "brothers and sisters" to refer to Mexicans and Mexican Americans does in *The Guardians*). Instead, her reinscription of familial bonds invokes an ethical responsibility opened out, unbounded by nation-state, by religious beliefs, or even by ethnicity. The metaphor of familial relatedness in *Desert Blood* takes upon itself fully the weight of ethical relatedness and responsibility, unmediated by other group identities to which we might owe allegiance.

Gaspar de Alba clearly hopes to blur group boundaries between "them"—the ones who are subject to the violence "on the other side" by virtue of their poverty and citizenship—and "us," the ones whom it does not touch, by making Ivon's sister, a U.S. citizen, a potential victim. As Irene, "playing wetback," bathes defiantly in the Rio Grande that marks the U.S.-Mexican border, her own body interrupts nation-state boundary lines that might define safety for some against risk for others (137). But if the ethics advanced in *Desert Blood* is fundamentally a humanist ethics, it is a *located* humanism. For one thing, Gaspar de Alba never loses sight of the ways in which citizenship does, in fact, have variable effects on the interpellation of subjects. When Irene bathes in the Rio Grande, after all, she is not arrested for illegally crossing the border, and her impunity is not because Border Patrol checks her papers (which she can't possibly have with her in the water), but because she does not *perform* as "undocumented": "No *mojado* would be swimming like that, back and forth, like it was a swimming pool. You think *la migra* doesn't know the difference?" (137).

Nonetheless, like Irene's body crisscrossing the length of the river boundary, Gaspar de Alba's ethical vision is, we might say, *loosely* bounded by geography, a sort of "border ethics." Near the novel's opening, Gaspar de Alba presents us with what is literally a sort of "bird's-eye view" of the border region, as Ivon overlooks it from flight:

> You can't see the chain-link fencing of the Tortilla Curtain, or the entrepreneurs in rubber inner tubes transporting workers back and forth across the Rio Grande, or the long lines of headlights snaking over the Córdoba bridge—one of the three international bridges that keep the twin cities umbilically connected. For the locals on

each side of the river, the border is nothing more than a way to get home. For those nameless women . . . the border had become a deathbed. For Ivon Villa, it was the place where she was born. (7)

While this perspective on the border, much like Anzaldúa's, does not "see" the dividing line (that is, does not recognize its legitimacy), it is still determinedly located; the border is a *place*, its cities—and its peoples—umbilically connected. The work of *Desert Blood* is to sketch a border ethics where the "locals on each side of the river," the "nameless women," and Ivon herself see themselves as intimately connected, as "family." Such a vision would unite the Juárez women not only with Mexican Americans like Ivon but also with, for example, the non-Latino rookie officer Pete McCuts from El Paso, whose sense of duty to the inhabitants of the border saves both Ivon and her sister Irene; and presumably, by extension, with non-Latino readers of detective novels like Gaspar de Alba's, as well.

Desert Blood—which, like *The Guardians*, resists heteronormative closure but which, unlike Castillo's novel, ends "happily"—closes with Ivon's words: "*¡Qué familia!*" (341), spoken as she surveys an extended family consisting of, among others, her rescued sister, her partner, and their soon-to-be-adopted son, Jorgito, claimed from the border's jaws of death. In a novel that is fiercely oppositional and antiheteronormative, the trope of family deployed here offers, perhaps, a new kind of "romance" in which the family image, presented as fluid, flexible, and heterogeneous, might come to stand for the border itself. If, as Schmidt Camacho argues, "Familial dislocation" due to undocumented immigration puts "identities . . . in crisis" (312), Gaspar de Alba's text offers a symbolic resolution of sorts by reimagining family and kinship as evoking notions of larger transnational responsibility. In Gaspar de Alba's text, kinship conceived at its broadest *can*, indeed, "mitigate against loss" (Schmidt Camacho 312). That this is, in its own way, an idealized and romantic symbolic resolution, through its hopeful and optimistic extension outward of the kinship metaphor, is a point that perhaps needs to be made.

The Caribbean Difference

Imagining Trans-Status Communities

Many scholars have noted that "illegal immigrants" are usually automatically associated, in popular understandings, with Mexicans.¹ For Caribbean Latinos (and in particular for Cubans and Puerto Ricans), the issue of legal status is quite differently inflected. Cubans have a distinctly different relationship to immigration law than Mexicans and Central or South Americans; through the early 1990s, Cubans were welcomed into the United States as political refugees, and even now, thanks to the "wet foot, dry foot" policy, there is virtually no such thing as an "illegal" Cuban in the United States. Puerto Ricans, of course, can move back and forth freely as U.S. citizens; absent the occurrence of family intermixture with other Latinos, the issue of undocumented immigration does not directly impact Puerto Rican communities. While Dominicans are the only Latino-Caribbean national origin group that *can* be "undocumented," in any significant numbers, in the United States,² even here there are some significant differences between undocumented Dominicans and other undocumented Latin American populations in the United States, including the role of Puerto Rico itself in Dominican undocumented migration. Dominicans who wish to come to the United States but lack authorization often reach U.S. soil precisely by traveling to Puerto Rico rather than the continental United States (Duany 245, 249). From Puerto Rico, furthermore, since a flight to the United States is considered domestic travel, there are no passport controls or customs inspections.³ Although Dominicans, like Cubans, may experience a dangerous and risky water crossing en route to U.S. soil (Castro and Boswell 1; Duany 249; Rohter), for none of these groups is the U.S.-Mexico *land* border an issue; nor is border patrol (the infamous "migra") the same specter for Cubans or Puerto Ricans that it is for other undocumented immigrant groups.

In this chapter, I consider how some Caribbean Latino/a writers have negotiated these significant differences among groups in their writing. How does the issue of undocumented immigration *register* in writing by Caribbean-American writers? I argue that several texts of Latino Caribbean writers reflect a highly attuned awareness of differences of status based on national origin, refracted through the lens of the family. Works by Caribbean Latina writers including Esmeralda Santiago and Achy Obejas highlight the divisions based on privilege that are created by legal status issues, in narratives that suggest the difficulties of stretching group identities across lines of national belonging. In Santiago's memoir, family remains sharply defined by biological connectedness and is not imaginatively extended to others. In Obejas's short story "The Spouse," by contrast, family as traditionally defined through legal relationships is jettisoned in favor of otherwise constructed families; but the net result is still a recognition of the significant obstacles in recognizing "familial" connections between Latino U.S. citizens and unauthorized immigrants. Junot Díaz's story "Negocios," from his debut collection *Drown*, is the first prominent text of Latino letters to explicitly narrate a story of *Dominican* undocumented immigration. Díaz's story probes the sore issues of illegality/illegitimacy in terms of the concentric circles of nation and family, such that anxiety regarding familial abandonment and illegitimacy is closely related to fears regarding national unbelonging. At the same time, the story ultimately downplays the significance of "illegal" status for Dominicans by imagining a larger Caribbean "family" the role of which is to "legitimize" Dominican presence in the United States. Finally, in extended treatments of undocumented immigrants in the novels of Cristina García, a Cuban American, and Julia Alvarez, a Dominican American, the authors imagine something like an ethics of cosmopolitanism that might be a basis of reconfiguring connectedness among Latinos of differing origin.

The Intra-Caribbean Difference

A host of scholars in recent years have commented on the second-class citizenship of Puerto Ricans, a citizenship which belies significant economic and social class disadvantages that are a result of their racialization, perceived foreignness, and colonized condition within the United States.[4] Nicholas De Genova and Ana Ramos-Zayas explain, "In spite of their U.S. citizenship, ... Puerto Ricans have been largely treated as ... incorrigibly inassimilable and fundamentally un-'American.' Thus, their birthright citizenship tends to be devalued and disqualified" (7). Yet these conditions have not necessarily led to panethnic solidarity with other marginalized Latino/a ethnic groups. De Genova and Ramos-Zayas document that Puerto Rican barrio youth in Chicago, for instance, reconfigured nationalist/activist forms of Puerto Rican cultural pride

> by embracing and boldly affirming their distinctive status as citizens of the United States. This "citizenship identity" was constructed in opposition to the "illegal immigrant" status attributed to the Mexicans, Central Americans, and other Latinos living in "the Puerto Rican neighborhood," regardless of their actual juridical statuses within the regime of U.S. immigration and naturalization law. Thus, in the effort to distinguish themselves from "foreign" Latinos, many Puerto Ricans tended to celebrate the U.S. citizenship which was an effect of their colonized condition. (58)

De Genova and Ramos-Zayas's findings suggest the possibility that Puerto Ricans who find themselves in close contact with other Latino-origin groups in urban centers, far from constructing a panethnic identity of solidarity with those groups, might be just as likely to *distinguish* themselves by virtue of the privileges and status of U.S. citizenship. One of Ramos-Zayas's respondents, for instance, explained, "I think that many [Mexicans and Guatemalans] ... are jealous of Puerto Ricans. My [Puerto Rican] neighbor told me: 'The thing with Mexicans is that they know they are wetbacks.' And, since we [Puerto Ricans] are [U.S.] citizens, they hate us because of that." This same woman, notably, did not rule out the possibility of cross-ethnic solidarity. She expressed her sense that in the building where she lived, "As Puerto Ricans, we help each other, we motivate each other," but then added, "And I've also helped Mexican people" (59). Nonetheless, her comments drew group lines between "wetbacks" and "citizens" and then framed interpretations of her social interactions based on those lines. Puerto Rican "help" was mutual, running both ways, while her aid to a Mexican apparently went in only one direction, from her position as benefactor to the Mexican objects of her help.

A remarkably similar dynamic is represented in Esmeralda Santiago's first memoir, *When I Was Puerto Rican*, which details Santiago's childhood of poverty in Puerto Rico and her arrival in the United States as an adolescent.[5] In a scene rather late in the memoir, Santiago participates in the construction of a "legal" citizen Puerto Rican identity within the continental United States that is formulated in opposition to "foreign" Latino identities. Santiago ("Negi") describes encountering non–U.S. citizen women of unspecified Latin American origin when she accompanies her mother to the welfare office in New York in order to translate for her:

> Women with accents that weren't Puerto Rican claimed they were so that they could reap the benefits of American citizenship. A woman I was translating for once said, "These *gringos* don't know the difference anyway. To them we're all spiks."
>
> I didn't know what to do. To tell the interviewer that I knew the woman was lying seemed worse than translating what the woman said. . . . But I worried that if people from other countries passed as Puerto Ricans in order to cheat the government, it reflected badly on us. (250–51)

Though it is not stated explicitly, the passage certainly raises the possibility that these women are not only *not* American citizens but are also unauthorized immigrants. What is at stake in the representation of this scene, then, is not just access to material benefits but also the lines drawn around belonging. The noncitizen woman certainly wants to draw group lines which oppose "the gringos" to a panethnic category of Latino solidarity: "To them we're all spiks." But although Negi also recognizes a fundamental commonality of experience based largely on socioeconomic status within the United States, noting that the women's "stories were no different from Mami's" and that "They needed just a little help until they could find a job again" (250), this recognition does not ultimately deter her own rejection (and, arguably, Santiago's) of the Latina woman's group boundaries; she worries that those who want to "cheat the government . . . reflected badly on us," thus redrawing a narrower line around "us" that includes Puerto Ricans, but not "people from other countries."[6] In *When I Was Puerto Rican*, Negi, faced with a miniature moral crisis of sorts at the individual level, falls back on the presumption that she is connected to her (immediate) Puerto Rican family by obligation, but not to a larger conception of ethnic family.

While Cubans lack the citizenship status of Puerto Ricans, they have historically benefited from an easy path to legalization and citizenship. Achy Obejas's first novel, *Memory Mambo,* presents the perspective of Caribbeans for whom legalization is not an obstacle; it gestures toward the benefits conferred by being a Cuban immigrant to the United States. In the novel, migrating Cubans are "caught" by sea while still trying to reach the U.S. shore: "My family and I came from Cuba to the U.S. by boat when I was six years old, in 1978. These are the facts: It was a twenty-eight-foot boat; there were fourteen of us; the trip lasted two days; we were picked up by the Coast Guard just a few miles from Key West" (9–10). In some ways, the story precisely parallels similar narratives of undocumented land crossings discussed in previous chapters; on the Cuban side, the crossers hide, waiting for the quiet cues that signal the arrival of transport across the "border": "We huddled at the beach, listening to the fear in one another's breathing, . . . waiting for the sound of the water to break ever so subtly . . . which signaled that our miserable little boat, its planks creaking against one another, had finally arrived to take us away" (9–10). Only in contrast with the narratives of land-border crossers does an additional detail stand in relief; when the fourteen migrants are caught by the U.S. Coast Guard, instead of being promptly returned to their country of origin, they are escorted to the United States. In other words, for Juani, the fictional narrator of *Memory Mambo,* being "picked up" by the Coast Guard while crossing the border is the *means of safe entry* into the United States, rather than the legal and state barrier to that entry. Neither the water border nor the Coast Guard have anything like the same signification for Juani that the land border and *la migra* do for undocumented immigrants coming north. As Ale, the narrator of Obejas's later novel, *Days of Awe,* comments without irony or self-reflection, "Cubans are always welcome here, always" (265).

Obejas's short story "The Spouse"—from her debut collection *We Came All the Way from Cuba So You Could Dress Like This?*—depicts a more explicit negotiation between a Latina citizen and a Mexican immigrant who is trying to acquire legal status. Remarkably, as the issues of legality/ illegality are foregrounded, the issue of *Cuban* legal status momentarily disappears; the story is about a Mexican American woman who is legally married to a Mexican immigrant so that he can apply for legal residency. Family here is not a metaphor for ethnic ties, however (which Cornell and

Hartmann call "family writ very large indeed [20]); the marriage turns out to be purely a "business deal" (85). The beginning of the story, which narrates the chance encounter of the legal spouses in a restaurant where the Mexican, Raul, works, depicts them as strangers to each other. (The Mexican American, Lupe, says, "I didn't realize you worked here" [83].) Thus the story would seem to support Lupe's later contention that they are not *really* related in any meaningful way merely by being "married," because the revelation to the reader that they *are* married is a rather surprising intrusion into the awkward conversation of obvious strangers to each other. Lupe repeatedly refutes any suggestion that marriage makes them family—"We're not family, no matter how many justices of the peace we stand in front of" (85)—or indeed that it imposes any obligations on them whatsoever. "You have your people and I have mine," she declares, and insists that the "bargain" of their legal marriage "doesn't include hanging around with you, your friends, or your family" (85), disavowing even the most tentative sorts of affiliation.

One layer of conflict between Lupe and Raul has to do with the tension between Raul's interpretation of their relationship and Lupe's. When Lupe insists that they are not family, Raul counters: "But of course we are!" (85). Apparently the narratives that *he* constructs suggest a more intimate relationship than the one Lupe acknowledges—as she hints when she shrugs that she "can't help it that you've spun all these stories for your family" (85). The story that Raul tells has to do not just with a meaningful "familial" relation but with an ethnic one—that is, with being bound by a "common culture." He tells Lupe, "You need me to help you stay in touch with your family, with your Latin self. . . . [The fact] that you're American is an accident of geography. . . . You're as Mexican as I am. . . . You need me to remind you about who you *really* are. You need me to remember all your real feelings" (86). That is to say, Raul spins a story of affiliative and cultural connectedness between himself, a Mexican, and Lupe, a Mexican American. In Raul's narrative they share a peoplehood, connected by "passion" and "music" and "poetry" (86); and this group identity also imposes obligations which Lupe ignores. Further, to refuse those obligations is for Raul an act of *cultural* denial.

In "The Spouse," Raul, though not a ghost, "haunts" Lupe with the specter of a culture of origin; Lupe, meanwhile, wants to exorcise his presence: "Cut this shit out, okay? And please, quit looking for me on the streets, quit following me out of restaurants . . . please don't bother me anymore"

(86, 89). From a certain perspective, Lupe's response is entirely in keeping with how some characters of ethnic fiction, according to Kathleen Brogan, regard their ghosts: "The most dreadful aspect of haunting is its involuntary nature; we cannot always choose our ghosts" (19). Raul wants to imagine himself in the restorative role that Brogan outlines for ethnic haunting, "bearing culture across linguistic and . . . geographic divides" (Brogan 16). Lupe's alternative narrative, however, casts doubt on the interpretation that this is a fully beneficial or even altruistic function.

Of course, as an argument for the connectedness of Mexicans and Mexican Americans across lines of citizenship, Raul's narrative of persistent cultural ties is perhaps *more* common than Lupe's insistence that "We're married in name only" (86). The notion that Mexicans and Mexican Americans are more united by culture than they are divided by a nation-state border is one that many Chicanos *and* U.S. dominant culture would recognize. In the story, however, Raul's narrative is a motivated one; a shared groupness on both sides of the border has implications for the obligations that it imposes on Mexican Americans. It is these obligations that Lupe rejects out of hand. For Lupe, they are connected "in name only" and should "just go our separate ways" (89). She insists on her right to choose her own forms of affiliation, having nothing to do with cultural identity. When she says she has her "people," Raul argues, "But . . . that's not your family. You need me to help you stay in touch with . . . your Latin self" (86). Indeed, a second layer of conflict has to do with the fact that Lupe is a lesbian, a fact that Raul literally refuses to hear ("He covered his ears with the palms of his hands[;] 'I don't want to hear that,' he shouted" [89]) and that also violates his sense of Mexican norms of gender and sexuality ("In Mexico, this wouldn't happen, and you'd have to do as I say" [86]). The entire microdrama, then, plays out the expectation on the one side of cultural solidarity and obligation based on transnational "latinidad," and on the other of a radical rejection of either expectation for new forms of "consent" and affiliation (to paraphrase Werner Sollors) that need not be circumscribed by the culture of origin.

A reading that even further complicates these two "sides" might involve scrutinizing a bit more carefully Lupe's contention that "we're not *really* married; we're only *legally* married" (88), an insistence that posits a fascinating distinction between the "real" and the "legal." In putting it this way, Lupe unlinks real identities from legal ones—a semantic strategy that, while she clearly does not consciously intend it, has implications for the issue of undocumented identities. In debates over illegal immigration, dominant discourse tends to simply take for granted that a "real" American is a "legal" one. But increasingly, counternarratives by immigrant activists challenge this assumption and attempt to wrest the definition of an "American" from a "legal" one to an experiential one. As Suzanne Oboler has suggested, for instance, while "granting citizenship continues to be the monopoly of the nation-state," this is "not without constant challenge from the members of the polity." She makes a case for "Rethinking citizenship in a way that fully incorporates Latino/as' historical presence . . . [and] fully takes into account their status and lived experience as residents" (21–22). William Perez's book about undocumented students in Southern California is titled *We ARE Americans.* A collection of YouTube videos featuring the voices of immigrants—including undocumented immigrants—bills itself through the tagline "We Are America." Jose Antonio Vargas, the Pulitzer Prize–winning journalist who revealed in the summer of 2011 that he was undocumented, subsequently launched the "Define American" project; in a YouTube video, he states, "I define 'American' as someone who works really hard, someone who is proud to be in this country and wants to contribute to it. I'm independent. I pay taxes. I'm self-sufficient. I'm an American. I just don't have the right papers" (Rojas). All of these sources offer strong, compelling counternarratives about what it means to be "American" that do not rest on legal permission to be a citizen granted by the state.

Arguably, then, Lupe's insistence to Raul on a strictly legal status, if read against the grain, has reverberations beyond their "marriage." Raul, it must be noted, is quite willing to *rely* on the equation between the legal and the real in order to bolster his own authority, even noting that in Mexico theirs would be a real marriage (complete with traditional patriarchal norms of behavior) because "There are laws, you know" (86). In relying on such a strict equation between legal and real, Raul attempts to bolster his male authority in a new context that does not recognize it (at least not for emasculated "illegal" Mexican immigrants) but shows no recognition of the ways in which the unyoking of "legal" and "real" is suggestive of different claims that he might make. Likewise, Lupe's insistence on keeping "legal" and "real" separate is within the fabric of the story only a manifestation of her willingness to inhabit and wield *her* privilege as a U.S. citizen and to reinforce the boundary lines that separate her from him. She reminds him that "I can put you right back on the wrong side of the river" (89) if he persists in bothering her, precisely by telling the truth about their fraudulent (that is, not "real") marriage. Nonetheless, Lupe's distinction between the "legal" and the "real" inadvertently implies, though it never explores, a mode of discourse that might potentially be quite useful in debates over what "counts" as a real American. To destabilize *those* definitions, of course, would have the rhetorical effect of potentially *diminishing* the lines of privilege and status that separate her from Raul—although again, this potential is never realized within the story itself.

"The Spouse" is about the conflict between a Mexican and a Mexican American (not a Cuban American), but some implications for a "Caribbean connection" might be suggested by the short story's context: the collection *We Came All The Way from Cuba So You Could Dress Like This?* and Obejas's authorship, invoked by that title. Within the context of queer theory, "dressing like this" might connote the performative aspects of identity; in the story, Lupe is (like Obejas) a self-identified lesbian, although not a Cuban American. Lupe also performs a peculiarly U.S. Latina identity, both at the mimetic level and at a metafictional one. For instance, at one point she warns Raul that she will "have you chopped like *picadillo,* baby" (88) when he seems to threaten physical force. It would seem that this form of code-switching, in which "picadillo"—a name for a Latin American dish of ground beef hash that actually takes very different forms in Cuba than in Mexico—is yoked to the slang "baby," would be a performance of a bicultural identity, with Lupe moving fluidly from a panethnic "Latin" ethnic marker ("picadillo") to an American colloquialism. In fact, as we learn in the next sentence, Lupe is supposedly speaking *Spanish* when she says this, since she now "yelled in English to the two men across the street" and only a bit later speaks to Raul again, "switching back to Spanish" (88). But if Lupe has been speaking in Spanish to Raul all along, this negates the possibility of literal, bilingual code-switching that "*picadillo,* baby" seems to suggest and moves that "performance" to the metafictional level—it is *Obejas* who performs as a Latina writer by code-switching here, rather than her character Lupe, who is performing Latina identity in a different mode by speaking in Spanish to Raul. That is to say, identity markers in this textual moment are quite fluid indeed, with some slippage between what Lupe is represented as doing (code-switching), what we are to understand her as "really" doing as a character (speaking in Spanish), and what Obejas is doing as an author (code-switching).

When Lupe makes reference to "picadillo," then, are we to understand this as Mexican picadillo (since Lupe is Mexican American) or as Cuban picadillo (since Obejas is Cuban American)? Readers who are cognizant that Obejas is the author who is "performing" the code-switching in her literary text might be forgiven for conjuring the Cuban dish, rather than the Mexican one.

This suddenly ambiguous moment—the use of code-switching in a scene where it is implausible and of reference to a dish that can "mean" quite differently according to national origin—might implicitly suggest *new* forms of Latina identity in the United States: for instance, bicultural and panethnic forms in which ethnic markers like *picadillo* cross-pollinate as they migrate across lines of national origin, and in which bilingualism is a recognized performance of Latino/a identity (including literary identity) across those same lines. This reading would suggest that Lupe does not need Raul to "remind" her of who she is, because "who she is"—what *kind* of Latina—is different from what Raul imagines. As a Mexican American who is portrayed as comfortably yoking the term *picadillo* with the slang *baby* (regardless of the literal impossibility of this particular "yoking" if Lupe is speaking in Spanish), Lupe is "culturally" very different indeed from Raul, with his rather old-fashioned Mexican notions of marriage and appropriate gender relations.

At the same time, the story as a whole invokes, in microcosm, a sense of the difficulties of building cross-*citizenship* solidarities. The story's slippage in this crucial passage can be read as metonymically reinforcing the slippage between Cuban American Latinas like Obejas herself and Mexican American Latinas like Lupe and consequently dramatizes for readers the possible interactions of *any* U.S. Latino/a "ethnic" group with those on the other side of the border and of belonging. Further, the exchange underscores the layers that might separate someone like Obejas herself from the Mexican immigrant about whom she writes. As a *Cuban* American lesbian, Obejas is even more removed than Lupe is, in terms of shared cultural experience or common identity, from the fictional Raul, although she attempts to imaginatively inhabit his perspective.

Near the end of the story, Lupe has calmed down enough to say to Raul, "If the cops get here and we're still fighting, you'll probably be in trouble, so let's just go our separate ways, okay?" And when Raul asks, "Don't you care?" she responds, "Yeah, I care. . . . That's why I'm telling you this. Please go back to the restaurant. I'll just leave, and when the cops get here there won't be anybody to file charges" (89). In the absence of conflict over male authority, Lupe is willing to get out of the way so as not to get Raul into trouble, suggesting *some* sense of obligation that extends beyond the business arrangement she sees herself as having signed on to. But that sense is highly attenuated, and involves, at best, a lack of active opposition—hardly suggestive of any grounds for a more active and politically engaged solidarity. As a whole, then, the narrative structure of the story works to underscore the significant barriers to solidarity across lines of citizenship status.

By contrast, in the writing of Dominican American writer Junot Díaz, the notion of Caribbean family writ large becomes a legitimizing trope. Díaz's much hailed debut collection of loosely connected short stories, *Drown*, centers on Yunior, a Dominican immigrant, in his formative years in the Dominican Republic and then in his adolescence and young adulthood in the United States. Yunior, like Negi, is the child of a splintering and eventually broken relationship, who comes (apparently legally) to the continental United States as an older child (Yunior tells readers he was nine when his father brought him over [70]). Unlike with Santiago's memoir, however, we never receive in *Drown* a recounting of the young protagonist's actual experience of migration from one land to the other. Rather, the concluding story, "Negocios," details the migrant experience not of Yunior but of his father, who is for a brief period an undocumented immigrant. In effect, "Negocios" is a story of "origins" that fills in some of the explanatory gaps about how Yunior and his family got from the Dominican Republic to the United States.

The barely concealed real concern that drives Yunior's story in "Negocios" is not his family's eventual migration but rather his father's near-abandonment of his family in the Dominican Republic. At base, "Negocios" might be said to contemplate in retrospect the trauma of familial separation, along with the specter of abandonment, that is such a looming issue in literary considerations of migration to the United States.[7] The theme of abandonment via migration, which haunts the entire collection, would seem to open up the possibility that Díaz is engaged in "dialogue with other disempowered groups," as Lucía M. Suárez suggests (91); and yet, I will argue, this "dialogue" is tenuous indeed. For the narrative also works hard to distinguish Papi's situation from that of other (Mexican and Central American) undocumented immigrants, and instead insistently groups him with "legal" Caribbeans. (Ylce Irizarry identifies *Drown* as firmly located "within the discourse community of Caribbean Latina/o America" [90].) "Negocios" portrays a profound "Caribbean connection" that in effect pulls Papi back to his "legitimate" Dominican family. While Marisel Moreno argues that *la gran familia* is a specifically *national* (Puerto Rican) model of identity that could link the Puerto Rican diaspora back to the homeland in imagination (3), I propose that in Díaz's *Drown* an even more extended trope of family—the *Caribbean* family, both "on the islands" and on the "mainland"—functions to grant legitimacy to Dominican presence in the United States and simultaneously to reinstate the legitimate nuclear family. Since legitimacy is crucial to the narrative of "Negocios," the Caribbean "family" must support/instantiate Papi's own "legitimacy"/legalization as it nudges him to move back in the direction of family legitimacy. Meanwhile, of course, potential ties to the undocumented Latin "others" are drastically attenuated in the narrative of "Negocios."

Marisel Moreno's study *Family Matters* offers an interesting lens through which to approach *Drown*, even though Moreno's focus is on Puerto Rican families rather than more broadly on Caribbean ones. Moreno contends that "the (virtual) absence of a father figure in many U.S.-Puerto Rican narratives . . . suggests that the fatherless model is more reflective of prevailing family structures in the diaspora . . . [reflecting] the high proportion of Puerto Rican female-headed households in the United States" (9). The analogies to Díaz's Dominican narrative are striking; in *Drown*, a highly patriarchal model of family is complicated by the fact that diaspora has rendered the Dominican nuclear family fatherless—except that, in this case, it is the father who has become part of the diaspora, leaving a female-headed household "back home." Various critics have noted that stories in *Drown* are characterized by a "crisis" or "loss" of masculinity (Frydman, Miller). John Riofrio points out that *Drown* represents "a situation in which survival depends upon fathers leaving the island to try and carve out a better life for themselves and their families . . . [leaving] an entire generation of Dominican boys forced to grow up without fathers" (26). "Negocios" details what happens to his father during his absence from his Dominican family—including his illegitimate second family (Papi never divorces his first wife, Yunior's mother, before "legally" marrying his second), which is ironically the source of Papi's eventual legality. In Yunior's motivated retelling of his father's story, "illegality" itself is portrayed as a technical condition, ostensibly incidental and easily overcome (albeit by the second marriage that constitutes Papi's betrayal of his Dominican family). Nonetheless, it is arguable that the relative ease with which Papi becomes "legal" in the story masks some profound anxiety (on Yunior's part, at least) surrounding issues of legality/legitimacy vis-à-vis the patriarchal nuclear family.

Strikingly, "Negocios" is narrated by Yunior himself, even though he is not present for most of its "action" and therefore can give readers at best a secondhand version, a conjecture of his father's experience in the United States as a new migrant. For most of the story Yunior's limited first-person voice recedes into the background, giving an impression of omniscience that is broken only by the reference to the central character by his familial title "Papi" (Dad)—reminding readers that he is Papi to *somebody* and that this somebody is telling the story. Yunior's narration of a story he was not "there" for underscores the significance of the unspoken tension between Yunior and the father whose life he narrates. As he explains in an earlier story, "Aguantando," "He had left for Nueva York when I was four but since I couldn't remember a single moment with him I excused him from all nine years of my life" (70). In "Aguantando," Yunior tells us, "On the days I had to imagine him. . . . He was pieces of my friends' fathers, of the domino players on the corner, pieces of Mami and Abuelo. I didn't know him at all. I didn't know that he'd abandoned us" (70). "Negocios," the final story, is in fact Yunior's effort to "imagine" his father—his projection of his father's experience in the United States during that period of abandonment. At times Yunior openly acknowledges the sources of his account ("There are two stories about what happened next, one from Papi, one from Mami" [174] or "Papi told me" [186]). At other times he is clearly speculating, producing a narrative entirely out of his own painful conjectures of his father's emotional resistance to bringing his original family over from the Dominican Republic (179, 199, 208).

The titular term *negocios*, literally "business," also invokes "transactions" or "dealings" ("affairs," as in business affairs).[8] The story details the various transactions and exchanges—economic as well as personal—that enable Papi's trajectory from Dominican husband and father to undocumented migrant and laborer in the United States to legalized resident who has abandoned his family and in effect abdicated his patriarchal role as "Papi." As Frydman puts it, "Papi's efforts to make it in the United States seem to consistently intersect in the text with his betrayal of Yunior's mother" (140)—that is, his business "negocios" are intimately interrelated to his "affairs." The story's title, however, alludes to the sorts of transactions ("affairs") that obscure or suppress prior familial arrangements and obligations and that allow Papi to indefinitely put off into the future the final, transnational transaction of bringing his Dominican family to join him in the United States. In other words, the story can be taken as Yunior's imaginative insertion of himself into his father's "business" (instead of "minding his own"). Further, Papi's transition from illegal to legal is marked by all sorts of business dealings—from the "cigar box stuffed with cash" that his father-in-law gives him in the Dominican Republic to make the trip (166); to his first employment at a Cuban sandwich shop; to the $500 "stuffed in a wrinkled paper bag" that he pays a Caribbean woman (he at first mistakes her for Dominican and then assumes she is Cuban) who agrees to marry him in order to legalize his status, a con job for which he "in return was given a pink receipt" but nothing else (191, 180); to his offer to pay a Dominican immigrant and U.S. citizen for English lessons (183), thus establishing a relationship with the woman who actually does becomes his new wife in the United States; to the remittances he sends home to his D.R. family, a financial transaction which allows him to suppress other kinds of obligations to them ("What in the world can I do? What does this woman want from me? I've been sending her money. Does she want me to starve up here?" [192]); to the plan for moving that family to the States that is outlined to him by his friend Jo-Jo: "Now that you have a place and papers. . . . Save some money and buy yourself a little business . . . then you get your familia over here and buy yourself a nice house and start branching out. That's the American way" (190). The chain of money exchanging hands throughout the story traces the route from Dominican to "American" via the debasement of one's personal "affairs," with all their emotional baggage, to economic exchanges (and the cigar boxes and paper bags that suggest their devaluation). Nonetheless, a striking fact of Papi's transactions is that they take place primarily with other *Caribbeans* in the United States.

Papi's best friend, Jo-Jo, is a Puerto Rican who insists on *legitimate* American Dreams for Papi, which combine the success of entrepreneurship and the ethos of pulling oneself up by one's bootstraps with the legitimacy of the patriarchal nuclear family:

> Jo-Jo had already rehabilitated two of his siblings, who were on their way to owning their own stores. . . . Jo-Jo spouted a hard line on

loyalty to familia.... Each scenario his friend proposed ended with Papi's familia living safely within his sight, showering him with love. Papi had difficulty separating the two threads of his friend's beliefs, that of negocios and that of familia, and in the end the two became impossibly intertwined. (190–91)

For Jo-Jo, the legitimacy of the American Dream rests on the two legs of the immigrant success story and the intact, legitimate immigrant family; a "nice house" and a "little business" are twin prongs of the "American way."

Notably, even while Yunior reconstructs his father's story in a way that will offer an explanation (however inadequate) for his failure to return to his Dominican family, he does not imaginatively group his father with other "illegals." Rather, the imagined community that Yunior constructs for his father consists mostly of Cubans and Puerto Ricans (all of whom are "legal") more than with other undocumented immigrants who share his lack of legal status. For one thing, Papi is able to travel to the United States legally on a tourist visa; he "passed easily through customs, having brought nothing but some clothes, a towel, a bar of soap, a razor, his money, and a box of Chiclets" (167). That is to say, Papi easily crosses the checkpoint into the United States because he does not look like he plans to stay; he does not look like an immigrant. Needless to say, there is no analogous experience for Mexicans and Central Americans who cross the land border into the United States, even without bringing substantial belongings; the racialization of the category "illegal immigrant" means that those at the border who look Mexican or Central American will be immediately targeted as "illegal."

Further, from the moment of Papi's arrival, Yunior links his father narratively with other *Caribbean* Latino migrants, rather than with other undocumented migrants; he notes, for instance, that Papi "intended to continue on to Nueva York as soon as he could" because "Nueva York was the city of jobs, the city that had first called the Cubanos and their cigar industry, then the Bootstrap Puerto Ricans and now him" (167). While Dominicans don't share the status of either group, apparently Yunior links his father more easily in his own mind with them than with groups more typically associated with unauthorized migration; he explains that "Dressed as he was, trim and serious, Papi looked foreign but not mojado"—that is, *not* like a "wetback," a term with its origins in the image of Mexicans trying to illicitly wade across the Rio Grande (170). If Puerto

Ricans are "citizens" and Mexicans are "wetbacks," Yunior's narration works hard to identify Papi with the former more than with the latter. Papi's first apartment is with Guatemalans, one of the very few moments in the story when non-Caribbean Latinos make a distinct presence; because it is next to impossible for working-class Guatemalans to secure authorization to enter the United States legally, it is likely that the roommates are undocumented. Yet the narrative "contains" this potential community by disrupting it through the information that *Papi* doesn't look "mojado"— a motivated observation which Yunior, of course, can only conjecture, even at this moment when his narrative poses as most "omniscient." At one point in Yunior's story, Papi, who is headed north, is stopped by federal marshals: "He'd heard plenty of tales about the Northamerican police from other illegals, how they liked to beat you before they turned you over to la migra." But Papi accepts and receives a ride in the car without being apprehended or even suspected of being undocumented (175). Instead, the marshals assume he is Cuban because he tells them he is from Miami (176). In other words, at almost every step where Papi's undocumented status is an issue, it is diffused or dissembled via comparisons to Cubans and Puerto Ricans who can narratively legitimize him (and thus, Yunior as well) by association.

Papi's unauthorized status becomes the pretext for his search for a new wife in the United States: "It was the old routine, the oldest of the postwar maromas," Yunior's narrative voice tells us. "Find a citizen, get married, wait, and then divorce her" (178). But as Yunior notes, the search for the citizen wife is also a way for Papi to forestall reunification with his Dominican family—a way to write postponement of unification into his narrative of the plan for unification. Yunior's retrospective reconstruction surmises that Papi "wasn't having fun but he also wasn't ready to start bringing his family over. Getting legal would place his hand firmly on that first rung. He wasn't so sure he could face us so soon" (179). Yunior understands, albeit reluctantly, that getting legal is only part of Papi's story; the other part, the part for which legalizing his status is just a sleight-of-hand, has to do with the more subterranean impulse to delay family reunification. Indeed, for part of Papi's narrative it appears that acquiring legitimacy in the United States entails suppressing his ties to the Dominican Republic, a psychological project that is never fully accomplished: "Papi should have found it easy to bury the memory of us but neither his conscience, nor the letters from home that found him wherever he went, would allow it. Mami's letters, as regular as the months themselves, were corrosive slaps in the face. It was now a one-sided correspondence, with Papi reading and not mailing anything back" (191). Yunior's story imagines ties to the home country as familial in nature and pervasive in tenor, even when the transnational connection is one-sided and truncated. And yet that connection persists *within* the United States. In Yunior's story, Papi is rendered so close to other Caribbean Latinos in the diaspora that he shares what could be considered an extended "familial" relationship with them; he is consequently deprived of any real excuse for his second marriage, which turns out not to be primarily about legalizing his status at all. It will be Papi's "Caribbean Connection" that eventually pushes him back toward his original Dominican family and toward "legitimacy" on all levels.

Nilda, the woman who eventually becomes Papi's wife in the States, is a Dominican who has "been in the States for six years, a citizen" (182); their arrangement is not financial (a "negocio") but affiliative. Nilda does not know about Papi's other family in the Dominican Republic; she learns about it "from a chain of friends that reached back across the Caribe" (187). But because it is marriage to Nilda that will regularize Papi's status, and because Papi's status will eventually allow him to bring over his Dominican family legally, it is logically Nilda who serves as the catalyst for the authorized entry of Yunior himself—a fact which, perhaps tellingly, is utterly elided by Yunior's narrative. Instead, Papi has seemingly always already been among a community of "legals," without papers only incidentally and for a brief period. When Papi injures himself at work, and the spectre of being fired looms, he says, "I'm not an illegal . . . I'm protected" (202), thus himself refuting community with unauthorized laborers (at least in Yunior's imagination), even though he was recently one of them, and claiming instead privileges of legality that he has accrued through illegitimate means (bigamy). The second wife, Dominican or not, must ultimately be suppressed and forgotten in this narrative, even though she is the originary instrument of legality. Just as it is "a chain of friends that reached back across the Caribe" (187) that introduces the unwelcome news of Papi's first and legitimate family into his new life in the United States, it is ultimately the same "chain" that insists on reinstating that original family *in* the United States. And yet that same connection also is responsible for forestalling legitimacy.

Papi's second marriage is the trauma at the heart of the story's retelling, since it is the concrete manifestation of the pervasive fear of abandonment via migration (see Dreby 202). It consequently also provokes the most glaring reminder that the story is actually narrated by Yunior's limited first-person perspective as Papi's son, rather than by an omniscient narrator. When Papi returns to the Dominican Republic for a visit with his new wife but never calls or visits his Dominican family—when, in other words, Papi gets too close for comfort to the younger Yunior as remembered by the retrospective narrator—the verb tenses slide from a definitive past tense to a speculative conditional: from Yunior's reporting of conjectures as factual (e.g., "Within a month Papi moved out of his apartment" [186] or "One day, he skipped his dinner and a night in front of the TV to drive south with Chuito into New Jersey" [194–95]) to his obvious struggle with speculation and attempts to explain his father's behavior to himself: "The air must have seemed thin. . . . He must have seen people he knew. . . . Maybe Papi stopped there and couldn't go on, maybe he went as far as the house. . . . Maybe he even stopped at our house and stood there, waiting for his children out front to recognize him" (199). This brief textual moment of speculation shatters the illusion of factual narration, cracking the narrative fabric, as it were, to remind readers that the story is Yunior's *projection* of his father's migrant experience. Through the stumbling narration Yunior highlights the trauma his father's absence has inflicted. Yet this trauma is, in fact, a salient characteristic of the condition of unauthorized migration which Yunior works so hard to separate his father's story from. At base—whether Yunior likes it or not—the trauma of fear of abandonment is one that many families divided by migration share. Thus Yunior's family story is haunted by the specter of illegality and illegitimacy: of the precariousness both of his reunified family and of the national belonging founded on that reunification. The story ends with Yunior's final speculation: "The first subway station on Bond would have taken him to the airport and I like to think that he grabbed that first train, instead of what was more likely true, that he had gone out to Chuito's first, before flying south to get us" (208). The postponement of legitimacy and familial unification via the Caribbean connection is the rupture that Yunior, in the end, cannot forgive.

* * *

As the foregoing fictions reveal, it is possible to find in the writing of Cuban, Dominican, and Puerto Rican authors in the United States a profound awareness of differences in legal status, and the benefits that difference confers, that might well serve as barriers to panethnic notions of Latino/a solidarity. When the trope of family becomes recycled to figure ethnic relatedness in such narratives, it most often serves to delineate the ways in which connection across *citizenship* lines is precarious indeed. It is notable that of the examples I have explored thus far in this chapter, the only instance in which a narrative uses family as a metonym that might potentially *integrate* "illegal" immigrants into a larger formulation of ("legal" and legitimate) community is *Drown*, the subject matter of which is Dominican migration, which does not carry the same access to "legal" status as Puerto Rican or Cuban migration. In the texts by Santiago and Obejas, by contrast, "family" tends rather to draw lines which separate the "legal" from the "illegal" and protect the privilege of "authorized" immigrants. In the following section, we will see how two novels by Caribbean writers, *A Handbook to Luck* by (Cuban American) Cristina García and *Return to Sender* by Julia Alvarez, both deploy what might be termed an ethic of *cosmopolitanism,* rather than the narrower ethic of filiation/affiliation, in order to suggest obligation *across* lines of citizenship and national origin.

Caribbean Texts and the Ethics of Cosmopolitanism

In contrast to works by Santiago, Obejas, and Díaz, Cristina García's *A Handbook to Luck* and Julia Alvarez's *Return to Sender* implicitly construct an ethics of solidarity *across difference* that is founded on a cosmopolitan perspective. For both García—a Cuban American writing about an "illegal" Salvadoran refugee—and for Alvarez—a Dominican American writing about an undocumented Mexican family—such an ethics reflects an understanding of how the forces spurring migration across nation-state boundaries are global in scope, rather than bounded by nation-state lines. Recognizing that the public sphere in which migration debates must be aired must necessarily be broader in scope than any single national citizenry, these two authors implicitly suggest the continued importance of *testimonio*—of personal witness to crisis as a means to change the given social and political landscape. But the nature of this particular *testimonio* on the part of the authors' imagined and undocumented characters is especially complicated by the authors' own heavily mediating positions.

Perhaps influenced by tenets of liberation theology, the novels by

Alvarez and García further imply that the "subaltern" need to consider *themselves* "worthy" of the project of *testimonio*, in the sense that they must *see themselves* as agents in their own lives who have the power to change, or at least modify, the circumstances they have been given. That is to say, both texts to some degree acknowledge a certain positionality of "ally-ship"; what is required of a cosmopolitan positioning is an acknowledgment of responsibility to others—including subaltern others—that does not erase the agency of those others. Indeed, as Caribbean Americans who for different reasons had fairly unhindered access to legalized status, both García and Alvarez are highly self-conscious of the gulf which separates them from undocumented migrants who cross a land border as they come North.[9]

* * *

A Handbook to Luck negotiates the Cuban "difference" in access to legal status in the United States through a narrative in which national origin differences are recognized and acknowledged yet ultimately downplayed in favor of a cosmopolitan sensibility necessitated by globalization.[10] The novel follows three protagonists from three parts of the world; the characters' lives intersect in the United States. Enrique came to the United States from Cuba as a child with his father, Fernando, a magician working in the hotels and cocktail lounges of Los Angeles and then Las Vegas. Marta is a Salvadoran living through the repressive 1980s who eventually migrates to the United States illegally, where she ends up working for Enrique as a nanny. Leila is an Iranian woman who shares a brief affair with Enrique before her arranged marriage takes her back to postrevolutionary Iran. The novel is fundamentally concerned with the global economic and political currents that bring people of different nations together in "unlikely" and seemingly random ways and in the new kinds of sensibility that are necessitated by such globalization.

While the characters' particulars (national origin, citizenship status) are distinct, they are not all-determining, and this is an important aspect of the novel's cosmopolitan orientation. As Cuban exiles, Enrique and his father never need to face issues of legality or citizenship in the United States—a fact which simply passes without commentary in the novel—while Marta must cross the border with a coyote and then negotiate the legalization process explicitly. Nonetheless, the novel suggests that

Marta's experiences and Enrique's intertwine and are interdependent on each other, such that the Cuban exile Enrique is actually instrumental in securing the U.S. citizenship of Marta's son. That is to say, the novel demonstrates how individual lives under globalized conditions are profoundly transnational, intercultural, and border crossing; thus the experiences of any one person cannot be understood apart from a globalized network of others.

The novel's title, of course, signals its concern with the theme of "luck"—that which is outside of our control—as do the casinos of Las Vegas and the cruise ships where Enrique works for a time as a professional gambler. Luck winds its way through the characters' lives in the form of highly unlikely events that profoundly shape the course of those lives. In a freak highway accident that serves as a grounding metaphor for the notion of random chance, Enrique is hit by an eighteen-wheeler and watches as

> the truck's back doors blew open and dozens of monkeys clambered out, screeching and scurrying into the desert like a pack of deranged jackrabbits. . . . Enrique thought of how random energies approached a common point before exploding. Chance intersecting with history and logic and reasonable expectations. . . . One hundred and twelve rhesus monkeys that should have been swinging in the jungles of India but were, instead, destined for research labs in southern California had been set free in the Mojave Desert. What were the fucking odds of that? (130–31)

"Chance," the explanation for how monkeys from India find themselves new inhabitants of the U.S. Southwest, becomes the novel's shorthand for the currents of globalization that bring people (and animals, too) from far distant lands into close proximity with one another in seemingly unlikely, "random" configurations. In this way chance partially writes the story of what is possible for the novel's characters.

Luck has its counterpart, however, in the trope of magic, the shaping by the human will of illusion that would seem to exceed all human power. In another of the novel's foundational metaphors, Enrique recalls how his mother died while performing a Houdini-inspired magic trick—an escape from a water tank—during which freak winds knocked an electrical cable into the water:

> On the day his mother died, a flock of storks, thrown off course by the strong autumn winds and looking like parasols, had landed in Colón Park, near the stage where his parents were performing. One of the storks got tangled up in an electrical cable and died at the same time as Mamá. What were the odds of that? (16)

On the one hand, there is the performance of "magic," in which every circumstance is carefully planned and controlled in order to achieve illusion. And on the other, there is "luck," in which the forces (historical, economic, social, natural) that converge in any given moment do in fact exceed any given individual's power to control or shape them. As we have already begun to see, "luck" serves as a placeholder for the crosscurrents of globalization which bring far-distant and disparate characters into contact with each other, and perhaps even for the random happenstance of nationality, the political and social circumstances into which one is born. But the novel is also quite invested in the ways in which human will and agency can bend "luck" into particular meaning (its own form of "magic"), thus creating unlikely new forms of cosmopolitan affiliation.

Kwame Anthony Appiah reminds us in *Cosmopolitanism: Ethics in a World of Strangers* that "cosmopolitan" originally meant "citizen of the cosmos," a paradoxical term in which ideas of belonging to a particular community (citizen) were yoked to the notion of cosmos, referring "to the world, not in the sense of the earth, but in the sense of the universe" (xiv). Cosmopolitans understand "the universe as a state, of which [all people] . . . are citizens" (Wieland 107; qtd. and translated by Appiah xv). Leo Tolstoy was derisive of the "'stupidity' of patriotism" and, as Appiah notes, plenty of contemporary scholars have also made the case that the "boundaries of nation are . . . accidents of history" (xvi). Western cosmopolitanism has traditionally invoked the notion that cosmopolitans are "citizens of the world" (Hagedorn xxxii, qtd. in Koshy 593).

It is thus possible to understand cosmopolitanism as an *ethical* framework, in which we are obligated to recognize that our interconnectedness with global others extends beyond the boundaries of *citizenship to a particular nation*. This formulation of cosmopolitanism frames it as an "ethics of care" (Koshy 607) or an "ideal" in which "every human being has obligations to every other" (Appiah 153, 144).[11] Though some recent articulations of a cosmopolitan ethics (e.g., Appiah, Koshy) resist the impulse to treat national affective ties as mere "stupidity" not worthy of respect,

I suggest that *A Handbook to Luck*, with its migration flows that bring together "A World of Strangers," understood not just as "those whom one does not personally know" but also as *extranjeros*, that is, "foreigners," does seem to push in the direction of a cosmopolitan disregard of nation as a source of loyalty or even as a meaningful category of identity. Nationalism is represented as hopelessly anachronistic. When Fernando reads in the newspaper about "Cuba's new constitution" (in 1976), he scoffs, "Another hoax in the name of patriotism!" (66). Another character expresses the opinion that "I think your childhood is more like your country than your actual country" (54), suggesting both that national origins need not be all-defining and that national ties, like childhood, can be "grown out of" and are thus only an early stage in the development of affiliation. The characters in the novel find their lives converging in unexpected ways and must decide whether to live within boundaries prescribed by hegemonic understandings of nation or to open themselves to new forms of identity formation that might be characterized as a sort of randomized "cosmopolitanism."

In both *A Handbook to Luck* and *Return to Sender*, birds serve as the primary metaphor for the national boundary crosser, suggesting migration that cannot be bound by geopolitical lines or notions of "belonging" to a particular geographical territory. Birds in *A Handbook to Luck* are frequently not where they belong, forming a sort of symbolic cross-tissue that connects one character's storyline to another at a level that has nothing to do with plot. In El Salvador, Marta hears a *clarinero* in a tamarind tree, "noisy and insistent," and asks herself, "What was it doing up at this time of night?" (61). In Iran, Leila glimpses "a dull brown thrush with thickset feathers singing off-key" and wonders, "What was it doing here in the bitter middle of winter[?]" (85). In Enrique's childhood Cuba, as we have already seen, a wayward flock of storks is "thrown off course by the strong autumn winds" (16). In all cases, the connective tissue is the presence of the birds where they are not supposed to be, gesturing toward the larger currents of global migration which does not necessarily respect the boundaries of belonging. The noisiness of the birds also carries symbolic valence. Birds make themselves heard, make a racket; they are "clamorous" and "bugle-loud," giving "signals of need and displeasure" (89, 92, 102)—suggestive of protest. A woman who tries to organize the workers at a shoe factory in El Salvador gets nicknamed "'Canary' because she stood ready to sing against injustices" (90). Thus singing becomes linked to *testimonio*; the "signals of need and displeasure" are one way of describing the eyewitness accounts of violence and trauma emerging from Central America in the 1980s and '90s. The trope of birds, then, brings together movement across borders *and* the notion of *testimonio* which clamors for attention and calls for ethical response.

This symbolic valence is particularly clear in Marta's brother Evaristo's case: "*A lot happens under my tree. Only the birds see what I see*" (28). With what is literally a bird's-eye view, Evaristo is able to observe what happens on the ground: "From his perch, he saw many things: two purse snatchings; a prostitute servicing a customer in the heliotropes . . . ; a group of protesting students rounded up by the police" (23). But what Evaristo witnesses in El Salvador gets increasingly disturbing. In italicized retrospective vignettes, he contemplates all he has seen: "*There's too much to tell, too much counting to do. This one dead, and that one, and that one. But where are the corpses?*" (148).

The crux of Evaristo's story, however, lies in the tension between seeing and *telling*—between witnessing and *bearing witness*, or put another way, between knowledge and *testimonio*, meant to somehow affect the reality he has observed:

> Evaristo was still shaken after having witnessed another abduction last Sunday. A group of soldiers dragged a young couple, shouting, into a van. The following morning, Evaristo found their mutilated bodies dumped behind the biggest department store on Paseo General Escalón. . . . Marta tried to make her brother swear that he wouldn't tell anyone about it. . . . Bodies were turning up everywhere, he insisted, heads in one place, limbs in another. Evaristo saw everything from his tree, everything that was supposed to go unseen. But who could he tell? Who would believe him? (89–90)

From his treetop vantage point, Evaristo witnesses what "was supposed to go unseen." But whether the witnessing translates into bearing witness (*testimonio*) remains a question. His sister Marta tries to ensure his silence for his own safety. But if Evaristo can't bear witness because the public sphere has been effectively destroyed, then what is the good of his witnessing (seeing) at all? Can *testimonio* exist without an audience?

Unlike the subversive "singing" of the organizer Sandra Mejía, the so-called Canary, Evaristo's birdlike qualities seem not to have a corollary in actual testimony. In yet another struggle between witnessing and bearing witness, Evaristo tells his sister that "the *guardias* had rounded up schoolgirls from a bus stop that day, called them Communists and whores. He said that he would do everything he could to find out who the girls were and memorize their names" (92). Is the memorizing of names a prelude to bearing witness, to passing the names on to the families of the disappeared so that they will know what happened to their daughters? Or is it an interiorized act of "witnessing" with no audience but Evaristo's *own* memory? (His brief vignettes of narrative present a similar ambiguity: while on one level they certainly testify to what he has seen *to the reader*, at the level of the narrative itself Evaristo seems not to have an audience for his testimony, or even to be bearing witness aloud; rather, these vignettes give the impression of being highly interiorized monologues.) Evaristo's recounting of the schoolgirls' kidnapping to Marta is immediately countered by her own plea that he "stay out of it," for his own safety, suggesting that his testimony in this instance may well go no further.

At the conclusion of the novel, Evaristo—still a young man at twenty-six, deported back to El Salvador and living in a house built on a hilltop that faces in all four directions (256–57)—is the figure of the bird's-eye witness who has seen too much in both countries: "Memories taunted him like sharp filaments of light. The priests with sticks up their asses. The schoolgirls taken away by the *guardias* and raped. The year in the border prison awaiting deportation" (258). Yet Evaristo's witnessing does not seem to translate into *bearing witness*:

> Evaristo had a difficult time remembering things . . . he was forgetting many lives' worth of detail and incident. Perhaps it was this forgetting that was congesting his skull, splitting it with pain and dizziness. If he didn't remember what he'd seen, nobody would. There were countless dead without anyone to speak for them, without anyone to say *I am your witness*. But it was no good for him to sit by himself in the mountains. His silence was killing them all over again. (256)

The names and crimes that Evaristo has "memorized," because they have remained interior and private rather than public, have died with his failing memory. This ethical failure of witnessing is the moral converse of a position of ethical cosmopolitanism; the mountaintop perch looks equally in all directions (suggestive of a global perspective) yet has no corresponding imperative in terms of intervening in *particular* public debates. In contrast to Appiah's insistence that cosmopolitanism is about both "curiosity" and "engagement" (168)—that "we have obligations to others" (xv) and that "if there are people without their basic entitlements . . . we are not meeting our obligations" (173)—Evaristo's culminating perspective is one that, seeing everything, does nothing; it has no ethical stakes. It is therefore utterly isolated and removed from the world, rather than being *part of it* as a moral actor.

In her discussion of totalitarianism, Nancy Fraser uses language that bears striking resemblance to Evaristo's ethical position; Fraser argues that totalitarian regimes are enabled by "affecting a God's-eye view from the commanding heights, above and outside the human world" (*Scales* 132). Indeed, Fraser points our attention to the possibility of new "quasi-totalitarian projects of bird's-eye view domination" (138) that are emerging in the twenty-first century. Analogously, by positioning himself *above* and *outside of* the public sphere where political discourse and debate over the good of the "polity" take place, and where the intrinsically political art of rhetorical persuasion is continually exercised, Evaristo strangely mirrors the way of "seeing like a state" (James Scott, cited in Fraser, *Scales* 132) that is the condition of the repressive Salvadoran regime in the late twentieth century and, arguably, of new seeds of totalitarianism in the twenty-first. It certainly cannot be said, of course, that Evaristo himself is "seeking to totalize a single vision" (Fraser, *Scales* 131); nonetheless, his is a vision that sees all and yet locates itself apart from any public space where debate and exchange might take place. He might speak for the subaltern—if he would just speak.

Despite Evaristo's own recognition that his self-imposed isolation prevents him from saying "I am your witness," the novel's conclusion suggests that he will not descend from his mountaintop home in order to bear witness. Instead, the concluding image depicts Evaristo as the sole auditor of the "woeful song" of a canary: "he imagined that the canary was his sister come to his side" (259). The image, of course, is highly ironic, since his sister had been the one attempting, for his own safety, to limit his speech. Indeed, this canary seems to silence Evaristo: when "the sound of his own voice startled him[,] [t]he canary stared at him until he grew quiet again" (259). Evaristo's fragments of interior monologue apparently have no audience but an imagined one; he thus conveys the moral danger, within a globalized landscape, of the witness who does not bear witness.

He may have a panoramic vision, but not an ethically cosmopolitan one. While birds (and monkeys as well) suggest the global crosscurrents of migration and a disregard of nation-state boundaries, the ways in which cosmopolitanism calls us to agency and to responsibility for larger circles of others must finally be invoked through other means.

As I have already suggested, *A Handbook to Luck* is centrally concerned with humanity's interconnectedness and with the global crosscurrents that make these connections a more palpable and inescapable reality than ever before. There is no character that more strongly emblematizes this theme than the Salvadoran refugee Marta, who defies U.S. borders with their imperative of exclusion and eventually re-creates herself as a citizen in her new land, in large part because of her formulation of a network of connections to (former) strangers from *other* homelands. Marta is the paradigmatic "world citizen" of the novel's vision, even while she herself inhibits her brother's participation and engagement in a global landscape of responsibility. After she leaves her homeland and the repressive terror tactics of its military regime (as well as her husband, Fabián, a *guardia* who is assigned to a firing squad under that same regime [91]), Marta thinks:

> It was remarkable how easy it had been to walk away from everything she knew: her family, her country, her habits, her belongings. Already, they were drifting away. . . . But maybe remembering was just a form of forgetting, of choosing one thing over another, turning green into yellow, day into night. If it was true that she was leaving behind everything familiar, could she leave herself behind, too? (98)

Marta's taking her life into her own hands, by leaving and indeed "forgetting" her husband in El Salvador along with "everything she knew," is a form of rewriting *herself* along narrative lines that do not conform to those of national belonging. Marta's narrative posits her relationship as an individual to a larger collective—in this case to cut the ties of obligation to home in a way that might be problematic, seen from the framework of *testimonio*. Nonetheless, it also suggests the ability to narratively redraw and redefine these connective lines. That is to say, Marta's allegiances are not bound by what she "knows"; in cosmopolitan fashion, she can extend the circle that her life encompasses to people and places that she does not "know." Although the path is much easier for the Cuban exile Fernando than for Marta, both have left their nations' repressive regimes to carve out entirely new futures for themselves that are characterized by new forms of transnational or transethnic alignments.

Marta's sense of agency defies the limitations of "nation" for an expansive, migratory view in which global intersections and the movement across borders become the mechanisms which help her define her identity. Once in the United States, Marta is able to contemplate the possibilities that her migration has opened up to her:

> In Los Angeles, it was possible to become someone other than who you started out to be. You could go from poor to rich and back again, learn to speak another language, accustom your tongue to different spices. . . . This couldn't have happened back home. Who dreamed of going beyond what they knew? In El Salvador, each generation repeated the patterns of the one before. Even her brother had a chance at a new life here. If he could make it, she thought, anybody could. (146)

Marta becomes the representative for the "new life" that is explicitly open to cross-cultural pollinations: new languages, different "spices," and the possibilities of diverging from the stale and stultifying patterns associated with national boundedness. While the novel plays with the trope of the random and the arbitrary, it also suggests that "luck" is, in fact, to some degree within human hands. Arguably, then, Marta's life story is itself the "handbook to luck." The novel might begin with Enrique's Cuban exile story, but it is Marta Claros, the "undocumented" immigrant who, by all dominant accounts, would not "belong" in the United States at all, who becomes the novel's central protagonist.

To say that Marta's story foregrounds the potential power of human agency to overcome the restrictive imperatives of nation-state and their control over individual subjects is not, however, to suggest that García's brand of cosmopolitanism erases significant global (or national) disparities. Rather than promoting an amorphous "humanist" perspective that obscures the very real obstacles to empathy across lines of difference, García in fact underscores differences of privilege that might separate Cuban Americans (like Enrique Florit and his wife, Delia) from an undocumented Salvadoran immigrant (like Marta). Reminders of differences of status between Marta and the Florits recur frequently in the novel. For example, when Marta becomes a nanny for Enrique and Delia, she thinks to herself that Señora Delia's problems are luxuries. "Since she couldn't agonize over basic things—like no money for food, or medicine for a dying baby—she drowned in a drop of water" (197). By contrast, one of the very first things we learn about Marta, as a young child vending used clothing on the streets of El Salvador, is that she "was hungry but she didn't dare go home yet" because she has not made enough money for the day; her mamá, we also learn, has "lost three babies in the past two years," as well as another who lived four days and then died of diarrhea (19). Marta's life history is characterized by agonizing over basic things like food and medicine, concerns that Señora Delia's experience cannot fathom.

There is no more powerful demonstration of the difference that difference makes than the issue of American citizenship in the novel. Marta secures U.S. citizenship during a period in which most Salvadorans were historically unable to secure legal status as political asylum cases.[12] Unlike Delia, who is simply identified as Cuban American, and Enrique, whose entry into the United States and subsequent legalization is unremarked on by the novel, Marta enters by illegally crossing the border, led by a coyote and risking her life in the process. Citizenship and "illegality," both of which are non-issues in Enrique's narrative, are thus foregrounded in Marta's. Significantly, however, she is able to obtain her citizenship—and, later, that of her adopted son, José Antonio, thanks in large part to her embeddedness in a web of interconnected relations with other subjects of global migration.

Her own status is seemingly secured by her marriage to a Korean American, Frankie Soon. At first, Marta thinks of Frankie just in terms of the privileges of status that he could provide: "She could do a lot worse than Frankie Soon.... [H]e was an American citizen, which meant that anyone who married him would become one, too" (106–7). Yet later, readers learn that Frankie "couldn't marry Marta because he had a wife in Korea and a divorce was impossible. Well, [Marta] wasn't officially divorced from her husband either," although she has heard that Fabián, the abusive *guardia*, has "remarried," which makes him "a bigamist on top of a *pendejo*" (145). Frankie's Korean wife eventually visits from Seoul and tells Marta that she will not stand in the way of his marriage to Marta (218), effectively releasing him. However, there is no indication that Frankie and his Korean wife actually secure a *divorce* prior to his marriage to Marta, since the marriage of Marta and Frankie takes place at city hall the same afternoon following his wife's announcement. Nor does Marta ever apparently divorce Fabián prior to marrying Frankie, even though earlier she disparaged Fabián for being a bigamist by having married again without a legal divorce. Marta's citizenship is enabled by Marta's and Frankie's marriage, but that marriage is itself apparently founded on a legal fiction, since both of them are already married to others. Thus new, interethnic alignments trump nation-state laws.

In a further tangling of family ties, Marta's son, José Antonio, whom she adopts, is the illegitimate child of her Salvadoran aunt (198–99). But the baby's birth in El Salvador (in 1984) makes his claim to "belonging" in the United States precarious indeed. Marta must lie by reporting to immigration that José Antonio is her biological child, with whom she had been pregnant when she returned to El Salvador for a visit; that the baby was born there prematurely; and that "If she'd waited the time necessary to get his papers in order, she would've lost her job. This was why she'd crossed the border illegally. Marta had a notarized letter from her employers, Mr. and Mrs. Enrique Florit, attesting to these facts" (219). Marta also draws on the help of another Latina of indeterminate national origin, Lety Sánchez, a "friend from church" on the U.S. side, to meet her near the Tijuana border as she returns north with José Antonio; Lety Sánchez uses her own newborn son's birth certificate to take Marta's son "across the border as her own child" (220).

The assumptions and legalities on which José Antonio's claim to citizenship rests are worth pausing over, since the claim entirely rests on, and thus undermines, the validity of documentation. José Antonio's citizenship depends on two sets of facts: (1) *Marta herself* is an American citizen at the time (hence her son has the right to citizenship from birth) and (2) he is her biological son, as documented by the "notarized letter" provided by Enrique. That is to say, José Antonio's citizenship rests on various sorts of documentation (marriage documents, citizenship papers, notarized testimonies) which turn out to be a hoax of "smoke and illusion" (Fernando's catchphrase for the art of magic [10]). Marta's story thus conjures a long string of filiative fictions into the legal "fact" of citizenship for her son. That transformation is *substantially aided by her encounters with other world migrants in a globalized landscape*; not only the Cuban Enrique but also the Korean Frankie (and even the Latina Lety Sánchez) are instrumental in creating a documented paper family that is for all purposes a "real" family.

The ease with which *A Handbook to Luck* glides over the details of the legal difficulties in obtaining citizenship for most undocumented immigrants, to focus narrative energy instead on the ways in which "legal" status is a collective performance in which various migrant strangers participate, has the effect of underscoring the "constructedness" of citizenship itself. The logistical and pragmatic realities of *actually obtaining citizenship* are, in the final analysis, elided in García's narrative, as citizenship becomes a sort of narrative fiction of identity—a collective fiction, with many storytellers. Marta's son José Antonio can "belong here" (240) because Frankie Soon and Enrique Florit and Lety Sánchez belonged first. Thus the welcoming fabric of a "nation of immigrants" makes room for one more in this vision of an inextricably globalized landscape.

* * *

Collective fictions of national identity have also been a powerful theme in the work of Julia Alvarez (*In the Time of the Butterflies, In the Name of Salome*). In *Return to Sender*, her young adult novel about an undocumented Mexican immigrant family that comes to Vermont to work as farm laborers, it is the national collective myths of the United States, rather than of the Dominican Republic, that are the subject of her attention. Like García's *A Handbook to Luck*, which crosses the more predictable lines of Cuban ethnic origin in its representation of a central Salvadoran protagonist, Alvarez's novel moves significantly beyond the subject matter of her earlier novels—including *How the Garcia Girls Lost Their Accents, Yo*, and *Saving the World*—all of which feature Dominican immigrant protagonists and writer figures like Alvarez herself.[13]

In my earlier discussion of Díaz's *Drown*, I noted that Dominican immigrants are the only Latino Caribbean national origin group with a significant undocumented population within the United States.[14] However, this statement obscures some fairly important differences among Dominican immigrants themselves which we now need to attend to. The beginnings of mass Dominican migration to the United States can be traced to the assassination of dictator Rafael Trujillo in 1961 and the U.S. military intervention in Santo Domingo in 1965. Prior to this point, most Dominicans who went abroad were of an elite or professional class (Duany 245–46). That is to say, in terms of legal status and economic privilege, Dominican immigrants prior to 1961 bore a much closer resemblance to

Cuban immigrants fleeing Castro's revolution in 1959 than to the bulk of Mexican or Central American immigrants reaching the United States today. Julia Alvarez's father, who fled the Dominican Republic with his family for New York in 1960 in the wake of his involvement in an underground resistance movement, was a physician, and the family had been relatively well off in the D.R. Arguably, this set of circumstances positions Alvarez's experience of immigration as analogous in many ways to that of Obejas or García; like these Cuban American writers who also came to the United States as children, Alvarez must negotiate borders of difference having to do with specificities of status, mobility, and access that separate her authorial position from that of the undocumented Mexican immigrants that she represents in *Return to Sender*. These lines of difference are inscribed into the text itself—although, notably, Dominicans and Dominican Americans for once do not make even an appearance in the narrative (a rarity in Alvarez's writing).

Instead, the negotiation of vastly different perspectives and life experiences is narratively rendered through the alternating young narrators of the novel: Mari, the eldest of three daughters in the Mexican family and the only sibling who is herself Mexican-born and therefore undocumented, and Tyler, a son of the family who owns the farm which desperately needs the labor of the undocumented workers when Tyler's father is seriously injured and can no longer contribute to the significant manual labor involved. While Mari provides the fictional "point of view" of a child scarred by her family's separation and her own undocumented status, it is Tyler, the white Vermont farm son, who undergoes an education and enlightenment process in the course of the novel, since he must come to grasp the complexities of the economic situation driving migration and the human costs of immigration policies that prevent migrant laborers from living and working openly. We might fault the novel for its emphasis on the moral development of the white citizen-son, who becomes enlightened by the Mexican other; but within the larger context of the U.S. climate on immigration it is clearly non-immigrant children that constitute a major target audience for Alvarez's novel, which is rooted in the premise that "the increased migration associated with globalization is now transforming the ethical-political self-understanding of many" (Fraser, *Scales* 135). The novel suggests the possibility of cosmopolitanism as an ethical commitment necessitated by global migrations, and it depicts the "transformation" of one of its two young protagonists to this "ethical-political self-understanding."

Mari, like Yolanda "Yo" García in Alvarez's earlier fiction, is the author figure in the novel, though of letters rather than of fictional stories. Like the "García girls" in general, Mari faces the difficulties of being regarded as foreign, as "other," as not belonging, in her new environment (20–21). As Mari thinks to herself when tracing her family's route from Mexico to the United States: "What a long journey to make to a place that does not welcome us but instead sends us away!" (26). Mari's remark of course invokes the novel's title, which alludes to mail "returned to sender" but also to "Operation Return to Sender," a government operation in which ICE raids swept up and detained and arrested thousands of immigrants beginning in 2006. Unlike the García girls, however, Mari also faces the overlay of being called an "illegal alien" (20)—a term which carries embedded *within* it the implied directive to "go back," to be returned. Mari understands that this particular insult means that she *legally does not belong*, whereas her two younger sisters "are little American girls as they were born here and don't know anything else" (21).

Return to Sender advances the possibility, through Mari, that *different* narratives of belonging, friendship, and loyalty are possible. And because Mari is the novel's only first-person narrator, her told story (her fictional *testimonio* of undocumented adolescence) takes on the status of one of these narratives that might differently imagine national belonging. One page before relating a nightmare about a "huge pen [that] came writing across the land, drawing a big black borderline" (29)—a scene that underscores the *imaginative* and *narrative* construction of the border as a line of inclusion and exclusion—Mari remembers the words of her missing mother, who is now in the metaphorical limbo of "the other side": "Whenever you feel sad or lonely or confused, just pick up a pen and write me a letter" (28). Mari frequently picks up a pen to write—to her disappeared mother, to the president, to her journal, to Tyler—composing a counternarrative that figures nation *differently* than the metaphysical pen drawing the borderline through the desert.

While *A Handbook to Luck* offers primarily a vision of global cosmopolitanism that transcends nation-state boundaries, Mari's counternarrative is strongly suggestive instead of Appiah's notion of "partial cosmopolitanism" (xvii). Appiah suggests that we do well to recognize that our sympathies and affective ties are never *im*partial. A cosmopolitan ethics, for Appiah, certainly invokes the nonnegotiable principle that "every human being has obligations to every other" (144); but on the other hand he also insists that "to say that we have obligations to strangers isn't to demand that they have the same grip on our sympathies as our nearest and dearest." On the contrary, a *partial* cosmopolitanism recognizes that we will in fact be "partial" to the communities closest to us, to those we belong to (158). Partial cosmopolitanism recognizes the pragmatic realities of affective communal ties.

The understanding that many contemporary crises are global in scope but also that people form strong attachments to particular circles of belonging is one that Alvarez rather explicitly plays out in the novel. The young Mari recalls how her teacher Mr. Bicknell "is always teaching us about saving the planet. We are all connected, he says, like an intricate spiderweb. If we dirty the air here in the United States, it will eventually blow over to Canada and maybe kill a bunch of people there. If some factory poisons a river in Mexico, it will flow into Texas and people will die there. . . . The other day in class, we learned how the ice caps are melting and the poor penguins and polar bears have nowhere to go" (59, 63). Mari's understanding of her environment acknowledges the reality of political borders but also notes that global capitalism has a global environmental impact. Implicit in Mari's vision is the notion that the guiding ethical principle should be "everyone potentially affected" (Fraser, *Scales* 5) rather than, more simply, everyone legally residing within particular nation-state boundaries.

For instance, in a letter she composes to the president, Mari notes that he claims to "want democracy for this whole world. . . . But that will mean that if everyone in this world gets a vote, the majority will not be Americans. They will be people like me from other countries that are so very crowded and poor. We would be able to vote for what we want and need" (60). In Mari's already rather advanced ethical system, she understands that the president's claim to want world democracy is circumscribed by national borders—democracy *within* nations, not between or among them—and thus highly limited. Evincing a budding understanding of the "all subjected" principle articulated by Fraser, Mari displays an awareness that as an unauthorized immigrant in the United States, she is subjected to laws that she literally has no say in. Echoing Mr. Bicknell's insight that "we are all citizens of one planet, indivisible with liberty and justice for all,"

Mari takes a specifically and identifiably nationalist rhetoric (the Pledge of Allegiance) and expands it into an ethos of global responsibility for mutual survival: "Viva los Estados Unidos del Mundo! . . . Long live the United States of the World!" (72). Already, Mari is reaching for a universalist cosmopolitan vision that does not let the laws of a single nation-state be the boundaries of her own notions of ethics.

Even when the small Vermont town in which Tyler and Mari live reaches toward more inclusive models of community which would include and embrace "foreign" migrant labor, however, the very rhetoric supporting inclusivity reveals lingering traces of a fundamental difference in the ability to participate in the public sphere that cannot be ignored or elided. It is once again Mr. Bicknell who, at a community town meeting, advances the cosmopolitan argument; Tyler's mother, Mrs. Paquette, congratulates the teacher by saying "You have my vote"—a colloquial phrase of support for his broad, humane vision, which nonetheless underscores the difference between Mrs. Paquette and the laborers she supports. No matter how much *they* might agree with the sentiment expressed by Mr. Bicknell, he cannot have *their* "vote," because they have no "vote," as Mari pointedly underscores in her letter to the president. They cannot participate in the debate on the status of the undocumented in a public sphere that recognizes citizenship as drawing the parameters around debates on matters of the public good. Consequently, Mari stays tellingly silent as Mr. Bicknell constructs his narrative history of the immigrant labor that built "this great nation" (191).

Tyler, the adolescent narrator who must be educated in cosmopolitanism, struggles with attachment to a nationalist frame of reference much more than Mari does. In the early pages of the novel, Tyler is still guided by the assumption that to be a good person is to be a "law-abiding citizen"—that is, to entirely adhere to the prerogatives of the nation-state: "All his life his parents have taught him to obey the laws and respect the United States of America" (56). Alvarez is keenly interested in how the nationalist framework conditions children to *see* things in certain ways—to emphasize, for instance, the boundaries between belonging and unbelonging. The book opens with Tyler's perspective when he first catches a glimpse of Mexican workers: "Some strange people are coming out of the trailer where the hired help usually stays. They have brown skin and black hair, and although they don't wear feathers or carry tomahawks, they sure look like the American Indians in his history textbook" (3).

Tyler instantly labels the Mexicans as "strange" based on their phenotype (the lesson of racism and xenophobia); he knows "instinctively"—without knowing anything at all at that point about their legal status—that they are interlopers in the nation, because he has been culturally conditioned to see *all* Mexicans as "foreign."

Correspondingly, Tyler's discovery that Mari's family may not be authorized to live or work in the United States immediately triggers his use of the pejorative "Illegal people," which defines human beings exclusively by their legal right to reside in a given geopolitical territory (57). At this point in the novel, Tyler still clings to the nationalist framework as the only ethical framework he knows: "I'd rather lose the farm than not be loyal to my country" (70), he says, interpreting tolerance of undocumented immigrants as a violation of patriotism. From this perspective, loyalty to nation (to paraphrase Appiah) rules out other kinds of loyalty—they are mutually exclusive.

Tyler's process of education is marked by the degree to which he learns to modulate and adapt a rigidly nationalist framework with an ethics of cosmopolitanism. Consider once again Tyler's response to the different phenotype of Mari's family. Alvarez builds irony into Tyler's initial view of the Mexicans through the analogy to "Indians," regarded as foreign "others" both historically and in present-day American dominant culture (which continues to represent them through stereotypes of feathers and tomahawks) despite their greater claim to territorial belonging. Within pages of Tyler's first disturbing view of the Mexicans, Tyler is thinking about his own family's potential loss of their farm and making a historical analogy: "If they left their home behind, it'd be like the Trail of Tears Tyler learned about in history class last year. How the Cherokee Indians had been forced from their land to become migrants and march a thousand miles to the frontier. So many of them had died" (6). The comparison is disturbing, given Tyler's automatic ascription of "foreignness" to those who look like "Indians" in his first glimpse of the Mexican laborers, suggesting a rather willful appropriation of an entire people's experience of forced migration. Apparently, in these early moments of the text, Tyler can appropriate the Trail of Tears—the trauma of another people's collective history—in order to dramatize his family's financial crisis, but he can only see "Indians" in the *present* as foreign, "Other."

Nonetheless, Alvarez clearly means to construct a text in which Tyler's initial ways of seeing are challenged, including by his own historical analogy. He doesn't see the irony in comparing his family to Cherokees driven from their ancestral lands while comparing Mexican migrants in the present to Indians as a form of derogation. In fact, the real comparison the text establishes is between the *Mexicans* and the Cherokees of the Trail of Tears; both peoples have been driven from the lands they once called home by circumstances of crisis having to do with the prerogatives of a nation-state to which they do not "belong." The comparison suggests that the fact that the migration is economic in nature does not mean it is not "forced" migration; it is economic desperation that drives Mari's family north. Tyler will need to be able to grasp *that* particular analogy in order to move beyond a blinkered nationalist paradigm.

Early on in the novel, Tyler is still embedded in a nationalist framework. For instance, he responds to the possibility that Mari's family is not legally present within U.S. boundaries with the invocation of the symbolic representatives of enforcement of the law: "Should we call the police?" (57). Eventually, however, Tyler reaches a point at which he can begin to see beyond a strictly legalistic "law and order" framework to distinguish between (nation-state) laws and (cosmopolitan) ethics and to recognize the possibility that it might be "right," morally if not legally, for Mari's family to be here: "He wants the law to be changed so that [Mari's family] can stay, helping his family as well as themselves" (133). At this point he invokes as historical analogy the "Underground Railroad: helping slaves find freedom" because it so perfectly illustrates that laws are not the measure of morality. This analogy suggests the ways in which Tyler continues to understand his *particular* brand of cosmopolitanism through the lens of national myths, values, and history. That is to say, when he looks to a moral precedent for violating the law in the service of a higher good, he still privileges his own nation's history.

Mari and Tyler repeatedly refer to historical analogies for the argument that national laws do not determine the parameters of ethics, even while relying upon *U.S.* history for their moral exemplars; the particularist history of the United States is still privileged as one that Alvarez's young readers will regard with moral authority and will have an affective connection to. The most obvious example is that of slavery. For Alvarez, history provides a longer view that is useful to apply to the present. Thus Mari notes of her own mixed status family, "It is just like the war of slavery in this country we learned about.... Mr. Abraham Lincoln said: 'United we stand, divided we fall.' Mr. B. explained that this statement is now true for our whole world" (59). In the extension of the analogy, just as the two sides of the "nation" needed to heal the rift and understand themselves as one, so now Mari's family must be permitted wholeness, rather than to be divided by citizenship status; and indeed, the world must come to recognize its global wholeness and mutual imbricatedness, with all the implications for ethical *world* citizenship.

Tyler comes to this analogy in a more roundabout way, through his curiosity about the constellations, which he views through the telescope that his grandfather gave him. In contrast to Tyler's earlier view of the universe as "scary" when he attempts to understand it through a nationalist framework, Tyler's interest in the physical universe is a trope for his development of a universalist or cosmopolitan perspective. Indeed, it is Mari who introduces the connection between the trope of space and the global or cosmopolitan perspective, reporting in her composed letter to the president on her teacher's warning that "'Our earth is already in trouble.' . . . Mr. B. says no other planet in our solar system has the water and air we need. 'We earthlings have to get our act together *pronto*'" (60). Shifting from the language of global crisis to the planetary perspective establishes the ways in which cosmopolitanism becomes represented through the trope of an interest in stellar and planetary space in the novel. Thus when, shortly thereafter, Tyler rejects Mari's overture of a "star lesson" with his telescope, it marks his resistance to the cosmopolitan perspective as he continues to struggle with the nationalist one (69). Tyler's enduring interest in the stars, however, offers him the grounds for the eventual formulation of a narrative that will counter and expand the "law-abiding citizen" framework. Tyler gets to the point where he wishes he could travel to "a planet with lots of farms and no borders" (120); he names a star after Mari (through the internet) as a birthday present (255–56); and he eventually gives her the gift of his own telescope. The universe literally becomes Tyler's new moral horizon, the constellations the "map" of his ethical framework, as he recalls his grandfather's lesson, "Anytime you feel lost, look up" (256–57). While *A Handbook to Luck* highlights globalized movements and transethnic allegiances as grounds for cosmopolitanism, *Return to Sender* literalizes the "universalist" cosmopolitan orientation through repeated recourse to images of the cosmos.

The universe as trope for a broader perspective or "bigger picture" also allows Alvarez to play with the notion of "illegal alien." Tyler's interest in space, naturally, extends to the possibility of spaceships: "Maybe some night he'll discover some new star cluster or spot a spaceship zipping around the stars" (51). But spaceships in turn imply aliens and new categories of belonging and unbelonging. When Tyler is cautioned not to talk too much about the new workers on his family's farm, he jokingly says, "If anyone asks I'll just tell them we've got us some Martians.... We hired extraterrestrials.... Excellent help. You don't have to pay them" (15). In this way Tyler stumbles on the rhetorical connection between "illegal aliens" and extraterrestrials, without fully understanding the implications of his substitution (though Alvarez obviously means to invoke it). Not only are "illegal aliens" exploited workers ("you don't have to pay them" hints at wage theft), but they also remain fundamentally, *essentially* foreign, in a categorical way that cannot be changed through incorporation into the national body. Indeed, Tyler goes on to wonder "if maybe being Martian is a lot easier to explain than being Mexican in Vermont" (16), suggesting the notion of the essentialized and unchangeable foreignness and unbelonging of the Mexican alien.

And in fact, in some senses at least, Mari's experience *will* always be fundamentally foreign to Tyler's. *Return to Sender* shares with the novels discussed in chapter 2 the theme of the trauma of loved ones who have disappeared while attempting to cross the border (e.g., Ana Castillo's *The Guardians,* Reyna Grande's *Across a Hundred Mountains*). Alvarez presents through Mari's eyes the trauma of a mother who has disappeared while attempting to return from Mexico, where she was visiting her own dying mother. This is a particular in which Alvarez emphasizes how very difficult it is for Tyler to empathize, or even to understand, Mari's experience, responding emotionally with sheer incredulity when he begins to learn that the family does not know where their mother is or even whether she is alive (120). When Mari answers the Paquette phone, hoping that it is her mother calling (it isn't), Tyler is confused to see that Mari and her two sisters "have the same stricken look on their faces, as if they have just heard that their mother has vanished without a trace" (119). Tyler fails to comprehend that his simile ("as if" the mother has vanished), which he regards as a preposterous and unlikely scenario, is in fact the reality. Tyler cannot in any way grasp, in other words, what it might mean for one's family member to vanish without a trace; the experience is so profoundly alien to him that he thinks in private retort, "How can you misplace your own mother, for heaven's sake?" (120). Vanishing, as a potential gesture toward the contexts of disappearances in Latin American histories of the late twentieth century, again links *testimonio* and *testimonio fiction* to the new undocumented terrain—for family members facing the disappearance of their loved ones, the emotional and psychological experiences are similar, despite the very different sociopolitical contexts.

Mari, too, stumbles upon the implication that her foreignness is so incomprehensible as to be irreducibly other. She needs to have explained to her that *alien*, the derogatory term she is called by some of the boys in her school, "is a creature from outer space who does not even belong on this earth! So, where am I supposed to go?" (21). Subsequently, Mari works hard to challenge, at least in her own mind, the nativist discourse that would consign her to "alien" status. When the Paquettes call Mari's family "Mexican Angels" for helping to rescue their farm (with their labor), Mari writes, in a letter to her lost mother, "Mexican angels, Mamá! How is that for being a special alien?" (32). Linking angels with aliens, Mari challenges the dominant understanding of "illegal alien" through the blended metaphor of space and heaven, deploying once again a universalist frame that implies concern for the welfare of all human beings, rather than just those of a certain nation. Angels have no citizenship.

But it is the particularist version of cosmopolitanism, not the universalist one, that wins the day in this novel. In the culminating symbolic performance of partial cosmopolitanism, Tyler ends up visiting Washington, D.C., "this nation's capital" (243), on a return trip with his aunt and uncle, who have agreed to transport Mari's mother back to her family from North Carolina, where she has been held hostage by unscrupulous coyotes or human smugglers. Alvarez downplays the fact that this transporting act could well be construed as illegal aiding of an unauthorized presence in the United States. Tyler, trying to calm his mother's anxieties, tells her over the phone that "it's no big deal. . . . We're just giving Mrs. Cruz a ride home" (229). But however "true" this may be to Tyler's family and to Mari's, the portrayal of Mrs. Cruz's transport as "*just* a ride home"—a domestication that renders it in highly familiar and quotidian terms for U.S. readers, as for Tyler's mother—elides the quite significant ways in which the simple "ride home" is significantly complicated by issues of legal status and immigration law. What the Mahoneys, Tyler's aunt and uncle, are doing in bringing Mrs. Cruz to her family could be interpreted as the unlawful transportation of an undocumented immigrant.[15] Yet the Mahoneys dismiss Tyler's mother's concerns (she is just being a "worrywart") and praise Tyler himself for having a more "adventurous" spirit (228). Reconstituted as an adventure rather than a crime, the trip north is represented as an integration of Mari, her mother, and, by extension, all unauthorized migrants into the very fabric of the nation.

The visit to Washington interweaves the most recognizable symbols of nation with a cosmopolitan perspective. One of the stops on the visit is the National Air and Space Museum, where they visit a planetarium—a setting that re-creates the trope of the cosmos (244). Another stop is the Vietnam Memorial, where Mrs. Cruz notes, "Each of those names left behind a grieving family" and Mari makes the connection to their own familial situation: "I know I was thinking of how we grieved for her during her absence" (245–46). In this way the meaning of a prominent national symbol is stretched and reconfigured to potentially include the situation of Mari's family. Mari's lost-and-found mother even visits the White House (a plot point which glosses over the necessity of providing social security numbers and tour requests months in advance), where she "could not believe she was inside a president's house, not to clean it, but as a guest!" (244). The incident ignores implausibility in order to narrate the possibility that the "guest workers," who supply the "cheap labor" on which the nation has been founded and now thrives, could in fact be treated as "guests" within the metaphorical house where they work.

As we have seen, Alvarez's narrative works hard to reconcile "patriotism"—those affective attachments to nation that children are taught from the earliest age—to an expansive, cosmopolitan view; and she does all this within a narrative structure the moral lessons of which are fairly overt, and therefore discernable by a young adult audience. If in so doing Alvarez elides the serious tensions that the history of nationalism, in practice, has always highlighted, she also refuses to fully abjure the psychological power of the affective ties that our particular, located experiences as human beings inevitably create for us. Rather than asking her young readers to set aside their inculcated respect for strongly affective symbols of nationhood including the flag and the Pledge of Allegiance, Alvarez attempts a counternarrative of what those nationalist symbols can *mean*.

* * *

I offer up some brief concluding remarks here about the vision that García's and Alvarez's novels provide as a corrective to the citizenship status distinctions that differently inflects Latino/a groups within the United States. Both novelists, arguably, represent characters from a group identity that is quite distant from their own, not *only* in terms of ethnicity but also in terms of access to legal status—to the right to belong. Nonetheless, both texts advance an ethics of solidarity *across difference*, based on a cosmopolitan perspective. These novels suggest that, however limited by the particularities of experience, we do well to understand the globalized and indeed universal nature of our responsibilities to each other.

4

Selling the Undocumented

Life Narratives of Unauthorized Immigrants

Although Arizona's notorious anti-immigration bill SB 1070 and the plethora of copycat legislation bills in several other states,[1] as well as the failure (to date) to pass any form of the DREAM Act at a national level,[2] have kept a spotlight on issues of undocumented immigration in national debates, the voices of the undocumented themselves have barely begun to register in this scene.[3] As I have suggested throughout this book, there is perhaps no population more silenced in the face of debates that most directly affect them than the undocumented. In his introduction to *Underground America: Narratives of Undocumented Lives*, editor Peter Orner foregrounds this problem: "We hear a lot about these people in the media. We hear they are responsible for crime. We hear they take our jobs, our benefits. We hear they refuse to speak English. But how often do we hear *from* them?" (7). In his foreword to the same collection, Luis Alberto Urrea points out, "Undocumented immigrants have no way to tell you what they have experienced, or why, or who they are, or what they think. They are, by the very nature of their experience, invisible. Most of us pass them by—some of us might say a prayer for them. . . . But nobody asks them what they think. Nobody stops and simply asks" (1). To speak *and be heard*, in ways that will not immediately invite the most serious of repercussions (e.g., detention and deportation), is a challenge that unauthorized immigrants face in ways that other populations with a direct stake in U.S. legislative battles do not. Thus the question of how undocumented stories might participate in the public sphere where immigration policy and legislation are debated becomes increasingly urgent.

Certainly, as we have already seen, in the last two decades there has been a dramatic increase in texts telling the stories of the undocumented so as to elicit empathy or even solidarity from readers. The new millennium saw the publication of collections of stories about undocumented individuals based on interviews—including *Crossing with the Virgin: Stories from the Migrant Trail* (2010), edited by Kathryn Ferguson, Norma A. Price, and Ted Parks, and *The Death of Josseline: Immigration Stories from the Arizona-Mexico Borderlands* (2010) by Margaret Regan—and of two compilations of oral testimony *by* the undocumented: *La Migra me hizo los mandados* (2002; translated as *The Border Patrol Ate My Dust* in 2004), edited by Alicia Alarcón, and *Underground America*, edited by Peter Orner. In this chapter, I consider in particular the collections by Alarcón and Orner, because these two make hearable, through direct discourse, the voices of the undocumented in order to insert these voices into the landscape of political debate.

Like other texts I have examined thus far, these collections too can productively be examined through the lens of Latin American *testimonio* study. Both compilations were published amid mounting debates over border security, as well as escalating raids and deportations. As we have seen in previous chapters, implications of the Gatekeeper era meant that border crossing became an increasingly dangerous and potentially traumatic experience. Meanwhile, under the last years of the Bush administration, a series of large workplace immigration raids to detain undocumented workers resulted in a dramatic rise in worksite arrests and detentions, from 485 in FY 2002 to more than 3,600 annually in FY 2006 and 2007. By some estimates, the raids cost taxpayers over $10 million a year (Capps et al. 10; Bennett).[4] A study of three major workplace raids estimated that for every two workers arrested, one child would be affected—and that close to two-thirds of all children of undocumented parents are U.S. citizens (Capps et al. 15, 17). Although Barack Obama had positioned himself during the 2008 presidential election campaign as advocating a more reasoned position on immigration, during his administration deportations skyrocketed to record levels, although worksite raids decreased (see O'Toole).[5] During the years 2001–2010, the number of removals rose to 2,794,946, compared with 946,506 during the 1990s (Kanstroom 12).

Nicholas De Genova and Nathalie Peutz have termed this state of affairs the "deportation regime"; it instituted a new, pervasive level of fear, a "culture of anxiety" (Orner 10), in undocumented and mixed-status families and in extended Latino communities. As Leo Chavez writes, "Undocumented immigrants are constantly aware that at any moment they could be apprehended and deported from the country" (*Shadowed Lives* 159). Alberto Ledesma, one of the few literary scholars to attend specifically to representations of undocumented immigration, takes a personal turn in describing "the fear that undocumented immigrants feel whenever the police are around, the fear that undocumented immigrant children feel when their parents don't return home at just the right time, the fear that immigrant workers feel when, though they might be fired or deported, they still speak up about the injustices they face at work. This is a fear my family has known" ("Narratives" 348). This sense of looming apprehension invading the fabric not just of individual lives but of families and communities has only increased with the escalation of enforcement measures in the U.S. interior. Immigrant communities where 287(g) agreements between state/local law enforcement and immigration have been implemented have become more likely to view police with suspicion and thus less likely to report crimes.[6]

In this chapter, I wish to argue that Alarcón's *Border Patrol* attempts to give testimony to the traumatic experience of border crossing (although, as I will argue, it fails for formal reasons), while *Underground America* is more concerned with testifying to the trauma of undocumented existence *within* the United States and to the "culture of anxiety" described by Peter Orner.

Testimonio has always faced the problem of constructing a sense of connection *across* identity categories such that readers in the United States would come to feel a sense of obligation and responsibility for what was happening "elsewhere." But this problem takes on new and complicated dimensions when the elsewhere is *here*—when the national "others" who are speaking are within the political boundaries of the intended readership's nation-state yet are regarded as *not belonging* there. The potential social power of *testimonio* resides largely in the ability of the personal story to construct empathy and identification in readers. *Testimonio* therefore needs insistently to anticipate the response of its imagined readership and to craft narrative strategies that will elicit the desired sense of ethical responsibility (see Nance, *Can Literature* esp. 50–59, 72–79). The peculiar status of the undocumented as perceived interlopers in the "nation" creates particular obstacles to the soliciting of empathy.

In a substantial revision of her earlier work on public sphere theory, Nancy Fraser has recently argued that traditional formulations of the public sphere—that metaphorical space in which matters of the social and political good are debated and "public opinion" is derived—have invariably taken for granted that "citizenship set the legitimate bounds of inclusion [in public deliberations], effectively equating those affected with the members of an established polity" (*Scales* 94). The noncitizen *has no voice* recognizable in the public sphere, as currently conceived, to participate in arguments about matters most pertinent to his or her own well-being, such as immigration policy and enforcement, possible routes to legal status, and so on (4–5). Peter Nyers turns his attention to the "acts of agency" involved when noncitizens do, in fact, insert their voices into debates directly impacting them and thus challenge their exclusion from a particular nation-state. He terms such practices "abject cosmopolitanism" (415, 417). In effect, they enact their "insertion into the public sphere" in order to "claim the idea of the state belonging to one"—the means by which, Gayatri Spivak suggests in her revisitation of her landmark essay "Can the Subaltern Speak?," the subaltern wrest agency for themselves (*An Aesthetic Education* 439). In insisting upon their "right" to speak on issues directly affecting them, undocumented migrants refuse their construction as "abject" by dominant discourses which relegate them to the position of silenced other and in effect reimagine the very terms of "citizenship" and "nation."

But such an understanding must come with qualifiers, as Nyers suggests through his probing questions, clearly influenced by Spivak: "Can the endangered speak for themselves? . . . For their agency to be recognized as legitimate and heard as political, does it require mediation from other citizen groups?" (415). We cannot assume that because the abject refuse their abjection they are therefore "speaking for themselves" in some pure form.

In this regard, a few preliminary words are in order on the precise nature of the "voices" that are represented in the collections I examine here. The collections inherit a legacy of transplanting and adapting *testimonio* to U.S. contexts, such as in the 1980s Sanctuary Movement (Westerman 228). But if *testimonio* provides a potential platform by which the subaltern can indeed speak, the very condition of subalternity generally necessitates the assistance of others in order to be made hearable—of those with institutional platforms for speech, greater access to publishing and media venues, and so on.

Agency, Spivak has insisted, is "institutional validation" (*An Aesthetic Education* 438); put this way, it is precisely what the undocumented lack but are striving to achieve. *Testimonio* is thus a highly mediated artifact. Referring to the most famous of all *testimonios*, *I, Rigoberta Menchú* (1983), Doris Sommer has pointed out that "From the introduction . . . we know that the testimonial is being mediated at several levels by Burgos, who records, edits, and arranges the information, so that knowledge in this text announces its partiality" ("Rigoberta's Secrets" 32). While Dave Eggers envisions the collection of undocumented stories contained in *Underground America* as a "partnership" between interviewees and interviewers, editors, and publishers (Gidley), the mediated relationship also of necessity bears the marks of the tension of a relationship of unequal power. The collections I consider here all certainly grant some degree of hearability to the voices of the undocumented; at the same time, none of them can be regarded as presenting those voices in some sort of pure essence.

Yet the traces of mediation are much more evident in some texts than in others. Detangling the "authentic" voices of the undocumented from the other forces that have shaped the final form of the text—the translation, editing, packaging, and marketing and the potential desire of the narrators/witnesses to accommodate an interviewer's presumptions—is thus beyond the scope of this chapter, even if it were a possible (and desirable) task.[7] I accept, then, the impurity of *all* of the final products, and seek to consider instead the narrative strategies advanced by the compilations as a whole—as mediated, composite texts which nonetheless clearly mean to advocate an "ethics of recognition" based on universal, shared humanity. As we shall see, that grounding sometimes sits uneasily with perhaps more pragmatic impulses and more circumscribed notions of identity.

In this chapter, I examine two compilations of direct undocumented testimony, *The Border Patrol Ate My Dust* and *Underground America*. As I shall discuss, while *Border Patrol* seems to provide the most unmediated testimony, it is in fact edited in ways that short-circuit its potential *testimonio* function; conversely, *Underground America*, which contains explicit editorial and framing materials, and thus seemingly foregrounds its mediated nature, has a strong *testimonio* function and overtly solicits readers to empathize with its subjects. Nonetheless, part of this text's dilemma of mediation is that it must make a case for empathy to a particular, nationally bound audience, and it cannot escape the constraints of that rhetorical situation.

"Direct" Testimony: *The Border Patrol Ate My Dust* and *Underground America*

John Beverley insists that the mediating relationships characteristic of Latin American *testimonio* need not indicate that the "real" voice is primarily that of the editor or compiler: "In the creation of the testimonial text, control of representation does not flow only one way" (that is, "downward" from the editor or interlocutor); further, "editorial power does not belong to the compiler alone" (38). Beverley posits instead an understanding of the (potentially) collaborative and mutually affective nature of the relationship between narrator and compiler in *testimonio* as suggesting "an appropriate ethical and political response" to the voicelessness of the subaltern, which is "the possibility of solidarity" (36). However imperfect that possibility remains in fact—or however uneven the direction of the "control" over meaning in any particular case—Beverley hypothesizes that, when it is a product of both a "witness"-speaker *and* a compiler who is not the same person (or a transcriber or editor—and, in some cases, perhaps *also* of a separate translator), "Testimonio involves a sort of erasure of the function, and thus also of the textual presence, of the 'author'" (35). Instead, the "final product," as it were, is that of a multitude of hands, whose particular contributions can blend (at times) seamlessly and may be indistinguishable in retrospect from each other. In the rest of this chapter, then, I wish to turn my attention to the functions served by textual compilations of direct undocumented testimony which, arguably, more closely resemble the genre of Latin American *testimonio*. Both *Border Patrol* and *Underground America* present the *testimonio* of migrants in the form of their transcribed stories.

The undocumented narrators who deliberately tell their stories to unknown and anonymous others in these books understand themselves in some sense as part of what critics would call a "public." "Publics are essentially intertextual," Michael Warner clarifies, "frameworks for understanding texts against an organized background of the circulation of other texts.... And that circulation ... is more than textual—especially now, in the twenty-first century, when the texts of public circulation are very often visual"—or (we might add) recorded (16). Every talk show host or politician whose comments rant against "illegals," every T-shirt, bumper sticker, or blog, as well as the more expected immigration-related newspaper articles, letters to the editor, and magazine covers, is a text in the circulating discourse of immigration. The narrating migrant subject's contribution then becomes another text, in an "intertextual" relationship with these—shaped by them, responding to them, challenging them. In the case of both *Border Patrol* and *Underground America*, I suggest that the packaging and framing of these collections is crucial in providing cues to readers for how to *read* these first-person accounts. The political valences of the two texts, as we shall see, come to seem quite different, despite the fact that both collections offer the putatively "direct" testimony of the subaltern migrant subjects.

Every testimony takes place within a specific rhetorical context and responds to that context in particular ways. In *Border Patrol*, the particular context that motivates and drives the shape of the narratives is public interest in the *act* of border crossing. By contrast, *Underground America* moves its focus from border to interior in order to address a different set of concerns: the ways in which the lives of undocumented individuals are made highly vulnerable and exploitable by their unauthorized status, *once they reside within the United States*. As we shall see, *Underground America* deploys both the rhetoric of human rights and that of national belonging to make its case. These dual rhetorical impulses in fact create a fairly dramatic tension within the structure of the text, which (I will argue) ultimately constrains the collection's ability to fully represent strategies of identification *not* based in national identity.

Border Patrol is the product of a question broadcast on the airwaves in Southern California, by radio host Alicia Alarcón, who invited her listeners to call in with their stories of coming to the United States. The text emphasizes *the physical journey itself* as the main topic of testimony: the English edition's cover, constructing immigrants primarily as "travelers," notes that "In this collection, Alarcón has recorded the footsteps of these travelers across deserts and rivers." In Spanish, the emphasis on physical movement is even more pronounced by its conversion into metaphor: "Alarcón muestra los pasos tomados por estos viajeros durante sus vuelos y caídas" [Alarcón demonstrates the steps taken by these travelers through highs and lows—literally, through *flights and falls*]. The forms of trauma to which the collection gives testimony, accordingly, are by and large those associated with the act of crossing: the violence or poverty in the home country that propelled migration as a "push" force, a bankrupt myth of the American Dream serving as a "pull" force, and the hazards and dangers of crossing itself. Yet the focus on movement means that the narratives rarely sustain a critique of immigration law or enforcement policy in the United States. Further, while a few of the accounts move toward an ethics of recognition by providing more sustained narratives that detail the struggle for a sense of agency on the part of respondents, most of them, told in fairly brief fragments often stripped of explanatory introductory material, mirror stylistically (through the flow of fragments and through openings in medias res) the "movement" that is the guiding principle of the volume, but at the expense of serving a *testimonio* function.

By contrast, *Underground America* is part of McSweeny's "Voice of Witness" series, which "allows those most affected by contemporary social injustice to speak for themselves" and "illustrates human rights crises through the stories of the men and women who experience them." The back cover of the volume explains that the series is dedicated to "Illuminating Human Rights Crises through Oral History." The names of both Dave Eggers and Luis Alberto Urrea feature prominently. In other words, *Underground America* is packaged and prefaced, and its oral histories are selected, as a contribution to the witness of "human rights crises" caused by current immigration laws and border security policies. By positioning itself in this way it urges readers to *frame* undocumented experiences as a "human rights" issue. It thus rather overtly presents itself as having a *testimonio* function, meant to move readers to a position where they can begin to engage in an ethics of recognition of underground existence as a form of trauma.

The Border Patrol Ate My Dust: Selling the Story of Crossing

The back cover of *Border Patrol* explains the collection's origin: "Southern California radio personality Alicia Alarcón invited her immigrant listeners to call in and share their stories. In this collection, Alarcón has recorded the footsteps of these travelers across deserts and rivers . . . on their way to a fabled 'América,' land of opportunity." While this is the only information readers get, in either edition, about the actual question that was asked over the airwaves to elicit these stories, we can hypothesize that the question contained within it an implicit (if not explicit) interest in the *act of migration* itself, which, for many of the responding listeners, was an "unauthorized" experience. After all, the stories, as the cover and even Alarcón's own website suggest, focus largely on the *act of crossing* itself. Hence the "Border Patrol" (or, in Spanish, the much more colloquial and familiar *la migra*) is the haunting presence against which many of the narrators tell their stories. At the very least, the selection of narratives places primacy on the literal movement from one side of a boundary to the other; the accounts are, with few exceptions, accounts of the experience of entering the country illicitly and of the difficulties encountered in the process.[8]

The compilation of these crossing testimonies in *Border Patrol* is assembled so as to mimic the original radio call-in format, creating an illusion of *immediacy* unfiltered by editing apparata. The narratives of the undocumented—the cover of the Spanish edition calls them *testimonios,* directly evoking that larger tradition of Latin American letters—are not prefaced by any remarks whatsoever (there is no introduction, preface, or foreword; the text begins with the first narrative), so that they appear to "speak for themselves" as straightforward first-person testimony. Indeed, some of the testimonies are particularly marked by oral "ticks" such as "¡Qué va mi amiga!" "Ya tú sabe," or "No m'ijita, qué va," which create an informal and conversational style between the speaker and supposed "listener" (Spanish ed., 185). Yet this presentation actually belies some fairly serious forms of mediation, with many of the stories clearly a hybrid of oral testimony and editorial interventions, additions, and deletions. The accounts are frequently interspersed with "texts"—from encyclopedia entries (39), written letters (50), and newspaper articles (51)—that belie their oral nature, since these would be highly unlikely to have been read aloud verbatim in a strictly oral account. Other accounts are punctuated by verbatim prayers (35–36, 145), song lyrics (79, 98), and the like—again anomalous for oral accounts broadcast on a radio talk show. The actual resulting text is, then, a mixture of transcribed oral forms (the spoken prayers, the songs, the story told on the radio) with written/"writerly" strategies.

The marketing and the covert forms of editorial manipulation in *Border Patrol* most often work to depoliticize the content of the narratives. The fragmented, truncated nature of many of the stories,[9] as well as the emphasis within the text (and on the book jacket) on stories of crossing—a product of the initiating radio "question"—and even the title's focus on the border patrol, all capitalize on readerly curiosity about the nature of "illegal" entry while potentially undermining the *resistant testimonio* functions of the text. It is worth noting that while the title of this collection, in both its English and its Spanish versions, suggests immigrant insouciance and a challenge to the authority of border patrol—characteristics that might well support preconceptions about the link between willful "illegality" and criminality—the title phrase appears nowhere in the actual testimonies, either in English or in Spanish. The rhetorical goals of *Border Patrol*, taken as a whole, are ambiguous and contradictory, despite the overt attempts to "package" them as *testimonio*.

Border Patrol addresses multiple audiences and is, at various points, alternately "inwardly" and "outwardly" directed; many of the stories do serve as counternarratives to dominant discourses about immigration. Some stories, for instance, challenge views of immigrants as public charges consuming resources, or they debunk the myth of the "American Dream" available to immigrants. Several accounts try to educate naïve American readers about the conditions of home countries that necessitated emigration, thus serving as *testimonio* about the *need* to cross, while sometimes they seem to address potential *immigrant* audiences to caution about the hazards of crossing and provide other forms of "advice."[10] Yet each of these rhetorical undertakings has its limitations, as I will argue; taken collectively, they fail to pose a forceful challenge to dominant discourses about undocumented immigration.

The stories are virtually all odysseys in brief, detailing dangers to safety and well-being (both environmental and criminal), encounters with and repatriation by Border Patrol, and means of evading detection. Stories recount migrants being robbed (54, 153); violently searched or extorted by Central American and Mexican soldiers and police (55, 91); piled into vans or garbage trucks without room to breathe (57, 91); strapped under train cars within inches of being sliced by the wheels (8); kept in "safe" houses and rooms that are invariably filled with the stench of excrement (58, 82, 86, 141); abandoned by coyotes (70); imprisoned and beaten in Mexican jails en route to the North (71); held hostage while awaiting exorbitant coyote fees (92); and even sold into modern-day slavery by coyotes (129–38). Accounts of rape or the threat of rape by coyotes and unscrupulous employers exploiting the vulnerability of the undocumented grimly punctuate the collection throughout (59, 77, 122, 135, 144, 159). In this respect, the text overlaps in its subject matter with the nonfictional journalistic narratives by Urrea, Ramos, Martínez, Nazario, and others.

But clearly the emphasis on border crossing is also a marketing tactic; the title emphasizes eluding the Border Patrol, which is given perhaps disproportionate prominence through the image of a Border Patrol agent, rather than a migrant, on the front cover. A certain amount of readerly interest in the *act* of unauthorized crossing in and of itself, as an illicit act, is thus both assumed and appealed to. Given the escalating rhetoric regarding "securing our borders," which focuses squarely on the moment of entry (visa overstayers are completely left out of such an equation, even though they constitute approximately half of undocumented immigrants),[11] as well as the efforts of "minutemen" vigilante groups to "protect our borders," that assumption about readerly curiosity hardly seems misplaced.

Several narratives in the collection depict the challenges of unauthorized crossing in terms of a fairly typical "American Dream" immigrant narrative, as obstacles to be surmounted. Conversely, challenges to the "American Dream" ur-text itself are the most obvious counternarrative constructed collectively by these accounts. Mae Ngai notes, "The telos of immigrant settlement, assimilation, and citizenship has been an enduring narrative of American history" even when not always realized in practice (5). The history of immigration laws in the United States bears evidence of policies that ostensibly supported the ideal of the American Dream for *some* immigrants (although the Chinese Exclusion Acts meant that the dream was not made available in any form to Chinese immigrants at the time). Prior to the 1924 Immigration Act, for instance, the emphasis on the exclusion of "undesirable" traits (chief among them disease or the likelihood of becoming a public charge) was perfectly compatible in theory with a narrative of liberal meritocracy whereby immigrants could come to the United States, work hard, and "get ahead" (Ngai 59, 77). The myth of American meritocracy further contributed to the labor needs of the fledgling nation, since "Unfettered migration was crucial for the settlement and industrialization of America" (Ngai 58). The Immigration Act of 1965, which abolished a racially biased, national-origin quota system, also gave preference to immigrants with family ties in the United States or to those who brought with them occupational skills (Ngai 227). Such laws, in theory if never completely in practice, suggested and supported values of family and work as crucial parts of the design of the national polity.

In a globalized economy spurred by the hegemony of American media such as television and movies, both of which ignore nation-state borders, versions of the American Dream narrative continue to be actively disseminated and have their own share in the construction of desire as a force propelling migration.[12] Some of the accounts given by the undocumented, accordingly, attempt a rhetorical self-presentation that is clearly engaging at some level with that "liberal" vision of the United States as a land of equality, where those who work hard and contribute in meaningful ways to American life have staked a compelling claim to be recognized as U.S. subjects. Teresa, for instance, suggests that it is her very belief in the value of meritocracy that drove her north: "I had grown up with the firm belief that material possessions would be my reward for honesty, integrity, and hard work" (35).[13] Teresa's prayers rhetorically position migration within the value system of meritocracy: "Let me love Thee, my Lord and my God, and see myself as I really am: a pilgrim in this world. . . . Make me prudent in planning, courageous in taking risks. . . . Keep me, Lord, attentive at prayer, temperate in food and drink, diligent in my work. . . . Let my conscience be clear, my conduct without fault, my speech blameless, my life well-ordered" (35–36). The English version of the prayer implicitly connects God's will to the act of migration itself (Teresa is a "pilgrim" who must be "courageous in taking risks"); simultaneously, it rhetorically opposes presumptions about the undocumented as taxing public resources with a counternarrative of industriousness, faith, and other moral values that make her (implicitly) worthy of the American Dream.

Heriberto from Los Angeles (originally from Mexico) concludes his brief account[14] with this narrative of hard work and success:

> Thanks to my wife's wise use of money, we were able to pay off the house that cost us $65,000 in seven years. . . .
>
> I would tell anyone who is coming here that things are difficult but not impossible. It's all about hard work and perseverance. If someone were to ask me how we did it, I would quote this phrase to them: "The basis of economic prosperity is hard work and spending wisely."

Just as we have succeeded, others can succeed as well. Immigrants don't come here looking for handouts; we are contributing a great deal to the prosperity of this country. (191)

As with many of the other accounts, Heriberto's story reveals an awareness of a dual audience. His "advice" suggests that he sees one audience as those who are planning to come north. At the same time, his insistence that "immigrants don't come here looking for handouts" is clearly not addressed to the immigrants themselves but to a dominant culture making erroneous assumptions about the undocumented becoming public charges on welfare. Heriberto counters the discourse of the immigrant as a costly public burden with his insistence that he and his family have prospered because of "hard work."

Other narratives in the collection, rather than trying to establish the worthiness of the speaker to inherit the American Dream, work instead to expose that dream as myth rather than reality. Martín's account displays naiveté about the promises of the United States offered up via popular culture: "The idea of going to the United States seemed more and more attractive to me with each passing day. I got even more excited when my father told me that we would be going to Los Angeles. I knew that Hollywood was in Los Angeles, and I thought that I might be able to meet some of the stars that came out on television" (3). Of course, this Hollywood fantasy utterly obscures the reality of the journey north, which for Martín involves clinging to a small space *underneath* a moving rail car. For Martín, the trauma of passage is literally embodied. After his long ride beneath the train car,

> It was as if someone had been pounding on our legs all night long. We examined our calves. It looked like a field of giant mushrooms, covered by the skin of our calves. There wasn't a single spot on our legs that didn't have some sort of protuberance.... Perhaps it was exactly the pretext I needed to get the weight off my shoulders from all of the horrors I had experienced over the course of my journey. (14)

The trauma is both physical and clearly psychological. Martín's life story reinforces the *difficulty* of the route as a warning to those who would follow. As he says directly to an imagined audience of migrant networks: "I tell you all of this so that those who are already here in the United States do not mislead those who are still in Mexico. The road is hard, very hard" (15). Martín's narrative emphasizes the dangers of a media-constructed image of an easy and glamorous America. This is a point also supported by Fabiola's account, which tells us that she wondered during her own extremely difficult crossing, "'Why doesn't any of this happen on television?' ... No one ever talks about it, either. All we know is that the United States is very beautiful and that people make a lot of money there. ... I began to suspect that the television had lied to me, too" (100). For Fabiola, as for Martín, the globalization of American popular culture is a very real "pull," even though it is also a highly deceptive one.

Several of the fragments that deflate the American Dream ur-text also bear some of the most visible traces of the otherwise rather invisible editorial hand in the rendering of supposedly unmediated oral narratives. Angélica's account, which is particularly striking for its references to U.S. popular culture in the form of Disneyland as iconic children's fantasy, opens with an epigraph (one of the more obvious of editorial interventions, as an epigraph is hardly an element of strictly oral testimony) that quotes the lyrics of the song "It's a Small World" in exaggerated style:

It's a small world after all
It's a small world after all
It's a small world after all
It's a smaaall smaaall woooorld! (79)

The song is not mentioned in the account itself, where the allusion to Disneyland comes from the father's efforts to gloss over the harsh realities of border crossing for his children by telling them that they are going to the famed amusement park. The narrative itself opens with the words, "They dragged him from his house[;] The boy cried" (79), a jarring contrast indeed to the immediately preceding lyrics of the song. Thus the choice of this particular epigraph suggests the editorial emphasis on irony: the Disneyland ride's rendering of a picturesque and untroubled diversity of cultures, which it is possible to "sail through" as a spectator/tourist, contrasts stridently with the ethnic and class strife of war-torn El Salvador with which the account opens and which would seem to demand a different form of ethical world citizenship in response. The editorial choice to juxtapose such accounts of violence, or of dangerous crossings, with idealized images of the United States arguably highlights ethical issues, creating a jointly constructed, deliberative text in Nance's sense—one meant to solicit readerly participation in a project of social justice. Moments such as these arguably constitute the text's clearest manifestations of a *testimonio* function.

And yet, if such accounts pose a critique of the American Dream mythology, it is perhaps worth considering that this mythology may well no longer be particularly persuasive or even hegemonic within American society. The pendulum in discourse seems most certainly to have swung away from a rhetorical emphasis on liberalism's valuation of the human pursuit of happiness (even for not-yet-citizens) and toward a much stronger weighing of the nation's "right to exclude" (Ngai 12), such that illegal immigration is now repeatedly couched as a threat to national sovereignty. Representations of immigration debates in mainstream media over the last two and a half decades would suggest that the persuasive power or currency of the American Dream as an argument for more liberal immigration policies has perhaps long been on the wane. Witness, for instance, a 1992 cover of the *National Review*, picturing the Statue of Liberty with her hand held out as a barrier to would-be immigrants and the headline, "Tired? Poor? Huddled? Tempest-Tossed? Try Australia" (pictured in Chavez, *Covering Immigration* 146). Though the argument is still deployed by both politicians and activists, immigration enforcement and sentiment in the nation as a whole has become more, not less, restrictive—leading one to believe that counternarratives to the American Dream are narratives that tilt at windmills. As a rhetorical centerpiece for immigration debates, either through the argument of possibility and fulfillment of the dream, or as an exposure of its failures, the American Dream seems increasingly bankrupt.

A more trenchant critique lies in the collection's inclusion of the narrative of María, titled "He Sold Me to the Armenian," which testifies to the extreme vulnerability of undocumented women. María's story is framed by the binary of fear and courage that marks her progression toward her own sense of personhood and agency, in a "literary" accounting of her path to the United States. The account opens, "I was paralyzed by fear" (129), laying the groundwork for a predictable assent into agency (nonparalysis). María's narrative of trauma is characterized by her repeated encounters with the possibility of rape, sexual abuse, and exploitation. This trauma is represented as *dehumanizing* her. Movement from the status of "slave" to that of person and agent largely involves resistance and rebellion: "A vestige of dignity and of rage started to grow inside me to the point that I began to fight and argue with Mr. Mike's daughters, who treated me as if I really were a slave" (133). Resistance results in improved conditions: "From slave I had been promoted to servant" (134). Eventually María finds the courage to "escape" her circumstances of enslavement entirely.

The ending of her printed account suggests a sort of "coming of age" marked by *laying claim* to an "American" identity:

> A border patrol agent boarded at one of the stops. One by one, he went around asking people for their papers. As he stood in front of me, I found the courage I had lacked all along. . . . I gathered it all up and used it to look him straight in the eyes and say, "American citizen." . . . We reached Los Angeles at sundown. (138)

As with the prototypical slave narrative trajectory, María represents herself as having embarked on a process of self-recognition which has taken her from the status of a "brute" and "slave" to that of a person, understood as having both identity and agency.

But María also *names* herself as a U.S. citizen in her story. As Arturo Arias has commented on acts of naming by the subjects of *testimonio*, "Teaching testimonio [and related genres] means helping students to understand and accept the words of others . . . both as their property in the process of *naming themselves* (which allows those 'othered' subjects to be the rightful 'owners' of their subjectivity) and as an enunciative strategy for the sake of *gaining agency*" (312). María's assertion that she is an "American citizen" constitutes a speech act of sorts, in which naming the self as "American" allows the possibility to be created in fact. It also, needless to say, counters and challenges dominant discourses that would construe her as "illegal" rather than as "American." In this way María's narrative represents a significant departure from other accounts in the collection that—through their formal and fragmented representations of dislocatedness—reinforce a standard narrative of illegal "unbelonging," as I will discuss shortly.

In a different sort of counternarrative, some of the stories of *Border Patrol* challenge dominant and exclusionary discourses about immigration. In perhaps the collection's single most powerful commentary on U.S. immigration policies, "Henry's" narrative appears to implicate U.S. asylum laws that keep those subject to violence in their home countries from entering legally. Henry recalls appearing before the U.S. Consulate to make his case for political asylum:

> My life was in danger. They couldn't deny me a visa. Irritated, the immigration officer replied in broken Spanish, "How do we know that you didn't write this [threatening] letter?" . . . Composing myself, I disputed the decision. . . . I didn't want to leave. I was being forced to do so.
> "This letter, *tú inventar*. Anyways, there is no political asylum in the *Estadous Unidous* for you people." (52)[15]

Accusing him of forging the letter that serves as evidence of his persecution, the immigration officer in effect challenges Henry's "authority" to *write himself* as a victim of political violence and thus a "proper" asylum claimant. Henry's oral account, transcribed into the text of *Border Patrol*, insists that this narrative exclusion is unjust, thus writing himself back *into* the proper boundaries of the U.S. nation. That is, he composes himself. After all, it is the immigration officer, not Henry, who cannot properly pronounce *Estados Unidos* in Henry's retelling.

Forced to confront U.S. political asylum policy, Henry responds viscerally—as in Javier Sanjinés's notion of *viscerality* as a mode of resistance to the West. In Arias's gloss on Sanjinés, he notes that it is "a bodily metaphor" through which readers are invited to experience "the emotions, anger, frustration, or dreams of revenge" of the traumatized subaltern subject (Sanjinés 5, qtd. in Arias 316). Certainly, Henry's physical response to the immigration officer can be understood as a bodily metaphor inviting identification with more profound emotions. In Henry's bodily reaction to the officer's rejection of his asylum claim, "An electrifying rage coursed through my body. . . . The muscles of my neck stiffened" (52).

The metaphor suggests through these *physical* manifestations Henry's resistance to his rejection from the body politic of the United States. Resisting both U.S. and Mexican immigration officials' naming of him as outside of the proper national body, as "wetback" (55), Henry follows his narrative re-inscription (his "composing himself") with a bodily one, as he rides a bus, a plane, and a van through Central America and Mexico to cross into the United States. Henry both figuratively and physically refuses to recognize the boundary lines which would exclude him from the U.S. polity.

Along slightly different lines, the narrative recounted by Rosa María contests the use of raids and deportation as an immigration law enforcement strategy—one of the rare moments in the text when U.S. immigration policies and their enforcement in the interior are directly indicted. Although *Border Patrol* focuses primarily on routes of crossing and immediate repatriations, Rosa María's story relates a raid on the factory where she worked. Her account is highly attuned to the ways in which stories about factory raids are deployed by mainstream media: "Somebody hollered to call the television station and the newspaper. The bust was a huge success for the border patrol. The . . . newspaper article that was published was thin on details: 'Raid in a garment factory.' No one reported the fear that we felt, nor did they cover the humiliation of being treated like common criminals" (117). In the media, the raids are portrayed in a self-congratulatory way as immigration enforcement "success" stories that suggest the appropriate identification and detainment of "common criminals," linking immigration "raids" terminologically with other kinds of crime "raids" (e.g., drug raids, prostitution raids). Left out of the reported story, which is "thin on details," is the psychological shock of this sort of an equation, which clearly has an impact on Rosa María, who equates her imprisonment with unjust captivity. Rosa María's *testimonio* offers itself as an alternative account of the raids—one which fills in the "details" of psychological suffering omitted by mainstream accounts and which reasserts the fundamental humanity (as against the criminality) of the undocumented worker. Near the end of her story, Rosa María underscores the distress created by the ever-looming threat of enforcement: "I didn't want to live any more with the uncertainty of whether or not the border patrol would come and arrest me" (120). Yet in the long run, as Rosa María imparts without detail, she changes her mind and decides to return to the United States, so listeners and readers can only assume that she continues to live indefinitely with this fear.

Most of the narratives, however, avoid presenting a critique of U.S. asylum law or immigration policy; instead, the *testimonio* function of the accounts, when it appears, lies largely in a recounting of the circumstances of violence and poverty *within* the countries of origin. The ways in which the first-person accounts of *Border Patrol* might be said to "bear witness" to trauma suggest a corollary focus on the conditions of the sending country (rather than on the hardships of immigrant life within the United States), with listeners apparently imagined as a largely Anglo-American "outsider group" uninformed about the conditions which propel migration. For instance, Julio, a Guatemalan living in Los Angeles, is committed to bearing witness to the circumstances of his home country in ways which will educate his U.S. audience, however briefly: "No one knew whether or not his own neighbor would decide to kill him on the following day. The green fields of Guatemala had been converted into cemeteries. Human remains became confused with the bones of the animals. There was no other choice: leave or die. I'm writing about this *because few understand the circumstances* under which people lived in Guatemala, mainly during the seventies and eighties" (103). Julio is clearly aware of the ways in which his *testimonio*, bearing witness to the violence he was forced to flee, could potentially contribute to larger debates with the public sphere. These stories of trauma, like the oral *testimonios* of the 1980s Sanctuary Movement, serve an educational function in recounting the histories of political violence in Latin America which have propelled people to leave their countries and seek refuge in the North. Yet I would suggest that Julio's account does *not* fully meet the criteria that scholars such as Nance and Beverley have associated with the most powerful and effective forms of *testimonio*. It does not, that is, present those circumstances as having anything to do with the reader's own world, rather than some distant "Third World" in which the reader (or listening audience) has no part (Nance, *Can Literature* 55); it does not call attention to U.S. involvement, much less culpability, in the "circumstances" about which U.S. audiences are ignorant.

In general, then, while the contextualization of narratives of migration within violent histories might serve to deepen an understanding of some causes of immigration, a limitation of *Border Patrol* in terms of its potential for intervention is that these *testimonios*, adept as they are at describing despair or repression, are often stripped of any larger globalized context. Nicholas De Genova and Nathalie Peutz consider our current "regime" of immigration and deportation practices deeply problematic precisely because it "elides the [receiving] state's role in producing the conditions of their migration, as well as the very circumstances of their need for state 'protection'" (24). The stories' ability to challenge what U.S. citizens think they know (or care to know) about the situation of Latin American civil strife is limited, in large part because these brief vignettes are largely stripped of any reference to the U.S. role in Central American violence, civil war, or instability. Indeed, while a larger question posited by the collection as a whole might be: "How do the people who migrate perceive the penetration of the U.S. economy into their lives?" (Chavez, *Shadowed Lives* 3), the migrants rarely attribute *push* forces to U.S. penetration into their home countries, even implicitly. By failing to implicate the United States in the root causes of migration *to* the United States, however, this collection largely accepts a "deportation regime" in which migrants sneak into the United States of necessity driven solely by circumstances in the home country. "Catch" and "evade" are understood as the terms of the game, but the game's rules are not substantially challenged. Thus the "outsider group" (U.S.-citizen readers) is potentially educated about the conditions that have driven migration but not about any degree of *U.S. responsibility* for those conditions.

This is an important point to make because, as Nance has argued, "an ethical response to witnesses suffering" in *testimonio* (*Can Literature* 62) is often negated by readerly responses of "absenting and abjection" (55), in which readers assume that the conditions being portrayed are so far removed from their own world that they cannot do anything about them. "Absenting," Nance writes, "assumes an incommensurable difference between speaker and reader, an uncrossable distance across which it is prohibitively difficult or even impossible to communicate. . . . [It] may be facilitated by critiques that emphasize the localization of speakers in their own cultural and geographic contexts, to the point of isolation" (55). The alternative is representational strategies that present conditions of social injustice as related to the reader's familiar world. When the narrators of *Border Patrol* focus on the forces compelling their leaving in terms of locally felt "pushes," without accompanying commentary on a global economic system that creates both pushes and pulls for which the host country has a significant responsibility, then the challenge that the testimonies can pose to mainstream discourses on immigration in the United States (which already focus on immigrants themselves) is accordingly more limited in nature. One effect is that the narratives cannot serve explicitly as testimonies to *global* forces of displacement.

Indeed, several of the Central American fragments present a foreshortened understanding even of the violence of the narrators' homelands, with politics of any kind all but erased from the accounts. Manuel, from El Salvador, reflects on his own former youthful self: "When you're fourteen years old, you really don't understand much about armed conflict; the one thing that was clear to me was that my life was in danger" (110). Manuel's ignorance regarding the details of history and politics translates to a lack of information that is never fleshed out by his adult self.

A different Manuel, also from El Salvador, notes that he is part of "a history of exodus, of fear, of repression for not belonging to a particular group. A history filled with protagonists and deserters. El Salvador riddled itself with bullets. The war, the filth, the helplessness" (64). What is remarkable about this "history" is how little history it actually contains or explains. El Salvador is a battleground, a violent country filled with "bullets"—but from whence come the bullets? Who are the protagonists, and who are the deserters? Who is the "particular group" that one might face repression for not joining? Later, this Manuel notes that "the newspapers in the United States would report" the wholesale deaths in El Salvador as a result of "conflicts between the left and the right wings" (67), but he does not provide readers with the tools for understanding why this supposedly "neutral" and "objective" representation might be problematic.

Pedro renders the Guatemalan repression similarly, as a war without clear agents: "In the midst of a civil war, even the innocent are guilty. Corpses appear on street corners. Their murderers go about freely, and no one dares to turn them in" (148).

José Luis deploys natural metaphors in order to render the Salvadoran conflict as a war without clear or even discernable antagonists:

> War is a terrible, terrible thing. It washes away everything, like an overflowing river. It causes everything to explode. It destroys everything. That's war. . . . During the rainy season in El Salvador, the rivers would overflow, and they would wash everything away. Just like the war, they would destroy the cornfields, the countryside, the livestock, and they would leave so many dead in their wake. (139–41)

In this metaphorical rendering, war is akin to a natural force, "just like" the rainy season—they are equally destructive but also equally random, equally depoliticized. Without historical and social context, however, there can be no *testimonio*. The absence of specifics, here as elsewhere in the collection, renders El Salvador an inexplicably violent country—violent without reason or explanation, a "heart of darkness" far distant from the United States, and about which readers could obviously do nothing.

The final account of the collection—the only one by a Cuban immigrant—underscores the degree to which appeals to readerly curiosity about the details of the border crossing journey trump political or historical contextualization (particularly about U.S. foreign policy and its implications for undocumented immigration) in *Border Patrol*. For the knowledgeable reader, an oral history by a Cuban in a collection of narratives about the Border Patrol holds a dubious status, since the regulations governing legal Cuban entry to the United States are strikingly different than those governing all the other represented nation-states in the collection. The United States has had a long history of admitting large numbers of Cuban exiles at different times since Fidel Castro's takeover in 1959. Historically, then, this account is an odd fit to other stories of eluding the Border Patrol by land routes; it is made to *seem* formally parallel only because the respondent traces a roundabout route through France and Spain to the United States. Differences in entry are glossed over with the simple concluding statement, "Later on, we finally arrived in the United States, and I got a chance to think about everything we had suffered through to have a better life" (203). A structural similarity consisting of tortuous paths of migration thus conceals a deeper disparity. The presence of this account undermines the capacity of the collection to testify, in any coherent way, to the circumstances of *unauthorized* immigration and highlights the ways in which this collection is *not* self-consciously crafted as a deliberative *testimonio* on issues of U.S. immigration policy. Only by *stripping* the accounts of the context of immigration and asylum laws that govern entry into the United States can the Cuban account be made in any way to reside comfortably alongside accounts by impoverished Mexicans or persecuted Salvadorans and Guatemalans, none of whom were permitted easy entry (or entry at all). But without sufficient context for understanding the role of the United States in these forms of migration and in their relative access, the accounts become *testimonios* about their own countries *only*.

Further, in ways that strikingly resemble the narratives of Ramón Pérez (*Diary*) and Yamileth (*Undocumented in L.A.*), as we shall see, these testimonies by American immigrants pose no significant challenge to the kinds of popular discourse that would ascribe them to a "nonbelonging" status with respect to their geographic *place* in the United States, although they certainly testify to the trauma of displacement. For the narratives of undocumented immigration in *Border Patrol*, the "place" is a journey—walks through the desert, rides hitched on the undersides of train cars, frantic journeys on buses, crawls through tunnels, walks through the racing currents of the Rio Grande. The very title, *The Border Patrol Ate My Dust* (or the Spanish *La Migra me hizo los mandados*), suggests rapid movement—the inability to "catch," place, or pin down. As such, the collection is part of a larger "movement discourse" partaking of "the American faith in 'mobility' as being ultimately redemptive and progressive" (M. Martinez 54). Such discourse hardly poses any kind of rhetorical challenge to forms of rhetoric that would deny occupation of place to undocumented immigrants. As Martinez has vehemently argued in this regard, "migrants seek 'to arrive.'" They want "not only a *sense* of stability, but an actual *place* of stability" (54). The ways in which migrant subjectivity is *dis*located, unanchored from place, are part of the larger trauma of unauthorized migration. Place in these narratives, however, is ever-changing; the stories are connected largely through the trope of movement rather than of stability or the story of creating a new home. It is the journey itself that is traced by these narrating "I"s (as shaped by the editorial hand of Alarcón). As such, the stories do fit comfortably with current articulations of transnationalism as a dynamic that pushes against traditional notions of national belonging and posits a more fluid, less geographically bounded sense of self. Deterritorialization, movement, and transnationalism have severe *strategic* limitations, however, as forms of contestatory counterdiscourse within the circulation of anti-immigrant rhetoric.

In general, as I am suggesting, mobility is not represented positively by the narrators in the collection. Several of the accounts end with lessons learned and messages to those who are thinking of coming over, suggesting that one possible implied audience is in fact those thinking of making the journey north (or their relatives who already reside here) rather than the dominant and non-immigrant American culture. The opening story in the collection by Martín serves as a sort of frame for a volume which otherwise has none:

> I cry out of sadness for all of those who now cross the border in a thousand different ways.... I tell you all of this so that those who are already here in the United States do not mislead those who are still in Mexico. The road is hard, very hard. God bears witness to how hard it truly is. (15)

It is true that Martín's story is not unambiguous in its message to would-be crossers (one implied audience); after all, Martín himself "made it alive" and is on the path to becoming a citizen (15). Nonetheless, the emphasis of the *testimonio* is on the trauma of crossing, not on the "American Dream." The final word is "how hard it truly is."

Fernando, a Honduran living in Los Angeles, echoes Martín's warning note: "My advice for all of those who are already here is: fight to get ahead, and please, do not convince anyone else to come and suffer in this country. We wouldn't want our families and friends to suffer as we have suffered" (183). Such "messages" to imagined audiences seriously limit the degree to which *Border Patrol*, taken as a whole, can be read as an interventionist text or counternarrative to U.S. immigration rhetoric, despite being narrated entirely by the "voiceless" undocumented. Accounts that serve as warnings *not to come* function, for all practical purposes, to reinforce the messages of ICE and more generally of the Department of Homeland Security.

As we will see in chapter 6, recent narratives by students and DREAM activists much more directly challenge constructions of the American "nation" that might exclude them, telling their stories in such a way that they write themselves *into* the nation: "We Are America."

Underground America: Selling an Ethics of Recognition

Peter Orner's *Underground America* is unprecedented in its scope, its explicit "human rights" agenda, and its high profile and reach. Including accounts by twenty-four immigrants of various national origins (not limited to Latin American countries), *Underground America* is published by McSweeney's as part of the "Voice of Witness" series founded and edited by human rights scholar Lola Vollen and by Dave Eggers, a prominent author whose other narratives of human rights crisis include *What Is the What?* (about southern Sudan) and *Zeitoun* (about civil rights in the aftermath of Hurricane Katrina). Luis Alberto Urrea, prominent Mexican American author of several books dealing with the border region (including *The Devil's Highway*) penned the foreword. The collection has been reviewed by the likes of NPR and *Publishers Weekly*. Thus, more than any other published book to date, *Underground America* attempts and to some degree has achieved a public hearing by mainstream audiences of the personal stories of the undocumented; it is engaged in an open debate within the public sphere.

Monisha Das Gupta has proposed that immigrant activists are perceived as "unruly" when they "struggle for rights in the face of their formal/legal and popular codification as noncitizens." At such times, they "provoke us to question the monopoly of citizenship on rights" (4). The undocumented immigrants of *Underground America,* I suggest, challenge the "monopoly of citizenship on rights" and insist on alternative notions of rights that do not stem from *codified* notions of national membership. Nonetheless, the pressure exerted on this collection as a whole by the circulation of vitriolic rhetoric about so-called illegal immigrants results in an ambivalent product in which reliance on human rights rhetoric coexists uneasily with notions of rights *precisely* based on national membership. The text thus ends up challenging not so much the idea that rights stem from national belonging as the idea that the undocumented narrators must be excluded from such notions of national belonging. The narrative of nation is rewritten, but notions of the rootedness of rights in nation are precariously maintained. The particular dilemma faced by the compilers and narrators of *Underground America* concerns how to solicit recognition and identification for the undocumented based on claims of a common humanity, when such claims are inherently circumscribed by the limits placed on national belonging.

Concepts of human rights have always been linked with notions of nation, even as they seemed overtly intended to stretch the limits of "rights" beyond national boundaries. Discourses of human rights and of national belonging have a fundamentally fraught relationship, relying on each other even as they seem to be pulling in opposite directions. *Underground America* displays a profound awareness of the imbrication of "human rights" with the construction of nationhood, and accordingly constructs an argument in which the undocumented should be "recognized" as fellow human beings precisely because they are part and parcel of a national narrative. The collection advances the premise that the immigrants it represents *are already* part of the "American nation," not only physically but in the more profound sense of collective belonging and participation in a national project, and that their claim to *human* rights ought therefore to be recognized on the grounds of *national* belonging. The text, that is, appears strategically shaped to anticipate and counter the unhearability of unauthorized immigrants for U.S. citizens and the potential inability of the latter to "recognize" the former as human beings with rights, precisely because they are "impossible subjects," inside and yet outside the boundaries of the nation-state. As I will suggest in the final portion of the discussion, to the degree that the rhetorical capacity of *testimonios* to invite identification with the subaltern narrator is ultimately limited, we might need to consider the possibility of an ethics of responsibility that depends less on identification and empathy and that requires, instead, "recognition" of *one's own* participation in a larger system of privileges and inequalities.

Underground America, like *The Border Patrol Ate My Dust*, is a relative rarity in the publishing world: a collection of oral history narratives of the undocumented. But it is not an exaggeration to state that, by bringing overt and explicit attention to a history of silences, *Underground America* is already breaking ethical ground that *Border Patrol* skirts, at best. Like *Border Patrol*, *Underground America* must be understood not *only* as the voices of the witness-participants themselves; it is also a product of mediation, with Peter Orner (the editor/compiler) collecting and introducing—and, in the process, also granting hearability to—the voices of the undocumented subjects. But in doing so, Orner has his own impact on the reception of these voices, as, to a lesser degree, does Urrea with his framing foreword. The fundamentally *collaborative* nature of *testimonio* is more overt in *Underground America*; simultaneously, as we shall see, the text as a whole more clearly manifests a deliberative *testimonio* function. A quick skim of the footnotes alone establishes that the collection is not politically "neutral"; it is packaged and presented in such a way as to serve a "deliberative" purpose: to move readers in their thinking about the issue of undocumented immigration and its "real" purposes and consequences.

The act of translation and editorial mediation is overtly signaled by prefatory remarks specifying the language in which each interview was conducted (19, 57, 101, 117, 139, 157, 205). Olga, one of the narrators, insists explicitly that she tells her story because she wants it to reach "Anglos," *in English*—in effect giving her consent not just to the interview but to its possible political purposes and reach (113). Editorial contextualizing is another manifestation of the overtly self-conscious collaborative project of *Underground America*. Unlike in *Border Patrol*, where the only information about home country conditions or U.S. immigration laws and enforcement must be gleaned from the snippets in the accounts themselves, Orner insistently supplements information within the oral histories with detailed editor's notes and footnotes that ground and contextualize the narrators' often politically charged references, including information on the H-2A visa program for seasonal employment of immigrants (193); boycotts by the Coalition of Immokalee Workers and by the Farm Labor

Organizing Committee resulting in better pay for farm workers (191); the requirement that any employee in the United States must have a social security number, leading to a situation where unauthorized immigrants must provide false numbers in order to work (189); complaints filed with the Department of Labor regarding workers who were cheated of pay by subcontractors involved in cleanup in the wake of Hurricane Katrina (136); the Violence Against Women Act, a provision of which allows undocumented women subjected to abuse by a citizen or permanent resident to apply for legalization (153), and so on.

I would suggest that *Underground America*'s packaging and marketing are part of a larger effort to "sell" a moral or ethical stance in response to the unhearability of the undocumented. Such a stance is commensurate with an "ethics of recognition," in which listeners and readers are called upon "to recognize the humanity of the teller and the justice of the claim; to take responsibility for that recognition; and to find means of redress" (3; Schaffer and Smith). Beverley has put the fundamental *call* to recognition at the very heart of his definition of the genre, the "dominant formal aspect" of which is "the voice that speaks to the reader in the form of an 'I' that demands to be recognized" (*Testimonio* 34). And E. Ann Kaplan postulates, "One has to learn to take the Other's subjectivity as a starting point, not as something to be ignored or denied. It is only in this way that we can gain a public or national ethics" (*Trauma Culture* 123).

At bottom, of course, an ethics of recognition which asks readers or listeners to recognize the humanity of the speaker as a first step in asserting rights claims is fundamentally a call to empathy. Orner postulates that the mere act of reading his collection of oral histories will constitute a "walk in someone else's shoes" (26), a phrase which assumes at least the possibility of empathy, the imaginative occupation of the subject position of another who is not oneself. Scholars such as Nance, Beverley, and Westerman concur that the creation of identification with subaltern subjects is an essential (if not necessarily a sufficient) aspect of the social justice project of *testimonio* (Nance, *Can Literature* 74; Beverley 37; Westerman 229). That is to say, *testimonio*'s aim of provoking an ethical response in the reader is arguably inextricable from a process that begins with empathy. Indeed, Lynn Hunt has argued that the eighteenth-century development in Europe and the American colonies of a concept of "human rights" relied precisely on growing cultural notions and practices of empathy, "the recognition that others feel and think as we do, that our inner feelings are alike in some fundamental fashion" (29). Hunt suggests that "imagined empathy serves as the foundation of human rights rather than of nationalism" (32).

Conversely, the failure of empathy might suggest the inability to engage in an ethics of recognition. Several critics have expressed skepticism about the idea that simply reading a narrative will result in empathetic identification—or that empathetic identification is generally likely (in and of itself) to lead to action on behalf of justice. On the one hand, Suzanne Keen doubts that the experience of empathy is as efficacious as some may think; she is particularly dubious of efforts "to connect the experience of empathy, including its literary form, with outcomes of changed attitudes, improved motives, and better care and justice" (207–8), in the absence of any verifiable evidence of such a connection. On the other, some critics fear the failure of the best narratives to even *elicit* the experience of empathy. Schaffer and Smith note that narrators of life testimonies in a human rights context "*hope for* an audience willing to acknowledge the truthfulness of the story and to accept an ethical responsibility to both story and teller" (6), which of course suggests the possibility of an audience *not* willing to take on this role. Kimberly Nance, in a similar vein, posits that a reader/listener may well "listen" to a life narrative of *testimonio* and yet *not* be prepared to imaginatively walk in someone else's shoes, for a host of reasons (*Can Literature* 50–51, 54–55). One possibility is that we will indeed ignore or deny the subjectivity of the Other through the "act of distancing," which lies in "the failure (or refusal) *to identify the self in the other*" (Ngai 133).[16] Nance, as I discussed in chapter 1, warns of the process of "absenting" on the reader's part, in which readers can view the speaking Other only across the other side of a distant divide. Whatever might be said about the dangers of an overly optimistic faith in the powers of empathy, it would appear that its opposite, distancing or absenting, immediately forestalls any project of engaging a responsive ethics.

Yet it is precisely the failure, across cultural and geographical distance, to identify the self in the Other, that is the threat posited by a national imaginary in which only those who are recognized as *belonging to* the "nation" can be heard as subjects *within* the nation-state with legitimate claims. Indeed, the substantial tension between the grounding of claims in the "humanity of the teller" (Schaffer and Smith) or contrarily in the notion of a "national ethics" (Kaplan) is part of the history of "human rights" discourse itself, as Samuel Moyn has astutely observed. On the one hand, as Moyn acknowledges, the concept of "human rights" today is regarded "as a set of global political norms" that is associated, almost without question, with notions of "human universalism": "the belief that humans are all part of the same moral group . . . the same 'family'" (10, 13). On the other hand, this universalizing discourse obscures the rootedness of "human rights" in notions of *national citizenship*: "Far from being sources of appeal that transcended state and nation, the rights asserted in early modern political revolutions and championed thereafter were central to the construction of state and nation, and led nowhere beyond until very recently"; there is thus an "essential connection between rights and the state" (12–13).

Ngai pertinently recalls Chief Justice Earl Warren's dissenting argument in *Perez v. Brownell* (1958): "Citizenship *is* man's basic right for it is nothing less than the right to have rights. Remove this priceless possession and there remains a stateless person, disgraced and degraded. . . . He has no lawful claim to protection from any nation, and no nation may assert rights on his behalf" (qtd. in Ngai 229). De Genova and Peutz, writing on the global uses of deportation as disciplinary practices that reaffirm state sovereignty, underscore the naturalized connection of concepts of "rights" with state belonging, postulating that deportation

> is premised on a normative division of the world into territorially defined, "sovereign" (nation-)states, and within these states, the ubiquitous division enacted between more or less "rightful" members (citizens) and relatively rightless nonmembers (aliens). . . . "Rights" . . . assume their meaning and substance only insofar as they have been stipulated within one or another normative or juridical framework. Rights are therefore inseparable from some form of political regime. (7–9)

They further argue that "the inscription and embodiment of human liberties within the inescapably nationalist mantle of citizenship serve precisely to *confine* human freedom" (8). Such scholars suggest that the very idea of universal and inalienable rights obscures the point that, until very recently, notions of "rights" have been attached almost exclusively to the granting and protection of those rights via citizenship, rather than to some concept of humanism that transcended the legal boundaries of the state.

I will note here, however, that in an intriguing counterpoint to Warren's assertion that rights only exist when ensured by the state, Jacques Rancière has suggested that the mere fact that a certain class of persons cannot actually access or enact their "human" rights does not render the concept meaningless. Rancière acknowledges that "rights" that have no guarantor "appear actually empty" and "of no use." Nevertheless,

> when they are of no use, you do the same as charitable persons do with their old clothes. You give them to the poor. Those rights that appear to be useless in their place are sent abroad, along with medicine and clothes, to people deprived of medicine, clothes, and rights. It is in this way, as the result of this process, that the Rights of Man become the rights of those who have no rights, the rights of bare human beings subjected to inhuman repression and inhuman conditions of existence. They become humanitarian rights, the rights of those who cannot enact them, the victims of the absolute denial of right. . . . The Rights of Man do not become void by becoming the rights of those who cannot actualize them. (Rancière, 307, qtd. in De Genova, "Queer Politics" 118)

Put another way, "human rights" are *called into existence by the insistence that they exist* and that therefore the most vulnerable do not have access to something they properly should have, by right. Nonetheless, such claims remain circumscribed in their *effectiveness* by the power of nation-states to act to ensure so-called human rights. While human rights are commonly understood as a challenge to the moral primacy of any one state, the preceding discussion underscores the possibility that the ability to recognize the claims of other human beings will—perhaps inevitably—be circumscribed by a national imaginary.

It is, arguably, for this reason that *Underground America* negotiates a precarious balance—via selection and editing, packaging, and framing materials, as well as the content of the narrated accounts themselves—between, on the one hand, constructing an argument for the human rights of the undocumented, and, on the other hand, recourse to a narrative that attempts to rewrite the boundaries of "nation" so that the undocumented are, indeed, understood to be a part of it (and therefore hearable, recognizable, by a U.S.-citizen readership). The first-person accounts themselves, as well as the editorial materials, manifest this dual thrust, pulling in two ways at once: toward a re-imagined narrative of "American" belonging and simultaneously toward a rejection of national boundaries as the binding parameters of ethical responsibility. Thus the rhetorical invocation of "human rights," conceived as nonterritorial, exists side by side with efforts to reconsider resident "aliens" as "Americans" in order to facilitate an ethics of recognition which might otherwise be bounded by notions of national belonging.

Certainly, *Underground America* can be understood as a text that attempts to contribute to creating a "common sense" understanding that immigrant rights are human rights. The accounts in *Underground America* are selected, as Orner explicitly notes, because they "demonstrate gross human rights violations" or the "dehumanizing lack of dignity afforded to undocumented people" (15). *Testimonio* is, of course, intimately linked to the effort—through personal storytelling—to insist upon an ethics that recognizes human rights. Indeed, one of the narrators of *Underground America*, Abel, a Mayan immigrant from Guatemala, links his insistence on "rights" to the very act of storytelling: "Now I demand my rights. With or without papers, I feel I have the same rights. . . . Some of us are more comfortable speaking up about our rights—we know what we are entitled to. . . . We speak to Americans, people who do have papers, people who work at organizations, people who can do something for us" (132). The assertion of "rights" is inextricably associated here with "speech," that is, with storytelling and *testimonio*, told to an audience who "can do something for us." The specific *source* of those rights—in Abel's case as in others—is not specified (it does not come from "papers"), suggesting that, in this instance at least, he sees them as *human* rights, attached to *personhood*, rather than as citizenship rights. He thus participates in the naturalization of a notion of human rights as both universal and *pre*-given, rather than bestowed by a nation-state. When undocumented narrators tell stories in which they insist on their rights, they participate in the very construction of those rights as a thing that can be claimed. Nonetheless, Abel also recognizes that in practical terms, the citizen's rights are more easily recognized and acknowledged than his own—that citizenship is *understood* as the "right to have rights," at least in U.S. dominant culture, while he lacks access to the rights that he claims. Thus he is willing to seek help from citizens in securing his unacknowledged rights.

Another narrator, Diana, also invokes her "rights"; when she is questioned by ICE, she recalls, "But I knew my rights from the meetings. . . . 'I need my lawyer. I have a right to a lawyer. I have the right to make a phone call'" (26). Diana's account insists on her own status as a legal subject with "rights," and demands an ethics of recognition, even though it is not forthcoming—part of her story is about the way her rights have been violated. Her lawyer, for instance, never "found" her in the New Orleans holding cell to which she was consigned when she was detained (26–27). Perhaps more striking, Diana's account, like Abel's, recognizes the currency of *stories* in the struggle over rights. ICE "wanted everyone's story," but Diana "knew I didn't have to tell them" (26). While ICE would use Diana's account of her country of origin and of her undocumented status as a story that "proves" her unbelonging, Diana withholds that story from them, yielding it, instead, to us as a *testimonio*, a story of the refusal of ethical recognition based on human rights. Thus embedded in her own account is a faith in the power of stories as a means to move others. At the same time, Diana's account suggests an awareness of the ways in which *testimonies* like her own might be ignored: "A few times I told the others that we have to report this. They told me to be quiet. 'But we're here in this country where human rights are respected,' I said. One woman said, 'Who told you that? Those are just stories'" (28). Diana's own words contain, in miniature, the tension between human rights understood as universal and their potential boundedness by nation and national belonging. If you are "in this country" but are not recognized as *belonging* here, are your human rights respected? Will your story be heard? Will you, indeed, be recognized as a human being with the "right" to tell a story that has some claim on other human beings? Echoing James Dawes's overriding concern, in *That the World May Know: Bearing Witness to Atrocity*, with the ways that "stories designed to shake us out of our self-absorption and apathy can fail" (10), Diana here betrays a grave concern with the possibility that her *testimon*io might itself be "just" a story, stripped of its political value, because she is not hearable "in this country."

At the opposite end of the spectrum from Abel and Diana, who insist on their "rights" and on the value and import of their stories, is a narrator referred to in the text only as "El Mojado" (the wetback). Accepting this derogatory pseudonym with its emphasis on nonbelonging, this narrator arguably participates in his own continuing erasure of self as an unauthorized national presence. El Mojado emphasizes his profound sense that he *has no rights* and therefore does not *feel recognized* as a person: "I can't fight for my rights. I have no rights here in the United States. I don't have a right to anything. I can't fight anything. I know I'm nobody important" (210). El Mojado displays a rather canny understanding that rights come with, and are ensured by, citizenship; in the absence of citizenship,

El Mojado feels, quite pragmatically, that he has no rights, because the nation-state will not guarantee them. He is "a stateless person, disgraced and degraded" (Warren, qtd. in Ngai 229)—in our modern era, barely a person at all. In contrast to El Mojado's lament, Abel's and Diana's stories about *speaking up for* their rights constitute a direct counternarrative to forms of discourse that deny rights based on the lack of citizenship: Abel challenges the claim of another that, "according to him, I didn't have a single right, nothing" (127), which is tantamount to saying that he is not human.

Nonetheless, it would seem that El Mojado's anxiety about nonrecognition based on the boundaries of nationhood might win the day; at the very least, such anxieties exert a considerable force on the structure of the overall narrative. In his introduction, Peter Orner, who is a former lawyer, describes presenting the asylum case of a Guatemalan immigrant, "Eduardo," in court, only to have the case denied. As Orner tells it, the government counsel suggested informally afterward that perhaps "the judge might have just simply seen one too many Guatemalans that day." Orner takes this incident as a jumping-off point for a meditation on the ethics of recognition:

> *One too many Guatemalans.* Over the next few months those words rattled around my head. Eduardo had survived a horrific experience only to be considered one of too many. Maybe Eduardo's essential problem was his very existence. His presence alone seemed to have pushed the judge over some imaginary line. . . . Afterward, I began to think about all those other people out there implied in the phrase *one too many Guatemalans*, which seemed to me another way of saying *one too many stories.* (7)

Orner's rhetoric here can be read as nothing less than an ethical rebuke to the position which would grant recognition or withhold it on the basis of national unbelonging. It intimately interweaves notions of hearability, and thus of fundamental humanity, with the lines drawn by the category of nation itself, such that to be an alien within that category is fundamentally to lack any claim to human recognition. In this moment, the editor of *Underground America* displays a profound concern that any ethics of recognition will fail, because "Guatemalans" are not "Americans." "They" are not "us."

The strategic response to such a pervasive anxiety is to make the case that they are us. Thus, battling for supremacy with the "human rights" discourse clearly evident in the collection, the tenor of much of *Underground America* is repeated affirmation that undocumented immigrants *are* part of a U.S.-American narrative and nation. Orner's introduction, which (along with Urrea's foreword) frames the accounts that follow and provides an interpretive lens by which to understand them, also insists that undocumented immigrants "are an integral part of this society and this economy" (12), even if not generally recognized as such.

Like Orner, the undocumented narrators included in the collection seem quite canny about the potential rhetorical power of insisting on their own "Americanness," and thus this theme is repeatedly echoed in the accounts themselves.[17] Abel, for instance, is quite aware of the rhetorical maneuvers that position immigrants as not belonging within the fabric of the nation; he makes reference to discourses in media and politics of "cleaning out immigrants" (130), as though they are pollution or trash to be disposed of. Like María in *Border Patrol*, Abel too insists on laying claim to an American identity: "I feel American—I have never felt like a Guatemalan, because I couldn't develop myself there" (132). Abel redefines what it might mean to be an "American" from a legal status to an *internally* defined state of belonging and identity. One becomes "American" through *self-identification*.

The accounts of Diana and Polo are testimonies of the ways in which, to recall Orner's introduction, undocumented immigrants "are an integral part of this society and this economy" (12) and yet are treated as disposable, contingent. Polo recalls working on Hurricane Katrina cleanup efforts in a naval base in Mississippi but never being paid because the boss disappeared (136). In her account, Diana relates being hired, like Polo, as cheap labor to help with rebuilding after Hurricane Katrina:

> When cleanup and reconstruction began there were a lot of jobs available.... It was hard, dirty work and by the end of that first week most of the whites and blacks had quit.... The construction people who'd offered us our jobs began to ask for more Hispanics to work on their crews: more Hispanics, more Hispanics, more Hispanics.... We exposed ourselves to diseases working those construction jobs.... I still have spots on my legs from ... the chemicals and insulation that came off the walls at those jobsites.

When the police passed by our construction sites they never stopped or said anything. The immigrant workers were necessary to get the work done. (24)

Diana's story encapsulates in brief the long history in U.S. immigration enforcement of turning a blind eye to the employment of undocumented immigrants when their labor was crucial to substantial economies (such as farming economies at harvest time), subjecting them to hazardous and substandard labor conditions that they had no power to protest or improve (pesticides, chemicals, unsanitary work and housing, insufficient drinking water, etc.), and then stepping up enforcement when the demand for labor dropped.[18]

But Diana is also a savvy subaltern subject, an agent in her own story; she invokes her "rights" when she is questioned by ICE: "But I knew my rights from the meetings. . . . 'I need my lawyer.'" These speakers see such rights as human rights, linked with *personhood* (rather than as citizenship rights), and by insisting upon them, even in their absence, they contribute to their construction.[19] Further, whereas human rights discourse implies the extension of rights *beyond* the territorial boundaries of the state, the adoption of human rights discourse by undocumented aliens shifts the notion of human rights to the noncitizen suffering *at home*. Peter Nyers calls these the claims of the "abject" because, as "the embodiment of exclusion," they are expected to be "speechless . . . , invisible and apolitical" (419).

Lorena, a young activist who crossed the border with her mother when she was six, insists on an ethics of recognition based on a common humanity rather than on citizenship rights. This ethical obligation begins with Lorena herself, who describes how an internship with an NGO in North Carolina helping farmworkers "opened my eyes to a lot of injustice that I didn't want to know about before that" (193)—invoking the metaphor of recognition (through *sight*) rather directly. Lorena explains that now her "job as a human being" is to give other undocumented immigrants "knowledge to defend themselves with," to "change one person's life" (194). That is to say, Lorena construes her ethical responsibility *as a human being* to be not just the ethical recognition of others but also the facilitation of *their* own demands for ethical recognition and thus for "rights." *Multiple* levels of an ethics of recognition, with attendant claims, define humanity for Lorena; it is her obligation not only to recognize others but to be a collaborative participant in *their* project for the demand of recognition.

Conversely, to not *feel recognized* as a person is linked to the sense that one has no "rights," as we have seen in El Mojado's admission that "I have no rights here in the United States" and that (therefore?) he is "nobody important" (210). In the absence of citizenship to serve as a guarantor of rights, El Mojado understands that he is "nobody," unrecognized. In one of the few accounts that devotes some attention to the actual act of crossing, the emphasis is on the liminality of the border space and the consignment of those who cross it without authorization to the margins of human recognition. Julio renders his experience in the desert in near-biblical terms, conveying the existential crisis of nonrecognition: "I was alone. I was crying, nobody saw me. I talked, nobody heard me. . . . A body nobody finds" (180). The anguish of not being recognized as a human being with claims is conveyed metaphorically through Julio's sense of disembodiment, of being a body that no one sees or hears. If a body is in the desert but no one sees it, does it exist? In a similar vein, Roberto, explaining how he had to demonstrate an unbroken record of living in the United States to support his application for "suspension of deportation," says, "I had to prove I had existed here for ten years" (72), thus converting a territorial claim about residence within the boundaries of a nation-state into an existential claim of humanity that risks being denied. Conveying his agony in the wake of his family's deportation back to Mexico while he has stayed on in the United States to support them, Roberto says, "Sometimes I laugh by myself, at myself. Sometimes I talk to myself. Sometimes I cry by myself. Sometimes I scream by myself. Who am I? I'm nobody" (74). The repeated refrains of being "nobody" underscore the speakers' visceral experiences of the ways in which the nation-state framework denies their claims to humanity. Because their testimonies bear witness to this erasure, they can be read on one level as a continuing refusal of the abject position to which the undocumented are consigned, even as they seem to inhabit it most thoroughly. At the same time, such textual moments of seeming existential crisis also suggest the narrators' pervasive anxiety about the potential failure of their own stories to elicit an ethics of recognition from readers.

As I have already suggested, the rhetorical invocation of a common humanity that ought to be recognized in itself, in passages such as these, continually rubs up against narrative efforts to reconsider resident undocumented immigrants as "Americans" so that their claims may be more readily recognized and acknowledged. Notably, considering the remarkable growth of transnational labor, as well as the resulting scholarly interest in transnational ties, affiliations, and communities that are considered the hallmarks of our current condition of globalization, a transnational sensibility is relatively absent from these narratives—a rather striking contrast from the thrust of the *Border Patrol* collection (or of the first-person accounts of Pérez and Yamileth in the next chapter). No doubt this shift in sensibility is strategic. Understandings of transnationalism tend to emphasize a sense of *dual* belonging, to two nation-states at once. Alejandro Portes, for instance, discusses the "dual lives" experienced by immigrants who "frequently maintain homes in two countries, and pursue economic, political, and cultural interests that require a simultaneous presence in both" (76). But for undocumented immigrants seeking legal status in the United States, overt suggestions of dual allegiances, to host *and home* countries, would be rhetorically dangerous, to say the least. Although many contemporary scholars "posit transnational perspectives as more politically engaged and nationalist ones as conservative, or even regressive" (Sugg 229), in this case it is precisely the politically pressing nature of the *testimonios* of the undocumented that dictates an eschewal of transnationalism in favor of narratives that emphasize national belonging.

In a similar vein, while *The Border Patrol Ate My Dust* focuses on stories of crossing, *Underground America* avoids extended representations of the act of border crossing itself. Such a focus, whatever else it might achieve in undermining traditional, highly bounded notions of national allegiances and identifications, would underscore the perceived "unbelonging" of the immigrants within U.S. territorial, nation-state boundaries—and, analogously, their unbelonging in a narrative of (American) nationhood. Complementing Sugg's critique of approaches that read "transnationalism" as automatically counterhegemonic, Manuel L. Martinez is scathing of border theory's generalized privileging of the trope and metaphor of border crossings as suggestive of movement, marginality, and hybridity, and of rootlessness over rootedness because, as he explains, such a theoretical approach to the borderlands "dismisses [the migrant's] desire for arrival and stability in the national sphere by instituting permanent displacement"; such a paradigm ignores or dismisses as indicative of a "colonized false consciousness" "the displaced migrant worker who searches for a stable space in which to achieve her objective—material stability" ("Telling" 54–56). Ngai has argued, further, that the act of crossing the border illicitly in the twentieth century became laden with a powerful negative symbolism that it had not held previously: "walking (or wading) across the border emerged as the quintessential act of illegal immigration" (89). Border crossing came to connote a larger willingness to violate the law, which made Mexican border crossers undesirable entrants on purportedly moral grounds. Crossing stories in *Underground America*, when they are provided at all, are often drastically downplayed. Diana simply states that she "made the decision to go back to the United States, this time for good," and leaves it at that (20). Roberto, Olga, and Abel each devote approximately one paragraph to their crossing stories, which are clearly not the heart of their accounts (58–59, 104, 121) but only a part of a much longer testimony.

Instead, we are presented with forms of American re-inscription. Rather than instantiating illicit border crossing as the center of the paradigmatic undocumented story, these accounts are seemingly elicited, selected, and edited with an eye to the ways in which they reinforce a narrative of national belonging. Lorena, a young activist who was brought to the United States by her mother when she was six, mocks the presumption that recent immigrants don't "want" to assimilate or to become American; discussing California's law providing in-state tuition for undocumented students who have graduated from California high schools, Lorena notes that she "had to sign an affidavit stating that . . . I would get legal residency as soon as I was able to. I think that last one is for those conservatives who think we're just educating terrorists. It's pretty ludicrous. I mean, who wouldn't want to get legal residency?" (190). Roberto attempts to relocate his children narratively *into* the United States (since they have been forced to return to Mexico) through a counterdiscourse of belonging; both his daughter, who came as an infant but was deported in the sixth grade, as well as his U.S. citizen son, "really grew [up] here in San Francisco. They spent their whole lives here. They learned to speak English, and they did very well in school. . . . Jennifer especially—since she had spent nearly ten years here, she had become very accustomed to things here. . . . My children did not want to leave" (71, 73). Roberto, that is, *places* his children narratively in the United States, even though they physically reside elsewhere; it is the United States that is the narrative context for their "whole lives" and filiative attachments, the frame by which we can understand their story.

And just as these accounts emphasize the ways in which the United States is the proper "place" for/in the life stories of the narrators, so too do accounts in the collection suggest the ways in which the stories of (undocumented) immigrants are part and parcel of the larger national story. The narratives by Diana and Polo about assisting in the cleanup efforts after Hurricane Katrina, for instance, underscore the role of undocumented labor in the aftermath of events that have become constructed as national disasters and forms of American cultural trauma. Such accounts reconfigure immigrant laborers not as transnational figures with a foot in two worlds but as already American in geography, loyalties, and participation in geopolitical events; they literally write themselves into a larger, ongoing national story of recovery and healing. Other narrators, such as Abel, insist not only on the economic value of their labor but on its *national* or *symbolic* value: "I've even made police uniforms, firemen's uniforms, government officials' uniforms" (131). Sewing the nation's uniforms, the clothing that simultaneously distinguishes different kinds of laboring bodies from each other and yet signals that they are all "authorized" by the nation-state, Abel stitches himself in a wonderfully metaphorical way into the "fabric" of the nation.

Notably, bodies in *Underground America* are a common trope both for a common humanity and—albeit more subtly—for American belonging; they suggest *embodied emplacement*. Lynn Hunt suggests that the concept of inalienable human rights arose out of a context of "greater respect for bodily integrity and clearer lines of demarcation between individual bodies" (29). Inextricably linked to the act of imaginative empathy, that according to Hunt was necessary in order for notions of universal human rights to emerge, was a growing concept of *bodily inviolability* (82). Hence one of the essential human rights recognized today is the right to protect our bodies: from extreme pain, from rape, and so on. Article 3 of the Universal Declaration of Human Rights declares that "Everyone has the right to life, liberty and security of person," and Article 5 states that "No one shall be subjected to torture or to cruel, inhuman or degrading treatment or punishment." To see the emerging discourse of human rights as intimately tied to these developing notions of the inviolable human body is also to understand the ways in which discourses *of* the body are part of a larger rhetoric of the demand for recognition based on an assumption of common humanity: if you recognize the pain of my body, you are recognizing me as a fellow human being entitled to protection from the infliction of pain.

Abel's story describes in bodily terms the psychological trauma caused by the "culture of anxiety" among the undocumented (Orner 10), moving from his own case to broader generalizations:

> There are still a lot of people here who have been left traumatized because their husband or their wife has been taken away. They think that every helicopter that goes by—it's Immigration hunting for them. Some of the people who were in jail [on immigration charges], they seem scared.... They hear the wind knocking on the door. They think every sound is Immigration. So their senses are not whole anymore.
>
> It is all about fear. Fear invades us. One is always afraid.... It's like poison in your brain. (129–30)

As with other instances of *testimonio*, trauma is described in terms of psychological effects that are marked *on the body*, that become embodied. Fear is a "scarring," a "poison" that "invades" the brain. The body testifies to the trauma of an underground, undocumented existence (the senses are not whole). It counteracts that trauma by insistently reminding readers of a fundamental, shared, *physical* humanity.

A typical interpretation of the ways in which undocumented immigrants are "seen" (or perhaps, "misrecognized") in American popular culture is that they are reduced to the sheerly physical. Their bodies are racialized, and race is read as precisely the "sign" of their unbelonging; as Lázaro Lima notes in *The Latino Body*, even as far back as the Zoot Suit Riots of the 1940s (and earlier), "the Mexican body had already been represented as an interloper on the national landscape" (61). The tautology of the racial marking of Mexican bodies is that "these people are not American because they are racially different from 'real' Americans, and they are racially different because they are not Americans" (5); it is precisely this tautology that has been at stake in outcries over Arizona's SB 1070 and other such legislation that raises charges of the potential for "racial profiling." Further, undocumented immigrants (and, in the mid-twentieth century, *braceros*) are identified synecdochically in terms of the strength of their bodies; the term *braceros*, referring to those who benefited from the guest worker programs of 1942–64, and who were regarded as in many ways interchangeable with "illegal" labor, limits the person precisely to the physical body, the arm or *brazo*. As Daniel Groody puts it, "hired overseers and their bosses often view immigrants as just arms and limbs without heart or soul, unrecognized bodies viewed in terms of their profit potential rather than their human potential" (72). "Illegal" immigrants, in the national imaginary, are understood to be *manual laborers*. (It is perhaps worthy of note that the common Spanish name Manuel is, in its Anglicized form, mispronounced as a homophone of *manual*.)

Nonetheless, the reduction of immigrant to physical body is a bit more complicated than this argument might suggest. Perhaps counterintuitively, the development of immigration policy and debate in the twentieth and early twenty-first centuries has increasingly *denied* the embodiment of the "illegal" immigrant and, to the degree that the body inevitably stands as a metonym for the person, thus denied the immigrant's personhood. Ngai argues that one of the notable shifts marked by the changes in immigration policy in 1924 was the shift from *physical* inspection of immigrants (to screen for physical illnesses) to the inspection of *documents*. As a result, "The system shifted to a different, more abstract register, which privileged formal status over all else. It is this system that gave birth to what we today call the 'undocumented immigrant'" (61). According to Ngai, "The illegal alien that is abstractly defined is . . . a body stripped of individual personage" (61). I would suggest, however, that part of the stripping of personhood has to do precisely with the abstraction of the body—that is, with the *dis*-embodiment of the immigrant via the shift to "documents," with their emphasis on "authorization" to be present within the territorial boundaries of the state, over physical and psychological "personage." Whereas formerly considerations that are eminently embodied—familial relations, long-standing residency, productive contribution to the U.S. economy—weighed against the practice of deportation, as the status of documents gained primacy, the immigrant's *embodied enmeshedness* in social relations *within the United States* was gradually effaced.

In response to such a dynamic, which refuses to *see* immigrant bodies as "signs" of personhood and to read them as belonging to a larger landscape, immigrant stories call insistent attention to the bodily trauma of being undocumented, and thus reinvest the body with its "individual personage." Undocumented immigration is, among other things, a *physical* condition. It is regularly characterized by bodily trauma, as we have already seen throughout this book (rape, dehydration, hyper- and hypothermia, injury), and it leaves its signs upon the body in other ways as well. That insistence on the body in *testimonios* of the undocumented, in narratives such as Abel's, can be read as a counternarrative to the abstraction of personhood into the authority of documentation. Furthermore, this embodiment is linked representationally to the *family ties* of the immigrant; embodiment is not only or reductively physical but also signals the ways in which the immigrant is utterly intertwined—physically, biologically, socially, and psychologically—within a geographically situated network of others, such that the severing of these ties (or the threat of it) is experienced bodily.

Consider, for instance, Abel's detailed account about a workplace accident:

> There were very bad accidents. I remember one of them that happened about ten years ago. I was nearby when it happened. At the plant, there was a machine for grinding the meat of the dogfish. We'd clean the fish. . . . And then we'd put it all in a machine to be ground up. This machine was very dangerous, and no one ever explained to us how it functioned. The temperature inside reaches 180 degrees. Once we were told to clean it, to clear out the bones. To do this we had to climb inside. It was like being inside an oven. I felt like I was being burned. I climbed out to save myself. And this other person, my friend, who was still in the machine—he died. . . . It was absolutely horrible. He was in the United States with his son. I left that place after my friend's death. (124)

Abel's narrative structure here works to insistently *rehumanize* the body, to invest the "bones" that are ground up in the machine with personhood. The account literally put the human being in the place of the fish that will be ground by the machine—Abel enters the machine, where he feels like he is being baked in an oven and must leave to save himself. By this point, when we learn that another man is crushed within the machine, we have already been primed to consider the physicality of the experience: the crushed bones, the intense heat, which renders a man into the equivalent of fish meat. Abel insists on the body's physicality, and invites readers to imaginatively place themselves inside the ovenlike machine with the man who dies.

But this is not the end of the account. Abel also *reinserts* that body into a larger social network. He was the man's friend. The man also had a son. Both were in the country together. (In the detailed appendix supplied by Orner, we learn that the son actually witnessed the accident that killed his father.) The accident, in fact, is so traumatic in its effects on the human relations within which Abel's friend was enmeshed that Abel must leave his employment with the fish-processing plant. The immigrant is decidedly a biological, physical body, but that body is part of a larger, meaningful network in which "bodies" are understood as fathers, sons, friends, co-workers—not just "bones." Embodiment then becomes a way in which some of the narratives reconcile claims to "American" belonging with claims to human rights. The body is above all *human*, but it is also *emplaced*, a body that exists in a particular place and has ties to that place through family, community, and social networks.

I close by returning to Orner's optimistic faith that readers, being willing to imaginatively inhabit the shoes of another, might consequently be more likely to participate in an ethics of recognition. It is worth noting that, with reference to undocumented migrants, the cliché about walking in another person's shoes is sometimes invoked to summon up the specter of the failure of empathy, rather than the condition of its possibility. El Curita (the priest), a man held in virtual modern-day slavery in the United States, insists, "No one can know what it was really like unless they were to walk in our shoes" (176). In El Curita's understanding, walking in his shoes cannot be mere metaphor. Thus he repeatedly invokes the impossibility of full empathy in the absence of common, shared experience: "No one could really understand unless they had experienced what we had. Truly, you would have had to have lived it firsthand to know how we suffered" (176). Part of the problem, for El Curita, is his awareness of a lack of "proof"—a lack that is strikingly transposed onto the body: "We didn't have physical marks we could point to, nothing outward to show how we were being abused. But we had scars in our souls" (169).

Such comments might be read as underscoring the need for *exotopy*, the corollary of empathy—that is, as Nance explains in her gloss on Bakhtin ("Let Us Say" 62–63), the ethical necessity of recognizing that identification can never be complete, precisely because the U.S. citizen cannot fully know on emotional, psychological, and physical levels the experience of the undocumented immigrant. And that recognition, too, is vital in an ethical response that would use the particular privilege and power of citizens to advocate on behalf of the undocumented in ways that the undocumented themselves cannot. As some scholars have persuasively suggested, empathy alone cannot constitute an adequate ethical response, given that such an ethics necessarily involves the *taking of responsibility* for the claims of others.

To illustrate using a related example: Sanctuary Movement citizen-participants in the 1980s often framed their involvement in terms of shared humanity with the oppressed refugees, while simultaneously pointing attention to the specific role played by U.S. foreign policy in cases of political migration from countries such as El Salvador and Guatemala—thus summoning the *responsibility* of listeners, as U.S. citizens, to address the situation they were hearing about (Cunningham 592, Coutin 69–70). Nance postulates that the ethics of our responses to the stories of other people's suffering is conditioned by a dual movement in and back, by which we

> must embark on an imaginative passage beginning with identification with the sufferer but conclude with an assessment of [our] ... own inclination and capacity to help. ... Readers must be induced to see the speaker's suffering by imagining themselves in that same situation. Those readers must then return to their own place in the world and consider the unique ways in which that position enables them to assist others. ("Let Us Say" 62–63)

As Bakhtin puts it, empathy "must be followed by a *return* ... to my own place ..., for only from this place can the other be rendered meaningful ethically" (25–26). Participants in the Sanctuary Movement were moved both by a sense of common humanity *and* by acknowledgment of a particular role as citizens of a specific nation-state—a role which marked their separation and difference from the sanctuary recipients who offered their *testimonios*.

This larger sense of an ethics of responsibility requires *self*-recognition in addition to recognition of the Other—that is, it requires recognition of the ways in which *our own* positions within the nation-state framework make us potentially complicit in the forms of oppression and denial to which the stories of *Underground America* testify. It is crucial to note that the accounts in *Underground America* bear witness to "rights" abuses (labor exploitation, hazardous working conditions, familial separations, etc.) that are *specifically* related to undocumented status in the United States.

This sort of witnessing (in contrast to the decontextualized accounts of Central American violence provided in *Border Patrol*) confronts the tendency for readerly "absenting" with a call to responsibility. As Orner puts it, the stories illustrate the "dehumanizing lack of dignity afforded to undocumented people" (15). The abuses we are witnessing are not far removed from us but rather are on our own home turf.

Yet the text's call for a broader ethics of responsibility that would move beyond empathy is potentially flattened through the concessions to a narrative in which common humanity can be made legible only through claims to national belonging. Urrea's foreword ends with an appeal to patriotism as an avenue to redress: "Real patriots are not afraid of the truth, and they are not afraid to love the stranger" (4). Orner's introduction, likewise, rests on a note firmly grounded within the conceptual space of the nation-state and its legitimating narratives: "The people in this book are struggling the best they can to get through the day, to keep their families safe, to make a little money. . . . Is there anything more American than this? . . . There's nothing very American about not being able to speak up" (13). The call is framed entirely in terms of ideologies of nation: "we" should empathize with "them" because they are pursuing the American Dream; "we" should ensure "they" have a voice because Americans value freedom of speech. The limitations of such a framing are that the rhetorical strategies urge nationally bound *identification*, at the possible expense of *responsibility*. The testimonies in *Underground America* ultimately suggest the fear that, because the (nonbodily) scars on the souls cannot be seen—because they are not *readable* within the context of a narrative of nation—no one will know (or care) that they are there.

Unauthorized Plots

Life Writing, Transnationalism, and the Possibilities of Agency

How can writers who have never been undocumented themselves really understand the experience of an undocumented immigrant? In earlier chapters I have explored the possibilities of representation and even of solidarity via empathy. This chapter turns to firsthand accounts of "unauthorized" lives in the United States. As a literary critic, I am particularly interested in the question of life writing *as narrative*—that is, not necessarily for the factual or historical accuracy of any given account so much as for the ways in which its construction, selection, and representation of events, framing, affective content, and so on, *give meaning* to the events and sociohistorical circumstances that the narrator recounts—that is to say, give particular *kinds* of meaning to these experiences (so that they register as meaning some things and not others). What *kinds* of stories do undocumented people make of their lives, through their "emplotment" and presentation of their life experiences? Through what lenses do they read these events? How do their narratives challenge, resist, or at times reaffirm and reinforce dominant narratives of illegality and immigration? How can we perceive those narratives operative in the background? How, in sum, do the narrators of life stories who are "undocumented" make *literature* of their lives? These are the questions hovering around the margins of this chapter.

Drawing on Freire's classic *Pedagogy of the Oppressed*, William Westerman writes, "Becoming the subject, the 'active participant' in one's own history requires . . . questioning, speaking out, being critical of one's own life" (231). But it is in fact often the case that a speaking subject can *confirm*, rather than substantially question, dominant ideologies about the marginalized group from which the subject speaks. Testimonies of undocumented existence in the United States are not by definition ideologically "resistant" in every case to mainstream narratives about the undocumented (however much celebratory scholarship on oral history might posit otherwise). Telling a story is, of course, in and of itself an act of agency and an effort to control a life story; but this does not mean that the story told is *necessarily* one of ideological resistance; further, challenging some forms of discourse may in the process confirm others.

The "Gatekeeper" era of the 1990s saw the publication of two full-length narratives of the lives of undocumented immigrants. In 1991, Ramón "Tianguis" Pérez published his memoir, *Diary of an Undocumented Immigrant*, with Arte Público Press; in 2003 it appeared in the original Spanish as *Diario de un mojado*. In 1997 Dianne Walta Hart published, also through Arte Público, an oral history she had taken of an undocumented Nicaraguan woman, Yamileth: *Undocumented in L.A.* Both accounts present detailed life narratives; both strongly assert the agency of the narrator, and they resist expected models or scripts of life narrative in order to assert control over the "plots" of their stories. In the process, even while these narratives do challenge various dominant discourses of immigration and of "illegality," they also reject a trajectory of American assimilation and belonging for a more resistant, transnational narrative. In so doing, however, they unexpectedly conform to and reinforce anti-immigration rhetoric that insists on the intractable foreignness of undocumented migrant subjects.

Diary of an Undocumented Immigrant: The Impossible Subject

When Ramón "Tianguis" Pérez published *Diary of an Undocumented Immigrant* in 1991 (already in translation), it was probably the first of its kind to be published in the United States. With Operation Hold-the-Line in El Paso only two years away, and Operation Gatekeeper in San Diego only three, Pérez was obviously capitalizing on a heated escalation of debates on undocumented immigration, in order to give the as yet "unheard" side of the story: that of the undocumented immigrant himself. As Alberto Ledesma notes, Pérez's memoir "articulates key situations that enable the reader to appreciate the undocumented immigrant's 'voiceless' condition" ("Undocumented" 92).

Diary draws on the fundamental assumption that, however excluded from the public sphere by virtue of being undocumented, Pérez does have the authority to speak on the undocumented condition. Sidonie Smith and Julia Watson explain in *Reading Autobiography*:

> In the case of . . . persons unknown and marginalized by virtue of their lack of public status, appeals to the authority of experience may be explicit. Such appeals may be made on the basis of sexual, or ethnic, or racial, or religious, or national identity claims. In other words, identity confers political and communal credibility. In such cases, a previously "voiceless" narrator from a community not culturally authorized to speak . . . finds in identification the means to speak publicly. (28)

To speak explicitly *as* an undocumented person, then, as Pérez does in his *Diary of an Undocumented Immigrant*, is to *claim* the authority to speak about an experience that, generally speaking, is (still) unheard in dominant U.S. culture. It is for this reason potentially troubling that the "actual veracity of [Pérez's] autobiography cannot be verified" (Ledesma, "Undocumented" 92)—since this issue would potentially call into question his authority to speak for/as the undocumented.[1] It is also troubling that *Diary* received little attention, at the time of publication or since, as a first-person narrative about illegality. In what follows, I examine Pérez's text rhetorically for the ways in which he *inhabits* the position of authoritative "undocumented" subject and, from that position, claims agency and challenges expectations. However, Pérez's text gives us surprisingly *little* testimony about the ontological status of being *mojado*. As we shall see, Pérez's strategic occupation of the undocumented subject position is never complete, and in many ways he actively resists that positioning. His is, I suggest, a remarkably "postmodern" life narrative which self-consciously undermines the authority of its "informant" to deliver accurate information *about being an undocumented immigrant*. Instead, in positioning himself as Subject (not illegal object) of his story—as story*teller* rather than told story—Pérez withholds *himself* from readerly scrutiny.

What It Is Not: *Diary's* (Lack of) Genre

The term *life narrative* is particularly suited to a discussion of *Diary of an Undocumented Immigrant*, which is neither written as a "diary" nor easily categorizable within any of a broad range of life-writing traditions.[2] To invoke Hayden White's characterization of "emplotment" as that which "transform[s] into a story a list of historical events" such that "the reader recognizes the story being told . . . as a specific kind of story" (43),[3] *Diary*'s "plot" is not easily recognizable in terms of already well-known life-writing forms that it might be expected to inhabit. Most obviously, it is not traditional autobiography, in that it does not emphasize the "autobiographer's role as a public presence" (Smith and Watson 114), nor is it a *testimonio* in which the author/speaker, as representative subject, bears witness to social injustices. *Diary* challenges such forms of self-narration.

Despite a firm basis in the narrator's experiences *as* undocumented throughout the bulk of the account—crossing the border illicitly, seeking work and housing, laboring in the fields, in a restaurant, in cabinetry, and evading immigration officials—*Diary* conveys very little of a conventional "self." This is because a sense of "interiority" is remarkably lacking in the text. Yet the representation of "interiority" is a crucial aspect of the discursive construction of self, as Smith indicates in her claim that "the interiority or self that is said to be prior to the autobiographical expression or reflection is an *effect* of autobiographical storytelling" ("Performativity" 109). In Pérez's account, however, the observing eye is always directed not inward in reflection but outward, toward the surroundings, the people, and the practices. There is remarkably little "opinion" offered explicitly in the text; much less is there the sort of self-reflection that Western readers have come to understand as part of the autobiographical impulse, in which the author reflects on the processes that have *shaped* him or her to be the coherent "self" that narrates the text. The "I" of *Diary* observes and acts but, on the whole, does not contemplate, ponder, philosophize, express emotion, form and describe personal attachments to others, or articulate a larger worldview—not even a resistant worldview.

One effect of this removal of the overt and coherent subjectivity of the subject is that, unlike in more conventional autobiography, the subject himself is not simultaneously an object of the text. Pérez willfully refuses to make himself the object of the *imagined reader's scrutiny and judgment*, even while writing about his daily life and activities as an undocumented immigrant. Precisely for this reason—that is, because Pérez does not, within his text, elevate himself as "representative" of the experiences he describes, regardless of the title—he refuses and negates his own authority, a postmodern strategy indeed for an undocumented writer. The unnamed narrator presents himself as possessing no greater degree of self-knowledge or social consciousness at the end of the narrative than at the beginning. What might be an explanation for such a refusal of the textual authority of experience?

What It Is: The Mappings of *Diary*

One possible way of understanding *Diary of an Undocumented Immigrant* is by approaching it with an eye to the geographies it maps—especially since, as a particularly exteriorized account, it pays a great deal of attention to the details of geographic locatedness. Drawing on the work of William Boelhower, Smith and Watson have suggested that some authors, "narrating their successive displacements in the new metropolitan centers . . . register the mobility of identity in transit in the fragmented, centerless spaces of the city and the resulting nostalgia for 'a proper dwelling'" (129–30; Boelhower 279, qtd. in Smith and Watson). While Smith and Watson betray their abiding interest in the narration and/or construction of a *self* in these remarks, their provocative remarks on the "centerless" metropolitan center confronted by the migratory subject is nonetheless useful in approaching *Diary* as a peculiar sort of postmodern narrative of the absent center.

After all, the narrative of *Diary* begins with the departure north to the United States, and it ends with the migration back to Mexico. In keeping with the text's lack of interiority, the first of these book-ending decisions apparently "didn't take a lot of thinking" and is given remarkably little personal context or textual deliberation; Pérez reports that he is merely "following the tradition of the village" in migrating north (12). In between the initial departure and the return are an abundance of continuing migrations, as the narrating "I" moves from city to city and from state to state in search of employment. In this way, *Diary* is a postmodern account of being a *migratory subject*—postmodern in that the narrative subject lacks a "center" or geographical "centeredness." It is worth noting that in the Spanish version of the title, the narrator is not "undocumented" but a *mojado* or "wetback," a term which emphasizes the act of migration and the subject in transit, un-"centered."[4]

To the degree that *Diary of an Undocumented Immigrant* is an ethnographic account of undocumented and migratory existence, it is quite contradictory in its presentation of what we might term a collective "undocumented people." It certainly makes some gestures in the direction of solidarity, particularly in some of its ethnographic details describing conditions in a migrant farmworkers' labor camp: "By the time the sun has come out from behind the hills, everybody is working. Some whistle, others sing.... Every few minutes, gusts of wind come through the orchard, raising great whirlwinds of dust that leave us looking like breaded veal cutlets" (198–99). Or consider Pérez's description of cleaning the camp: "Some of the guys pull the mattresses outside and hang them in the sun; later, they beat them with sticks, creating veritable clouds of dust.... I go into the shack and, not seeing any mattresses, I pull one out of the tarps.... [W]ith some branches, we sweep the floors of the shacks until they are presentably clean. Then we prepare what will be our beds during the season" (195). Such passages as the ones above seem to be operating on a strategy that incorporates the "I" into a larger, collective "we" (even while there is little overtly critical commentary on the larger social conditions that create the possibility of labor camps such as these). To the degree that autoethnography rhetorically asserts the existence of a *self* in the context of a *community of others*, this is arguably Pérez at his most "conventional"—like other life writers of the past two hundred odd years, he is conceivably painting a *self*-portrait through this exteriorized and detailed description.

Yet Pérez is relatively uninterested in the dynamics of *testimonio*, by which one subaltern stands as synecdochic representative in a text that bears witness to injustice. Indeed, the fact that Pérez calls himself a *mojado* hardly signifies a resistant solidarity with other undocumented workers. At one point in the text Pérez actually emphasizes his *lack* of radicalization: seeking assistance with finding employment, he is told by a Cuban that they help the undocumented at a nearby church. When he finds himself at the church, he asks a woman,

> "Is this the place where you help wetbacks?" As always I use the word *mojados*.
> "*Mojados?*" she says to herself.
> Some light wrinkles cross her forehead and her eyes look to the walls, as if she expected to find an answer there. The she turns toward me with her eyes wide open, as if she was having trouble seeing. Her slight smile has vanished and now her lips are tightly shut. I feel her looking at me from head to foot.

"*Mojados?*" she repeats. . . .
"Yes," I say, baffled, "somebody told me that here you help *mojados*."
"No!" she says with cold emphasis. "Here there are no *mojados*." (72)

When the narrator, confused, returns to the Cuban, the Cuban tells him, "Undocumented worker is the correct term" (72). But the narrator continues throughout the rest of his account to use the term *mojados* (or, in the English translation, "wets" and "wetbacks"), thus thwarting any readerly expectations about a resistant coming into consciousness. If "there are no *mojados*" at the church but he calls himself a *mojado*, he is on some level erasing his presence, his capacity to be *seen* and comprehended by others, even those most likely to stand in solidarity with him.

While certainly this incident can be read as an acceptance of the label for undocumented immigrants defined by their wading or swimming through the Rio Grande—and thus of the group identity it invokes—the term *mojado* turns out to be a fluid identity rather than a stable one. At the end of his account, Pérez writes that he returned to Mexico, and "the inconveniences of a wetback's life last only until he gets home again" (237). This is to say, there is no actual *identification* between the narrator and the wetback category or label, all ethnographic impulses aside. This particular identity label is temporary and thus not one that Pérez views as grounds for a stable sense of self.

It turns out that the role the narrator occupies as "wetback" is, in fact, a fairly self-conscious performance—and one not even solidified by the accrual of repetitions. Even when speaking *as* a *mojado*, the positioning that Pérez embraces is a remarkably isolated and individualistic one which downplays solidarity with other *mojados*. In one episode, he recounts an encounter with a Peruvian undocumented immigrant who critiques U.S. society on the grounds that "They don't know that for a man to survive, he's got to have help." Yet this is a responsibility that the narrator himself is unwilling to take on: "When we reach the center of town, I say so-long to the Peruvian. He's looking for somebody to help him in the United States, and I can't be his friend" (67). The passage is intriguing for the ways in which it holds forth, albeit briefly, the possibility of "centering" or centeredness (they "reach the center of town") via cooperative solidarity and the tentative bonds forged by a shared group identity. But this possibility is just as quickly fractured as it is aired, along with the rejection even of the possibility of friendship (much less identity).

On a fundamental level, the narrator does not *identify* with other undocumented immigrants. When he explains why he has decided to leave Houston, he notes that he has no successful narrative models to buttress his hope for success there: "I have for examples young men like Chesperito, who I have seen drag his misery to the corner, feeding himself with what they give away in the mission; ... Abel, who despite his determination remains without steady work; and the old man in black gabardine, who almost certainly will end his days in nostalgia for his youth in Mexico" (86). The narrator cannot see in any of these cases any patterns for developing a satisfactory life narrative of his own; thus he distances himself from them, both literally and figuratively. The passage contains in brief, then, an illustration of what I have suggested about this memoir as a whole: that it fails to subscribe to the patterns or expectations presented by other models (or genres) of life narrative. Pérez implies that the narrating "I" actively refuses identification with the other undocumented workers around him. Without a script to follow or an interiorized, self-reflective consciousness constructing a sense of "self," Pérez's text lacks a cohesive center.

The decentered self is particularly on display in two scenes in which the narrator is expected to play the "Indian." In one, he describes his interaction with two white women in a bar. "When they ask where I come from, I tell them that I come from the state of Oaxaca, and just like the Chicanos in San Antonio, they admiringly repeat, 'Oaxaca! Oaxaca!' They, too, ask me about the magic mushrooms of María Sabinas. . . . I lie. I tell them that I am from the same town and that I eat the mushrooms regularly" (204). In another scene, he relates an exchange with some coworkers who have nicknamed him "Indian Geronimo," because he "looks like him." Of course, the only sense they have of what "Geronimo" might look like is from mainstream media—that is, it is a stereotype: "Just to tease me, every now and then one of them will begin dancing and whooping when I come by, in the manner of Indians they've seen in movies" (124). Yet the response of the narrator in both of these instances is to ironically inhabit the stereotyped role that both the white women and his workmates have constructed for him. For the white women he lies, making himself into a shamanistic "Indian"; for the coworkers, he describes appropriately barbaric customs such as hanging criminals from trees and slowly "cut[ting] pieces of flesh from [their] extremities until only [their] . . . torso and head were left" to which his companions "listen with open mouths" (124).

In this strange textual moment—in which the text self-consciously inhabits the guise of an ethnography but simultaneously admits the lie to the reader—the narrating "I" quite explicitly undermines his own authority as a reliable informant. Arguably, Pérez's narrative resists dominant scripts in the degree with which it underscores the ironic and temporary *performance* of "undocumented" stereotypes. "Undocumented" and "Indian" are both labels that Pérez can parody in order to mock readerly assumptions that they will "know" the undocumented (or the Indian) via such performances.

Yet behind the performative and postmodern aspects of the text, there is, as it turns out, a fairly predictable plot: the plot of migration *and return*. This is a plot Pérez has been familiar with before ever leaving his village:

> I noticed that going to the U.S. was a routine of village people. People went so often that it was like they were visiting a nearby city. I'd seen them leave and come home as changed people. . . . People came home with good haircuts, good clothes, and most of all, they brought dollars in their pockets. . . . It was natural for me to want to try my luck at earning dollars. (13–14)

Although Pérez describes his desires as "natural," what his own description reveals is the way in which they are *constructed* by the "plots" made available to him—plots about going to the United States, making it good, *and then coming back*. Pérez clearly *does* see his life as a story; by pointing us back, in the end, to his original motivations for going north ("Ever since the day in which I made my plans to come to the United States, it has been with the idea of earning dollars to change into pesos when I go back"), he is simply reaffirming and reifying his own life "plan," which is to make it good and then *return*. Thus, the conclusion to his story to some degree recenters this decentered "illegal" subject. His refusal of the immigrant narrative is rendered as a deliberate *decision* in which he is an agent who "plans," and it substitutes the trajectory of return for the more traditional and readily recognized immigrant story of assimilation and integration. Moments of parody aside, the emplotment of Pérez's life in narrative is not a script of immigration but of circular migration.

While the "we" that encircles undocumented immigrants in the United States is an ambiguous one, the first-person plural of Pérez's description of the Mexican village of his home is always profoundly collective, without parody or distancing: "In our village. . . . Families decorate their houses and family altars with figures cut out of paper, and they make crowns with the leaves of a type of maguey that grows in the mountains" (128–29). *Families* and *communities*—not just isolated individuals—engage in these practices, in stark juxtaposition with the relatively isolated nature of the way in which the narrator describes his situation in the North: "I also feel melancholy, because I am alone, far from my family and friends" (128). Pérez's narrative ends up not being so much a narrative of identification with undocumented immigrants in the United States as a narrative of temporary migration and return "home," thus confirming Alberto Ledesma's observation that "Although Chicana/o and Mexican narratives [about migrants] give voice to similar immigrant experiences . . . they tend to draw opposite conclusions about what immigration means, conclusions that justify permanent versus temporary migration to the United States" ("Undocumented" 87).

Preeminent in Pérez's ethnographic descriptions of his home village, however, is the necessity of detailing a culture that has already been irreparably affected by the impact of mass migration north. He begins his explanation of Carnival with the observation that it "used to be the responsibility of the village's Society of the Young, but now, everybody takes a responsibility, because so few young people remain in the village" (167). Similarly, he describes how "the old and the very young inhabit the village, because most of the young adults are wetbacks in the United States." Thus at festival time, "There are not enough people now to fill the streets with noise . . . and at night, it's as quiet as a desert" (130). Such details serve as powerful underpinning of a more modernist "nostalgia for 'a proper dwelling'" (Smith and Watson 129–30)—it is a nostalgia born not so much of the fact that *he* has left the village through migration, but of the fact that the village itself is ceasing to exist *as* "proper dwelling" because of migration. Thus the cultural traditions that Pérez describes already bear the indelible trace of their own dilution and modification. Read from this light, even the revolving-door migrant narrative is not fully available to Pérez, since the landscape when he "revolves" back will look nothing like the home he left.

Undocumented in L.A.: Unauthorized Plots

While *Diary of an Undocumented Immigrant* is a narrative written by the migrant subject himself, and then mediated by translation, *Undocumented in L.A.: An Immigrant's Story* is an oral history, mediated by transcription, selection, and organization processes, and the framing of the text with editorial commentary—as well as by translation. As a form of life narrative, oral history seems both driven by and a challenge to Karl Marx's sentiment that "they cannot represent themselves, [therefore] they must be represented" (qtd. in Fuchs and Howes 4). Oral histories of course *do* ask that the subjects represent themselves, though often in highly mediated forms which mean that they are at the same time (still) being represented by others. Because of this mediation, a central question of life writing in general is the one that has persisted for some time with regard to Latin American *testimonio*: "Any ethnographic or autoethnographic approach to life writing must . . . explore the relationship between the person who has led the life and the person or persons recording and preparing it for publication" (Fuchs and Howes 5).

Unlike *Diary of an Undocumented Immigrant, Undocumented in L.A.: An Immigrant's Story* is a much more overtly "mediated" text; it was published in 1997 "by" the transcriber/compiler/oral historian Dianne Walta Hart, who thus preserves for herself the author function—an important point for understanding the shape and thrust of the narrative taken as a whole. In general, in *Undocumented in L.A.* as a transcribed oral history that has been published in book form, questions of how framing materials may themselves shape the "plot" of the oral history narrative rise to the fore. Yamileth's testimony was transcribed in the late 1980s through early 90s, before the advent of Operation Gatekeeper and attendant rise in migrant deaths beginning in 1994. The text makes self-evident the "constructedness" of the oral history of Yamileth, which is influenced as much by the interviewer/transcriber as by Yamileth herself. Hart's introductory comments, for instance, explain her "decisions about what testimony to include in the manuscript"; selection choices were made "to provide the reader with a smoothly flowing oral history" (xxvii). Of course the criteria of what makes a "smoothly flowing" narrative are clearly subjective; we are more likely to believe, for example, that a story moves along smoothly if it fits pre-given narrative models.

The book's foreword by Ray Verzasconi, as well as the introduction by Hart, both seem to assume a narrative of gradual assimilation and integration, in which the subject of the oral history becomes ever more inextricably tied to life in the United States. Yamileth's strongly mediated text, taken as a whole, thus betrays a struggle for "authority" over the telling and interpretation of her story. Hart and Verzasconi frame it in terms of a fairly standard narrative of Americanization and eventual assimilation, even though elements of Yamileth's own telling strongly contradict this plot, suggesting instead (as in Pérez's telling) a story of transnational pulls, revolving-door migration, and a planned return to the home country. But as the combined text progresses, Yamileth's story gives signs that she feels she has lost control over its telling and trajectory, leading to a loss in her own sense of authority and agency.

The Struggle over Plot: An Immigrant's Story?

The title of the work itself—*Undocumented in L.A.: An Immigrant's Story*—runs contrary to Yamileth's sense of her own life story. While Yamileth might perhaps have had no difficulty with the term *undocumented*, as she herself narrates a persistent sense of unbelonging while within the United States, the subtitle "An Immigrant's Story" runs entirely counter to her repeated insistence that she is *not* an "immigrant"; that is, she does not plan to settle permanently in the United States but sees it as a temporary sojourn, with the "end" that she sees for herself being a permanent return to Nicaragua. In his foreword, Verzasconi notes the persistence of "Yamileth's attachment to Nicaragua"(xvi) and her original plan to "make money and return to Nicaragua where she would have a better life" (xvii). Clearly Yamileth views her departure as a temporary, not a permanent step: Verzasconi also quotes Yamileth herself as declaring, "You are made to be in your own land" (xvii), which suggests not just mere intent but philosophy, the very purposiveness of a life. As Yamileth tells her own life story, she explains that when she decided to go to the United States, her family and friends "wanted to have a farewell party, but I told them not to do that because a farewell party is when you're never going to come back.... My fear was that I might not be able to return because I'd be so far away" (10). Like the narrator of *Diary of an Undocumented Immigrant*, Yamileth clearly "plots" a return migration in her own life narrative.

Yet Verzasconi apparently takes issue with Yamileth's own view of her life pattern:

> But, as she switches from her dishes of rice and beans to hamburgers, and as she decides to learn English, one can only wonder if she, too, . . . has decided that there is no future in Nicaragua, however bleak her prospects are in South-Central Los Angeles. One wonders if she and her son will not, in an effort to overcome overt discrimination and the disadvantages of being "outsiders," become more "American" than most Americans. (xvi)

In this speculative passage, "one" surely stands in for Verzasconi, who generalizes *his* viewpoint on Yamileth's life, which clearly diverges from that offered by Yamileth herself; Yamileth's perspective, by contrast, is rendered as simply her own, individual—what she "says," rather than what a generalized "one" thinks.

Hart echoes these assumptions about the course of Yamileth's life—its predictable "plot"—in her introduction to the oral history. Hart frames Yamileth's decision to come to the United States as follows:

> That call . . . [from Yamileth to her sister up north] symbolized the beginning of her life in the United States and of the recognition of the end of her personal dream for the success of the Nicaraguan Revolution; nonetheless, had anyone had the foresight at that moment to point that out to her, she would have fiercely denied any such significance. (xxv)

Hart insists on occupying the position of knowledge *about* Yamileth's narrative that Yamileth herself, in this construction, could never provide. In giving her own interpretation of the significance of Yamileth's phone call to her sister primacy over *Yamileth's* interpretation, Hart fits Yamileth's narrative (retrospectively, of course) into a "plot," with "symbolic" meaning, that is decidedly *not the plot* Yamileth herself would choose to give her story (as both Hart and Verzasconi understand). Hart's interpretive structure suggests to readers that the possibility of Yamileth's eventual and permanent return to Nicaragua, her home country, is increasingly unlikely; instead, the conclusion of the "plot" beyond the told story itself, it is implied, will be assimilation and a life that remains here.

Yet this plotting of the "raw materials" of Yamileth's story is quite remarkable for the ways in which it denies Yamileth herself the agency to determine her own plot. For Yamileth's expressed goals, like Pérez's in *Diary of an Undocumented Immigrant*, have always been to return to her home country. Indeed, at one point late in the text, Hart notes that Yamileth "lived with what she called 'the illusion' of being able to return to Nicaragua" (124). Yet even this rendering of what would seem to be a straightforward translation of Yamileth's words (presumably "la ilusión") contains a distortion. In Spanish, *tener la ilusión de* is a false cognate of "to have the illusion of." In English, *illusion* implies falsity, as opposed to reality. In Spanish the meaning is more along the lines of having a "dream," as in Martin Luther King's "I have a dream" or Langston Hughes's "dream deferred." It might be challenging to obtain such a dream, but the possibility is nevertheless still held out as a *real* one, not a delusory fantasy. For Yamileth, returning to Nicaragua is her "dream"—a challenge, but by no means necessarily impossible. For Hart, who renders Yamileth's words in translation, it is an "illusion" that masks the "real."

Late in the text, Hart comments retrospectively on her own presumptions and attitudes about the "plot" of Yamileth's life story:

> Toward the end of the year, I realized that Yamileth and her family were becoming Nicaraguan Americans, whether they wanted to or not, and for the first time I found our cultural differences troubling.... [In Nicaragua,] as I listened to their struggle against the Somozas, to their defiance of the Contras, and to all that they lost in their hope to be free, I saw them as admirable, even virtuous.... Their roles were modest and down-to-earth, but they and thousands like them overthrew a dictator and his henchmen.... Their transition to living in the United States was awkward for me.... While they imitated the culture of the industrialized world..., it seemed to me that they often imitated the worst parts of it. (110)

Hart's description of the "awkwardness" of the trajectory of her subjects' lives suggests that those lives have deviated somewhat from the plot she *wanted* them to have. She was untroubled when they were revolutionaries in Nicaragua, fitting the script of an outgunned resistance movement fighting for a noble cause; she finds it awkward, however, when (in her eyes) they come to the United States and cease to be resistance fighters. Hart understands that Yamileth's narrated history *as an undocumented woman* is less "resistant" than it could be—less resistant, for example, than much literature of the Chicano Movement of the 1960s and 1970s. What she doesn't seem to understand is that Yamileth's story *is* in certain ways resistant, although the resistance, as with Pérez, is to the very narrative of immigrant assimilation that Hart adopts to understand her story, even while being dismayed by it.

Although I have suggested that the authorized voice in these framing narratives is that of the scholars who analyze Yamileth's narrative, Verzasconi also maintains that "Yamileth's testimony is not a Nicaraguan story; it is a universal one that has been lived and suffered by millions of immigrants over the centuries and, no doubt, will be lived and suffered by millions more" (xviii–xix). Stripping the oral history of its social and historical specificity, so that Yamileth's story can stand in for the story of immigrants "over the centuries," despite the fact that the *particular* nature of current "illegal" immigration, with its accompanying pervasive threat of deportation (which clearly haunts Yamileth's narrative), began to take shape only in *this* century (De Genova, "Legal Production" 161, 163, 167–69). Verzasconi rhetorically strips it also of any political valence with which it might be charged. Recommending the book, Verzasconi notes that "because Hart's sole concern is to provide us with in-depth insight into a recent immigrant and not to enter the debate on the pros and cons of current immigration policy, Yamileth's story allows readers to come to their own conclusions. Consequently, it is a most welcome addition" to the body of scholarship on "the subject" (xix), which remains only vaguely specified. Yamileth's story is "most welcome" because, according to Verzasconi, neither the story nor Hart's "concern" in documenting it is political; it is valuable to the degree, precisely, that it is not perceived as wading into the very debates which are likely to provide any kind of readership for the text. Yamileth's story, that is, is ostensibly valuable for being *outside of* politics. Instead, it is framed as valuable to the degree to which it conforms to the generalized script of an immigration narrative.

Verzasconi, needless to say, does not similarly refrain from politics in his foreword to the text. In long footnotes he observes, for example, that HR 123, the English Language Empowerment Act, was a "totally mangled" English-only bill; that "Despite overwhelming evidence that the vast majority of immigrants (documented and undocumented) is determined to learn English" (xiv), English-only has become a lightning rod in immigration debates; and that "many of us who are children of immigrants . . . remember how ludicrous it was . . . that, while we were required to study a foreign language in high school, we were not allowed to use any language other than English outside of the classroom" (xiv–xv). In more politically ambiguous (but still certainly political) discussion of the costs versus benefits debate, he contends that recent waves of immigrants have more access to, and therefore use more, public benefits than previous waves, of the nineteenth and early twentieth centuries (when such benefits, on the whole, did not exist) (xv–xvi). Verzasconi seems to feel it is the *job* of an introduction to lay out and delve into the "pros and cons of current immigration policy," while it is the job of the interviewee such as Yamileth *not* to do this, but to keep her narrative strictly limited to the (nonpolitical) immigrant trajectory. Thus the implicit hierarchy between scholar and "informant" is preserved and reified, and the scholar's interpretation is given priority over the "informant's," even when the scholar appears to be fairly sympathetic about egregious examples of nativism.

The Resistant Narrative

Yamileth's own account, however, bears witness to how the "personal" is in fact political, yielding traces everywhere of how immigration policy has affected her own life story. In this way, Yamileth's story, like Pérez's, is resistant in its very existence, by refusing to conform to the scripts into which it is so clearly expected to fit. Early on in the narrative, she describes her fear of dying during a border crossing—an annually increasing phenomenon that, as we have seen in other chapters, has become its own narrative of cultural trauma for the communities left behind: "I also worried about crossing the border. . . . Others said you had to cross a river, and many had drowned. Sometime earlier, five people going to the States . . . all drowned" (10). While Verzasconi rejects the importance of politics in the narrative, Yamileth displays a pressing awareness of a narrative that is quite different than that of assimilation: it is the story of death by crossing. The prominence of this narrative for molding a "life story" is underscored when Hart describes how Yamileth's sister Leticia "called from Los Angeles, her voice heavy with sadness" and told Hart that Yamileth and her nieces (with whom she was traveling) "had left Nicaragua, but that was a few weeks ago; she had heard nothing from them and was worried that they had met with some disaster" (27). It turns out, however, that Leticia and Yamileth are playing a practical joke on Hart, and that all have arrived safely. In this case, Leticia uses the knowledge of the narrative of border deaths to *subvert* it, creatively playing with the models of "undocumented narrative" that are already available to her and her sister.

Yamileth also challenges the generalized criminalization of the "illegal" immigrant in dominant discourses. Indeed, Yamileth resists doing *anything* "illegal" beyond the simple act of crossing the border (or overstaying her visa):

> People tell me I can get false documents, but I've been afraid to do that because *la migra* can catch me. They say I can deceive the government, though, but what I can't do is deceive myself. My conscience tells me not to. Besides, they'd find out and that would make me more ashamed. I don't want anyone in Nicaragua to say that we did anything dishonest. It's better to stay quietly undocumented, quietly looking for work, and not doing things we shouldn't. (95)

Clearly Yamileth is acting partly out of fear—"*la migra* can catch me"; "they'd find out"—but she lays claim to her decision as primarily one of *conscience,* that is, as an ethical one in keeping with her own system of values, in which being "dishonest" is a particularly grievous offense. By her own code of ethics—not by that of *la migra*—Yamileth sees falsification of identity as "wrong" in a way she does not of overstaying her visa. One wonders how nativist anti-immigration activists might respond to such a distinction, as it runs so counter to dominant perceptions of "illegals" as being in a *perpetual state* of illegality.[5]

Another narrative that this oral history subverts is the common one of the opportunities available in the United States. Repeatedly, Yamileth's account refers to the myth of the United States as a land of opportunity. Yamileth relates how her son, Miguel, also "wanted to go [north] because he believed, from what Leticia (Yamileth's sister) and others had told him, that it'd be like going to another world, to a paradise where everything would be within our reach" (10). Her first view of Los Angeles is described as follows: "He drove us to Los Angeles. I didn't expect the city to look like that. I had seen postcards that people sent to Nicaragua. Some of them had tall buildings with beautiful lights and the card said 'New York,' so I thought all cities, no matter what they were called, looked like that. But Los Angeles wasn't like that at all" (26). The realization that, in the fabled North, her sister's entire family lives in a single room—a grave decline in standard of living from what Yamileth and Miguel are used to in Nicaragua—brings on a particularly striking narrative treatment:

> I simply didn't know. It hadn't occurred to me that they all, including Sergio's two brothers, two sisters, and mother, lived in one room.... Imagine my surprise.... Miguel had come with all sorts of dreams, illusions, and so had the girls. All of us had our own imagined world in our heads, an image different from what was in front of us.... Leticia couldn't explain it. She tried, but for me it was too much of a surprise. (28–29)

Yamileth's *formal* presentation of her narrative here bears witness to how the collision of Leticia's deployment of the "opportunity" narrative with the perceived reality creates cultural shock for her, through the repetition of such phrases as, "I simply didn't know," "It hadn't occurred to me," "Imagine my surprise," and "I still couldn't believe it" (28–29). Yamileth repeatedly returns to the shock of recognizing that her sister's own construction of life in the United States is not true to the facts of their lives—for this narrative has clearly had a great sway over her own decisions in propelling her to come north.

The foreword by Verzasconi offers one possible explanation for the distortion of this particular narrative; it, like any story, is *motivated* in its telling:

> The vast majority [of immigrants] views the United States as a land of opportunity and, in the process, tends to exaggerate those opportunities when contacting family or friends in their native land.... [T]hose who wrote home often played up their own success as a way of "saving face." And that vision, of an America whose streets are "paved with gold," was and is reinforced by the fact that many immigrants were and still are able to send money home. (xii–xiii)

Further, Leticia also shapes her story in a particular way, because she tells the story to urge her sister to join her. For Leticia, then, the story of immigrant success becomes a strategic means of achieving certain goals, as well as of constructing her own story in the way she prefers; for Yamileth, this version of the story is a "lie" that has induced her to make decisions she understands that she would not otherwise have made.

In Yamileth's own story, the narrative of the American Dream is persistently resisted. Repeatedly throughout the oral history, for instance, she compares Nicaragua to the United States to find them equally problematic, rather than seeing the latter primarily as the land of hope: "The situation in Nicaragua is like it is everywhere. There's food, but you need money to buy it. Here in the United States there are so many things to buy, but how can you buy them without money? Here [in the United States] I feel more tension, so much so that it makes me want to cry, and I feel a desperateness" (97). Elsewhere she compares gang violence and crime in the United States to the hazardous political situation in Nicaragua:

> In Nicaragua we know who our enemies are. I can spot them by how they're dressed, by the guns they carry.... The enemy in Pico-Union is different from the enemy in Nicaragua. It's hard for me to tell what kind of person I'm meeting up with, what kind of evildoer—a rapist, a murderer—will confront me. (55)

In part, of course, Yamileth's sense that the perils of the United States are just as great as those in Nicaragua comes from her own sense of unbelonging in the former, her inability to know "what kind of person I'm meeting up with," to read whatever social cues of identification might be more available to a native. Nonetheless, comparisons hardly reaffirm the traditional immigrant narrative of America as the promised land; instead, the text continually repeats the refrain that her sojourn in the United States is temporary and that it offers her different problems—though no lesser in degree—than those in Nicaragua. Indeed, in some senses, Yamileth's account suggests a greater degree of agency available in Nicaragua than in the United States, even for women—a reversal of the standard immigrant account of women as achieving greater freedom and self-fulfillment in a post-liberation-era United States than in "machista" Latin America cultures of origin. Yamileth recalls, for instance, how "I went all over Nicaragua talking about the rights women should have, but my own nieces aren't interested. They think that since they're in the United States, a Prince Charming will give them everything they desire. The prince, though, is only a story, a legend made for children, and he doesn't exist" (106). Fully aware of the power of stories to shape the reality that we imagine for ourselves, Yamileth challenges a classic story of gender ideology with her own contrasting narrative of feminist empowerment, associating the latter with Nicaragua and the former with the United States.

By contrast, in an analytical chapter penned by Hart called "Thoughts along the Way," we get a very different accounting of the nature of differences between the two lands:

> I [Hart] remember watching her [Yamileth] one day as she approached a sink that had faucets that even those of us who have always lived here would consider unusual. She stood back and looked at the faucets, then slowly and deliberately reached out and lifted the main one. It worked! Next, she turned it to the right and felt the water, then to the left. She stepped back and smiled. (99)

From Hart's perspective, Yamileth is represented as a sort of modern-day noble savage, primarily fascinated by U.S. technology. But Yamileth presents much more of a challenge to narratives of American progress than Hart gives her credit for. When Leticia urges her to remain in the United States, rather than returning to Nicaragua, by saying, "Don't go[;] The future's here," Yamileth responds with a challenge: "What future? . . . Tell me what future you have here and what future your children have. Give me some proof. Is being in debt having a future? Not being able to pay the rent? Not being able to buy food? Never having any rest, always running? Never spending one day with your children? That's the future?" (77). Her response to her sister, as narrated in her oral history, is a direct challenge to the narrative of making good in the United States that Leticia continues to endorse and reproduce, despite all evidence to the contrary.

The Lost Subject

While the "authorizing" texts that frame Yamileth's narrative cast it as a story of assimilation and incorporation (albeit reluctant), Yamileth never narrates herself as an American or as rightfully belonging in the United States, but always as a subject plagued by unbelonging and disorientation. In one particularly resonant scene, Yamileth recalls being literally lost in a system that she cannot figure out how to navigate her way through:

> We got on the bus. The driver . . . was trying to tell me it was the wrong bus, but I didn't understand. We got another bus, and even though the driver spoke Spanish, it was the wrong bus, too. . . . After that, we ran. It was getting late, and I knew we were going to miss the train. . . . We kept running. One person told me the station was in one direction, but I was careful and asked another, who told me

> the opposite direction. . . . Could we still catch the train? . . . [The agent] told us to run. I kept saying "But where, where? I don't know where!" . . . [On the train] They handed out one of those map-like papers telling where the train went, . . . but I understood nothing. (32–33)

The passage could be a scene from a novel, so resonant with symbolism is it. Yamileth is repeatedly thwarted by her lack of understanding, even when those attempting to help her are speaking Spanish, suggesting that her confusion is not (or at least not solely) a linguistic effect but a more profound cultural one. Her disorientation is geographical in nature—she is unable to map her way through space, unable to read the maps—but it also clearly takes on existential meanings, as she is repeatedly made to "run" but doesn't "know where" to run to. Thus geographical "lostness," in Yamileth's meaning-making, becomes metonymic of a larger cultural lostness in which Yamileth senses she is in the "wrong" place but cannot find her way to a "right" one—that is, to a place of belonging.

Such rhetoric of lostness resonates with Yamileth's concern over her "illegal" status, which is a persistent strain in her self-narration. As Ngai asserts, the construction of "illegality" for the undocumented is largely dependent upon the threat of deportation, which by being nebulous and seemingly random is also omnipresent. We see the operations of the resulting, all-pervading (and regulatory) fear at work in Yamileth's account:

> I get nervous when I go near MacArthur Park. I'm afraid the authorities will catch me and send me out of the county without my being able to say good-bye. It'd be all right if *la migra* caught me with Miguel, but the possibility of being caught alone worries me so. I couldn't protest because I don't have the right. I'd have to leave without saying anything or asking for anything. . . . I don't know which people are *la migra*. I don't know who, of the people dressed in military clothes, has the right to kick someone out. I'll leave this country still not knowing who's who. So I'm afraid of going out, of even going to a restaurant, especially in Los Angeles. Many times, people have been caught in Latino restaurants and coffee shops. Whenever I go to a restaurant, I'm afraid that will happen to me. I know I'll be leaving, but I don't want them to throw me out. (56–57)

Yamileth's sense of unbelonging is intimately related to her inability to identify the *boundaries* of belonging—of "who's who." She knows, for instance, that deportations have occurred in Latino businesses, even though presumably many of these businesses are actually owned by citizens. How are the Latinos distinguished from the "illegals"? What separates them? Yet while this blurring of boundaries challenges hegemonic boundaries of belonging, Yamileth never goes so far as to challenge the fundamental claim that she doesn't have "the right" to be in the country or to protest.

Thus while on one level her insistent *refusal* to conform her narrative to the classic immigrant assimilation story can be interpreted as a form of resistance, it is surely a resistance largely conditioned by the primary premise that she cannot and never could "belong." Yamileth represents her resistance to deportation as a form of agency, but not as a challenge to constructs of the nation and its boundaries; she knows she will leave eventually to return to her home, but wants to do so on her own terms and in her own time, rather than being thrown out.

Authorized Subjects and the Loss of Authority

By contrast, the foreword by Verzasconi and the introduction by Hart both read Yamileth's return to the United States and postponement of the "final" return to Nicaragua through the lens of an immigrant assimilation plot that is clearly imposed upon Yamileth's story in opposition to her own interpretation of events. Yamileth represents her sojourn in the United States as a deliberate decision to *postpone* her return; Verzasconi and Hart, however, interpret her as falling into a narrative plot over which she exerts little control or agency. Verzasconi, for example, notes of her original decision to come north: "In her own mind, Yamileth's decision to emigrate to the United States [was] . . . a decision seemingly made without great forethought" (xvii; parentheses removed). Hart similarly notes that when Yamileth returns to the United States with her son in 1990, Hart "asked her about her resolutions to make changes in her life, [but] she would tell me only that they had left Nicaragua out of hunger" (82). While Hart is not specific about which "resolutions" she is referring to, it is clear that she reads her own question as pushing Yamileth on the subject of an agency that Yamileth has failed to live up to; Yamileth's response about leaving Nicaragua because of hunger is apparently insufficient in itself to suggest the fulfillment of any deliberate "resolutions," at least for Hart.

In general, Hart's representation of Yamileth smacks of the Western scholar-subject who "knows better" than the native informant and can play the role of judge (thus perpetuating uncomfortable dynamics within hegemonic discourses whereby the voices of the subaltern-undocumented are given no weight, are not *really* listened to). In a late episode in the oral history, for instance, Hart recounts a conversation with Yamileth about Hart's own diagnosis of cancer:

> For years I had shaken my head in dismay as I watched Yamileth and her family make major decisions based on small personal, and at times seemingly overstated, problems with the family. This time, I carefully explained to her, with the hope that someday she would apply this to her own life, that my brothers had good jobs, and that if they were to quit them in the Nicaraguan-López style to rush to my side, then we would really have problems. (103)

In this recounting, Hart clearly permits herself to judge whether Yamileth's decisions are sound or unsound, rather than allowing Yamileth to be the voice delivering judgment on her own decisions. Yamileth is cast as the naïve child, still in need of maturing and being educated by the wiser and benevolent Westerner. In this way, while seemingly more sympathetic than dominant discourses toward the plight of undocumented immigrants, Hart nonetheless composes a narrative that conforms to presumed national-cultural hierarchies of knowledge and "development." To do things according to a Nicaraguan cultural ethic, rather than a U.S.-Western one, would be to "really have problems."

What I am suggesting, of course, is that Yamileth's narrative is framed in such a way that the authority of the undocumented "voice" is repeatedly undermined in the text as a whole, despite its ostensible airing of that voice—such that the text may well end up reinforcing, rather than challenging, stereotypes that denigrate "illegals" and take for granted the superiority of U.S. citizens. The comments of one anonymous reader/reviewer on Amazon.com who self-identifies as a college student, reading the text for a class, may be particularly illuminating in this regard:

> Yamileth herself comes across as a strange character; many of the actions she takes throughout the text would very kindly be described

as "misguided" if not outright stupid. The greatest example of this is her decision to leave Oregon (where she had a satisfying job, and her son was truly happy), and return to live with her manipulative sister in Los Angeles. . . . Perhaps even more confusing is her ultimate decision to return to Nicaragua, which in some senses proves to be even worse than Los Angeles. Yamileth comes across as consistently indecisive, as well as impractical. Her dithering would be acceptable were she only by herself, but her continued decisions to deny her son happiness and stability in life reek of irresponsibility, as well as juvenility.

This response of what might be termed a "naïve" (that is, nonexpert) reader, of course, takes no account of the ways in which it is Hart's commentary, rather than Yamileth's narrative in and of itself, that *creates* the impression that Yamileth is "'misguided' if not outright stupid." After all, it is *Hart's* guidance, interjected in her own editorializing, that Yamileth is ignoring, *Hart's* preferred choices that Yamileth is rejecting. From Hart's framing, a reader may well come away with the impression that Yamileth is misguided, irresponsible, and immature.

Another way of putting this is to note that Hart judges Yamileth's actions according to a *different system of cultural values* than the one that Yamileth herself holds. Yamileth seems to resist criteria assigned by dominant U.S. culture, such as when she relates that "most parents [from her children's school] don't go to school meetings, and the school says that having to work isn't a justification to miss meetings" (58). The school touts a class- and culture-inflected ascription of "value"; Yamileth challenges it with various hypothetical counternarratives:

> Sometimes teachers don't realize what sacrifices parents make to support their children. They don't know if the head of the family is a single woman who'd have to leave work to go to the meeting, or if the day of the meeting isn't her free day, or if her children's food depends on her work. For Latinos, there must be a way to find an alternative. (58)

Yamileth does not accept the dominant culture's "value" system as her own; in its place, she poses a system where having a job that provides food for her children is of more value than the occasional parent-teacher meeting.

When Yamileth returns to the United States, this time pregnant with a daughter who is born in the United States and therefore an American citizen, her fears of deportation recur:

> I don't go out in the street, partly because I'm afraid if I go with my daughter that they might take her from me or something will happen. I don't know, there are so many things in my mind that I, instead of maturing, have become more childlike for fear of something happening to my daughter. So I don't go. I prefer to call Marisa and say, "Marisa, if you have money, bring such and such a thing." (94)

In this self-plotting of her story, Yamileth *self-consciously* narrates the precise opposite of a bildungsroman form marked by growth, knowledge, maturity, and agency. Instead, what Yamileth has "learned" that increasingly shapes her own subjectivity, according to her account, is her unbelonging and resulting helplessness—she is (in *her own* self-perception) more childlike, less able to make decisions about her movement through space, more dependent on others. Though perhaps not overtly radicalized, Yamileth's words surely present a critique of a "deportation regime" (De Genova and Peutz) that robs people of agency and freedom.

Further, as time passes, Yamileth is seemingly less *able* to narrate her own story, which becomes marked by the withholding of secrets—not from the reader but from central people in her life. And while some withholdings, such as those of Rigoberta Menchú can be read as purposeful, deliberate, and thus as manifestations of agency (Sommer, "No Secrets"), Yamileth portrays her withholdings not as motivated or strategic but instead as a consequence of shame and embarrassment at her own life decisions, suggesting a loss of control over her story. She tells Dianne Hart that when she first decided to migrate to the United States, she explained her decision to her lover, David, in Nicaragua, as follows:

> I told David I was coming here—I don't like to hide anything—but I told him it was just for three months. I'm a bit ashamed to tell him I stayed this long, a year.... [In a letter he sent me] he told me he never thought I'd do such a thing as to tell him I was leaving for a short time and then not return.... He asked if I had decided to stay here, if I no longer wanted to live in Nicaragua. That hurt. It bothered me a lot. What could I say? (72)

While one possible lens by which to understand Yamileth's actions is a feminist framework, it is important to note that, in terms of her *life narrative*, this is not the meaning that she herself gives to the events she narrates. Rather, she describes her decisions as a source of shame which inhibits her control over her own story—she doesn't like to "hide" things, but her shame drives her to conceal portions of her story, such that *narrative fails*: "What could I say"? For Yamileth, her control as a subject over the outlines of her own story seems to begin to break down as her time in the United States continues.

The most dramatic instance of what we might term Yamileth's failure of narrative occurs when she is persuaded by her sister Leticia to leave Oregon, where Yamileth has found a good position with a loving and supportive family, in order to return to Los Angeles for a "job" that, it turns out, doesn't exist. Later, Yamileth explains, "I didn't want to return to Oregon because I didn't want to see them after I had dropped everything to find a better job—after everything there had been so good—and found no job at all. . . . I'd cry at night because I didn't have enough courage to tell Miguel, 'Let's go [back] to Oregon, little one. Let's go'" (48). Once again, Yamileth's sense of shame precludes her ability to narrate: she "didn't have enough courage to *tell*." And her inability to tell the story she *wants* to tell about her own life in turn conditions her inability to *shape* her life in the way she wishes she could. It is fascinating to observe that in Yamileth's account of this moment in her life it is not any external circumstances which limit or constrain her decision making. The family she worked for in Oregon wants her back; her son urges her back; and she herself wants to return. It is, rather, a profound sense of *shame* at the course of her own life trajectory that keeps her from returning, because, in a metadiscursive way, to return would entail the necessity of *telling* this shameful narrative, as she understands it. Ironically, then, her unwillingness to *tell* a part of her narrative to a particular audience keeps her from living her life *according to* the plot she has already "told." Retrospectively, Yamileth judges her own decisions: "I made the biggest mistake of my life when I left Oregon and came back here to Los Angeles. I believed that what Leticia told me was true. . . . My head filled up with lies" (47). Increasingly, Yamileth's narrative struggles with a sense of loss of agency born of her circumstances as an undocumented migrant, despite her efforts to assert narrative control and—above all else—to resist plots imposed upon her by others.

Simultaneously, the text gives the effect of her story increasingly being wrested from her by Hart. The final chapter of the oral history, titled "The Changing Face of Los Angeles," inserts Yamileth's life narrative into the historical context of the 1992 Los Angeles Riots triggered by the verdicts in the Rodney King trial. But, although Hart tells readers in her epilogue that Yamileth gave a "lengthy testimony" in 1992, this testimony is virtually absent from the narration of the L.A. Riots, which is provided almost entirely from Hart's perspective. In this chapter, Yamileth is portrayed as caught up in a whirlwind of events occurring "outside" of her own personal story, but not as an *interpreter* of those events. Hart, for instance, notes that "There was no way for [Yamileth] to anticipate the role that the police, the gangs, an African American named Rodney King, the economy, the schools, *la migra*, and Proposition 187 would play in her future" (113). Of course there would have been no way for *anyone* to anticipate such a convergence of events, but the advantage of writing a retrospective narrative about them is that it allows the writer to "make meaning" from them. Yamileth is, for all practical purposes, denied such meaning in the book: "The immigration debate swirled around" Yamileth and other immigrants (115), without the reader ever being told how they took a position in those debates. It is Hart who reviews for us the content of the "swirling" immigration debates, the changing demographics of Los Angeles and of those who actually participated in the riots, the attitudes of Latinos themselves about the latest waves of immigration, the statistics about how many children were born to undocumented parents in Los Angeles County, and so on (113–16, 120). Hart describes Yamileth's attitudes in response to the riots through indirect discourse, with Hart as the main narrator.

Yet the one instance when we hear Yamileth commenting on the riots offers a contradictory perspective: "We're part of the family. We're all Latinos. It's not my country, but I am still ashamed of what has happened. Those of us who live here have all come with the hope of learning and advancing and not going backward, but what these people did was to go backward instead of going forward. There's no reason to come here to rob. They could have learned that in their own country and not shame the rest of us here. We're representatives, and even though we don't come from the same countries, we're all Latinos" (120–21). When Yamileth speaks through direct rather than indirect (filtered) discourse, what she "wonders" is not why Latinos did not steal more food, but why Latin American immigrants have "shamed" themselves and each other by stealing in the first place. Indeed, in this (relatively rare) moment in the narrative, Yamileth lays claim to a panethnic and cross-generational "Latino" identity, in a way that utterly contradicts Hart's implication that Yamileth distances herself from the Latino/a migrant community. It is impossible, of course, to know whether Yamileth's own attitudes were contradictory or changed over time, or whether Hart casts her own particular interpretive lens over Yamileth's expressed thoughts, and in so doing distorts them.

* * *

As I have argued, both Ramón "Tianguis" Pérez and Yamileth tell their life stories in a way which resists or refuses the immigrant assimilation story. Both Pérez and Yamileth fundamentally refuse to see themselves as immigrants who have arrived at their "destination" when they reach the United States, instead understanding themselves as part of much longer-lived and circular, revolving-door migration patterns. In this sense they provide us with more profoundly transnational sensibilities than either the narrators from *Underground America* (previous chapter) or the undocumented youth whose testimonies I discuss in chapter 6. At the same time, while Pérez maintains control over his own life story by following the "plot" he has laid out for himself, Yamileth increasingly reflects on her own sense of dramatically attenuated agency by suggesting an increasing inability to properly tell her story, and the fabric of this text, as a whole, conveys her loss of narrative control. As we shall see, the sense in which unauthorized presence in the United States entails a more or less automatic loss of voice has become an increasingly contested issue, as undocumented immigrants and activists take on the struggle to tell their own stories in compelling—and politically effective—ways.

Undocumented Testimony

American DREAMers

In *¡Marcha! Latino Chicago and the Immigrant Rights Movement*, Amalia Pallares writes, "The undocumented have always faced the fundamental question of whether they can be represented, much less represent themselves, given their lack of legal standing" (222). The undocumented have been compelled to remain in the shadows, underground, below the radar (the metaphors are numerous) because to call attention to their own situation in any public way is to immediately risk deportation. Indeed, it is for this reason that citizen Latino/as have at times felt called upon to speak out on issues of legalization (and against restrictive or punitive measures such as SB 1070) on behalf of the undocumented, who are often members of their own families or communities. (We saw how this relationship is manifested literarily in chapter 2.) Protestors who marched for immigrant rights in 2006 and 2007, marches triggered in large part by punitive bills then being considered in Congress, described themselves as having a duty and responsibility to speak for those who were unheard and "seem to have no voice in this country" (Flores-Gonzáles 206, 208–9).

Not only are the potential repercussions of speech—especially political speech—severe for the undocumented but also, because the undocumented are generally understood to be outside of the "nation" (even if inside the geographical nation-state boundaries), their speech is often given no official outlet, no possibility for a public hearing. Dominant discourse in the United States tends to construct only citizens as having rights. But to not be able to assert an *undocumented identity* as a subject, with authority on the very topic of legalization and deportation issues (which, after all, affect the undocumented most directly), is to be unable to assert subjecthood *as an undocumented person*. As Pallares has argued, activism for legalization measures on the part of unauthorized residents "clearly presents particular difficulties not only because the activists are noncitizens whose presence the state considers unlawful but also because they are viewed as the excludable Others who help to define and delimit the nation" (220)—that is to say, they are defined by dominant discourse precisely as the *non*-nation.

Because the undocumented subject is not a subject whose trauma is viewed as worthy of being recognized in the U.S. legal system, and because popular discourse denies undocumented immigrants any connection to other historical civil rights struggles with unjust laws (Pallares 223), undocumented immigrants are placed "outside of history, outside of [recognized narratives of] exploitation, and outside of the law"; thus "there is no figurative or real space in which [they] can claim any rights from the state" (224). As subjects who are physically present yet never recognized *as* subjects worthy of rights or protections, they are the "present absents" in U.S. mainstream discourse (233). Pallares comments, "It is not possible to not be seen and not be heard and [simultaneously] become a political subject" that can agitate for rights (226).

As Nancy Fraser has argued in *Scales of Justice*, noncitizens have been positioned outside of *any* theoretical understanding of the "public sphere" and thus excluded from participating in arguments about matters most pertinent to their own well-being (such as immigration policy and enforcement, possible routes to legal status, and so on). In the current model of the public sphere that still governs much theory, Fraser argues that "the subjects of justice could only be fellow members of a territorialized citizenry." Such a framing is clearly problematic, given the multiple manifestations of "globalization" and of concerns (climate change, migration) that exceed the bounds of any single nation-state. Pressing issues of this kind "prompt many to think in terms of functionally defined 'communities of risk' that expand the bounds of justice to include everyone potentially affected" (4–5). To conceive of undocumented immigrants as "outside" the nation proper is also to conceive of them as "outside" the public sphere in which the policies shaping their own life stories are debated and held up to scrutiny.[1]

Peter Nyers also raises such issues about the voices of noncitizens in debates about policies which shape their own life stories:

> Who represents those in need of protection? Can the endangered speak for themselves? What are the possibilities and constraints that (dis)allow political activism by non- or quasi-citizens? For their agency to be recognized as legitimate and heard as political, does it require mediation from other citizen groups? Most important, what implications does the activism of abject migrants have for regimes of the political that operate on the assumption that such acts of agency are, in fact, impossible? (415)

Nyers terms "abject cosmopolitanism" the practices by which undocumented immigrants (and other "abject" noncitizens) challenge their exclusion from a particular nation-state and thus in effect reimagine the terms of citizenship (417, 422).

In Bonnie Honig's conception of a democratic cosmopolitanism in *Democracy and the Foreigner*, she argues that "democracy is a form of politics in which power is not received by grateful subjects but rather is taken, redistributed, reenacted, and recirculated by way of liberty, that is, by way of popular political action" (99). Honig suggests that the issue at stake is "who has the status of a speaking being and . . . how those who are denied such a status can nonetheless make their claims or make room for themselves" (100). The concept of democratic cosmopolitanism as articulated by Honig involves "subjects who are not fully included in the system of rights and privileges in which they live" (99) who determine to lay claim to those rights and privileges, not via a preexisting claim to citizenship or belonging but via their own political activism. The narrative of democratic cosmopolitanism that Honig wants to tell is one in which the "heroes are not nationals of the regime but insist, nonetheless, on exercising national citizen rights while they are here. . . . The nation [is] not their telos. . . . [It is] a story of illegitimate demands made by people with no standing to make them, a story of people so far outside the circle of who 'counts' that they cannot make claims within the existing frames of claim making" (101). Honig's "democratic cosmopolitanism" and Nyers's "abject cosmopolitanism" both suggest subjects and activists that refuse their exclusion from full democratic participation, with all its rights and privileges, based on the principle of nation-state belonging. These formulations dovetail in intriguing ways with Appiah's "ethics of cosmopolitanism," which I discussed in chapter 3. While the latter implies the need to testify and act on behalf of others, Honig and Nyers make central the primacy of subalterns speaking for themselves.

We might understand the emerging voices of the undocumented within public debates as precisely this sort of refusal, a direct challenge to currently dominant conceptions of the public sphere. The undocumented, and particularly undocumented youth, are increasingly representing *themselves*, and telling their own stories, in response to raids and deportations that have separated undocumented parents from U.S. citizen children and undocumented spouses from citizen spouses. Arguably, this move to storytelling for political effect marks a significant development in the political agency of the undocumented, as William Westerman suggests in his contention about *testimonio's* narrators: they are "rising from a condition of being victims, objects of history, and taking charge of their history, becoming subjects, actors in it" (230). This is what Tamara, an undocumented DREAM activist that I interviewed in the fall of 2010, insisted upon as the baseline for her own activism:

> It wasn't until I started organizing with a group of undocumented people that I realized that what was missing from my organizing before was a clear perspective that it should be undocumented people who are at the head of the movement. Because the group that I'm in now and that I helped start is precisely a group where we want to say that it's about undocumented young people leading, and their decisions—our decisions—being respected. Of course, with the importance of allies and all of that stuff, but in the organizing before, what I think was really frustrating was that there are all of these citizens saying no, like you're wrong, this is the best option for you, and us thinking there's something here that doesn't make sense.[2]

Tamara insists on the right to be an activist, on her own behalf and that of other undocumented youth, rather than being an "object of history" for whom others can speak.

In a recent article decrying the infamous Arizona Senate Bill 1070 criminalizing undocumented presence in Arizona and explaining the motivation of protesters, Roberto Cintli Rodriguez suggests, "For many of us, the right to our own narrative—the right to memory" is a core value "worth getting arrested for." This sentiment—the paramount importance of the right to tell one's own story—is expressed repeatedly by DREAM activist youth. Cesar, a youth activist whom I interviewed in fall 2010, emphasized (like Tamara) that what has been absent in dominant discourses about undocumented immigration is precisely *their own narratives*:

> Many don't understand why we come to this country in the first place, or the root causes of migration, and they don't hear enough about stories such as mine. They don't understand. Just seeing, around that age [in high school], the things on the media. I just knew that this isn't right, and I knew that as immigrants, wait a minute, where's *our* voice in this whole—everything that's going on? And so that's when I decided, you know what, I need to share my story because it's stories like mine that will change people's minds and hearts.

At base, we can understand the impulse for the undocumented to begin to tell their own stories in their own way, and to lay claim to their own memories as a meaningful framework for understanding events, as in itself a challenge to processes of making history.

As Robert Perks and Alistair Thomson have explained, quite pertinently here, "Oral history has been used [by marginalized social groups] . . . to recover the experiences of the silenced; to assert new ways of understanding past and present; to engage members of an oppressed group in projects which explore experiences of both injustice and self-assertion" (184). We can understand the oral histories of DREAM activists in this dual manner—that is, as geared both toward fighting injustice with regard to immigration policy and enforcement *and* toward "self-assertion." The stories of the undocumented, thus understood, are meant not only to politicize people on immigration *but also* to demand recognition as voices worthy to speak on this subject and be heard. As we will see, the process of "self-assertion" in this case is not exclusively—or even primarily—an individual one.

Undocumented DREAMers: A New Counterpublic

While the texts I have examined thus far foreground the traumas of deaths, family member disappearances, and a "culture of anxiety," in this chapter I turn to the particular underground existence of undocumented youth. Children who had come to the United States with their undocumented parents, and who were therefore themselves undocumented, learned to live in secrecy and fear that their own status would be discovered. While other adolescents worried about dating and driving, undocumented students learned, as part of their "growing up" process, that they could not legally drive or work in the United States and could not qualify for federal financial aid. Even if they could find a way to afford college, they would not be able to legally work after graduation. Thus years in public education, sometimes an entire K–12 career, followed by a college education, led to an inevitable dead end.

The DREAM Act (Development, Relief, and Education for Alien Minors), a version of which was first proposed in Congress in 2001 (the same year as the September 11 attacks which dramatically impacted public discourse on immigration), would have granted a path to legalization for undocumented youth who had come to the United States before age sixteen, been resident in the United States continuously for at least five years, graduated from U.S. high schools, and gone on to complete at least two years of college or service in the military. But this and subsequent versions repeatedly failed to pass (Adams 545; Barron 631–35). For undocumented children, the situation has in the decade and a half since then seemed to be increasingly without hope.

I posit in this chapter that DREAM activist students are what Nancy Fraser, Michael Warner, and others have characterized as a "counterpublic"— a group that does not have equal access to the main routes of public discourse and debate. As Warner explains, counterpublics "are defined by their tension with a larger public. Their participants are marked off from persons or citizens in general. Discussion within such a public is understood to . . . [be] structured by alternative dispositions or protocols, making different assumptions about what can be said or what goes without saying. This kind of public . . . maintains at some level, conscious or not, an awareness of its subordinate status" (56). In this case, by virtue of their unauthorized presence within U.S. borders, the undocumented generally cannot even speak publicly about their status without fear of deportation, although the DREAM activists, as well as prominent figures such as journalist Jose Antonio Vargas and activist Elvira Arellano, have challenged this prohibition.

Nancy Fraser adds to our consideration of counterpublics a heightened awareness of the "dual character" of *subaltern* counterpublics: "On the one hand, they function as spaces of withdrawal and regroupment; on the other hand, they also function as bases and training grounds for agitational activities directed toward wider publics" ("Rethinking" 67–68). It is precisely this "dual character" with which I am particularly concerned in this chapter—that is, the ways in which the writing and the stories of undocumented youth are both "inwardly" and "outwardly" focused, both an intragroup exchange that helps to constitute a strong sense of group identity and a means of activism with a *testimonio* function, "directed toward wider publics." I suggest that to understand DREAM activist undocumented youth as a subaltern counterpublic is to consider not *only* the ways in which their stories function as a counternarrative to dominant discourses within the larger public sphere but *also* to take into account the ways those stories "function as spaces of withdrawal *and regroupment*"— that is, the ways in which they might operate to *construct* the identity of a particular "group" that is seen as separate from the larger civic "group" of U.S. citizens—even while, paradoxically, the ultimate goal of this subaltern counterpublic is to be included within the boundaries of that larger group. Spivak has insisted that subaltern attempts to wrest agency within the public sphere involve, precisely, "the effort to create the possibility of metonymizing oneself for making oneself a synecdoche, a part of the whole" (*An Aesthetic Education* 439). DREAM activists see their voices and stories very much as synecdochic of the larger group identity which they have painfully constructed (and continually construct) *through* the sharing of stories. They have even developed a shared repertoire of metaphors, critiques and life story "plots" in the telling of their stories, so that "self-assertion" is in fact "group assertion." I argue that the stories of undocumented activist youth engage directly with dominant discourses about "illegal" immigration but also function as forms of *group construction* and community building. The latter process is clearly a vital one in galvanizing a political movement that could then direct itself toward mainstream social views on immigration.

Further, the life narratives of DREAM activist youth of the early twenty-first century bear certain discernable similarities of form and function. They are meant to tell a *collective* story of oppression, disenfranchisement, and nonrecognition (in the existential sense: nonrecognition of the humanity of the Other and the validity of his/her claims, as in Schaffer and Smith's ethics of recognition) through individual examples that closely resemble each other despite differences in details. All the stories told in this way—even the ones that I solicited in private interviews with DREAM activists—are *meant* to be "political," in that they are clearly intended to have an impact on public discourse and on the shaping of national politics and immigration legislation.

The stories told by DREAMers are important to examine as *stories*—as narratives with particular plots and trajectories. As Perks and Thomson have noted, "Social memory and narrative form have become pivotal interpretive interests for oral historians" (270). My own study of the narratives of undocumented youth underscores the ways in which *narrative form* is intimately related to the ways in which these activists construct "social memory." Undocumented youth narratives reveal many of the same "themes," and the counterdominant discourses about unauthorized immigration in similar ways. For example, even partial narratives about the experience of undocumented youth emphasize their "innocence," their achievements, and their general worthiness of character, in opposition to the "criminality" trope that infuses much anti-immigrant rhetoric. The DREAMers also underscore their profound sense of "Americanness" rather than transnational ties or continuing allegiances to home countries—a challenge to the argument that the latest waves of Latino/a immigrants are resistant to assimilation. But in addition to noting the ways in which DREAM stories can be seen as direct counternarrative to anti-immigration discourse, it is also important, I propose, to see them as counter*narratives*—that is, to look at the *shape of the stories* themselves, their "narrative form." DREAM narrators tell stories that in many ways resemble the traditional bildungsroman plot—the coming-of-age story in which the narrator/protagonist must pass from childhood to adulthood and from innocence to knowledge or awareness.

The stories of undocumented activist youth trace an enlightenment trajectory. For instance, DREAMers often note the trauma of "first recognition" of their "illegal" status and what this means for them—in the senses of being unrecognized, unable to talk about their situation with others, limited in their human potential, lacking in shared experiences with their peers, and fundamentally alone. Part of the "plot" of the DREAMer's story is about a shedding of the *fear* of being undocumented; for undocumented activist youth, time and time again, the "enlightenment" plot is transformed into a plot about metaphorically *coming into the light* from "underground"—of moving toward the sentiment conveyed in the activist slogan, "undocumented and unafraid."

The DREAM story of coming into the open, modeled as it is on the coming-out trope of LGBTQ activists, depends on a mutual recognition and construction of a *collective* story; the *testimonios* of DREAMers are never about just themselves. Thus, as these activists tell their story, part of its coming-of-age "plot" is about the stitching together of a *new* community of undocumented activist youth. This community—they call themselves the "DREAMers"—is constructed through stories of shared experiences of marginality which are remarkably similar across state location or national origin, as well as through an invigorated sense of ethical commitment. United We DREAM, the nationwide organization, is a broad network of students who have literally created a community of undocumented youth that previously might have felt alone, isolated, ashamed—they frequently use metaphors such as living "underground" or "in the shadows"—for fear of deportation. Their slogan, in community, is "undocumented and unafraid," and they have partaken in state and national action including sit-ins, walks, and "graduation" ceremonies, calculating that deporting high-achieving undocumented students who have never known any other place as "home" could quickly become a public relations nightmare for ICE. They have spread their stories in the media, on websites (dreamactivist.org, weareamericastories.org, unitedwedream.org), on YouTube, with political representatives (including President Obama), in publications such as *Underground Undergrads* and *Papers: The Book*, and anywhere they can, in the perhaps idealistic belief that if people actually understood their stories, as human beings, they might reconsider their stance on immigration issues—or, at the very least, might come to see these youth as fundamentally "American."

Life Plots: American Dreams

What is the place of children who have spent virtually their entire lives in the United States (in many cases, literally their entire remembered lives) but who have no legal right to be here? What is their place in what Benedict Anderson calls the "imagined community" of the nation? As Leo Chavez has suggested, "The notion of imagined communities raises important questions concerning undocumented immigrants. Does the larger society imagine undocumented immigrants to be part of the community? And to what extent do undocumented immigrants imagine themselves part of the larger community?" (*Shadowed Lives* 5).

To answer the first part of Chavez's question, we might reconsider the reverberations of the terrorist attacks of September 11, 2001, on the imagined community of the nation. In the wake of 9/11, immigration enforcement was repositioned as an essential part of the war on terrorism. The functions of policing immigration both at the border and in the nation's interior were reassigned by the Homeland Security Act of 2002 to the new Department of Homeland Security (Kanstroom 96; Golash-Boza, *Immigration Nation* 47); with immigration repackaged in this manner as a "security" issue and potential terrorist threat, statistics on deportations were now touted as evidence that the United States was making itself safe from terrorists (Regan xxvii; Chertoff; Kanstroom 83; see also Cornelius). We were now to understand "terrorists" as a subset of "illegal immigrants" (L. Smith), who could never—by virtue of their inextricable association with criminal threats to the nation—actually belong to the nation.

The particular dilemma of undocumented youth—especially but perhaps not exclusively those who have become political activists on immigration issues—is that they "imagine" themselves fully as part of the larger community understood as "American" and yet *are not imagined* by the larger community as belonging to that community. This creates an irreconcilable tension in the stories of DREAM youth, who inevitably probe this contradiction like a sore wound.

In response, undocumented youth activists, fully aware of the dominant myths of American society, package their stories of "origins"—that is, of arrival within the United States—by framing these narratives in terms of the classic "American Dream" immigrant story, which they insist still belongs to them. Indeed, the name of the DREAM Act itself, and thus of the "DREAMers," relies entirely upon its evocation of this primary myth of what "America" means and stands for as a nation. The website of the "DREAM Activist Undocumented Students Action and Resource Network" quotes Harvey Milk—in an appropriation of LGBTQ rhetoric that, as we will see, is a dominant strategy of current undocumented rhetoric:

> On the Statue of Liberty it says "Give me your tired, your poor, your huddled masses yearning to be free." In the Declaration of Independence it is written, "All men are created equal and endowed with certain unalienable rights." For Mr. Briggs and Mrs. Bryant and all the bigots out there, no matter how hard you try, you can never erase those words from the Declaration of Independence! No matter how

hard you try you can never chip those words from the base of the Statue of Liberty! That is where America is!

<blockquote>Harvey Milk, DREAM Activist, "National Coming Out of the Shadows Week"</blockquote>

The fundamental rhetorical appeal of DREAM activist youth is that they *are American* already, and thus they lean heavily on forms of nationalist symbols, myths, and narratives such as those symbolized by the Statue of Liberty and encoded in notions of the "American Dream."

Cesar's life story, as he himself underscores repeatedly, "encompasses what the American Dream is about"; but more specifically, it is a story of an American Dream gone wrong through the vagaries of fate. His grandfather emigrated from Venezuela, where "he was able to realize his American dream" by working his way up in the hotel industry. He started as a banquet hall manager in the New York Hilton and, according to Cesar, he "was quite successful. He had become a citizen in '58, and by the time he was retired he was well-off. . . . He had two houses, he had accumulated some wealth." Cesar's story emphasizes success and the accumulation of property; it also emphasizes the grandfather's citizenship as a prelude to the story of his own family. Cesar's father (the grandfather's son) came to the United States when the grandfather became ill to take care of him; legalization proceedings were underway, but the grandfather (the "sponsoring" citizen family member) died before they could be completed. The father received a sizable inheritance in U.S. property and "figured that we'd be able to legalize our situation soon"—apparently not immediately realizing that his father's death had permanently shut down all avenues for legalization: "It was tough for my father to get work because with my grandfather's death, that legal process had ended, and really, he had no other . . . he didn't have any options to legalize his situation." This particular narrative, then, takes the form of an American Dream randomly interrupted by an external event beyond anyone's control or will: the death of the single U.S. citizen family member, after the family had already relocated. Later, Cesar once again returns to the theme of a failed meritocracy in telling the trajectory of his own life: "I remember I even got accepted to this magnet school, and it's for the arts. And I didn't go, because I was like, no, what's the point? It's tough, it really is tough. You lose a lot of hope. That happens to a lot of students."

James closely echoes Cesar's observations about the failed American Dream, which for him is a story of the unfulfilled promise of agency—of the ability to modify one's circumstances:

> It always just seemed so absurd to me, because—immigrants that I grew up with, that I related to, that I worked with, that I went to school with, they were people who gave their entire lives to work, to create—to make something happen, you know? I mean, we get here, and we're taught about the American Dream, and we're taught that if we show the effort, if we demonstrate our commitment, and our passion, and our determination, and resilience, that anything is possible. And we *believe* in that, from the very first day we're here. So many of us kind of hit a brick wall one day when we realize, well, yeah, you can accomplish anything you want in this country—if you have the right paperwork, if you are given the access to those privileges.

The American Dream story, as James understands it, is a story of agency and meritocracy. Based on hard work, effort, and "passion," one can achieve proportionately. For James, then, the story of his and other DREAMers' relationship to the American Dream is the story of disillusionment—the story of believing a dream that turns out to be a myth.

The failure of the American Dream becomes a key trope for undocumented activist youth, who repeatedly raise the disparity between American immigration practices and American ideals. Putting current immigration debates in the context of previous periods of American history, James expresses the view: "So little has changed. We really don't notice that we keep going in circles in the history of this country. America is supposed to be better than that." Like many other undocumented activist youth, James has developed a broad view: one which not only includes a subaltern counterpublic but also understands the situation of that counterpublic as part of a longer history of marginalized peoples. He understands, like so many before him, that the ideals and mythology of America don't always measure up to the realities of its practices. He is willing to continue to rely on the rhetoric of an "American Dream" to measure our distance from the ideals, but he is somewhat cynical that the gap can ever close.

The Recognition Scene

Another common and recurring theme in stories by undocumented youth, which initiates their narratives of enlightenment, is that many did not actually *realize* they were undocumented—or, at least, did not understand the implications of this status for their life potential and possibilities—until their teen years. James relates how "I didn't even have any idea about the fact that I had no status until I was graduating from high school." Katrina recalls that "our family had never really talked about immigration stuff. All I knew was, our immigration status was 'pending.' That's all I'd been told. That's all I really knew. It's the moment that you kind of realize that you're a DREAMer, even though you don't *know* that you're a DREAMer yet and you don't really *call* it being a dreamer." Cesar's coming to recognition about his condition is more metaphorical, a matter of realizing its significance rather than of learning factual information. He notes, "From a young age, I was aware of what was going on, I knew that we were undocumented"—but then adds the qualifier, "I really didn't know what it was, or really didn't fully comprehend it until I reached high school."

DREAM narratives often emphasize that a full understanding of their undocumented status and what it means is, in reality, a full understanding of the limitations that inhibit them. Part of James's recognition (in his discussion of the uncompleted American Dream), for example, is the realization of his limitations, of the circumstances that prevent his full agency as a human being. Alicia concurs, describing how by definition, "To me, being an undocumented immigrant meant less opportunities, less things I could do. At the end of college, I stopped studying as much, I just felt like I didn't really have a way to go. I mean what was I going to do with this degree I had? So at the end of my college career my grades dropped more because I felt like there was no real future for me." This form of realization, then, is not "enlightenment" in the sense that it is not coupled with metaphors of illumination or "seeing the light"—it is, rather, a realization of limits on one's full development.

Leo Chavez discovered in *Shadowed Lives: Undocumented Immigrants in American Society* (1998) that the undocumented migrants he interviewed used "metaphors of confinement"—including living within a circle, in a chicken coop, or in jail/a cage—to convey "what it is like to live in a state of almost constant fear" (159–60). Chavez's finding suggests the degree to which metaphorical images of this kind profoundly imbue the thinking of the undocumented. Metaphors in DREAM youth narratives frequently refer to underground, darkness, shadows, and closed doors—that is, to darkness rather than literal "enlightenment." Describing his own coming-into-awareness of his condition, Cesar notes that in his freshman year of high school

> I was filled with optimism, but by the time I had reached senior year, I remember that I really had no hope, I had lost all hope for getting a degree in higher education or just any, a bright future, basically. I really—All these doors had closed on me. And really I had no aspirations, or I didn't see the light. I really didn't fully comprehend it until I reached high school. But in high school, that's when you hit that brick wall, that's the way that we describe it. Because you just can't do, basically, you see all these closed—these doors close on you. You can't apply for scholarships, you can't do simple things, like taking driver's ed class—you're thinking oh, what's the point?

The metaphors Cesar uses to describe his growing awareness of the limitations placed on him—limitations that, he noted, were exacerbated by the event of 9/11 and the change in political climate that it precipitated regarding immigration reform—are quite striking. There is a sense of structural barriers—"all these doors had closed," "you hit that brick wall"—and a corresponding cutting off of light: no hope of "a bright future," "I didn't see the light."

The metaphor of walls that serve as visual reminders of limits and barriers is repeated later in Cesar's story, when he describes how he was part of an activist group protesting student deportations outside a detention center. "We looked over the exterior wall of the detention center, [and] we could see how they were actually expanding its construction. And that, for us, was, you know, just a visual representation of things, that things were not going the way that we wanted them to—that things were just getting worse." Cesar, who is a strikingly metaphorical thinker, even recounts an incident during a job while he was cleaning toilets and thinking "how reflective of" his situation this was, "how looking down, seeing the toilet flush, it reminded me of my *life*."

A point worth noting here is that Cesar's story also is suggestive of the degree to which the rhetoric of walls, doors, and the blocking of light (if not of flushing toilets) is already a *shared* rhetoric, crafted over time within a subaltern counterpublic: "That's the way *we describe it.*" Tamara, too, underscores the ways in which the rhetoric she draws upon to describe limitations is a shared one, learned through collective conversation and debate. She recollects, for instance, a conversation with classmates in which she tried to bring home the idea that immigrants are not just a distant, foreign other. "It's not just like those immigrants that you imagine over there in the shadows—I don't think I actually used the word *shadows*. I think that's something more recent." Tamara's rather tangential observation about her use of the word *shadows* suggests her self-consciousness about her adoption of rhetoric that has been developed by a larger community: "coming out of the shadows" has become one of the central metaphors of undocumented, DREAM activist youth.[3]

An Ethics of Recognition

For James, another DREAM activist, coming out of the shadows constitutes a direct challenge to the failure of mainstream American society to recognize the fundamental humanity of the undocumented. His story is thus, at its core, a narrative plea for what Schaffer and Smith call an "ethics of recognition." Indeed, it would seem that James's entire existential condition is shaped by the sense that he has never been recognized as "belonging" to a nation, and this was not only in the United States. James's story actually begins with a different "illegal" immigration: from Colombia, the country of his birth, to Venezuela: "And so the earliest memories of my life are of me being an infant in a country where I really wasn't allowed to be." It is this condition which later extends to his life in the United States, where in high school he started to realize the impact of his undocumented status. As with so many other DREAM youth, James's narrative emphasizes his achievements, merit, and potential social contributions, invoking an ideal of meritocracy that DREAM youth have found hollow:

> 'Cause I was at the top of my class, and I started out my senior year as valedictorian of the school, and a Golden Seniors nominee [award name changed], and hundreds of hours of community service, and recommendation letters from practically all of my teachers. As we got closer to graduation and some of my friends started

getting accepted to Ivy League schools—you know, friends that I had tutored in physics and calculus and things like that—I started hearing back from the schools that I wanted to go to, and they were telling me, "I'm sorry, but if you don't have any status, we can't allow you to register for classes." My Colombian documents had expired, so I didn't even have a passport from my home country. I literally had absolutely no form of identification from anywhere. So it was very depressing and very scary to build up so much in my life and work so hard, you know—to get to my high school graduation and then suddenly realize one day *that I practically didn't exist*, and my presence in this country wasn't really acknowledged by the system.

As with other narratives, James's "realization" is in part of *nonrecognition*—of options closing, doors shutting, lights turning off: the opposite of enlightenment. James realizes that he "practically didn't exist," that he is not *seen* by "the system" as existing, that he belongs nowhere (since even his birth country doesn't recognize his existence with proper documentation).

Eventually James was able to be legalized thanks to his stepmother, a U.S. citizen, who sponsored his application. But his related memories about finally receiving legal status are infused with his sense that he had never been recognized as belonging—or even existing:

> Because the day that the letter came in the mail, you know, it's a letter that says, "Welcome to the United States of America." And it comes with your green card. And when I got that, I really only just started crying. It felt very insulting to me, that only after thirteen, fourteen years was I going to begin to be acknowledged in the country that I called home and that I loved.

To James, being "welcomed" in a country that he does not remember ever entering is a textual denial of his entire prior existence; it is a way of saying, "Only now do we see your presence in this country; only now, for us, do you exist."

James's understanding of his situation gives the lie to a particular narrative of "illegal" immigrants as lawbreakers by their very presence. In this dominant construction, the undocumented immigrant undermines the principle of "consent" to the governing institutions of the nation-state which underlies liberal democracy, because he or she

> never consents to American laws, and "we" never consent to his presence on "our" territory. . . . He takes things from us and has nothing to offer in return. He takes up residence without permission; he is interested in social welfare state membership . . . , not citizenship . . . ; she takes services without payment. . . . In short, the "illegal" . . . slides from being a person defined by a juridical status that positions him as always already in violation of the (immigration) law into being a daily and willful lawbreaker. (Honig 96)

For DREAM students, this narrative of nonconsent and criminality is a particularly difficult one to process. Undocumented youth raised partially or entirely in the United States *do* understand and represent themselves as having "consented" to the nation, its ideals, and its prerogatives, and their narratives are replete with the ways in which they see themselves as having "given" to the social good; they thus see the withholding of consent *on the part of the nation* to be a particularly painful and arbitrary one that casts them as having violated some foundational principle by their presence which they never, in fact, "consented" to violate.

For Alicia, the in-state tuition law that was passed in her state at just the time that she entered college was pivotal, not because of the money but because it constituted a recognition *of her*, in her identity as a *student*:

> What you're giving students [with in-state tuition] is so much more than the money . . .—it was being able to become a woman . . . the feeling of being kind of American. Nobody saw me as an immigrant first, they saw me as a student first . . . and kind of that idea of you couldn't pick me out of a line of students. . . . If I was standing there, in a line of students, you could not pick me out. . . . I was a student, I went to class, . . . I did stupid things like students do.

In effect, being eligible for in-state tuition took Alicia, in her own terms, out of a metaphorical "line-up" (an image replete with criminality) and mainstreamed her. By allowing her to pay tuition as a resident of her state, the legislation acknowledged Alicia's identity on terms that she herself felt comfortable with. In effect, it gave her de facto recognition as an "American."

Identity and/in the Written Word

For undocumented students, coming to a full existential understanding of their condition is inextricably linked to the written word; undocumented youth emphasize the power of *written documents* to bestow—or withhold—a sense of identity. James explains that, because of his undocumented status, "I literally had absolutely no form of identification from anywhere. So it was very depressing [to] ... suddenly realize one day that I practically didn't exist." As we have already seen, the arrival of James's green card was a moment that provoked crisis for him, since—acknowledging for the first time his legitimate presence in the United States—it simultaneously functioned to deny all the prior years of his existence as someone who has always felt "American." James recounts crying on receiving the card because it felt so "insulting" to him. Alicia responded to her own legalization with a similar sense of outrage: "Finally, they can't do anything to me. You know, I have—I have rights. . . . Because of this . . . I remember getting the green card, and it's this stupid little card. And I was like . . . this stupid . . . fucking thing. . . . I'm sorry, but that's the word you would use. It's so stupid. It's just a card." All these young activists are pressingly aware that their identity is only recognized and legitimated by the written word, even while they react with resentment and hostility to a recognition that hinges so fully on "official" texts and documents.

Similarly, Katrina's "recognition" scene stresses the moment in which—having no memory of a time before her presence in the United States—she fully came to realize the ways in which the larger American society does not "recognize" her:

> In junior year of high school we started to take our first advanced placement tests and things like that, and like the college discussions started ... I took my SATs and did all of that good stuff, and I scored pretty well. And so the beginning of senior year, like right around Thanksgiving is when I started applying to all the different places and first, my parents being their overachiever selves, wanted me to apply to ... all of the Ivy League schools. . . . So I looked up their applications and then I noticed ... for citizenship status it was ... are you a citizen, are you a permanent resident, or are you an international student? And those were the only three options. . . . And our family had never really talked about immigration stuff. All I knew

was our immigration status was "pending." That's all I'd been told. That's all I really knew.... So with that application I was just like, well, I'm not really in any category and there's no *other* box.... It seems like from hearing other DREAMers' stories, it's the moment that you kind of realize that you're a DREAMer, even though you don't *know* that you're a DREAMer yet and you don't really *call* it being a DREAMer, it's still kind of the first time that most of us are just like, well, there *is* no box for me, so I don't really know what to do.

Katrina's narrative of her recognition scene indicates her understanding that in the "identification" documents, she literally had no identity. Teresa de Lauretis has described the role that such forms have in "identifying" us, in interpellating us into a given set of social relations (de Lauretis refers specifically to gender relations); if there is no box, it logically follows that there is no recognized set of relations to the larger social whole. It is this dilemma that Katrina encountered when she first "realized" what it means to be undocumented.

DREAMers as a Subaltern Counterpublic

But Katrina's account is also fascinating for the ways in which she clearly, retrospectively, inflects her story with a sense that she *has* found—or constructed—a set of social relations within which she sees herself as belonging: the DREAMers. Katrina moves from feeling that "*I'm* not really in any category" to noting that "from hearing other DREAMers' stories" she knows that "it's still kind of the first time that *most of us* are just like, well, there *is* no box for me." The hearing and sharing of stories *among* the undocumented youth has created a sense of group identity and vocabulary (they call themselves "DREAMers" *now*, though they might not have called it that "then")—that is, a sense of a subaltern counterpublic. For Alicia, her sense of belonging within a larger community of the "subaltern" is a more pronounced shift—from being in a relatively more dominant and privileged social class in Mexico to being a "minority" in the United States:

> For the first time I was a minority. I had always been a majority. I have always been this girl who was popular and can make fun of people. And suddenly I was not that any more.... Without thinking consciously about it, you have to make a decision about what your

values need to be and who you really want to be.... You have to kind of grow up.... I think if I would have stayed in Mexico I would be a worse person for it; I would have never had to evaluate those things.... [In Oaxaca] if you're whiter, you were thought of as being better. That's kind of something that's just engrained in the culture of Mexico.... The people that are here, a lot of them are indigenous, from little towns in Oaxaca and other places, and I had a lot in common with them.... I realized ... why have I been thinking that these people are so much different? I don't understand, because ... I have more in common with them. And suddenly there's really no difference between us.... When I'm in the store ... and somebody from a really small town, an indigenous town from Oaxaca, is in the store, they don't see me and them as different. They see us as being immigrants. And so we're in the same boat.

For Alicia, the shift in perception begins with an external gaze that homogenizes "immigrants" and places them "in the same boat." But the group identification is one that Alicia herself has accepted and internalized. Alicia connects this "realization" to her own current activism related to immigrant rights. In other words, having been inserted into a situation where she was forced to identify with the experience of the Other has been crucial to Alicia's larger sense of empathy and social responsibility, driving her to continue to do work with and for undocumented immigrants even after she herself has become legalized. Alicia has come to recognize herself in indigenous "others," in her new U.S. context.

In James's story, similarly, his activism is explained as originating in an ethics of recognition and of the construction of a subaltern counterpublic. James's profound sense of the condition of nonrecognition spurs his initial politicization: "I never wanted anybody to be treated like just a number.... We're all human beings." He describes how his own entry into the immigrant rights movement was triggered by reading the story of another undocumented youth, who was detained for his status:

When I read his story in the newspaper, it shocked me, because we were practically identical. I mean, we were the same age, from the same country, the same city, came to this country at the same age— we were the same age when we arrived to the United States, had the same grades, we lived in the same city, I mean it was just absolutely absurd. But he was in detention and I was living my everyday life.

And that's when it hit me that at any moment I could be picked up by an immigration official. At any moment.... And so I really felt like, well, if I would ever want anybody to help me in my situation, then I have to be willing to stand up for his rights.... And so that's how I got involved, working on that campaign and meeting other people in the movement.

Notable here is how James's insight reenacts moments both of profound empathy and (perhaps more unexpectedly) of exotopy as well. While James fully identifies with the student who was detained for his status, he also recognizes the differences between them: the student is detained, while James, for the moment, is not and is thus *able* to "stand up for his rights." Even in this example then, which we might construe as being about *common* cause within a particular "in-group" rather than solidarity across group lines, we can see how empathy is only part of the process of creating the impetus to act toward social justice; a return to an informed occupation of one's own social position is also crucial. (This is clearly also true of Alicia, who felt much more empowered to act on behalf of undocumented others when she herself had been legalized and could use that position, and the more risk-free voice it enabled her, on their behalf.) Nonetheless, it is also clear that, despite having never met this fellow undocumented student, James identifies with him as "the same"—the beginning of a formulation of a sense of subaltern group identity for the undocumented in James's understanding of his own situation. For James, the activism that results is one that transforms "I" into "We": his recollection that "I felt a very desperate need to take action and to do something just out of the ordinary ... something very drastic to bring attention to the issue" becomes the narrative of the origin of the "Trail of Dreams" march in which "*We* wanted it to be the start of the new decade—*we* wanted [to tell] our stories."

And, in the same way as reading the story of another undocumented youth proves pivotal for James, literally propelling him to action, he sees the telling of undocumented stories as crucial for moving to action those outside the "group," the mainstream American culture. Describing his own participation in the Trail of Dreams, James notes that "we wanted the new year to start with us telling our stories from our own mouths, not allowing the media to frame the message of who immigrants are—are supposed to be." The direction of James's comments here are twofold. Obviously he is concerned with how immigrants are "framed" by the media, that is, with how they are portrayed by, and will therefore be understood by, mainstream culture. On the other hand, his wording also reveals a concern with the process of framing itself—with *who gets to tell the story*. There is an emphasis on agency—"telling our stories from our own mouths" as opposed to "allowing" the media to have full control of the story. The words, then, point two ways—toward their representational meaning (*what* they represent, the content of their stories) and toward the politics of *who* gets to represent the undocumented. They express the exhaustion with a politics of representation in which groups with more social power or status (Latinos who are U.S. citizens, journalists, and the like) get to "represent" (in both senses) those who presumably cannot speak for themselves. One of the strident calls of undocumented activist youth is that they can.

A Culture of Anxiety

For activist youth to emerge from living an "underground" existence, in which others speak for them, to speaking for themselves, they must struggle to overcome what Orner has labeled a "culture of anxiety" in which speech about one's status is immediately associated with risk of deportation. But even to describe such a culture in retrospect is, itself, an act constitutive of group identity. James's story, for instance, posits an "in-group" that lives within this "culture" and understands it, as well as implying an "out-group" to whom it must be explained. Like many undocumented narrators, James is at pains to explain to potential mainstream audiences that, as he puts it,

> People are forced to take certain courses of action for their survival, and to care for people that they love, and to seek opportunities. And so really, when you listen to the whole story . . . you'd see that it's not as simple as: Is a certain course of action a crime or not? Should these people be punished or not? It's so much more complex than that, because there were forces, there were systems that brought people to that moment where they . . . were forced to leave their

countries, or were forced to enter countries where they were not accepted.

Pronouns in narratives of the undocumented, as I have noted throughout this book, are always telling. Here the "you" James addresses is clearly an imagined mainstream U.S. citizen audience that might assume that it's "as simple as" the word *illegal* (as in the slogan: "What part of *illegal* don't you understand?"). James hopes to complicate that projected "mainstream" understanding of unauthorized migration.

Like narrators in *The Border Patrol Ate My Dust*, James contextualizes his account with history—in this case, with the history of violence in Colombia that eventually prompted his father to leave the country permanently:

> The reason why we came to the United States was because of the situation in Colombia. It was a lot of political instability and violence. There was some sort of group in Bogota that assumed that my family had money for some reason. . . . There was a maid that worked at our house and a few times we came home and we found her tied up. They had threatened to murder her. And we got a call from the neighbors one day and they told us, just flat out, not to come home. You know, there's these men in leather jackets holding guns in front of your house and they're waiting for you to arrive from work—so please don't come. Beyond just the risk of getting hurt, in Colombia, there's always the risk of being taken. You know, Colombia's a country where one-third of the kidnappings in the world occur every year, and that's just very common—family members to be taken into the mountains and then someone else in the family will get a call demanding ransom money.

As is typical of James's account, and that of so many other undocumented narrators, he moves from his specific family history to the generalized case: the "men in leather jackets holding guns" are only a synecdoche for a larger "risk of being taken" in Colombia.

What is striking, however, is how much this language of violence—of forcible and traumatic family separation—echoes his later description of what happened when his family's political asylum applications in the United States were denied:

The letters started coming in the mail that everybody's political asylum cases were being denied. And the way the immigration system works is that once your asylum case is denied, it's like a double-edged blade. Either you get it, or you get an order of deportation. So the letter came, and they generally say you have either 30 or 60 days to pack up your things, get a plane ticket, and leave. And if you stay beyond the time that they give you, then immigration officials show up at your workplace or they show up at your house in the middle of the night and take people out of their beds and put them in the backs of vans. . . . My family that had grown to be about 22 individuals all throughout the region, little by little, everybody started being taken away and having to leave.

Narratively the scene dramatically echoes James's description of the earlier fears of "being taken" that characterized the reasons the family fled the home country to begin with.

While James was the only DREAM student I spoke with who described the possibility of deportation in precisely this way—creating a thematic and metaphorical continuity with the violence of the Latin American home country that is strikingly absent from the *Border Patrol* narratives—he was by no means the only one to underscore the profound sense of anxiety and fear that constitutes the lives of the undocumented. Cesar, too, discusses his recollections of his family's living in a "culture of anxiety": "I remember . . . living in this omnipresent fear of, if you'd get pulled over, or something like that. I still remember a couple of times in which that happened, and just my parents being really afraid, because they didn't have any papers." Alicia recollects that while she herself—perhaps (she speculates) because of her youth—did not feel as pressingly the fear that immigration would come into her house and "take" her, her mother did: "My mom was, I feel like, always the most aware and afraid of it, and you know, and she came up with a code. . . . When we first moved, she was like, if immigration is there or grabs you or something, say that 'goat legs' grabbed you." The fear was apparently so insidious that Alicia's mother felt it could only be expressed covertly, even if the worst had in fact happened.

Silencing and Trauma

For Cesar, the main impact of this omnipresent fear on his own life was *silence*—the inability to tell any portion of his story to anyone—which is one of the fundamental aspects of many definitions of trauma:

> It's a very difficult time period, because not only are you dealing with the pressures of being a teenager, but at the same time you're dealing with these additional pressures that *you don't tell anybody about*. You don't tell your high school counselor, or your professor, or your teachers that you're undocumented—it's not something that you're public about.... You're almost ashamed about it. So *you don't tell anybody*.... And *most undocumented people don't like to share stories*.

Cesar's story recollects Leigh Gilmore's assertion that autobiographical narratives of trauma are characterized by "an impossible injunction to tell what cannot, in this view, be spoken" (133), suggesting the degree to which growing up as undocumented *is* experienced as traumatic for these youth, a condition which (from the very beginning) inhibits them from shaping a life story that they can share publicly.

Similarly, for Katrina, a constitutive element of her childhood as she recalls and retells it is the silence that surrounded her—a tacit familial prohibition on talking about things openly that has prevented her from fully understanding her own life story: "No one ever tells me anything because—I guess for a lot of it maybe they just don't want to remember, or maybe they just don't want to revisit the past, I'm not really sure.... So I only know it as I've kind of pieced it together." Katrina struggles to explain the reasons for her family's silence and seems to connect it only tangentially to issues of their undocumented status:

> Our family—and I think it's partly a cultural thing and partly just a weird family thing, but I always complain that no one ever tells me anything.... I feel like always in our family—and I don't know if it's because we were so separated at the beginning, or I don't really know what it was, but it just seems like there's always kind of been a lack of personal communication. So between these two it's just kind of hard to randomly strike up a conversation, like, you know,

"What's for dinner, and why did you send me here?" . . . I have a list of things I want to know . . . *after* all this is over.

Of course, the explanations Katrina wants have precisely to do with issues of their status and the longer story of why they came to the United States. The fact that Katrina is uncertain about basic facts of her own life story is a repeated refrain in her narrative: "I was sent here. I'm not even sure if the intention was for me to stay here permanently. I'm not sure what the reasoning was. All I know is they shipped me off here." At another point, she comments that she does not actually know if her parents are still "really married" or not, because "we don't talk about things in my family . . . just because no one ever tells me." For Katrina, a constitutive factor in her narrative is precisely what cannot be told, what can never be told.

Alicia talks about the sense of silencing specifically with regard to her "abject" position as a noncitizen, excluded from the public sphere:

> I always felt like I couldn't talk. . . . I could never talk, you know. When they challenged the in-state tuition law after it passed, I became a member of LULAC so we could countersue. I was in the legal document that appears . . . listed as Member A. And we met with the lawyers . . . [but] I was never fully involved because I thought I couldn't. I was so afraid that anything would happen to me or my family that I should never really talk much. But I always felt like I had so much to say, I always felt like saying something. And I loved politics. And suddenly there was this policy that affected me directly and I couldn't talk. I could never say anything. I felt like I had really no voice, and it was so frustrating, so frustrating to me.

For Alicia, the inability to comment explicitly even on policy matters most directly impacting her is more than disenfranchisement; it is a denial of her sense of her own identity as someone who "loved politics." Indeed, she speaks of her lack of political voice in haunting terms: "I really would dream, when I was running or something, . . . I would think of what I would say to the senators who were trying to pass the DREAM. I would make up these things." Silencing, for Alicia, is experienced as deeply traumatic and personal—not only an inability to register an opinion but an encroachment on her own most deeply imagined sense of self.

Alicia actually denies having felt *fear* as an undocumented child; yet she recounts a high school episode with anorexia in terms of a lack of control over her life:

> I couldn't really tell people, like my friends, that I was undocumented; it just felt . . . [like my] life had completely changed. . . . I had my friends [in Mexico] . . . everybody [knew me] in my school . . . and no longer was I *that*, so what was I? . . . It's kind of holding on to something that you know, that you know you have control over. . . . I didn't have control over what would happen to me, really—if somebody decided to take my parents . . . I couldn't control anything else. I didn't have a car, I couldn't control where I was going, even. . . . I don't even understand that person . . . it's just not me . . . it wasn't me before and it's not me now.

Though Alicia insists that she never felt that ICE would come knocking on her door to take her or her parents—that this was a fear her mother felt more than she did—her explanation of her experience with anorexia is replete with a sense of lack of agency (she could not control what would happen to her or her parents) and voice (she could not tell her friends that she was undocumented), resulting in a profound loss of a sense of identity itself (that person was "not me"). The traumatic silence imposed on undocumented youth, who grow up feeling that they literally cannot *tell who they are*, much less fully understand and interpret their stories, must be countered with speech, as a crucial step in the growth and "enlightenment" of these youth.

Self-Education

Part of the process also involves learning to understand one's own story as *not just one's own* but as part of a larger story—not a random occurrence but a product of larger social and legal systems and intimately interconnected with the stories of others. As Barbara Myerhoff elucidates in a more general register:

> Conditions sometimes make the members of a generational cohort acutely self-conscious, and then they become active participants in their own history; they provide their own sharp, insistent definitions

of themselves, their own explanations for their past and their destiny. They are then knowing actors in a historical drama which they themselves script, rather than subjects in someone else's study. (qtd. in Westerman 230)

This is the process Cesar describes when he explains how a crucial aspect of his growth into an agentive and political *subject* involved a process of self-education:

And so I began this process of political education, through the organization as well as deconstructing everything . . . or basically just educating myself. . . . To a large extent we're ignorant to this subject. . . . Most people really don't know, don't understand the issue, because of its complexity. And to this day, I can't say I know it all, but—and the more I know, the more I realize how much I *don't* know.

Notable in Cesar's account here is (once again) a slippage of pronouns: "educating myself" slips imperceptibly into "we're ignorant to this subject" which in turn becomes "most people." It is unclear, when Cesar refers to the ignorance of most people on the subject, whether he means the American populace in general (at face value, he seems to be gesturing toward the process of the "political education" of the public, which doesn't "understand the issue") or whether he means, more specifically, *undocumented youth*, prior to their "process of political education." I would suggest that, in fact, he does not primarily have a "dominant American public sphere" in mind—at least, not yet. For bracketing his comments about the ignorance of "people" on the topic of illegal immigration are comments reflecting on *his own ignorance*. Cesar shifts from "I" to "we," clearly referring to the undocumented but still talking about an "education" process. The pronoun shifts highlight the question: *who* doesn't understand the issues? For all it seems to refer to what Fraser calls "wider publics," Cesar actually seems to be thinking first and foremost here about a subaltern counterpublic in the process of constituting itself. As Cesar says near the end of his interview, "I didn't understand my story. For many years I blamed my father for not legalizing our situation, but I didn't realize then that it's the system. . . . And those are things that I didn't understand, and I don't fully understand them now, but I see things much clearer."

Constructing a Subaltern Counterpublic

Seeing things more clearly is, of course, a more typical metaphor of enlightenment, suggesting light rather than shadows, expansiveness rather than barriers and enclosed spaces. Notably, in discussing this stage in a process of politicization and mobilization, undocumented youth have adopted and adapted from the LGBT community rhetoric associated with "coming out of the closet" as a way of suggesting an emergence from the "underground" existence of living as an undocumented person. Consider, for instance, the following call to action published on the website DREAMactivist.org:

> Congratulations! You have decided to come out of the shadows about your undocumented status. Perhaps you have finally decided to tell your friends why you haven't signed up for your drivers' ed. class or why you still don't drive to school. Maybe, you will come out to your guidance counselor, who has asked you repeatedly to turn in your college application, but you were too afraid to tell him/her that you don't have a social security number and that you still don't know how you will pay for college without financial aid. Please remember you are not alone. You are part of a large community of courageous undocumented youth who have decided to come out of the shadows about our immigration status. We live every day in fear and we are tired of it. We want to be able to talk about our lives and our stories without fearing persecution or deportation. We are not free to travel, go to school, work, live, *but we refuse to be helpless*. In the same way the LGBTQ community has historically come out, undocumented youth, some of whom are also part of the LGBTQ community, have decided to speak openly about their status. Your courage will open the way to having even more conversations about your immigration status. Sharing your stories will allow us, as a movement of undocumented youth, to grow, as we continue to learn to accept ourselves. By being more open we will begin replacing fear with courage and, ultimately, be united in our demands for change. (New York State Youth Leadership Council)

This rallying cry stresses the strength, communal identity, and agency found in the sharing of stories. Telling one's story comes to represent a conquering of the culture of anxiety in which fear of discovery renders one "helpless" (without agency to change circumstances). The site also openly promotes the stitching together of individual stories into a larger story ("even more conversations") and, eventually, an address directed outward, as well as to others in the group—as a tool in "our demands for change." Thus emergence from the underground is profoundly tied to the notion of telling one's story—both as a marker of belonging within a group identity ("undocumented") and as a *constitutive* action that participates in the building of a subaltern counterpublic (undocumented activist youth).

Indeed, part of the assertion involved in coming out is increasingly not just of identification within a particular group but of a *positive* valence to that group identity. One DREAM activist has been reported in the media (by Cuban American writer Achy Obejas) as explaining: "Last year undocumented youth began to think of undocumented as *an intrinsic part of our identity*, of who we are, and of how we experience our lives. . . . We sat in a room and said to each other that we were undocumented, and told our stories" (Obejas, "DREAM Act"). The move from "undocumented" as a shameful status to be kept hidden to an "intrinsic part of our identity" gives worth to that identity. As Alicia puts it, her "confidence that we can change something" comes, in part, *from* the more profound understanding she feels she has as a result of having been undocumented: "I have been in this spot, and I in a way know a little bit more. The wisdom that this gave me is something you can't take away from me by telling me that I was an undocumented, that I was an illegal—you cannot take it away from me."

The move to invest undocumented identity with value is echoed in some of the content of blogs and websites posted by DREAMers:

"Being undocumented is something that has given us strength and patience throughout the years. Nobody, not even the Senate, can stop us. We're here and we're not leaving, be proud and be loud!"

Angy, New York State Youth Leadership Council ("DREAM Act")

"This year, not only are we undocumented and unafraid, but we are also unapologetic. We are and we deserve to be a part of this country, and we won't let anyone tell us differently."

Reyna, Immigrant Youth Justice League, National Immigrant Youth Alliance ("DREAM Act")

While the assertion of being "unapologetic" about being unauthorized may not fit comfortably with the insistence that "we deserve to be a part of this country," the overriding rhetoric here is one which, closely paralleling moves in the LGBTQ community, replaces shame and fear with proud identification and belonging. In this sense, "undocumented and unafraid" is the rhetorical equivalent of "coming out of the closet."

"Coming out" is of course a spatial metaphor for a quality of existence that is in some sense not spatial at all—just as, Michael Warner has underscored, is "the closet" itself:

> "The closet" is a misleading spatial metaphor . . . a name for a set of assumptions in everyday life as well as in expert knowledge: assumptions about what goes without saying . . . what can be known about a person's real nature through telltale signs. . . . Yet ironically, common mythology understands the closet as an individual's lie about him- or herself. We blame people for being closeted. But the closet is better understood as the culture's problem, not the individual's. No one ever created a closet for him- or herself. People find themselves in its oppressive conditions before they know it, willy-nilly. (52)

It is certainly worth considering the ways in which this analogy might be usefully extended to the lives of the undocumented, and especially of undocumented youth who came here with their parents as children. "What goes without saying"—in this case, the normative status of citizenship—is of course in the case of the "closet" the very thing that turns out not to be true. "What can be known about a person's" *status* (that is, whether the person is "legal" or "illegal") is supposedly indicated, on some level, by degree of "Americanization." But in this case, by far the majority of DREAM activists can "pass" as citizens; they have grown up here, and many do not remember life in any other country. They wear U.S. styles, listen to U.S. music, pay attention to U.S. politics (far more than to the politics of any "home" country), and have been educated—including, quite largely, about U.S. history—in U.S. schools. They speak perfect, accentless English. The closet (or perhaps, the "underground") for them is constructed by the assumption that kids who act, dress, and speak like Anglo Americans are also Americans—unless they "come out" and reveal themselves otherwise. Undocumented youth do not move from one "space" to another when they "come out" (any more than gays or lesbians do). Rather, as is clear from the above examples, they *declare* their identity as undocumented;

"coming out" is declarative in nature. It is a speech act. When you declare your identity as undocumented, you have "come out"; simultaneously you have marked your membership in a group that is always in the process of being constituted: a subaltern counterpublic of the undocumented. In another sense, however, the condition of being undocumented is highly spatialized; typically, the undocumented have moved from a geographical space where they are authorized to be (the home country) to one where they are not (or no longer are).

While *the act of* "coming out" as undocumented does not suggest literal movement from one space to a different one, undocumented activist youth do often employ tactics related to the symbolic occupation of space in their activism—for example, by occupying a government space in a sit-in (a visual and symbolic demonstration of their insistence on the right to "be here" and of "coming out" of secret "spaces") in order to force authorities to remove them, or by declaring themselves undocumented with signs and chants as they march through city streets and plazas. "Coming out" as undocumented can, in this sense, suggest particular ways of moving through public space while identifying oneself in relation to that space.

The stories told to me by DREAM activist youth repeated and extended this complicated nexus of the overcoming of fear, the claiming of voice and authority to speak on the issue, the telling of stories, the orientation "inward" of the stories through the stitching together of group identity, and the orientation "outward" to what Fraser calls "wider publics." Tamara, who mentions late in her narrative that she "came out as part of the queer community," actually seems to view her revelation of her undocumented status as the more "personal" and difficult coming out. Tamara's full explication of her "coming out" story is fascinating and worth reproducing at some length. In this segment, she begins with discussing why, after significant media attention had already been given to her story of her undocumented status, she avoided political activism on immigration issues:

> I think that I just wanted to be a normal student, quote unquote, whatever "normal" means. And actually when I started college I also came out as part of the queer community, and I think I started focusing my activism and everything on that. I became president of a feminist organization; we organized a huge conference on

sexuality—you know, which is great, and I love, and I was a gender studies major. But I think part of me was also avoiding diving back into immigration, 'cause it felt so personal. And so it actually wasn't until my last year of college that I was taking a sociology of immigration class, and people were going around saying, "Well, isn't it true that the immigrants are taking our jobs? That they're driving down the wages?" And I just remember sitting there feeling like I couldn't seriously have a conversation with people if they didn't know what my experience was—like I feel like I couldn't talk about immigration in the abstract, 'cause it wasn't abstract. [laughs] And so that's the first time that I remember raising my hand and saying that I was undocumented and that when we're talking about immigrants, we have to realize that it's not just *those* immigrants that you imagine over there in the shadows—I don't think I actually used the word *shadows*, I think that's something more recent, but you know, that we were in the classroom, next to you. [laugh] And afterwards, my teacher told me that I should be careful, right, that I never knew like who was listening, and, you know, he was just warning me that I should be careful.

In this narrative, while *coming out* is used specifically with reference to Tamara's queer identity, rather than her undocumented identity, every other reference suggests the degree to which the latter felt more private, intimate, and personal to her (less "normal") than the former. "Diving back to immigration" is "personal," in contrast to her queer and feminist activism, in which arenas she feels she can be openly political. Tamara's undocumented status is "in the shadows" while her feminist and queer identity can be harnessed in the organizing of a conference—an arena for the *open* sharing, discussion, and debate of ideas. Even when she reveals her identity as an undocumented person in the classroom, a much more contained and localized space than a conference, although certainly still a "public" one, the revelation is immediately followed by her teacher's warning to be cautious about revealing herself—essentially, to stay in the shadows. Nonetheless, Tamara's story also highlights her sense that as an undocumented person *she* has a particular authority to speak on these issues, and she claims voice precisely on those grounds.

While Tamara's story emphasizes her individual "coming out," coming out of the shadows is also an essentially community-building process. It is about the fact that *"we* [are] in the classroom next to you," not just that "I" am. Cesar, who sees his process of "political education" as inextricable from the shedding of fear, also emphasizes from the very beginning the collectivity of this process: "Really we were beginning this process of losing the fear of being undocumented. Above all we were transforming ourselves." He describes participating in a campaign with other activist youth: "We had about 100 undocumented youth there. We're all wearing undocumented T-shirts that say, 'Undocumented,' with the words 'Notice Me' on the back." Cesar's description constitutes what theorists such as Schaffer and Smith might characterize as a demand for recognition at an ethical level; the demand to be "noticed" is of course, at its base, the demand to have the legitimacy of claims recognized. But to have impact, this demand must be collective, not just individual—a demand that requires numbers ("100 undocumented youth") for social legitimacy.

Cesar emphasizes his own coming into being as a storyteller as part of his larger process of the claiming of agency for himself:

> I knew I had to do something about it. I just knew that things weren't right.... It didn't feel right. And I felt that it was important for individuals such as myself *to share our stories,* so that people can begin this process of comprehension, and looking at things differently, *or hearing our voices as undocumented individuals.* And that's when, around that time . . . I wrote this letter that I basically sent out to national contacts, or everybody I could find online. I even sent it to Bush and Cheney.... I basically depicted my story.... I really didn't know anything about struggle. All I knew is that I just wanted to do something and advocate for immigrant rights.

Cesar's process of politicization begins with his twofold recognition that (1) "things weren't right"—that is, that there is an unjust social situation which *goes beyond his own personal situation* and which needs to be addressed—and that (2) a step in rectifying the larger situation is the *sharing of his own story,* which he immediately sees as intrinsically connected to others' sharing of their stories as well. In other words, while the first action that Cesar actually takes (in his life narrative) is the writing of a letter about his own situation to the representatives of political power and agency, even the framing of this individual act is already put in terms of a collective, although it wasn't yet collective—not the sharing of "my story" but the sharing of "our stories" and "our voices." In telling his story, even in this early instance, in other words, Cesar already was beginning to understand himself as part of a larger collective. Whether or not this accurately represents his understanding at the time—whether it accurately represents the "history" of Cesar's psychological and political development—is not as important here as the fact that this is how Cesar, in retrospect, *represents his life story*—as always-already collective.

Like others, Cesar credits that collective, communal identity with his own individual survival process and notes its necessity for those who have not yet discovered that group identity. Retrospectively, Cesar notes the impact on his own life of

> hav[ing] a support group—if you for example know that there are other students fighting for the DREAM Act and doing things about the situation, that gives you hope. And you may see things in a different light. But for most undocumented youth that are in high school, they don't know what's going on, or they don't talk about this. They don't share this with their friends. Your best friend might be undocumented as well and you can go through high school without ever sharing it. It creates this sense of isolation.

Clearly for Cesar, a first and crucial *effect* of the sharing of undocumented stories is the *overcoming of isolation* to form a "support group"—a group of people who share experiences, both in the sense of having had similar ones and in the sense of exchanging with each other the stories of those experiences, as a way of constituting group identity. It is the group identity which imbues a sense of agency and "hope," while the experience of being undocumented seems much harder to overcome in isolation. Cesar himself invokes Paulo Freire at the end of his narrative—a sign, perhaps, that his life story has indeed been shaped, retrospectively, by the reading and "political education" he has undergone (one in which Freire has been flagged as a foundational thinker), but also perhaps an indication that he accepts this framework as a legitimate one for the telling of his life story.

In Cesar's narrative, it is immediately after the writing and sharing of his individual story for the media and politicians that he brings up becoming involved with activist organizations addressing immigrant rights, an involvement he relates in terms of clear agency: "We've been fighting for the DREAM Act, advocating for immigrant rights. *We basically did it all.* . . . We did the lobbying, we did the rallies, we did the protests, we did everything. We even stopped student deportation cases. We stopped five deportations." At this point, Cesar has clearly become the subject of his own story, the agent, but also a *collective* agent; what is emphasized over and over again in his sentence structure is what "we did."

Yet while the constitution of a self-aware community or counterpublic is a positive outcome for Cesar, it is clearly not enough. At some point, the counterpublic wants to change not just self—or selves—but world: "The one thing that we realized, though, was that we were transforming ourselves, and it was good in that aspect, but things weren't changing systemically." This outwardly directed goal—toward "wider publics"— prompted a plan for undocumented youth to "walk" across the country to Washington D.C., which became the "Trail of Dreams." His description of the genesis of the "Trail of Dreams" again emphasizes the agency of his and his friends' collective activism:

> We took something that was demoralizing, and we did something about it. We weren't going to take it, and we said to ourselves, you know what, we have to do something. And José was the one that first said, "You know what? I'm walking. I'm walking to D.C. We were active. We wanted to participate. It was just a brilliant idea. It just made so much sense to me. The risks were enormous. We were talking about risking our lives, walking through the Deep South, which still has many parts which are—which have Klan activity, for example.

Cesar's description of the walk is of a refusal to accept life circumstances as they are and to commit to changing them—the very core of a definition of agency. Cesar relates his decision in terms that self-consciously reproduce his sense of agency and of calculated decision making. For Cesar, then, his life story follows a clear trajectory: from a recognition of limitations, to a growing awareness of conditions through the sharing of stories, to a sense of a larger community of undocumented youth, to a sense of collective agency.

Alicia, too, understands agency and activism as intimately linked to her ability to find her voice. Although Alicia profoundly felt her own silencing as an undocumented student, she relishes the voice she feels she was able to obtain with legal residency. She describes how, on receiving her green card, "Right then and there, I was like, I'm never—I'm *not* going to be quiet anymore. I'm not going to—I can't be afraid." She discusses the profound significance for her of "Being able to go to the House and the

Senate and tell my story." And she reflects on the ways in which she sees her voice as a tool for collective struggle:

> Now that I'm on the other side of the coin, it's like, what are we gonna do to change this horrible injustice? My story I think relatively to other people is fairly okay. But what are we going to do with immigrants that have U.S. citizen children. I feel I have a voice finally and I didn't always. And now my job is to give a voice to that, and to understand, and to hear stories and be able to talk, and to help, just one on one. Undocumented students want to hear it from somebody who's gone through it.

Having been a college student in the first year that her state passed an in-state tuition law that could potentially benefit undocumented students, Alicia knows that by sharing her "voice" with others like her she can impart crucial information about the pragmatic steps to take to benefit from the law: "If I can just take them to the office where they have to [go] and tell them what to say, and navigate them through the system, then that feels so great." The contrast to her sense of lack of control or agency when she had no voice is striking. Alicia also discussed her work with a local community activist organization that had been constituted in order to defeat proposed state anti-immigrant legislation modeled on Arizona's SB 1070. A central part of Alicia's life story, then, as she herself narrates it, is the way in which finding her own voice was a way of contributing to a collective community of undocumented immigrants.

That sense of agency, in turn, is dramatized in the sharing of stories with a larger "public sphere," in which this time the clear focus is on effecting change *external* to the group. Cesar reports:

> By the time that we started the walk, people realized its magnitude. There began to be this awareness about it, and people began noticing. We made the *Times*, *USA Today*, local newspapers, we made it in many media outlets, and it began getting a lot of attention, and people were noticing. Millions of people found out about it. It was a great success. We talked to immigrants everywhere. We would do a lot of speaking in churches, community centers, you name it. We really wanted to reach people and talk about the issue, even with people who didn't necessarily agree with our position, and really just create an awareness about it.

Cesar's account emphasizes the sharing of multiple stories (or "testimonies") as a way of *changing people*: "People were noticing." In other words, stories themselves become a form of agency, in that they change the DREAMers' environment. He ends the narrative describing activist efforts to boycott Phoenix, Arizona, in the wake of SB 1070 as well as to end 287(g) programs "which have been so harmful and detrimental to our communities." That is, Cesar's own sense of the trajectory of his narrative points to both his own profound sense of "our communities"—of subaltern counterpublics—and to the efforts of those communities to change their environments in response to political circumstances.

Failure of Stories?

A cautionary note is in order here. It is worth recalling the possibility, as Dawes worries in *That the World May Know*, that stories can fail. This is hardly a possibility toward which DREAM activists are oblivious. James, for instance, is gravely aware of the risk that the life stories shared by undocumented youth, moving and powerful though they are, might fail to provoke the required and desired response; and he conveys that anxiety, fittingly, through a story. This is his recounting of a meeting between DREAM activists and Obama: "He told me, 'Listen, I understand that you have a beautiful story of an incredible undocumented immigrant in this country who has done wonderful things and who can do so much for our nation. But just like you can tell me that story, I could find for you a million other stories of a million other people in the world that wish that they could come to the United States.'"

Rhetorically, this is a fascinating moment in James's narrative, in which Obama's discourse is integrated *into* the undocumented story and made part of its fabric, suggesting both the multivoicedness of oral histories and the reframing of speech within the context of other speech and another person's story. As Samuel Schrager argues, oral histories such as James's are polyvocal in nature. Public discourses are often integrated into oral histories, including as "quotations" interwoven into the fabric of the story, to which the narrators themselves respond (291–92). Indeed, the DREAMers are often "quoting" or indirectly paraphrasing dominant viewpoints on immigration, such as those captured by the phrasing "illegal aliens" or ascriptions of "crime" to the state of being in the country illegally—in order to reframe and counter such viewpoints. James's speech "quotes" Obama's speech as characteristic of a larger stance which he hopes to counter through his own discourse.

More to the point, however, the interweaving of Obama's words into James's narrative is a rhetorical counterpoint to the point of view that James has, up to this point, expressed regarding the power of stories to move people. This instance of polyvocality suggests, rather, the failure of stories. Because, as Dawes puts it, there are *too many* stories, those stories might not in the final analysis be effective as tools of advocacy. James's response to Obama's words is to note that "I honestly don't see that as an excuse to take away the humanity of millions of people that are living within your country." For James, the fundamental issue is the *nonrecognition of the humanity of the undocumented*; his story insists on an ethics of recognition as a counterweight to the impulse to erase the undocumented from consideration because they are not "written" into the official story of mainstream America.

James's account, and that of other DREAM activists, gives new meaning to the term *undocumented*. Some critics have pointed out that, while there are grievous problems with the labeling of unauthorized immigrants as "illegal," neither is "undocumented" unproblematic as a descriptor. For one thing, as Orner points out (12), the "undocumented" have many documents of their lives: birth certificates, baptism records, high school diplomas, family photographs. These just aren't the "right" documents, the ones that are legally recognized as authorizing their presence and belonging within the United States. For another, it can seem euphemistic, as though being without documents is an accident rather than a result of choices made (Downes). (And we might add that those choices certainly include the passage of some pieces of legislation rather than others, not just the choice to enter the country or not.) But to read the narratives of undocumented youth is to understand the ways in which they are trying to *document themselves*—to tell stories that have not been told, and to tell those stories explicitly as *part of a national story*. "Undocumented" in this larger, symbolic understanding, becomes itself an appeal for an ethics of recognition: We are here. We are a part of you. Do not ignore us. Take account of us. Take us into account.

Conclusion

Although the dominant rhetoric in the media about "illegal" immigration continues to be that undocumented immigrants are not, and can never be, part of the "American" nation, as we have seen, stories by Latino/a writers as well as by the undocumented themselves are increasingly challenging such discourse. The New Sanctuary Movement constituted an effort to give a public hearing to the personal stories of families at risk of being separated because of immigration proceedings (Caminero-Santangelo, "The Voice"). It was inspired in part by Elvira Arellano, an undocumented Mexican immigrant and the mother of a young U.S. citizen son. Arellano became the first prominent spokesperson of the undocumented when she took sanctuary in a Chicago church in 2006–7 in order to avoid deportation. As she explained later, "I wanted to talk about what was happening in my case in particular and to call attention . . . to what is going on . . . and ask what we want to do about it. I wanted to give us a voice" (Terry 43). Upon leaving her yearlong sanctuary, Arellano declared in a public statement:

> I believe . . . that we must come forward in the witness of faith to bring a resolution to this crisis. . . . On September 12th, I will go to Washington, D.C. I will go to pray and fast in front of the Congress. . . . But I ask my community, the families facing separation, to join me. . . . I ask all people of conscience and good will to join me. . . . Together in faith and prayer I hope that we can join together to heal the will that is broken in Congress. (Arellano, "Statement")

Arellano's call imagined forth a collective "people" formed out of the challenges of immigration legislation and enforcement, and recognized that this collective extended—that it *must,* of necessity, extend—beyond the undocumented themselves.

Arellano's very public "coming out of the shadows" was eventually followed by an even more public statement by Pulitzer Prize–winning journalist Jose Antonio Vargas, who revealed his own undocumented status in 2011. Vargas launched the "Define American" campaign in a specific effort to present a challenge to the dominant narratives that define the U.S. "nation" in narrow and exclusive ways. In a similar vein, the "We Are America" project posts personal stories of the undocumented on its website and in YouTube videos. A *Time* magazine cover for June 25, 2013, featuring a picture of Jose Antonio Vargas leading a crowd of others, carried the headline "We Are Americans" and then, asterisked and in smaller print, "Just Not Legally."

In a Facebook post in summer 2012, Vargas wrote, "In this golden age of story-sharing—powered by social media and technology—storytelling has been at the heart of the modern immigrant rights movement. Led by DREAMers, who insist on being seen and heard fully and humanely, telling our stories, individually and collectively, has been a true game-changer. Let's keep doing it." Immigrant rights movements such as the New Sanctuary Movement and the Dream Activist movement, and prominent undocumented figures such as Elvira Arellano and Jose Antonio Vargas, have in the past decade begun to make undocumented voices more "hearable." The United We DREAM website has claimed credit for having pressured Obama to issue the memo which instantiated the new DACA (Deferred Action for Childhood Arrival) provisions, announced by Obama in June 2013, allowing undocumented youth who arrived in the United States as children to defer deportation and obtain work permits. No doubt, the persistent efforts of DREAM Activists and others raising their voices were instrumental in this development. In June 2013, the "Immigration Modernization Act," an immigration reform bill that would have offered many undocumented immigrants a path to citizenship, was passed by the U.S. Senate in a bipartisan vote, but it was never brought to the floor of the House of Representatives. In November 2014, declaring frustration at congressional failure to pass comprehensive immigration reform, Obama announced a new executive action granting temporary legal status and work permits to qualifying undocumented immigrants.

In December, seventeen states filed a constitutional challenge to the action in federal court.

And the struggle continues.

James Dawes asks, "When does the story become real enough to change you?" (7). Perhaps it is fair to speculate that no one story by itself can change the landscape of immigration in the United States. What is needed, and what we have witnessed, is a mass mobilization of stories, including the stories of Latino/a writers who have come to see themselves as inextricably tied to this larger community. Perhaps it is just possible that this unprecedented telling of the stories of the undocumented might, in fact, change lives.

Notes

Introduction

1. Anzaldúa was, of course, hardly ignorant when she was writing *Borderlands/La Frontera* of the situation of undocumented immigrants and border crossers—indeed, the first chapter of *Borderlands* ends with a section titled "*El cruzar del mojado*/Illegal Crossing."

2. Under the 1986 Immigration Reform and Control Act, those who knowingly employed undocumented workers could for the first time be subject to sanctions under federal law (Ellingwood 25). In practice, however, since employers did not need to ascertain the validity of documents, the employer sanction provision simply generated an industry in the production of fraudulent documents (Golash-Boza, *Immigration Nation* 38; Andreas 86, 101).

3. Between 1987 (after the passage of IRCA) and 1989, three news magazine covers featured the topic of immigration. By contrast, between 1992 and 1994, eighteen magazine covers featured the topic of immigration (Chavez, *Covering Immigration* 134–36).

4. Launched in 1954, Operation Wetback involved massive sweeps to deport undocumented agricultural workers in the U.S. Southwest. In the first three months alone, approximately 170,000 laborers were deported to Mexico (Andreas 34; Ngai 156).

5. See, for example, Weisberg and Adler.

6. In 1993 Immigration and Naturalization Service commissioner Doris Meissner told Congress, "Responding to the likely short- to medium-term impacts of NAFTA will require strengthening our enforcement efforts along the border" (qtd. in Nevins, *Dying* 114).

7. In the original Sanctuary Movement of the 1980s, U.S. churches offered "sanctuary" to refugees fleeing repressive Central American regimes.

8. A note on terminology: while "American" can certainly refer to all those who live on either North or South American continents, in the context of "imagined communities" the term has particular weight and heft, whether rightly or wrongly, as a term referring to *national belonging*. In this context, it has a valence that is without substitution; to say "I am a U.S. citizen" is to assert legal status, not the *feeling of belonging to a nation*. U.S. citizens have no English equivalent for the term *estadounidense* [a United States-er]

to express such belonging; it can only be conveyed by saying, "I am American." I therefore use the term throughout this book when I wish to invoke such a constructed sense of national membership, belonging, and participation.

9. See, for example, Debra Castillo, *Redreaming America*, 2, 8, 10.

10. During the Chicano movement, the interests of Mexican nationals within the U.S. borders (whether *braceros* or undocumented laborers) and those of Chicano workers were fundamentally opposed, with the latter seeing the former as cheap labor competition who disrupted their ability to organize (Ngai 158).

11. Observing that trauma victims "frequently remark that they are not the same people they were before they were traumatized," Brison notes that one paradigmatic concept of the "self"—inherited from Locke—has to do with "a set of continuous memories, a kind of ongoing narrative of one's past that is extended with each new experience" (41). A disruption of the *narrative* of self (through the intrusion of an event that does not "fit") is therefore coextensive with the disruption of self itself.

12. See, for instance, Povinelli, esp. 111–21.

Chapter 1. Narrating the Non-Nation: Literary Journalism and "Illegal" Border Crossings

1. Arizona's SB 1070, signed into law by Governor Jan Brewer in April 2010, required law enforcement officers to check immigration status if officers have "reasonable" suspicion that the person detained is undocumented. It became a crime for noncitizens to be without their immigration papers and the law prohibited undocumented immigrants from seeking work. AZ SB 1070 sparked significant protest as well as boycotts of travel to Arizona.

2. See, for instance, Auster, Buchanan, Dougherty, Brimelow, and Huntington.

3. On *testimonio* as a first-person, witness-participant account, see Yúdice 54. On *testimonio* as giving voice to the subaltern, see Beverley 19, 82–84; Yúdice 42; Craft 185; Sommer, "No Secrets" 134.

4. Urrea's *The Devil's Highway* was a finalist for the Pulitzer Prize; the six-part *Los Angeles Times* series upon which *Enrique's Journey* was based won Nazario the 2003 Pulitzer Prize in feature writing; Martínez was awarded a Lannan Literary Fellowship in 2002 after the publication of *Crossing Over*. All three books made several "best books" lists.

5. See, for instance, the following reviews: Bilger; Cowie; Dunham; Manuel Martinez, "Humanizing"; Medina, "Baptism" and "Families"; Montgomery-Fate; Ribadeneira; Turakhia; Urrea, "Lost"; Wildman; Wilson.

Chapter 2. The Lost Ones: Post-Gatekeeper Border Fictions and the Construction of Cultural Trauma

1. Two days later the same volunteer, Dan Millis, was issued a ticket for "littering" for leaving gallon jugs of water at strategic points in Buenos Aires National Wildlife Refuge. This scenario was repeated in 2009 with the cases of several other volunteers who were charged with "knowingly littering" for leaving water in the desert. Most of the latter cases were eventually dismissed.

2. Estimates are, for example, that by 1985, the dead and disappeared in Guatemala numbered 75,000 (Gonzalez 138); in El Salvador, the estimated number of dead and

disappeared reached 87,000 by 1991 (Stephen 808). In Argentina, the Mothers of the Plaza de Mayo place the total figure at 30,000 (Feitlowitz ix, 257).

3. Urrea and Ramos describe the stages of death by hyperthermia; Nazario details the many hazards—including theft, rape, and loss of limbs by train—that accompany crossing the border; Annerino includes photographs of corpses found in the desert.

4. On the testimonial novel and its relation to *testimonio*, see Craft.

5. The novels by Castillo, Grande, and Straight have yet to be the subject of significant literary scholarship.

6. "Corpses," Katherine Verdery observes, are an "important means of *localizing* a claim" about violence or injustice (27–28).

7. Feldman notes that the Mothers of the Plaza de Mayo in Argentina have "refuse[d] a final state-sponsored memorial for their disappeared children precisely because such commemoration would subject the politically deleted and absent to biographical closure, and thus excuse the state from ongoing historical accountability" (166). Participants of border vigils, likewise, insist performatively upon the recurring and repeated nature of such deaths, holding government policies accountable.

8. The words are an obvious allusion to Tomás Rivera's short story cycle of migrant workers, *Y no se lo tragó la tierra*.

Chapter 3. The Caribbean Difference: Imagining Trans-Status Communities

1. See, for instance, De Genova, "Legal Production."

2. Of the Dominicans living in the United States, 56 percent are immigrants and only 48 percent of this immigrant population are U.S. citizens (Brown and Patten).

3. Duany reports that the percentage of undocumented to documented Dominican immigrants in Puerto Rico is close to six times higher than in the continental United States (249). Many may also eventually regularize their status once they are in Puerto Rico through marriage to U.S. citizens or legal permanent residents (249–50).

4. See especially Juan Flores.

5. On Santiago's portrayal of assimilation and her ostensible rejection of Puerto Rican identity in *When I Was Puerto Rican*, see Sánchez González; Marshall; Socolovsky; Khader.

6. Bonnie Honig distinguishes between representations of "good" immigrants who reaffirm dominant narratives of the nation as welcoming and inclusive and of "bad" ones, meaning "illegal" immigrants who want only to "take" from the nation and undermine its laws (96).

7. Some scholars have focused attention on the linguistic code-switching and interplay between English and Spanish of *Drown* as a "violent enterprise" (Céspedes and Torres-Saillant 902, qtd. in Frydman 134; Torres 83); but at least one critic argues that because *Drown* "does not rehearse the traditional immigrant narrative of assimilation," the critical focus on the English-Spanish opposition is reductive (Frydman 138, 135; see also Irizarry, "Making It Home" 90–91).

8. As Lucía M. Suárez points out, the collection's translation into Spanish takes the name of this story, "Negocios," rather than the translation of the word *drown* (92).

9. Dominicans did not migrate to the United States in large numbers for economic

reasons until the 1980s; and even after Trujillo's assassination, in the 1960s visas were comparatively easy for Dominicans to get because "the Dominican and U.S. governments saw emigration as a safety valve that could dissipate still virulent political tensions" in the D.R. Further, the earlier waves of Dominican migration included professionals and skilled workers (Suárez 93–94).

10. *A Handbook to Luck* has yet to acquire significant scholarly attention.

11. In a somewhat different formulation, Monisha Das Gupta has pointed out that "cosmopolitanism" implies a level of status, privilege, and mobility that would seem to preclude subaltern or marginalized cosmopolitans (11).

12. Only 2.6 percent of asylum applications from Salvadoran refugees were granted between 1983 and 1990 (Gonzalez 131).

13. *Return to Sender* has thus far received almost no critical attention.

14. Dominicans in the mid-1990s had become the eighth largest undocumented population in the United States (Department of Homeland Security 6).

15. Section 274 of the Immigration and Naturalization Act (INA) imposes criminal penalties on anyone who "knowingly or in reckless disregard of the fact that an alien has come to, entered, or remains in the United States in violation of law, transports, or moves or attempts to transport or move such alien within the United States by means of transportation or otherwise, in furtherance of such violation of law."

Chapter 4. Selling the Undocumented: Life Narratives of Unauthorized Immigrants

1. After the passage of SB 1070 in April 2010, five states passed similar omnibus legislation (Segreto et al.). Alabama's HB 56, now hailed as the most restrictive and punitive of state anti-immigration laws to date, became law in June 2011.

2. The DREAM (Development, Relief, and Education for Alien Minors) Act would provide a path to citizenship for undocumented youth who came to the United States with their parents and who have attended U.S. colleges or served in the military.

3. Elvira Arellano, an unauthorized Mexican immigrant who took sanctuary in a Chicago church during 2006 and 2007, became the most prominent undocumented spokesperson for immigrant rights until the revelation that journalist Jose Antonio Vargas is undocumented. Undocumented student activists for passage of the DREAM Act have maintained a prominent web presence and have engaged in public demonstrations.

4. High-profile worksite raids included six raids on Swift meatpacking plants in December 2006 (Capps et al. 11) as well as the May 2008 raid at the Agriprocessors slaughterhouse and meatpacking plant in Postville, Iowa (Camayd-Freixas; Kanstroom 57–58).

5. In place of the Bush-era massive workplace raids, Obama escalated fines to employers from $675,000 in FY 2008 to $6.9 million in FY 2010 (Bennett).

6. The 287(g) program was created under a section of IIRIRA that allows for cooperative agreements—or memoranda of understanding—between police departments and ICE, whereby police officers may carry out immigration enforcement functions (Chishti 1–2).

7. According to Orner, "The people we finally chose for [*Underground America*] were people who were very invested in having their story told publicly. They wanted to be heard in some way. . . . Especially when there was an egregious human rights issue

involved, people really did want to get that out, because they had no other way to tell that story" (Joiner). Further, reportedly the Voice of Witness series of oral history collections does not publish final accounts without the narrators' approval and allows them to make changes and modifications to their original testimonies later (Gidley).

8. Stories that don't fit neatly into the organizing rubric of the collection include an account of a woman who must cross *back* to Mexico when she is caught in a factory raid and deported ("Rosa María," 117–20); the narrative of a man who himself is a legal resident but whose girlfriend is subsequently smuggled in illegally ("James," 172–78); the account of a woman whose crossing is really a narrative occasion for her to rehearse the "life that flashed before me like a movie" ("Iginia," 121–28); and the story of a Cuban who arrives eventually in the United States via a tortuous route through France and Spain ("Pilar," 201–3).

9. Stories in the collection often begin in medias res, obviously *not* at some rhetorical "beginning" point, as they would be if called into a radio show.

10. Implicit advice and instruction abound: coyotes will hold migrants hostage for exorbitant fees (92); don't cross at Mexicali because you risk closer inspection (186); gas stations are good places to go for directions (22); missions can provide food, coffee, and shower facilities (23–24); buses heading north from San Diego to Los Angeles will be stopped and checked at the military base at Camp Pendleton (29); it's a good idea to use false names when detained by Border Patrol—and even a false country of origin, if you are from Central America (29, 72–73); bluffing might actually work with customs agents in airports (48); it's wise to split up your money and put it in different places (54); and a variety of other creative strategies.

11. Visa overstayers account for roughly 45 percent of the undocumented population (Pew Research Center).

12. Several accounts are marked by a tension between the beloved memories of the home country and an account of the conditions that make leaving necessary (e.g., Alarcón 104, 129, 182).

13. English quotations are from the English translation/edition of this text. If the English translation raises significant issues of meaning-making (the speaker's) or interpretation (ours), I will comment on this fact and, where necessary, provide an alternative translation.

14. The idea that *any* of these witnesses "conclude" their accounts in any particular way is, of course, a rhetorical fiction. We do not know how they concluded their accounts; we know how their accounts conclude in the text that has assembled them, but it is fairly obvious that accounts have had material cut from them in the editorial process.

15. In the original Spanish, the immigration officer actually *speaks* in "broken Spanish," continuously using the infinitive forms of Spanish verbs instead of conjugating them ("¿Cómo sabemos tú no escribir esa carta?").

16. Ngai cites Todorov 157, 185.

17. It is impossible to discern how much of this effect is a product of the editing of *Underground America*. The narrators might have been prompted by questions which specifically directed them to speak about the degree to which they felt "American"; the

inclusion of some accounts over others might also have been guided by this thematic principle.

18. See, for instance, De Genova and Peutz; De Genova, "Legal Production"; Bacon.

19. As Hunt argues, for inalienable human rights to be seen as "self-evident," people had to *agree* that they were self-evident, a given (19–20).

Chapter 5. Unauthorized Plots: Life Writing, Transnationalism, and the Possibilities of Agency

1. According to Christina Sisk, Pérez was invited to write about his experiences as a resistance guerilla in Mexico and as an undocumented immigrant by Rick Leavis, a journalist who translated both *Diary of an Undocumented Immigrant* and *Diary of a Guerilla* into English. The earlier-written memoir, *Diary of a Guerilla* (Arte Público 1999), was actually published later than *Diary of an Undocumented Immigrant* (see Sisk 14).

2. Smith and Watson use the term *life narrative* for a broad range of texts including autobiography, memoir, *testimonio*, and autoethnography (2–3).

3. Emplotment, White argues, is one aspect of the "production of meaning," because "any given set of real events can be emplotted in a number of ways, can bear the weight of being told as any number of different *kinds of stories*" (44).

4. Sisk suggests that in the English translation of the title, *Immigrant* suggests "arrival," whereas *mojado* does not imply either arrival or departure (17).

5. A ruling in a 2007 case before the Kansas Court of Appeals found that "while an illegal alien is subject to deportation, that person's ongoing presence in the United States in and of itself is not a crime unless that person had been previously deported and regained illegal entry into this country" (Unruh).

Chapter 6. Undocumented Testimony: American DREAMers

1. For Fraser, the question "What, if anything, should delimit the bounds of justice?" is answered by the *all-subjected principle* which proposes that "all those who are subject to a given governance structure have moral standing as subjects of justice in relation to it" (*Scales of Justice* 65).

2. The stories of undocumented youth activists that I draw on here are taken from a series of interviews I conducted by phone and in person during 2010 and 2011. The interview format was simple: I asked the activists to tell me their life stories, beginning where they thought appropriate and leading up to their current activism. After that point I kept any interruptions to a minimum, since I was interested in large part in the ways my interviewees selected and arranged what they felt was important to include, although I asked follow-up questions for clarification when they were finished. In most cases, in my transcriptions, filler words such as *like, you know*, or *um* have been silently removed from the text of the interviews, except in cases where I felt they were an indication of hesitation or reservation on the topic.

3. For instance, the Immigrant Youth Justice League, in coordination with other immigrant-rights community organizations, has for several years organized national "Coming out of the Shadows" events (Immigrant Youth Justice League; Obejas, "DREAM Act").

Works Cited

Adams, Joyce. "The DREAM Lives On: Why the DREAM Act Died and Next Steps for Immigration Reform." *Georgetown Immigration Law Journal* 25.2 (2011): 545–49.

Adler, Jerry. "Sweet Land of Liberties: If Everyone Has His Own Niche, What Do We Have in Common Anymore?" *Newsweek* 10 July 1995: 18. Web.

Alarcón, Alicia, ed. *The Border Patrol Ate My Dust*. Houston: Arte Público Press, 2004.

———. *La Migra me hizo los mandados*. Houston: Arte Público Press, 2002.

Alexander, Jeffrey C. "On the Social Construction of Moral Universals: The 'Holocaust' from War Crime to Trauma Drama." *Cultural Trauma and Collective Identity*. Ed. Jeffrey C. Alexander, Ron Eyerman, Bernhard Giesen, Neil J. Smelser, and Piotr Sztompka. Berkeley: U of California P, 2004. 196–263.

———. "Toward a Theory of Cultural Trauma." *Cultural Trauma and Collective Identity*. Ed. Jeffrey C. Alexander, Ron Eyerman, Bernhard Giesen, Neil J. Smelser, and Piotr Sztompka. Berkeley: U of California P, 2004. 1–30.

Allatson, Paul. *Latino Dreams: Transcultural Traffic and the U.S. National Imaginary*. New York: Rodopi, 2002.

Alvarez, Julia. *Return to Sender*. New York: Alfred A. Knopf, 2010.

Anderson, Benedict. *Imagined Communities: Reflections on the Origin and Spread of Nationalism*. New York: Verso, 1991.

Andreas, Peter. *Border Games: Policing the U.S.–Mexico Divide*. Ithaca: Cornell UP, 2000.

Annerino, John. *Dead in Their Tracks: Crossing America's Desert Borderlands*. New York: Four Walls Eight Windows, 1999.

Anzaldúa, Gloria. *Borderlands/La Frontera*. 2nd ed. San Francisco: Aunt Lute Books, 1999.

Appadurai, Arjun. *Modernity at Large: Cultural Dimensions of Globalization*. Minneapolis: U of Minnesota P, 1996.

Appiah, Kwame Anthony. *Cosmopolitanism: Ethics in a World of Strangers*. New York: W. W. Norton, 2006.

Arellano, Elvira. "Statement of Elvira Arellano on August 15, 2007." 20 August 2007. Los Angeles Independent Media Center. Web. 20 September 2011. <http://la.indymedia.org/news/2007/08/205070.php>.

Arias, Arturo. "Teaching Testimonio: A New, Ex-Centric Design Emerges." *Teaching Life Writing Texts*. Eds. Miriam Fuchs and Craig Howes. New York: Modern Language Association of America, 2008. 310-317.

Ashcroft, Bill, Gareth Griffiths, and Helen Tiffin. *Post-Colonial Studies: The Key Concepts*. New York: Routledge, 2000.

Associated Press. "System for Tracking Visa Overstays Is Almost Ready." *Washington Times* 6 March 2012. Web. 9 July 2012.

Auster, Lawrence. *Erasing America: The Politics of the Borderless Nation*. Monterey, VA: American Immigration Control Foundation, 2003.

Bacon, David. *Illegal People: How Globalization Creates Migration and Criminalizes Immigrants*. Boston: Beacon Press, 2008.

Bakhtin, Mikhail. "Author and Hero in Aesthetic Activity." *Art and Answerability*. Ed. Michael Holquist and Vadim Liapunov. Trans. Vadim Liapunov. Austin: U of Texas P, 1990. 4-256.

Bal, Mieke. Introduction. *Acts of Memory: Cultural Recall in the Present*. Ed. Mieke Bal, Jonathan Crewe, and Leo Spitzer. Hanover, NH: UP of New England, 1999. vii-xvii.

Barron, Elisha. "Recent Development: The Development, Relief, and Education for Alien Minors (DREAM) Act." *Harvard Journal on Legislation* 48.2 (Summer 2011): 623-55.

Bencastro, Mario. *Odyssey to the North*. Trans. Susan Giersbach Rascon. Houston: Arte Público Press, 1998. Published in original Spanish as *Odisea del Norte* in 1999.

Bennett, Brian. "Republicans Want a Return to Workplace Immigration Raids." *Los Angeles Times* 27 January 2011. Web. 10 July 2012. <http://articles.latimes.com/2011/jan/27/nation/la-na-immigration-raids-20110127>.

Beverley, John. *Testimonio: On the Politics of Truth*. Minneapolis: U of Minnesota P, 2004.

Bhabha, Homi K. Introduction. *Nation and Narration*. Ed. Bhabha. New York: Routledge, 1990.

Bilger, Pam. "Unusual Subjects Make These Books Winners." *Charlotte Observer* 13 April 2006: 5K. *America's Newspapers*. NewsBank. U of Kansas, Lawrence. 27 July 2008. <http://www.infoweb.newsbank.com>.

Boelhower, William. "Avant-Garde Autobiography: Deconstructing the Modern Habitat." *Literary Anthropology: A New Interdisciplinary Approach to People, Signs, and Literature*. Ed. Fernando Poyatos. Philadelphia: Benjamins, 1988. 273-303.

Boyle, T. C. *The Tortilla Curtain*. New York: Viking Press, 1995.

Brimelow, Peter. *Alien Nation: Common Sense about America's Immigration Disaster*. New York: Random House, 1995.

Brison, Susan J. "Trauma Narratives and the Remaking of the Self." *Acts of Memory: Cultural Recall in the Present*. Ed. Mieke Bal, Jonathan Crewe, and Leo Spitzer. Hanover: UP of New England, 1999. 39-54.

Brogan, Kathleen. *Cultural Haunting: Ghosts and Ethnicity in Recent American Literature*. Charlottesville: UP of Virginia, 1998.

Brown, Anna, and Eileen Patten. "Hispanics of Dominican Origin in the United States, 2011." *Pew Research Hispanic Trends Project.* 19 June 2013. Web. 20 December 2014. <http://www.pewhispanic.org/2013/06/19/hispanics-of-dominican-origin-in-the-united-states-2011/>.

Buchanan, Patrick J. *State of Emergency: The Third World Invasion and Conquest of America.* New York: Thomas Dunne Books, 2006.

Camayd-Freixas, Erik. "Interpreting after the Largest ICE Raid in U.S. History: A Personal Account." 13 June 2008. Web. 13 July 2012.

Caminero-Santangelo, Marta. *The Madwoman Can't Speak; or, Why Insanity Is Not Subversive.* Ithaca, N.Y.: Cornell UP, 1998.

———. *On Latinidad: U.S. Latino Literature and the Construction of Ethnicity.* Gainesville: UP of Florida, 2007.

———. "Responding to the Human Costs of U.S. Immigration Policy: No More Deaths and the New Sanctuary Movement." *Latino Studies* 7.1 (Spring 2009): 112–22.

———. "The Voice of the Voiceless: Religious Rhetoric, Undocumented Immigrants, and the New Sanctuary Movement in the United States." *Sanctuary Practices in International Perspective.* Ed. Randy Lippert and Sean Rehaag. New York: Routledge, 2013. 92–105.

Capps, Rany, Rosa Maria Castañeda, Ajay Chaudry, and Robert Santos. *Paying the Price: The Impact of Immigration Raids on America's Children.* Washington, D.C.: Urban Institute and the National Council of La Raza, 2007. Web. 11 July 2012.

Caputo, John D. "The End of Ethics." *The Blackwell Guide to Ethical Theory.* Ed. Hugh LaFollette. Malden, MA: Blackwell, 2000. 111–28.

Caruth, Cathy. *Unclaimed Experience: Trauma, Narrative, and History.* Baltimore: Johns Hopkins UP, 1996.

Castillo, Ana. *The Guardians.* New York: Random House, 2007.

———. *So Far from God.* New York: W. W. Norton, 1993.

Castillo, Debra A. *Redreaming America: Toward a Bilingual American Culture.* Albany: State U of New York P, 2005.

Castillo, Debra A., and María-Socorro Tabuenca Córdoba. *Border Women: Writing from La Frontera.* Minneapolis: U of Minnesota P, 2002.

Castro, Max J., and Thomas D. Boswell. "The Dominican Diaspora Revisited: Dominicans and Dominican Americans in a New Century." *North-South Agenda* 53 (January 2002):1–25.

Céspedes, Diógenes, and Silvio Torres-Saillant. "Fiction Is the Poor Man's Cinema: An Interview with Junot Díaz." *Callaloo* 2000: 892–907.

Chavez, Leo R. *Covering Immigration: Popular Images and the Politics of the Nation.* Berkeley: U of California P, 2001.

———. *The Latino Threat: Constructing Immigrants, Citizens, and the Nation.* Stanford, CA: Stanford UP, 2008.

———. *Shadowed Lives: Undocumented Immigrants in American Society.* Fort Worth: Harcourt Brace College, 1998.

Chishti, Muzaffar A. *Hearing on Examining 287(g): The Role of State and Local Law En-*

forcement in Immigration Law. Washington, D.C.: Committee on Homeland Security, House of Representatives, 4 March 2009. Web. 13 July 2012.

Cohen, Roger. "The Cry of the Disappeared." *International Herald Tribune* 14 June 2007: 8.

Conniff, Ruth. "The War on Aliens." *Progressive* October 1993: 22ff. Web. 10 July 2012.

Cornelius, Wayne. *Extended Interview: Wayne Cornelius.* Frontline/World. Web. 13 July 2012.

Cornell, Stephen, and Douglas Hartmann. *Ethnicity and Race: Making Identities in a Changing World.* Thousand Oaks, CA: Pine Forge Press, 1998.

Coutin, Susan Bibler. "The Oppressed, the Suspect, and the Citizen: Subjectivity in Competing Accounts of Political Violence." *Law and Social Inquiry* 26.1 (Winter 2001): 63–94.

Cowie, Jefferson. "Death in the Desert." Rev. of *The Devil's Highway. Chicago Tribune* 4 April 2004: Books 1. *America's Newspapers.* NewsBank. University of Kansas, Lawrence. 27 July 2008. <http://www.infoweb.newsbank.com>.

Craft, Linda J. *Novels of Testimony and Resistance from Central America.* Gainesville: UP of Florida, 1997.

Craps, Stef. "Linking Legacies of Loss: Traumatic Histories and Cross-Cultural Empathy in Caryl Phillip's *Higher Ground* and *The Nature of Blood.*" *Studies in the Novel* 40.1–2 (Spring/Summer 2008): 191–202.

Craps, Stef, and Gert Buelens. "Introduction: Postcolonial Trauma Novels." *Studies in the Novel* 40.1–2 (2008): 1–12.

Cruz-Malavé, Arnaldo. *Queer Latino Testimonio, Keith Haring, and Juanito Xtravaganza: Hard Tails.* New York: Palgrave Macmillan, 2007.

Cunningham, Hilary. "The Ethnography of Transnational Social Activism: Understanding the Global as Local Practice." *American Ethnologist* 26 (August 1999): 583–604.

Danticat, Edwidge. *The Farming of Bones.* New York: Penguin, 1998.

Das Gupta, Monisha. *Unruly Immigrants: Rights, Activism, and Transnational South Asian Politics in the United States.* Durham, NC: Duke UP, 2006.

Dawes, James. *That the World May Know: Bearing Witness to Atrocity.* Cambridge, MA: Harvard UP, 2007.

De Genova, Nicholas. "The Legal Production of Mexican/Migrant 'Illegality.'" *Latinos and Citizenship: The Dilemma of Belonging.* Ed. Suzanne Oboler. New York: Palgrave Macmillan, 2006. 61–90.

———."The Queer Politics of Migration: Reflections on 'Illegality' and Incorrigibility." *Studies in Social Justice* 4.2 (2010): 101–26.

De Genova, Nicholas, and Nathalie Peutz, eds. *The Deportation Regime: Sovereignty, Space, and the Freedom of Movement.* Durham, NC: Duke UP, 2010.

De Genova, Nicholas, and Ana Y. Ramos-Zayas. *Latino Crossings: Mexicans, Puerto Ricans, and the Politics of Race and Citizenship.* New York: Routledge, 2003.

Department of Homeland Security. *Illegal Alien Resident Population.* 1996. 21 February 2012. <http://www.dhs.gov/xlibrary/assets/statistics/illegal.pdf>.

De Lauretis, Teresa. *Technologies of Gender: Essays on Theory, Film, and Fiction.* Bloomington: Indiana UP, 1987.

Díaz, Junot. *Drown*. New York: Riverhead Books, 1996.

Doland, Gwyneth. "Fact Check: 9/11 Terrorists Did Not Enter U.S. from Canada." *New Mexico Independent* 17 June 2010. Web. 9 July 2012.

Dorfman, Ariel. "Código politico y código literario: El género testimonio en Chile hoy." *Testimonio y literatura*. Eds. René Jara and Hernán Vidal. Minneapolis: Institute for the Study of Ideologies and Literature, 1986. 170–234.

Dougherty, Jon E. *Illegals: The Imminent Threat Posed by Our Unsecured U.S.-Mexico Border*. Nashville: Thomas Nelson, 2004.

Downes, Lawrence. ""What Part of 'Illegal' Don't You Understand?" *New York Times*, 28 October 2007. Accessed 30 August 2011 <http://www.nytimes.com/2007/10/28/opinion/28sun4.html>.

"DREAM Act." n.d. Web. 25 May 2015. <http://dreamactnow.tumblr.com/post/3298304598/are-you-undocumented-and-unafraid-time-to-come>.

Dreby, Joanna. *Divided by Borders: Mexican Migrants and Their Children*. Berkeley: U of California P, 2010.

Duany, Jorge. "Dominican Migration to Puerto Rico: A Transnational Perspective." *Centro Journal* 17.1 (2005): 242–69.

Dunham, Jillian. "Danger Permeates These True Tales from Afar." Rev. of *Enrique's Journey*. *Chicago Tribune* 18 June 2006.

Durand, Jorge, and Douglas S. Massey. "The Costs of Contradiction: U.S. Border Policy, 1986-2000." *Latino Studies* 1.2 (2003): 233–52.

Ellingwood, Ken. *Hard Line: Life and Death on the U.S.-Mexico Border*. New York: Random House, 2004.

Erikson, Kai. *Everything in Its Path*. New York: Simon and Schuster, 1976.

———. "Notes on Trauma and Community." *Trauma: Explorations in Memory*. Ed. Cathy Caruth. Baltimore: Johns Hopkins UP, 1995. 183–99.

Escandón, María Amparo. *Esperanza's Box of Saints*. New York: Simon & Schuster, 1991.

Eschbach, Karl, Jacqueline Hagan, Nestor Rodriguez, Ruben Hernández-León, and Stanley Bailey. "Death at the Border." *International Migration Review* 33.2 (Summer 1999): 430–54. Web. 2 August 2012.

Eyerman, Ron. "Cultural Trauma: Slavery and the Formation of African American Identity." *Cultural Trauma and Collective Identity*. Ed. Jeffrey C. Alexander, Ron Eyerman, Bernhard Giesen, Neil J. Smelser, and Piotr Sztompka. Berkeley: U of California P, 2004. 60–111.

Feitlowitz, Marguerite. *A Lexicon of Terror: Argentina and the Legacies of Torture*. New York: Oxford UP, 1998.

Feldman, Allen. "Memory Theaters, Virtual Witnessing, and the Trauma-Aesthetic." *Biography* 27.1 (Winter 2004): 163–202.

Ferguson, Kathryn, Norma A. Price, and Ted Parks, eds. *Crossing with the Virgin: Stories from the Migrant Trail*. Tucson: U of Arizona P, 2010.

Flores, Juan. *From Bomba to Hip-Hop: Puerto Rican Culture and Latino Identity*. New York: Columbia UP, 2000.

Flores-Gonzáles, Nilda. "Immigrants, Citizens, or Both? The Second Generation in the Immigrant Rights Marches." *¡Marcha! Latino Chicago and the Immigrant Rights*

Movement. Ed. Amalia Pallares and Nilda Flores-González. Urbana: U of Illinois P, 2010. 198–214.

Forth, Christopher E., and Ivan Crozier, eds. *Body Parts: Critical Explorations in Corporeality.* Lanham, MD: Lexington Books, 2005.

Fraser, Nancy. "Rethinking the Public Sphere: A Contribution to the Critique of Actually Existing Democracy." *Social Text* 25/26 (1990): 56–80.

———. *Scales of Justice: Reimagining Political Space in a Globalizing World.* New York: Columbia UP, 2009.

Fraxedas, J. Joaquín. *The Lonely Crossing of Juan Cabrera.* New York: St. Martin's Griffin, 1993.

Frydman, Jason. "Violence, Masculinity, and Upward Mobility in the Dominican Diaspora: Junot Díaz, the Media, and DROWN." *Columbia Journal of American Studies* 8 (Spring 2007): 133–43.

Fuchs, Miriam, and Craig Howes, eds. *Teaching Life Writing Texts.* New York: Modern Language Association of America, 2008.

García, Cristina. *A Handbook to Luck.* New York: Alfred A. Knopf, 2007.

Gaspar de Alba, Alicia. *Desert Blood: The Juárez Murders.* Houston: Arte Público Press, 2005.

Gidley, Ruth. "Breaking the Silence." *Guardian* [U.K.], 24 June 2008. Accessed 12 December 2011. <http://www.guardian.co.uk/books/2008/jun/25/history.society?INTCMP=SRCH>.

Gilmore, Leigh. "Limit-Cases: Trauma, Self-Representation, and the Jurisdictions of Identity." *Biography* 24.1 (2001): 128–39.

Golash-Boza, Tanya. *Due Process Denied: Detentions and Deportations in the United States.* New York: Routledge, 2012.

———. *Immigration Nation: Raids, Detentions, and Deportations in Post-9/11 America.* Boulder, CO: Paradigm, 2012.

Gonzalez, Juan. *Harvest of Empire: A History of Latinos in America.* New York: Penguin, 2000.

Graham, Shane. "'This Text Deletes Itself': Traumatic Memory and Space-Time in Zoe Wicomb's *David's Story*." *Studies in the Novel* 40.1–2 (Spring–Summer 2008): 127–45.

Grande, Reyna. *Across a Hundred Mountains.* New York: Atria, 2006.

Groody, Daniel. "The Drama of Immigration and the Cry of the Poor: The Voices of *Alambrista* Yesterday and Today." *Alambrista and the U.S.-Mexico Border: Film, Music, and Stories of Undocumented Immigrants.* Ed. Nicholas J. Cull and Davíd Carrasco. Albuquerque: U of New Mexico P, 2004. 59–78.

Gutiérrez-Jones, Carl. *Rethinking the Borderlands: Between Chicano Culture and Legal Discourse.* Berkeley: U of California P, 1995.

Hagedorn, Jessica. Introduction. *Charlie Chan Is Dead 2: At Home in the World.* New York: Penguin, 2004. xxvii–xxxii.

Hall, Stuart, ed. *Representation: Cultural Representations and Signifying Practices.* Thousand Oaks, CA: Sage, 1997.

Hart, Dianne Walta. *Undocumented in L.A.: An Immigrant's Story.* Wilmington, DE: SR Books, 1997.

Herrera-Sobek, María. "The Corrido as Hypertext: Undocumented Mexican American Films and the Mexican/Chicano Ballad." *Culture across Borders: Mexican Immigration and Popular Culture.* Ed. David R. Maciel and María Herrera-Sobek. Tucson: U of Arizona Press, 1998. 227–58.

Hing, Bill Ong. *Defining America through Immigration Policy.* Philadelphia: Temple UP, 2004.

Hondagneu-Sotelo, Pierrette. *God's Heart Has No Borders: How Religious Activists Are Working for Immigrant Rights.* Berkeley: U of California P, 2008.

Honig, Bonnie. *Democracy and the Foreigner.* Princeton: Princeton UP, 2001.

Hunt, Lynn. *Inventing Human Rights: A History.* New York: W.W. Norton, 2007.

Huntington, Samuel. *Who Are We? The Challenges to America's Identity.* New York: Simon and Schuster, 2004.

Immigrant Youth Justice League. "Who We Are." *Immigrant Youth Justice League.* Web. 27 May 2015. <http://www.iyjl.org/whoweare/>.

Interfaith Worker Justice. *For You Were Once a Stranger: Immigration in the U.S. through the Lens of Faith.* Chicago: Interfaith Worker Justice, 2007.

Irizarry, Ylce. "Making It Home: A New Ethics of Immigration in Dominican Literature." *Hispanic Caribbean Literature of Migration: Narratives of Displacement.* Ed. Vanessa Pérez Rosario. New York: Palgrave Macmillan, 2010. 89–103.

Johnson, Kevin R., and Bill Ong Hing. "The Immigrant Rights Marches of 2006 and the Prospects for a New Civil Rights Movement." *Harvard Civil Rights–Civil Liberties Law Review* 2007: 99–138.

Joiner, Whitney. "Not Quite Americans." Interview with Peter Orner. *Salon,* 11 June 2008. Accessed 14 December 2011. <http://www.salon.com/2008/06/11/orner/>.

Kanstroom, Daniel. *Aftermath: Deportation Law and the New American Diaspora.* Oxford: Oxford UP, 2012.

Kaplan, E. Ann. *Trauma Culture: The Politics of Terror and Loss in Media and Literature.* New Brunswick: Rutgers UP, 2005.

Keen, Suzanne. "A Theory of Narrative Empathy." *Narrative* 14.3 (Oct. 2006): 207–236.

Khader, Jamil. "Subaltern Cosmopolitanism: Community and Transnational Mobility in Caribbean Postcolonial Feminist Writings." *Feminist Studies* 29.1 (Spring 2003): 63–81.

Kim, L. S. "Invisible and Undocumented: The Latina Maid on Network Television." *Aztlán* 24.1 (Spring 1999): 107–28.

Koshy, Susan. "Minority Cosmopolitanism." *PMLA* 126.3 (2011): 592–609.

Koven, Seth. "Remembering and Dismemberment: Crippled Children, Wounded Soldiers, and the Great War in Great Britain." *American Historical Review* 99.4 (October 1994): 1167–1202.

LaFollette, Hugh. *The Blackwell Guide to Ethical Theory.* Malden, MA: Blackwell, 2000.

Lakoff, George, and Sam Ferguson. "The Framing of Immigration." Berkeley: Rockridge Institute, 2006. Web. 22 Feb 2016. <http://afrolatinoproject.org/2007/09/24/the-framing-of-immigration-5/>.

Ledesma, Alberto. "Narratives of Undocumented Mexican Immigration as Chicana/o Acts of Intellectual and Political Responsibility." *Decolonial Voices: Chicana and Chi-*

cano Cultural Studies in the 21st Century. Ed. Arturo J. Aldama and Naomi H. Quiñonez. Bloomington: Indiana UP, 2002. 330–54.

———. "Undocumented Crossings: Narratives of Mexican Immigration to the United States." *Culture across Borders: Mexican Immigration and Popular Culture.* Ed. David R. Maciel and María Herrera-Sobek. Tucson: U of Arizona P, 1998. 67–98.

Lerner, Melvin J. *The Belief in a Just World: A Fundamental Delusion.* New York: Plenum, 1980.

Lima, Lázaro. *The Latino Body: Crisis Identities in American Literary and Cultural Memory.* New York: New York University P, 2007.

Limón, Graciela. *The River Flows North.* Houston: Arte Público Press, 2009.

Lyon-Johnson, Kelli. "Acts of War, Acts of Memory: 'Dead-Body Politics' in U.S. Latina Novels of the Salvadoran Civil War." *Latino Studies* 3.2 (2005): 205–25.

Madera, Gabriela, Angelo A. Mathay, Armin M. Najafi, Hector H. Saldívar, Stephanie Solis, Alyssa Jame M. Titong, Gaspar Rivera-Salgado, Janna Shadduck-Hernández, Kent Wong, Rebecca Frazier, and Julie Monroe, eds. *Underground Undergrads: UCLA Undocumented Immigrant Students Speak Out.* Los Angeles: UCLA Center for Labor Research and Education, 2008.

Marcus, Steven. "Freud and Dora: Story, History, Case History." *Literature and Psychoanalysis.* Ed. Edith Kurzweit and William Phillips. New York: Columbia UP, 1983.

Marosi, Richard. "Border Jumpers Leave Their Imprint on a Besieged Town." *Los Angeles Times* 3 June 2004. Web. 8 May 2015. <http://articles.latimes.com/2004/jun/03/local/me-borderhomes3>.

Marshall, Joanna Barszewska. "'Boast Now, Chicken, Tomorrow You'll Be Stew': Pride, Shame, Food, and Hunger in the Memoirs of Esmeralda Santiago." *MELUS* 32.4 (Winter 2007): 47–68.

Martin, Philip L. "The United States: The Continuing Immigration Debate." *Controlling Immigration: A Global Perspective.* Ed. Wayne A. Cornelius, Takeyuki Tsuda, Philip L. Martin, and James F. Hollifield. 2nd ed. Stanford: Stanford UP, 2004. 51–85.

Martinez, Manuel L. "Humanizing the Issue of Immigration—A Poignant New Book Focuses on People Rather than Statistics." Rev. of *Crossing Over. Chicago Tribune* 21 October 2001: 3. *America's Newspapers.* NewsBank. University of Kansas, Lawrence. 27 July 2008. <http://www.infoweb.newsbank.com>.

———. "Telling the Difference between the Border and the Borderlands: Materiality and Theoretical Practice." *Globalization on the Line: Culture, Capital, and Citizenship at U.S. Borders.* Ed. Claudia Sadowski-Smith. New York: Palgrave, 2002. 53–68.

Martínez, Rubén. *Crossing Over: A Mexican Family on the Migrant Trail.* 2001. New York: Picador, 2002.

McKenna, Teresa. *Migrant Song: Politics and Process in Contemporary Chicano Literature.* Austin: U of Texas P, 1997.

Medina, David D. "'Baptism into a New Life': Journalist Chronicles Life of Migrant Mexican Family." Rev. of *Crossing Over. Houston Chronicle* 9 December 2001: 19. *America's Newspapers.* NewsBank. U of Kansas, Lawrence. 27 July 2008. <http://www.infoweb.newsbank.com>.

———. "Families Face Great Divide." Rev. of *Enrique's Journey. Houston Chronicle* 26 March 2006: 21. *America's Newspapers.* NewsBank. U of Kansas, Lawrence. 27 July 2008. <http://www.infoweb.newsbank.com>.
Migration Policy Institute. "Immigration Enforcement Spending since IRCA." November 2005. Web. 9 July 2012.
Miller, Matthew L. "Trauma in Junot Díaz's DROWN." *Notes on Comtemporary Literature* 41.1 (2011). *Literature Resource Center.* Web. 23 Feb. 2016.
Montgomery-Fate, Tom. "To Hell and Back." Rev. of *The Devil's Highway. Boston Globe* 25 April 2004: D8.
Moreno, Marisel. *Family Matters: Puerto Rican Women Authors on the Island and on the Mainland.* Charlottesville: U of Virginia P, 2012.
Moyn, Samuel. *The Last Utopia: Human Rights in History.* Cambridge, MA: Belknap Press of Harvard UP, 2010.
Nance, Kimberly A. *Can Literature Promote Justice? Trauma Narrative and Social Action in Latin American Testimonio.* Nashville: Vanderbilt UP, 2006.
———. "Let Us Say That There Is a Human Being before Me Who Is Suffering: Empathy, Exotopy, and Ethics in the Reception of Latin American Collaborative Testimonio." *Bakhtin: Ethics and Mechanics.* Ed. Valerie Z. Nollan. Evanston, IL: Northwestern UP, 2004. 57–73.
Nazario, Sonia. *Enrique's Journey: The Story of a Boy's Dangerous Odyssey to Reunite with His Mother.* 2006. New York: Random House, 2007.
Nevins, Joseph. *Dying to Live: A Story of U.S. Immigration in an Age of Global Apartheid.* San Francisco: City Lights Books, 2008.
———. *Operation Gatekeeper: The Rise of the 'Illegal Alien' and the Making of the U.S.-Mexico Boundary.* New York: Routledge, 2002.
New York State Youth Leadership Council [NYSYLC]. "Coming Out of the Shadows Week: How to Guide." Web. 12 June 2015. <http://www.nysylc.org/2010/03/coming-out-of-the-shadows-week-how-to-guide/>.
Ngai, Mae M. *Impossible Subjects: Illegal Aliens and the Making of Modern America.* Princeton, NJ: Princeton UP, 2004.
No More Deaths/No Más Muertes. "Crossing the Line: Human Rights Abuses of Migrants in Short-Term Custody on the Arizona/Sonora Border." 2008. Web. 27 July 2012.
———. "A Culture of Cruelty: Abuse and Impunity in Short-Term Border Patrol Custody." 2011. Web. 30 September 2011.
Novak, Amy. "'A Marred Testament': Cultural Trauma and Narrative in Danticat's *The Farming of Bones.*" *Arizona Quarterly* 62.4 (Winter 2006): 93–120.
Nyers, Peter. "Abject Cosmopolitanism: The Politics of Protection in the Anti-Deportation Movement." *The Deportation Regime: Sovereignty, Space, and the Freedom of Movement.* Ed. Nicholas De Genova and Nathalie Peutz. Durham, NC: Duke UP, 2010. 413–41.
Obejas, Achy. *Days of Awe.* New York: Ballantine, 2001.

———. "DREAM Act/Coming Out of the Shadows Day Rally Today; Will Rahm Listen?" 10 March 2011. Web. 8 August 2011. <http://www.wbez.org/blog/achy-obejas/2011-03-10/dream-actcoming-out-shadows-day-rally-today-will-rahm-listen-83477>.

———. *Memory Mambo*. Pittsburgh: Cleis Press, 1991.

———. "The Spouse." *We Came All the Way from Cuba So You Could Dress Like This?* Pittsburgh: Cleis Press, 1994.

Oboler, Suzanne. "Redefining Citizenship as a Lived Experience." *Latinos and Citizenship: The Dilemma of Belonging*. Ed. Suzanne Oboler. New York: Palgrave Macmillan, 2006. 3–30.

Orner, Peter, ed. *Underground America: Narratives of Undocumented Lives*. San Francisco: McSweeney's Books, 2008.

O'Rourke, Allen Thomas. "Good Samaritans, Beware: The Sensenbrenner-King Bill and Assistance to Undocumented Migrants." *Harvard Latino Law Review* (2006): 195–208.

Ortega, Bob, and Erin Kelly. "Politics of Border Security Hamper Immigration Overhaul." *U.S.A. Today*, 24 June 2014. Web. 29 December 2014.

O'Toole, Molly. "Analysis: Obama Deportations Raise Immigration Policy Questions." Reuters 20 September 2011. Web. 10 July 2012.

Pallares, Amalia. "Representing 'La Familia': Family Separation and Immigrant Activism." *!Marcha! Latino Chicago and the Immigrant Rights Movement*. Ed. Amalia Pallares and Nilda Flores-González. Urbana: U of Illinois P, 2010. 215-36.

Pérez, Ramón "Tianguis." *Diary of an Undocumented Immigrant*. Trans. Dick J. Reavis. Houston: Arte Público Press, 1991.

Perez, William. *We ARE Americans: Undocumented Students Pursuing the American Dream*. Sterling, VA: Stylus, 2009.

Perks, Robert, and Alistair Thomson, eds. *The Oral History Reader*. New York: Routledge, 1998.

Pew Research Center. "Modes of Entry for the Unauthorized Migrant Population." 22 May 2006. Web. 26 May 2015. <http://www.pewhispanic.org/2006/05/22/modes-of-entry-for-the-unauthorized-migrant-population/>.

Portes, Alejandro. "Global Villagers: The Rise of Transnational Communities." *American Prospect* (March-April 1996): 74–77.

Povinelli, Elizabeth. *Economies of Abandonment: Social Belonging and Endurance in Late Liberalism*. Durham, NC: Duke UP, 2011.

Ramos, Jorge. *Dying to Cross: The Worst Immigrant Tragedy in American History*. New York: Rayo, 2005.

Rancière, Jacques. "Who Is the Subject of the Rights of Man?" *South Atlantic Quarterly* 103.2–3 (2004): 297–310.

Regan, Margaret. *The Death of Josseline: Immigration Stories from the Arizona-Mexico Borderlands*. Boston: Beacon Press, 2010.

Ribadeneira, Diego. "Dying for the Chance to Work in America." Rev. of *Crossing Over*. *Record* [New Jersey]: E3. *America's Newspapers*. NewsBank. U of Kansas, Lawrence. 27 July 2008. <http://www.infoweb.newsbank.com>.

Riofrio, John. "Situating Latin American Masculinity: Immigration, Empathy, and Emasculation in Junot Díaz's DROWN." *Atenea* 28.1 (June 2008): 23–36.

Rivera, Rick. *Stars Always Shine*. Tempe, AZ: Bilingual Press, 2001.

Rivera, Tomás. *Y no se lo tragó la tierra*. 1971. Houston: Arte Público Press, 1987.

Rodríguez, Néstor. "The Social Construction of the U.S.-Mexico Border." *Immigrants Out! The New Nativism and the Anti-Immigrant Impulse in the United States*. Ed. Juan F. Perea. New York: New York UP, 1997. 223–43.

Rodriguez, Roberto Cintli. "The Root of Youth Civil Disobedience in Arizona." *New America Media*. 10 July 2010. Available on *Alternet*. 25 May 2015. <http://www.alternet.org/story/147439/the_root_of_youth_civil_disobedience_in_arizona>.

Rohter, Larry. "Puerto Rico's Coastline: New York's Back Door." *New York Times* 13 December 1992. Web. 15 February 2012. <http://www.nytimes.com/1992/12/13/us/puerto-rico-s-coastline-new-york-s-back-door.html?pagewanted=all&src=pm>.

Rojas, Leslie Berestein. "Jose Antonio Vargas: 'I'm an American, I just don't have the right papers.'" 23 June 2011. *Multi-American: How Immigrants Are Redefining 'American' in Southern California*. 24 May 2015. <http://www.scpr.org/blogs/multiamerican/2011/06/22/7223/jose-antonio-vargas-im-an-american-i-just-dont-hav/>.

Sadowski-Smith, Claudia. *Border Fictions: Globalization, Empire, and Writing at the Boundaries of the United States*. Charlottesville: U of Virginia P, 2008.

Saldívar, José David. *Border Matters: Remapping American Cultural Studies*. Berkeley: U of California P, 1997.

Saldívar-Hull, Sonia. *Feminism on the Border: Chicana Gender Politics and Literature*. Berkeley: U of California P, 2000.

Sánchez González, Lisa. *Boricua Literature: A Literary History of the Puerto Rican Diaspora*. New York: New York UP, 2001.

Santa Ana, Otto. *Brown Tide Rising: Metaphors of Latinos in Contemporary American Public Discourse*. Ithaca: Cornell UP, 1998.

Santiago, Esmeralda. *When I Was Puerto Rican*. New York: Vintage Books, 1994.

Scarry, Elaine. *The Body in Pain: The Making and Unmaking of the World*. New York: Oxford UP, 1985.

Schaffer, Kay, and Sidonie Smith. *Human Rights and Narrated Lives: The Ethics of Recognition*. New York: Palgrave Macmillan, 2004.

Schmidt Camacho, Alicia. *Migrant Imaginaries: Latino Cultural Politics in the U.S.-Mexico Borderlands*. New York: New York UP, 2008.

Schrager, Samuel. "What Is Social in Oral History?" *The Oral History Reader*. Ed. Robert Perks and Alistair Thomson. New York: Routledge, 1998. 284–99.

Schreiber, Evelyn Jaffe. *Race, Trauma, and Home in the Novels of Toni Morrison*. Baton Rouge: Louisiana State UP, 2010.

Schwab, Gabriele. "Writing against Memory and Forgetting." *Literature and Medicine* 25.1 (Spring 2006): 95–121.

Scott, James. *Seeing Like a State: How Certain Schemes to Improve the Human Condition Have Failed*. New Haven: Yale UP, 1998.

Segreto, Joy, April Carter, and Ann Morse. "2011 Immigration-Related Laws and Resolutions in the States (January–June)." National Conference of State Legislatures. 19

September 2011. Web. 10 December 2011. <http://www.ncsl.org/default.aspx?tabid=23362>.

Sisk, Christina L. "Toward a Trans(national) Reading of Ramón 'Tianguis' Pérez's *Diario de un mojado.*" *Aztlán: A Journal of Chicano Studies* 34.1 (Spring 2009): 13–34.

Sklodowska, Elzbieta. "Spanish American Testimonial Novel: Some Afterthoughts." *The Real Thing: Testimonial Discourse and Latin America.* Ed. Georg M. Gugelberger. Durham, NC: Duke UP, 1996. 84–100.

Slaughter, Joseph R. *Human Rights, Inc.: The World Novel, Narrative Form, and International Law.* New York: Fordham UP, 2007.

Smelser, Neil J. "Psychological Trauma and Cultural Trauma." *Cultural Trauma and Collective Identity.* Ed. Jeffrey C. Alexander, Ron Eyerman, Bernhard Giesen, Neil J. Smelser, and Piotr Sztompka. Berkeley: U of California P, 2004. 31–59.

Smith, Lamar. "Immigration Enforcement and Border Security Are the First Line Defense against Terrorists." *Fox News* 12 September 2011. Web. 9 July 2012.

Smith, Sidonie. "Performativity, Autobiographical Practice, Resistance." *Women, Autobiography, Theory: A Reader.* Ed. Sidonie Smith and Julia Watson. Madison: U of Wisconsin P, 1998.

Smith, Sidonie, and Julia Watson. *Reading Autobiography: A Guide for Interpreting Life Narratives.* Minneapolis: U of Minnesota P, 2010.

Socolovsky, Maya. *Troubling Nationhood in U.S. Latina Literature: Explorations of Place and Belonging.* New Brunswick: Rutgers UP, 2013.

Sollors, Werner. *Beyond Ethnicity: Consent and Descent in American Culture.* New York: Oxford UP, 1986.

Sommer, Doris. "No Secrets: Rigoberta's Guarded Truth." *Women's Studies* 20.1 (November 1991): 51–72. Reprinted in *The Real Thing: Testimonial Discourse and Latin America.* Ed. Georg M. Gugelberger. Durham, NC: Duke UP, 1996. 130–57.

———. "Rigoberta's Secrets." *Latin American Perspectives* 18.3 (Summer 1991): 32–50.

———. "Taking a Life: Hot Pursuit and Cold Rewards in a Mexican Testimonial Novel." *Signs* 20.4 (Summer 1995): 913–40.

Sontag, Susan. *Regarding the Pain of Others.* New York: Farrar, Straus and Giroux, 2003.

Soto, Sandra K. Seeing through Photographs of Borderlands (Dis)Order." *Latino Studies* 5.4 (Winter 2007): 418–38.

Spivak, Gayatri Chakravorty. *An Aesthetic Education in the Era of Globalization.* Cambridge, MA: Harvard UP, 2012.

———. "Can the Subaltern Speak?" *Marxism and the Interpretation of Culture.* Ed. Cary Nelson and Lawrence Grossberg. Urbana: U of Illinois P, 1988. 271–313.

Stephen, Lynn. "Women's Rights Are Human Rights: The Merging of Feminine and Feminist Interests among El Salvador's Mothers of the Disappeared (CO-MADRES)." *American Ethnologist* 22.4 (1995): 807–27.

Straight, Susan. *Highwire Moon.* New York: Anchor Books/Random House, 2001.

Suárez, Lucía M. *The Tears of Hispaniola: Haitian and Dominican Diaspora Memory.* Gainesville: UP of Florida, 2006.

Sugg, Katherine. "Literatures of the Americas, Latinidad, and the Re-Formation of Multi-Ethnic Literatures." *MELUS* 29.3/4 (Autumn-Winter 2004): 227–242.

Taylor, Diana. "Trauma and Performance: Lessons from Latin America." *PMLA* 121.5 (2006): 1674–77.
Terry, Diana. "The New Sanctuary Movement." *Hispanic* August 2007: 42–45.
Todorov, Tzvetan. *The Conquest of America: The Question of the Other*. Trans. Richard Howard. New York: Harper Perennial, 1992 [1984].
Torres, Lourdes. "In the Contact Zone: Code-Switching Strategies by Latino/a Writers." *MELUS* 32.1 (2007): 75–96.
Turakhia, Vikas. "Policy Blamed for Deaths along Mexican Border." Rev. of *The Devil's Highway*. *Plain Dealer* [Cleveland] 11 July 2004, J10.
Unruh, Bob. "Court Rules: Illegal Aliens Not Really 'Illegal.'" *WND* 22 August 2007. Web. 27 May 2015. <http://www.wnd.com/2007/08/43154/#3dmi7Z4Jko1Y7xba.99>.
Urrea, Luis Alberto. *The Devil's Highway: A True Story*. New York: Back Bay Books/Little, Brown, 2004.
———. Foreword. *Underground America: Narratives of Undocumented Lives*. Ed. Peter Orner. San Francisco: McSweeney's Books, 2008.
———. *Into the Beautiful North*. Boston: Little, Brown, 2009.
———. "The Lost Children." Rev. of *Enrique's Journey*. *Washington Post* 26 March 2006: T8.
Van Denburg, Hart. "Drawing a Line in the Sand: Organization Offers Water, Aid to Desert-Crossing Illegal Immigrants from Mexico." *Denver Post*, 4 August 2002: L-01.
Vare, Robert. "The State of Narrative Nonfiction." *Nieman Reports* (Fall 2000): 18–19.
Vargas, Jose Antonio. "My Life as an Undocumented Immigrant." *New York Times*, 22 June 2011. Web. 11 July 2012.
Verdery, Katherine. *The Political Lives of Dead Bodies: Reburial and Postsocialist Change*. New York: Columbia UP, 1999.
Verzasconi, Ray. Foreword. *Undocumented in L.A.: An Immigrant's Story*. By Dianne Walta Hart. Wilmington, DE: SR Books, 1997. ix–xix.
Viramontes, Helena María. "The Cariboo Café." In *The Moths and Other Stories*. Houston: Arte Público Press, 1985.
———. *Under the Feet of Jesus*. New York: Penguin, 1995.
Warner, Michael. *Publics and Counterpublics*. Brooklyn: Zone Books, 2002.
Weisberg, Jacob. "Xenophobia for Beginners." Review of *Alien Nation*. *New York Magazine* 24 April 1995: 24–26. Web. 12 July 2012.
Westerman, William. "Central American Refugee Testimonies and Performed Life Histories in the Sanctuary Movement." *The Oral History Reader*. Ed. Robert Perks and Alistair Thomson. New York: Routledge, 1998. 224–34.
White, Hayden. *The Content of Form: Narrative Discourse and Historical Representation*. Baltimore, MD: Johns Hopkins UP, 1987. E-book.
Wieland, Cristoph Martin. "Das Geheimniß des Kosmopolitenordens." *Teutscher Merkur*. August 1788.
Wildman, Sarah. "Coming to America." Rev. of *Enrique's Journey*. *New York Times Book Review* 7 May 2006: 21.
Wilson, Frank. "Death in the Desert at the Southern Border." Rev. of *The Devil's Highway*. *Record* [Hackensack, NJ] 6 March 2005: E03.

Wirshing, Irene. *National Trauma in Postdictatorship Latin American Literature: Chile and Argentina*. New York: Peter Lang, 2009.

Young, James E. "Interpreting Literary Testimony: A Preface to Rereading Holocaust Diaries and Memoirs." *New Literary History* 18.2 (Winter 1987): 403–23.

Yúdice, George. "Testimonio and Postmodernism." *The Real Thing: Testimonial Discourse in Latin America*. Ed. Georg Gugelberger. Durham, NC: Duke UP, 1996. 42–57.

Index

Abandonment, 44–45, 60, 76; in *The Guardians*, 81–84; in "Negocios," 117–24

Abject cosmopolitanism, 224

Absenting: in *Crossing Over*, 41; in *testimonio*, 168, 176

Across a Hundred Mountains (Grande): amnesias in, 76–77; deaths in, 64; dis(re)membered body in, 85–86; *el otro lado* in, 64–65; narrative breakdown in, 103; religious faith in, 98, 101

Activism, 24–25, 222–24; agency and, 256–58; of Arellano, 261–62; religious faith and, 98–99. *See also* DREAM activists

African Americans, 79, 103

Agency, 24, 163–64, 233; cosmopolitanism and, 133–34, 152; deportations and, 218, 256–57; stories and, 258–59; in *Undocumented in L.A.*, 206–7, 212, 215–16, 218; voices and, 152–53, 242–43

Agriprocessors slaughterhouse, 268n4

Aid, 43–44

Alabama, 268n1

Alambrista! (film), 15

Alarcón, Alicia. See *The Border Patrol Ate My Dust*

Alexander, Jeffrey, 20, 29, 35–36, 63. *See also* Cultural trauma

Alien Nation (Brimelow), 4

Aliens, 9, 28, 35; in *Return to Sender*, 139, 145–46

Allatson, Paul, 13

Alvarez, Julia. See *Return to Sender*

American, 114, 265n8

American Dream, 159–63, 193, 232; agency and, 233; in *Crossing Over*, 39–40; in *Undocumented in L.A.*, 210–12

Amnesias, 76–79

Amnesty, 3

Amnesty International, 53

Anderson, Benedict, 230

Andreas, Peter, 4

Annerino, John, 53, 62, 267n3

Anxiety, 166, 245–46; culture of, 27, 67, 150–51, 188, 243–45

Anzaldúa, Gloria, 1–2, 74, 265n1

Appiah, Kwame Anthony, 30, 128

Arellano, Elvira, 261–62, 268n3

Argentina, 75, 266n2, 267n7

Arias, Arturo, 164–65

Arizona, 34, 54; deaths in, 58–59; SB1070 in, 33, 149, 188, 225, 258–59, 266n1, 268n1

Ashcroft, Bill, 8–9

Assimilation, 204–5, 215–16

Astronomy, 144–45, 147

Asylum law, 244–45; in *Border Patrol*, 164–65; *testimonio* and, 95–97

Attribution, of responsibility, 68–69

Bacon, David, 10

Bakhtin, Mikhail, 35–36, 192

Bal, Mieke, 19–20

Belief in a Just World (Lerner), 35

Belonging, 214–15, 220–21. *See also* National belonging
Beloved (Morrison), 84–85
Bencastro, Mario, 59–61, 91–97
Beverley, John, 23, 35, 154, 167, 175
Bhabha, Homi, 8–9, 34
Bigamy, 118–19, 123–24
Bilingualism, 115–16
Birds, 129–30, 132–33
Blame, 86–94
Bodies, 70–71, 86, 191; *braceros* as, 188–89; documents or, 189; human rights and, 187–88; identity related to, 84–85; pain and, 52–53, 62, 187–88; personhood and, 189–90
The Body in Pain (Scarry), 52–53
Border corpses, 267n6; details of, 71–72; physicality of, 70–72; vigils and, 56–57; violence of, 71; women as, 70–72
Border ethics, 105–6
Border Fictions: Globalization, Empire, and Writing at the Boundaries of the United States (Sadowski-Smith), 11
Border Games (Andreas), 4
Borderlands, 11–13
Borderlands/La Fronter (Anzaldúa), 1–2, 74, 265n1
Border Matters: Remapping American Cultural Studies (Saldívar), 11
Border Patrol, 51, 54, 164, 269n10
The Border Patrol Ate My Dust (La migra me hizo los mandados) (*Border Patrol*) (Alarcón), 30, 151, 153, 269nn13–14; asylum law in, 164–65; without context, 168–70; crossing in, 155–57; fantasy in, 161–62; hazards in, 158–59, 161–62, 171–72; ignorance in, 168–69; irony in, 162–63; marketing of, 157–59; meritocracy and, 159–61; origins of, 156–57; place in, 170–71; readers of, 158, 161, 166–67, 171–72; responsibility in, 167–68; slavery in, 163–64; style of, 157; *testimonio* and, 164, 166–70; *Underground America* compared to, 174, 185, 192–93
Borders: decontextualization of, 68–69; *el otro lado* and, 64–65; fluidity of, 1–2; impermeability of, 2, 28; locatedness and, 11–12; symbolism of, 5, 12; water crossing as, 111. *See also* Deaths
Border *testimonio*: blame in, 86–94; environmentalism in, 91; odyssey in, 91–93; restaurant raid and, 93–94
Border Women: Writing from La Frontera (Castillo, D. and Córdoba), 11
Bowden, Charles, 68
Braceros, 188–89
Brewer, Jan, 266n1
Brimelow, Peter, 4
Brison, Susan J., 19, 266n11
Brogan, Kathleen, 19–20, 113
Buelens, Gert, 16, 26
Buenos Aires National Wildlife Refuge, 266n1
Bush, George W., 150, 255, 268n5

California, 3, 186
Can Literature Promote Justice? (Nance), 35
Caribbeans, 29–30; difference among, 108–25. *See also* Cosmopolitanism
Caruth, Cathy, 16, 18–19, 101
Castillo, Ana, 1, 58. See also *The Guardians*
Castillo, Debra, 11, 13
Cause-and-effect narrative, 18–19
Change: from *testimonio*, 23, 25, 35; from testimony, 24–26, 31–32
Chavez, Leo, 3, 90, 92, 151, 230; on Latino threat, 34–35; metaphors of, 234–35
Chávez, César, 98–99
Chicano/a authors, 12, 14–15; collective trauma of, 73–74
Chicano/a identity, 14–15
Chicano movement, 69, 266n10
Citizen children, 57, 150
Citizens, 105, 172–73, 265n8; *The Devil's Highway* and, 52–54; family and, 118–25; in *A Handbook to Luck*, 135–37; human rights and, 177; by marriage, 111–17, 135–36; noncitizens, 222–24; privilege of, 114–15; rights and, 180–81
Ciudad Juárez, Mexico, 70
Clinton administration, 4
Coast Guard, U.S., 111
Code-switching, 115–16
Cohen, Roger, 57, 63

Collective, 202–3
Collective agency, 256–57
Collective fiction, 136–37
Collective identity, 79, 102–3
Collective representation, 20
Collective rhetoric, 235–36
Collective trauma: of Chicano/a authors, 73–74; collective identity in, 79; of community, 17–19; disappearances and, 72–84; in *The Guardians*, 79–80, 84, 102–3; in *Highwire Moon*, 81–84; human rights and, 74; personal identity and, 74–77
College, 227, 234, 238, 239–40, 250
Colombia, 244
Coming out, 250–54
Communication, 246–47; code-switching in, 115–16; in raids, 87–88
Community: collective trauma of, 17–19; of DREAMers, 230–31; fragmentation of, 85; imagined, 104–5, 121–23, 230; queer, 250–54
Compassion, 43–44
Consumerism, 39–40
Córdoba, María-Socorro Tabuenca, 11
Cornell, Stephen, 79, 103, 111–12
Cosmopolitanism, 30, 268n11; abject, 224; agency and, 133–34, 152; ethics of, 125–47; framework of, 128–29; in *Return to Sender*, 139–44, 146–47. See also *A Handbook to Luck*
Cosmopolitanism: Ethics in a World of Strangers (Appiah), 128
Counternarratives, 28; in *Return to Sender*, 139–40
Counterpublic. See Subaltern counterpublic
Coutin, Susan Bibler, 94–95
Coyotes (human smugglers), 59–60, 88–89, 269n10
Craft, Linda J., 22–23
Craps, Stef, 16, 26–27
Criminals, 3–5, 9–10, 166, 268n15
Cross-citizen solidarity, 116–17, 147–48
Crossing, 111; in *The Border Patrol Ate My Dust*, 155–57; in *Underground America*, 185–86. See also Borders
Crossing Arizona (film), 55, 87
Crossing Over: A Mexican Family on the Migrant Trail (*Crossing Over*) (Martínez, R.), 28, 266n4; absenting in, 41; American Dream in, 39–40; estrangement in, 40–42; identification in, 39–42; informants in, 40–41; intrusion in, 41–42
Crossing with the Virgin: Stories from the Migrant Trail (Ferguson, K., Price, and Parks), 60, 150
Crozier, Ivan, 84–85
Cruz-Malavé, Arnaldo, 41
Cubans, 169–70; legal status of, 107–8
Cultural trauma, 16–19, 29, 57–58, 61; in *Into the Beautiful North*, 80–81; construction of, 63; disappearance as, 63, 74–75; *el otro lado* in, 64–67; narrative of, 63; personal identity and, 74–77; representation of the traumatic and, 20–21. See also Deaths
Cultural values, 216–17
Culture: of anxiety, 27, 67, 150–51, 188, 243–45; commonality of, 112–13; indigenous, 40–41; life narratives in, 28, 35

DACA. See Deferred Action for Childhood Arrival
Dawes, James, 25, 180, 263; on failure, 259–60; on genocide, 21–22
Days of Awe (Obejas), 111
Dead in Their Tracks: Crossing America's Desert Borderlands (Annerino), 53, 62
The Death of Josseline: Immigration Stories from the Arizona-Mexico Borderlands (Regan), 150
Deaths, 2, 27, 69, 266n2, 267n3; border corpses, 56–57, 70–72, 267n6; in *The Devil's Highway*, 51–53; doubling of, 34; by drowning, 209–10; *el otro lado* as, 65–68, 76–77; enforcement and, 5–6; in Gatekeeper era, 58–59; in *Across a Hundred Mountains*, 64; NMD, 5–6, 9, 38, 43–44, 55–56; of sponsor, 232; symbolism and, 61–62, 190–91; urgency about, 34; vigils for, 56–57; of women, 89–90. See also Disappearances
Declaration of Independence, 231
Decontextualization, 68–69
Deferred Action for Childhood Arrival (DACA), 262

De Genova, Nicholas, 109, 150–51, 167, 177
de Lauretis, Teresa, 240
Democracy and the Foreigner (Honig), 224
Democratic cosmopolitanism, 224
Department of Homeland Security, 231
Deportations, 6, 27, 214, 270n5; agency and, 218, 256–57; asylum law and, 245; disappearances by, 67–68; DREAM activists and, 244–45
Deportations regime, 150–51
Desert Blood: The Juarez Murders (*Desert Blood*) (Gaspar de Alba), 70–71; border ethics in, 105–6; family in, 106; humanism in, 104–5; religious faith in, 100–101; responsibility in, 89–91
Detention centers, 235
Development, Relief, and Education for Alien Minors. *See* DREAM Act
The Devil's Highway (Urrea), 28, 266n4, 267n3; citizens and, 52–54; death in, 51–53; effects of, 55; empathy in, 51–54; ethics in, 54; identification in, 50–54; imagination in, 51–53; language in, 51–52; universalization in, 50–52
DeVivo, Dan, 55
Diary of an Undocumented Immigrant (*Diario de un Mojado*) (Pérez, R.), 30–31, 195, 270n1, 270n4; authority in, 196; collectivity in, 202–3; genre of, 196–98; identification in, 199–201; interiority in, 197–98; mappings of, 198–203; nostalgia in, 203; plots of, 196–97, 202, 221; positioning in, 196; representation and, 197–98; responsibility in, 200; solidarity and, 198–200; *testimonio* and, 199–200; *Undocumented in L.A.* compared to, 204
Díaz, Junot. *See Drown*; "Negocios"
Differences: among Caribbeans, 108–25; in testimony, 22–23
Disappearances, 29, 130–31, 266n2; closure and, 57; collective trauma and, 72–84; confirmation about, 57, 77–78, 85–86; as cultural trauma, 63, 74–75; by deportations, 67–68; *el otro lado* and, 64–66; in El Salvador, 57–58; in *The Guardians*, 64, 79–80; imagination about, 79–80; military regimes and, 57, 61; in *Odyssey to the North*, 91–92; pictures about, 73; in *Return to Sender*, 145–46; shrines and, 62; transborder solidarity over, 58
Disorientation, 213–14
Dis(re)membered bodies, 84–86
Distance, 36, 176
Documents, 189
Dominicans, 267nn2–3; legal status of, 107–8, 137–38; undocumented, 137, 268n14; in U.S., 267n9. *See also* "Negocios"
Dorfman, Ariel, 23
DREAM Act (Development, Relief, and Education for Alien Minors), 31, 149, 268nn2–3
DREAM activists, 225, 232–33; college for, 227, 234, 238, 239–40, 250; deportation and, 244–45; LGBTQ community compared to, 250–54; oral history and, 226, 259–60; out-group and, 243–44; recognition of, 234–42; self-education of, 248–59; silence of, 246–48; trauma of, 246–48
DREAMers, 226; community of, 230–31; counterpublic of, 227–28; group identity of, 240; narrative form of, 229; stories of, 228–29, 259–60; subaltern counterpublic of, 227–28, 233, 240–43, 250–59; trajectory of, 229–30
Dreby, Joanne, 76
Drown (Díaz), 27, 117–18, 125, 267n7
Drowning, 209–10
Duany, Jorge, 267n3
Dying to Cross: The Worst Immigrant Tragedy in American History (Ramos), 34, 61–62

Editing, 157; mediation as, 203–4; of *Underground America*, 174–75, 269n17
Education, 31, 248–49, 251–59; college, 227, 234, 238, 239–40, 250
Eggers, Dave, 153, 172
El otro lado, 139; in cultural trauma, 64–67; as death, 65–68, 76–77
El Salvador, 92, 266n2, 268n12; disappearances in, 57–58; testimony about, 95–97; violence in, 168–69. *See also A Handbook to Luck*

Empathy, 44–45, 103–4; in *The Devil's Highway*, 51–54; exotopy and, 28, 36, 50, 191, 241–42; identification and, 35–36, 38–39, 176; Nance on, 26–27, 35–36, 40–41, 191–92
Emplotment, 197, 202, 270n3
Enforcement, 166; by Border Patrol, 51, 54, 164, 269n10; deaths and, 5–6; literature against, 7–8
English language, 208–9
English Language Empowerment Act, 208
Enrique's Journey: The Story of a Boy's Dangerous Odyssey to Reunite with His Mother (*Enrique's Journey*) (Nazario), 28, 266n4, 267n3; aid in, 43–44; compassion in, 43–44; conclusion of, 48–49; empathy in, 44–45; estrangement in, 45–49; family separation in, 44–49; humanism in, 42; identification in, 44–46; morality in, 47–48; plot in, 47–48; resentment in, 48–49; return in, 48; structural conditions and, 49–50; synecdoche in, 42–43
Entrepreneurship, 119–21
Environmentalism, 99–100; in border *testimonio*, 91; in *Return to Sender*, 140, 144
Erikson, Kai, 17, 20
Escandón, María Amparo, 60
Esperanza's Box of Saints (Escandón), 60
Estrangement: in *Crossing Over*, 40–42; in *Enrique's Journey*, 45–49
Ethics, 49, 54; activism and, 24–25; of cosmopolitanism, 125–47; empathy and, 26–27, 35–36, 40–41; of recognition, 25–26, 175, 183–84, 191–92, 236–40; *testimonio* and, 24; in *Undocumented in L.A.*, 210, 220–21; of witnessing, 103–6. *See also* Empathy
Exclusion, 10
Exotopy, 28, 36, 50, 191, 241–42
Exploitation, 182–83
Eyerman, Ron, 19–20

Facebook, 262
Failure: of stories, 259–60; of *testimonio*, 26–27
Faith. *See* Religious faith

Family, 106; citizens and, 118–25; marriage and, 111–17
Family Matters (Moreno), 118
Family reunification, 78; in "Negocios," 122–24
Family separations, 6–7, 44–49, 76; by deaths, 68; by deportations, 67–68; as fracture, 78–79; trauma of, 72–73
Fantasy, 161–62
Fears, 209–10, 214–15, 218
Feldman, Allen, 62, 267n7
Feminism on the Border: Chicana Gender Politics and Literature (Saldívar-Hull), 11
Ferguson, Kathryn, 60, 150
Ferguson, Sam, 9
Fiction, 8, 60–61, 136–37
Film, 15, 55, 87
Fines, 268n5
Forth, Christopher, 84–85
Fragmentation, 85
Framing, 35, 165; in *Undocumented in L.A.*, 208, 216–17, 220
Fraser, Nancy, 150, 227, 253, 270n1; public sphere and, 10, 132, 152, 223
Fraxedas, J. Joaquín, 8
Freire, Paul, 194, 256
Frontera de Cristo, 56, 74
Frydman, Jason, 119–20

García, Cristina. *See A Handbook to Luck*
Gaspar de Alba, Alicia. *See Desert Blood: The Juarez Murders*
Gatekeeper era, 60–61; deaths in, 58–59; Operation Gatekeeper, 4–5, 33
Genocide, 21–22; Holocaust as, 17, 35–36
Genre, 196–98
Ghosts, 112–13
Gilmore, Leigh, 246
Globalization, 33, 167–68; in *A Handbook to Luck*, 126–27
God's Heart Has No Borders: How Religious Activists Are Working for Immigrant Rights (Hondagneu-Sotelo), 97–99
Gonzales, Rodolfo "Corky," 28
Grande, Reyna. *See Across a Hundred Mountains*
Great Depression, 69

Griffiths, Gareth, 8–9
Groody, Daniel, 189
Group construction, 228
Group identity, 29–30, 228; of DREAMers, 240; of immigrants, 240–41
Group support, 256
The Guardians (Castillo, A.), 1; abandonment in, 81–84; appearance in, 82–83; border corpses in, 71–72; collective trauma in, 79–80, 84, 102–3; decontextualization and, 69; disappearances in, 64, 79–80; dis(re)membered body in, 85–86; *el otro lado* in, 65–66; hazards in, 59, 89; humanism in, 103; identity in, 82–84, 89; memory in, 82–83; narrative breakdown in, 101–2; religious faith and, 99–100; resentment in, 83; responsibility in, 88–89, 91; synecdoche in, 85
Guatemala, 167, 169, 181, 266n2
Gupta, Monisha Das, 172–73, 268n11
Gutiérrez-Jones, Carl, 12–13

A Handbook to Luck (García, C.), 29–30, 125, 268n10; birds in, 129–30, 132–33; citizens in, 135–37; collective fiction in, 136–37; globalization in, 126–27; intersection in, 126–27, 133; luck in, 127–28, 134; nationalism in, 129; privilege in, 134–35; redefinition in, 133–34; responsibilities in, 130–32; witnessing and, 130–33
Hart, Dianne Walta, 31, 195, 204–5. See also *Undocumented in L.A.: An Immigrant's Story*
Hartmann, Douglas, 79, 103, 111–12
Hazards, 59–60, 89; in *The Border Patrol Ate My Dust*, 158–59, 161–62, 171–72
Herrera-Sobek, María, 15
Highwire Moon (Straight): collective trauma in, 81–84; deaths in, 64; dis(re)membered body in, 85–86; *el otro lado* in, 66–68; humanism in, 104; religious faith in, 97–98; responsibility in, 86–89; shrine in, 62; uniqueness of, 81
Hing, Bill Ong, 88
History, 244. See also Oral history
Holocaust, 17, 35–36

Holy Week, 98–101
Hondagneu-Sotelo, Pierrette, 97–99
Honig, Bonnie, 224–25, 267n6
HR 4437, 6–7
Humane Borders, 43–44
Humanism, 106; in *Desert Blood*, 104–5; in *Enrique's Journey*, 42; in *The Guardians*, 103; in *Highwire Moon*, 104
Humanitarian rights, 178
Human rights, 37–38, 175–76, 270n19; assurance of, 177–79; bodies and, 187–88; collective trauma and, 74; nation related to, 172–73; in *Underground America*, 178–83
Human Rights and Narrated Lives (Schaffer and Smith, S.), 94
Human smugglers (coyotes), 59–60, 88–89, 269n10
Hunger, 46
Hunt, Lynn, 175–76, 187, 270n19
Huntington, Samuel, 9
Hurricane Katrina, 175, 182–83, 187

I, Rigoberta Menchú (Menchú), 153, 218
"I am Joaquin" (Gonzales, R.), 28
Identification, 14, 182, 193; of border corpses, 70–72; in *Crossing Over*, 39–42; in *The Devil's Highway*, 50–54; in *Diary of an Undocumented Immigrant*, 199–201; empathy and, 35–36, 38–39, 176; in *Enrique's Journey*, 44–46; ethics and, 49; Holocaust and, 35–36
Identity, 14–15, 102–3, 251–52; amnesias and, 78–79; bodies related to, 84–85; in *The Guardians*, 82–84, 89; narratives of, 73, 163–64; reality of, 113–15; representation of, 27; silence and, 247; undocumented, 222–23; of U.S., 9. See also Group identity; Personal identity
IIRIRA. See Illegal Immigration Reform and Immigrant Responsibility Act
Illegal immigrants, 9, 35; consent to, 237–38; as Other, 11. See also DREAM activists
Illegal Immigration Reform and Immigrant Responsibility Act (IIRIRA), 6, 268n6

Imagination, 81; in *The Devil's Highway*, 51–53; about disappearances, 79–80; nations related to, 8, 265n8; in "Negocios," 119–22, 124
Imagined community, 104–5, 230; in "Negocios," 121–23
Immigrants, 267n6; as criminals, 3–5, 9–10; group identity of, 240–41; invasion of, 3–4, 90; reframing of, 35, 165
Immigrant Youth Justice League, 270n3
Immigration Act of 1924, 159
Immigration Act of 1965, 159–60
Immigration and Naturalization Act (INA), 268n15
Immigration and Naturalization Service (INS), 33, 265n6
Immigration Modernization Act, 262
Immigration policy, 49–50, 163, 166; 9/11 and, 6, 231; in *Undocumented in L.A.*, 208–9; about visa overstayers, 159, 210, 269n11
Immigration Reform and Control Act (IRCA), 2, 265nn2–3
INA. *See* Immigration and Naturalization Act
"Indians," 141–43, 201–2
Indigenous culture, 40–41
INS. *See* Immigration and Naturalization Service
Into the Beautiful North (Urrea), 61; abandonment in, 81; cultural trauma in, 80–81
Intra-Caribbean difference, 108–25
Invasion, 3–4, 90
Iowa, 268n4
IRCA. *See* Immigration Reform and Control Act
Irony, 162–63

Jesus, 43–44
Jews, 35–36
Judicial review, 6

Kaplan, E. Ann, 18, 73–74, 103–4
Keen, Suzanne, 176
Kidnapping, 244–45

Kim, L. S., 15
King, Rodney, 220

Lakoff, George, 9
Language, 87–88, 165, 269n15; bilingualism, 115–16; in *The Devil's Highway*, 51–52; English, 208–9
The Latino Body (Lima), 188
Latino Dreams: Transcultural Traffic and the U.S. National (Allatson), 13
Latino solidarity, 109–10
Latino threat, 9, 34–35
Leavis, Rick, 270n1
Ledesma, Alberto, 14–15, 151, 195, 203
Legal identity, 113–14
Legal status, 210; of Cubans, 107–8; of Dominicans, 107–8, 137–38; literature and, 10–11; of Puerto Ricans, 107–9
Lerner, Melvin J., 35–36
LGBTQ community, 250–54
Liberation theology, 99
Life narratives, 28–29, 35, 270n2
Life pattern, 205–6
Lima, Lázaro, 188
Liminality, 11
Literature: against enforcement, 7–8; illegality in, 10–11; legal status and, 10–11
The Lonely Crossing of Juan Cabrera (Fraxedas), 8
Los Angeles Riots (1992), 220
Lyon-Johnson, Kelli, 61

Mappings, 198–203
!Marcha! Latino Chicago and the Immigrant Rights Movement (Pallares), 222–23
Marcus, Steven, 76
Marketing, 157–59
Marriage, 111–17, 135–36. *See also* Bigamy
Martinez, Manuel Luiz, 12, 171, 185–86
Martínez, Rubén, 28, 39–42, 266n4
Marx, Karl, 204
McKenna, Teresa, 10–11
Media, 163, 166, 242–43, 265n2
Mediation, 203–4
Meissner, Doris, 265n6

Memory, 19–20, 69, 131; amnesias and, 76–79; in *The Guardians*, 82–83
Memory Mambo (Obejas), 111
Menchú, Rigoberta, 153, 218
Meritocracy, 159–61, 233, 236–37
Metaphors, 234–35
Mexican Child Protective Services, 76
Mexicans, 3–4, 188–89. See also *Crossing Over: A Mexican Family on the Migrant Trail*
La Migra me hizo los mandados. See *The Border Patrol Ate My Dust*
Migrant Imaginaries (Schmidt Camacho), 72–73, 80
Migrant Song: Politics and Process in Contemporary Chicano Literature (McKenna), 10–11
Military regimes, 57, 61
Milk, Harvey, 231–32
Millis, Dan, 266n1
Mojado. See Wetbacks
Morality, 47–48, 142–44
Moreno, Marisel, 118
Morrison, Toni, 84–85
Mothers of the Plaza de Mayo, 75, 266n2, 267n7
Motivation, 211
Moyn, Samuel, 176–77
Myerhoff, Barbara, 248–49

NAFTA. See North American Free Trade Agreement
Nance, Kimberly, 24–25, 86, 168, 176; on empathy, 26–27, 35–36, 40–41, 191–92
Napolitano, Janet, 2
Narration, 34
Narrative breakdown, 101–3
Narrative form, 229
Narrative memory, 19–20
Narratives, 18–19, 63, 266n11; counternarratives, 28, 139–40; of identity, 73, 163–64; life, 28–29, 35, 270n2
National belonging, 186–87, 265n8
National identification, 14
Nationalism, 11, 129, 171, 185; in *Return to Sender*, 141–44, 147

Nations: homogeneity of, 8–9; human rights related to, 172–73; imagination related to, 8, 265n8; narration of, 34
Nativism, 33–35
Nazario, Sonia, 28, 54. See also *Enrique's Journey: The Story of a Boy's Dangerous Odyssey to Reunite with His Mother*
"Negocios" (Díaz), 29–30, 108; abandonment in, 117–24; appearance in, 121–22; bigamy in, 118–19, 123–24; entrepreneurship in, 119–21; family reunification in, 122–24; imagination in, 119–22, 124; imagined community in, 121–23; transactions in, 119–21
Nevins, Joseph, 2–3, 33–34, 68
New Sanctuary Movement (NSM), 7, 261–62
Ngai, Mae, 159, 177, 186, 189, 214
Nicaragua, 205–6; U.S. compared to, 212–13. See also *Undocumented in L.A.: An Immigrant's Story*
No More Deaths (No Más Muertes) (NMD), 5–6, 9, 38, 43–44; Frontera de Cristo and, 56; volunteers for, 55
Noncitizens: activism of, 222–24; democratic cosmopolitanism and, 224; rights of, 222–24
North American Free Trade Agreement (NAFTA), 4–5, 89–90, 265n6
Nostalgia, 203, 269n12
Novak, Amy, 84
Novels of Testimony and Resistance from Central America (Craft), 22–23
NSM. See New Sanctuary Movement
Nyers, Peter, 152, 183, 223–24

Obama, Barack, 150, 259–60, 262, 268n5
Obejas, Achy, 27, 111–17
Oboler, Suzanne, 114
Odisea del Norte. See *Odyssey to the North*
Odyssey: in border *testimonio*, 91–93; post-Gatekeeper era and, 60. See also *Enrique's Journey: The Story of a Boy's Dangerous Odyssey to Reunite with His Mother*
Odyssey to the North (*Odisea del Norte*) (Bencastro), 61; disappearance in, 91–92;

hazards in, 59–60; synecdoche in, 93–94; time in, 93; transition in, 92–93; voice in, 95–97
Operation Blockade, 4
Operation Gatekeeper, 4–5, 33
Operation Hold-the-Line, 4, 33
Operation Return to Sender, 139
Operation Río Grande, 4
Operation Safeguard, 4
Operation Wetback, 265n4
Opportunity, 210–11
Oral history, 203–5; DREAM activists and, 226, 259–60
Orner, Peter, 260, 268n7. See also *Underground America: Narratives of Undocumented Lives*
Out-group, 243–44

Pain, 52–53, 62, 187–88
Pallares, Amalia, 222–23
Parks, Ted, 60, 150
Participatory journalism, 41–42
Paying the Price: The Impact of Immigration Raids on America's Children, 81, 87–88
Pedagogy of the Oppressed (Freire), 194
Penitentes, 101
Pérez, Ramón "Tianguis," 30–31, 195, 221. See also *Diary of an Undocumented Immigrant*
Perez, William, 31, 114
Perez v. Brownell, 177
Perks, Robert, 226, 229
Personal identity: cultural trauma and, 74–77; recognition of, 77, 175
Personhood, 189–90
Peutz, Nathalie, 150–51, 167, 177
Physicality, 70–72
Plots: of *Diary of an Undocumented Immigrant*, 196–97, 202, 221; emplotment, 197, 202, 270n3; in *Enrique's Journey*, 47–48; in *Undocumented in L.A.*, 206–7
Political asylum. See Asylum law
Portes, Alejandro, 185
Positioning, 196; of *Underground America*, 156, 172, 175, 182, 193

Post-Gatekeeper era: fiction on, 60–61; odyssey and, 60
Postmodernism, 198
Price, Norma A., 60, 150
Privilege, 134–35; of citizens, 114–15; ethics and, 49
Proposition 187, 3
Prostitution, 75
Publics, 154–55, 252
Public sphere, 10, 132, 152, 223
Puerto Ricans, 118; distinction of, 109–10; legal status of, 107–9
Puerto Rico, 267n3
Pulitzer Prizes, 262, 266n4

Queer community, 250–54
Queer theory, 115
Quinteros, Josseline Jamileth Hernández, 5

Raids, 81, 93–94, 268nn4–5; citizen children and, 57, 150; communication in, 87–88; crimes and, 166
Ramos, Jorge, 34, 61–62, 267n3
Ramos-Zayas, Ana, 109
Rancière, Jacques, 177–78
Rape, 89
Rastreo (search for missing bodies), 70–71
Readers: of *Border Patrol*, 158, 161, 166–67, 171–72; of testimony, 25–26
Reading Autobiography (Smith and Watson), 196
Reagan, Ronald, 2
Recognition, 153, 180–81, 193; of DREAM activists, 234–42; ethics of, 25–26, 175, 183–84, 191–92, 236–40; of personal identity, 77, 175
Redefinition, 133–34
Redreaming America: Toward a Bilingual American Culture (Castillo, D.), 13
Reframing, 35, 165
Regan, Margaret, 150
Religion, 43–44; Jews, 35–36
Religious faith, 160; activism and, 98–99; in *Desert Blood*, 100–101; *The Guardians* and, 99–100; in *Highwire Moon*, 97–98; in *Across a Hundred Mountains*, 98, 101

Repatriation, 74
Reporting: participatory journalism as, 41–42; testimony as, 22
Representation, 13–15, 20; of counternarratives, 28; *Diary of an Undocumented Immigrant* and, 197–98; of identity, 27; undocumented testimony and, 222
Republican Party, 3–4
Resentment, 48–49, 83
Resistance, 207–15, 221
Responsibilities, 200; in *Border Patrol*, 167–68; in *Desert Blood*, 89–91; in *The Guardians*, 88–89, 91; in *A Handbook to Luck*, 130–32; in *Highwire Moon*, 86–89; IIRIRA, 6, 268n6; self-recognition and, 192–93
Restaurant raid, 93–94
Rethinking the Borderlands: Between Chicano Culture and Legal Discourse (Gutiérrez-Jones), 12–13
Return, 48, 139
Return to Sender (Alvarez), 29–30, 125, 268n13; aliens in, 139, 145–46; astronomy in, 144–45, 147; cosmopolitanism in, 139–44, 146–47; counternarrative in, 139–40; disappearance in, 145–46; *el otro lado* in, 66, 139; environmentalism in, 140, 144; morality in, 142–44; narrator in, 139; nationalism in, 141–44, 147; universalism in, 140–41, 144, 146; white perspective in, 138–39, 141–46
Reyes, Silvestre, 4
Rights: citizens and, 180–81; of noncitizens, 222–24; voices and, 179–80; of wetbacks, 180–81, 184. *See also* Human rights
Riofrio, John, 118
Rivera, Rick, 8
Rivera, Tomás, 267n8
Rodríguez, Néstor, 5
Rodriguez, Richard, 14–15
Rodriguez, Roberto Cintli, 225
Rwandan genocide, 21–22

Sadowski-Smith, Claudia, 11
Saldívar, José David, 11
Saldívar-Hull, Sonia, 11
Sanctuary Movement, 152, 167, 192, 265n7; NSM, 7, 261–62
Sanjinés, Javier, 165
Santiago, Esmeralda, 108–10
SB1070, 33, 149, 188, 225, 266n1, 268n1; DREAM activists and, 258–59
Scales of Justice (Fraser), 223
Scarry, Elaine, 52–53, 62
Schaffer, Kay, 25–26, 94, 236
Schmidt Camacho, Alicia, 72–73, 80, 106
Schrager, Samuel, 259
Schreiber, Evelyn, 17
Schwab, Gabriele, 73
Search for missing bodies (*rastreo*), 70–71
Secrets, 218–19
Self-education, 248–59
Self-recognition, 192–93
Sensenbrenner Bill, 6–7
September 11, 2001, 6, 231
Sexual norms, 113, 116
Shadowed Lives: Undocumented Immigrants in American Society (Chavez), 92, 234–35
Shame, 219–21
Shrines, 62
Silence, 14–15, 22, 96–97, 149; of DREAM activists, 246–48
Sisk, Christina, 270n1, 270n4
Sklodowska, Elzbieta, 76
Slaughter, Joseph, 94
Slavery, 163–64
Smelser, Neil, 29, 63, 86
Smith, Sidonie, 94, 196, 198, 270n2; recognition and, 25–26, 236
So Far from God (Castillo, A.), 99–100
Solidarity, 27, 74, 154; of Chicano movement, 69; cross-citizen, 116–17, 147–48; *Diary of an Undocumented Immigrant* and, 198–200; Latino, 109–10; transborder, 58; trauma and, 20–21. *See also* Cosmopolitanism
Sommer, Doris, 36, 38, 45, 153
Sontag, Susan, 86
Soto, Sandra K., 64, 68
Spivak, Gayatri, 152–53, 228
Sponsor, 232
"The Spouse" (Obejas), 111–17

Stars Always Shine (Rivera, R.), 8
Statue of Liberty, 3, 231–32
Stereotypes, 201–2
Stop the Out-of-Control Problems of Immigration Today (STOP-IT), 3
Stories: agency and, 258–59; of DREAMers, 228–29, 259–60; failure of, 259–60; in *Underground America*, 179–81, 269nn8–9
Straight, Susan, 64, 74. See also *Highwire Moon*
Structural conditions, 49–50
Suárez, Lucía M., 117, 267n8
Subaltern counterpublic, 227–28, 233, 240–43, 255–59; coming out of, 250–54
Subalterns, 10; in *testimonio*, 37–39, 125–26, 152–54, 173–74
Sugg, Katherine, 185
Swift meatpacking plants, 268n4
Symbolism, 106, 187; of borders, 5, 12; deaths and, 61–62, 190–91; of Statue of Liberty, 3, 231–32
Synecdoche, 64; in *Enrique's Journey*, 42–43; in *Odyssey to the North*, 93–94; in *testimonio*, 41, 84–85

Taylor, Diana, 56, 63
Territoriality, 68–69
Terrorist attacks, 6, 231
Testimonial function, 23–24
Testimonio, 24, 151, 266n3; absenting in, 168, 176; agency and, 164; asylum law and, 95–97; *Border Patrol* and, 164, 166–70; challenges of, 30; change from, 23, 25, 35; definitions of, 37–38; *Diary of an Undocumented Immigrant* and, 199–200; distance and, 36; failure of, 26–27; interlocutor in, 38; subalterns in, 37–39, 125–26, 152–54, 173–74; synecdoche in, 41, 84–85. See also Border *testimonio*
Testimony: change from, 24–26, 31–32; coherence about, 21; differences in, 22–23; about El Salvador, 95–97; need for, 21; readers of, 25–26; as reporting, 22; *testimonio* compared to, 23–24; transition of, 21–22; unhearable, 94–97; voice of, 22

That the World May Know: Bearing Witness to Atrocity (Dawes), 21–22, 180, 259–60
Thomson, Alistair, 226, 229
Tiffin, Helen, 8–9
Totalitarianism, 132
"Trail of Dreams," 242, 257
Transborder solidarity, 58
Transition, 92–93; of testimony, 21–22
Transnationalism, 171, 185
Trauma, 103, 188, 266n11; agency and, 24; cause-and-effect narrative of, 18–19; definitions of, 16, 18, 84; of DREAM activists, 246–48; of family separations, 72–73; narrative breakdown and, 101–2; narrative memory of, 19–20; range of, 17–18; reenactment of, 16–17; solidarity and, 20–21. See also Collective trauma; Cultural trauma
Traumatic, 17–18, 20–21
Traumatic history, 73–74
Traumatic memory, 19
287(g) program, 151, 259, 268n6

U.S. See United States
UCLA Center for Labor Research and Education, 7–8
Underground America: Narratives of Undocumented Lives (*Underground America*) (Orner), 30–31, 149, 151, 153, 268n7; ambivalence of, 173; bodies in, 188, 190–91; *Border Patrol* compared to, 174, 185, 192–93; crossing in, 185–86; editing of, 174–75, 269n17; exploitation in, 182–83; humanity in, 184–85; human rights in, 178–83; national belonging in, 186–87; positioning of, 156, 172, 175, 182, 193; stories in, 179–81, 269nn8–9; transnationalism and, 185
Underground Undergrads: UCLA Undocumented Immigrant Students Speak Out, 31
Under the Feet of Jesus (Viramontes), 1
Undocumented, 225, 260. See also DREAM activists
Undocumented Dominicans, 137, 268n14
Undocumented identity, 222–23

Undocumented in L.A.: An Immigrant's Story (Undocumented in L.A.) (Hart), 30–31, 195; agency in, 206–7, 212, 215–16, 218; assimilation in, 204–5, 215–16; assumptions in, 205–7; belonging in, 214–15, 220–21; cultural values in, 216–17; disorientation in, 213–14; ethics in, 210, 220–21; fears in, 209–10, 214–15, 218; framing in, 208, 216–17, 220; illusions in, 207, 210–12; immigration policy in, 208–9; intention in, 205, 213; judgment in, 216–17, 219; legal status in, 210; life pattern in, 205–6; motivation in, 211; opportunity in, 210–11; oral history in, 204–5; perspective and, 206; plot and, 206–7; resistance in, 207–15, 221; secrets in, 218–19; shame in, 219–21
Undocumented testimony, 222
Unhearable testimony, 94–97
United States (U.S.), 33, 111; Bush and, 150, 255, 268n5; Dominicans in, 267n9; identity of, 9; Nicaragua compared to, 212–13; Obama and, 150, 259–60, 262, 268n5
United We DREAM, 230
Universal Declaration of Human Rights, 187
Universalism, 140–41, 144, 146
Universalization, 50–52
Urban Institute, 57
Urrea, Luis Alberto, 31, 61, 80–81, 149; *The Devil's Highway* by, 28, 50–55, 266n4, 267n3

Vare, Robert, 44
Vargas, Jose Antonio, 114, 262, 268n3
Verdery, Katherine, 267n6
Verzasconi, Ray, 205–6, 208–9, 215
Vigils, 56–57. *See also* Mothers of the Plaza de Mayo
Violence, 175, 212; of border corpses, 71; in Colombia, 244; in El Salvador, 168–69. *See also* Deaths
Viramontes, Helena María, 1

Visa overstayers, 159, 210, 269n11
Voices, 10, 22, 150; agency and, 152–53, 242–43; of Alicia, 247–48, 257–58; authenticity of, 153; in *Odyssey to the North*, 95–97; rights and, 179–80. *See also* Silence
Vollen, Lola, 172
Volunteers, 55, 266n1

Walls, 235–36
Warner, Michael, 154–55, 227, 252
Warren, Earl, 177
Water crossing, 111
Watson, Julia, 196, 198, 270n2
We ARE Americans: Undocumented Students Pursuing the American Dream (Perez, W.), 31, 114
We Came All the Way from Cuba So You Could Dress Like This? (Obejas), 111–12, 115
Westerman, William, 194, 225
Wetbacks (mojado), 121–22, 198, 265n4, 270n4; rights of, 180–81, 184
When I Was Puerto Rican (Santiago), 109–10
"While You Were Sleeping" (Bowden), 68
White, Hayden, 197, 270n3
White perspective, 138–39, 141–46
Who Are We? The Challenges to America's National Identity (Huntington), 9
Wilson, Pete, 3
Wirshing, Irene, 16–17
Witnessing, 103–6, 130–33. *See also* Testimonio
Women, 175; as border corpses, 70–72; deaths of, 89–90
Workplace raids. *See* Raids

Yamileth. *See Undocumented in L.A.: An Immigrant's Story*
Y no se lo trago la tierra (Rivera, T.), 267n8
Young, James, 21
YouTube, 114

MARTA CAMINERO-SANTANGELO is the Director of the Center for Latin American and Caribbean Studies and professor of English at the University of Kansas. She is the author of *On Latinidad: U.S. Latino Literature and the Construction of Ethnicity* and *The Madwoman Can't Speak: Or Why Insanity Is Not Subversive*.

www.ingramcontent.com/pod-product-compliance
Lightning Source LLC
Chambersburg PA
CBHW031429160426
43195CB00010BB/670